Listening in the Language Classroom

CAMBRIDGE LANGUAGE TEACHING LIBRARY

A series covering central issues in language teaching and learning, by authors who have expert knowledge in their field.

Listening in the Language Classroom

John Field

CAMBRIDGE
UNIVERSITY PRESS

CAMBRIDGE UNIVERSITY PRESS
Cambridge, New York, Melbourne, Madrid, Cape Town, Singapore, São Paulo, Delhi

Cambridge University Press
The Edinburgh Building, Cambridge CB2 8RU, UK

www.cambridge.org
Information on this title: www.cambridge.org/9780521685702

First published 2008

Printed in the United Kingdom at the University Press, Cambridge

A catalogue record for this publication is available from the British Library

Library of Congress Cataloguing in Publication data
Field, John, 1945–
Listening in the language classroom / John Field.
    p.   cm. – (Cambridge language teaching library.)
Includes bibliographical references and index.
ISBN 978-0-521-86678-1 hardback
ISBN 978-0-521-68570-2 paperback
1. Language and languages – Study and teaching.   2. Listening – Study and teaching.
3. Second language acquisition – Study and teaching.   I. Title.   II. Series.
P53.47.F54   2009
428′.0071 – dc22   2008045463

ISBN 978-0-521-68570-2 paperback
ISBN 978-0-521-86678-1 hardback

Contents

Contents

*In recognition of all I owe to my mother
Maud Henrietta Field (1910–1983),
the best of listeners*

Acknowledgements

This book has a long history. It grew from an interest in second language listening that goes back over 25 years, and from an idea that was first mooted ten years ago. I had expected the writing to take eight months but it finally lasted three years. Unsurprisingly, I have built up more than a few debts of gratitude along the way.

As often happens, putting words on the page had the chastening effect of showing the author how little he knows. I rethought ideas that had seemed set in stone and questioned lines of argument that had once been utterly convincing. I also had to find ways of making information relevant to teachers in the field. In circumstances such as these, one badly needs to put one's ideas past an informed listener who has a complete grasp of the issues. I cannot think of anybody more competent to fulfil that role for L2 listening than Gillian Brown, who commands enormous respect among all who work in the area. Gill was enormously generous with her time; and it was a great pleasure and privilege to work with her on the final draft of the book. I cannot stress enough how much poorer the book would have been without the benefit of her experience and without her insights, always perceptive, invariably frank ('*Omit*' featured quite often, and she was always right), and punctuated at well-timed intervals by coffee and walks round the garden.

I also owe a considerable debt to Alison Sharpe of Cambridge University Press for her continuing faith in me and in the book, ever since the time we first discussed it on a train all those years ago. During the writing, I greatly appreciated the sound advice – not to mention the understanding and patience – of Jane Walsh, my editor. The presentation of the material has benefited considerably from the expertise of Jacqueline French, the copy editor, who showed great sensitivity towards both text and author.

Many of the ideas in the book were first developed during a three-week summer school on second language skills that the British Council ran at Oxley Hall in the University of Leeds. (Sadly, like much of the enlightened work that the Council once did, it has now been axed.) I taught there for ten years and remain grateful to the Director, Niall Henderson, for employing me on what was undoubtedly the most rewarding teacher-development experience of my career. Oxley Hall gave me the opportunity of exchanging views on listening with teachers from all over the world. Many of those attending taught in difficult conditions. Some (from Tanzania, Vietnam, Cambodia, the poorer parts of South America) had to make do with the most limited of resources. Others (from eastern Europe, from Palestine, from South Africa, from the Sudan) had been the victims of occupation or intimidation. I developed a huge respect for their commitment and for the enthusiasm with which they embraced the idea that second language listening might be handled more productively – even where they had no reliable power supply or their books and equipment had been destroyed. I hope that former Oxley Hall students will come across this book and remember some happy and stimulating times.

Another much-valued source of ideas has been the relatively small group of teachers, writers and researchers who specialise in second language listening. Over the years, I have been fortunate to work with some and to engage in fruitful discussions with others at conferences or via email. I imagine that traces of all these exchanges can be found somewhere in the pages that follow. I add the usual rider that any errors of interpretation are entirely my own – but (given the topic of the book) I can always fall back on the defence that listeners and readers have no choice but to remake the message.

Finally, it is not surprising that a project that took up so much time and was so important to me put a severe strain upon my personal life. I am lucky indeed to have a group of loyal friends who have kept faith with me over many years; and I cannot thank them enough for their concerned enquiries and their tolerance of my prolonged absence from the scene. Above all, I would like to thank Paul Siedlecki for the support and understanding that has helped me to get through what has been a very long haul.

Publisher's acknowledgements

The authors and publishers acknowledge the following sources of copyright material and are grateful for the permissions granted. While every effort has been made, it has not always been possible to identify the sources of all the material used, or to trace all copyright holders. If any omissions are brought to our notice, we will be happy to include the appropriate acknowledgements on reprinting.

Page 20: text 'Contextual ambiguity' and page 233: Table 12.9 'Sample exercise: text-level reference', from A. Maley and A. Duff, *Variations on a Theme* (1978). By permission of Alan Maley.

Acknowledgements

Page 82: extracts from G. Brown and G. Yule, 'Investigating listening comprehension in context', *Applied Linguistics* 7/3 (1986): 284–302; page 282: extracts from M. Underwood, *Listen to This!* (1975), and page 306: extract from C. Goh and Y. Taib, 'Metacognitive instruction in listening for young learners', *ELT Journal* 60/3 (2006): 222–32. By permission of Oxford University Press.

Pages 103–5: text adapted from Dawn Daly, 'Learner evaluation of a ten-session intensive listening programme', unpublished paper presented at the BAAL/CUP seminar, 'Research perspectives on listening in L1 and L2 education', University of Warwick, 12–13 May 2006. By kind permission of the author.

Page 147: Table 9.2 'Weak forms grouped by word class', adapted from A. C. Gimson, *Gimson's Pronunciation of English* 5th revised edition (1994), ed. Alan Cruttenden, Hodder and Arnold. Reproduced by permission of Edward Arnold; page 154: extract adapted from Richard Cauldwell, *Streaming Speech: Listening and Pronunciation for Advanced Learners of English* (Student Workbook), speechinaction 2003 © Richard Cauldwell.

Pages 229–30: text transcribed from the *Today* programme, 26 October 2005, BBC Radio 4 and page 280: text transcribed from *Any Questions*, 25 January 2008.

Pages 232–3: extracts from Joanne Collie and Stephen Slater, *Listening 3 Student's Book, Cambridge Skills for Fluency* (1993) © Cambridge University Press.

Page 242: extract from M. Geddes, 'A visit to Nepal', in *How to Listen*, BBC Publications.

Pages 300–1: Tables 15.3 'Avoidance and achievement strategies' and 15.4 'Repair strategies', adapted from Z. Dörnyei and M. L. Scott, 'Communication strategies in a second language: definitions and taxonomies', *Language Learning* 447/1 (1997): 173–210. By permission of Blackwell Publishing.

Introduction

The word is half his that speaks and half his that hears it.
Michel de Montaigne (1533–1592), French essayist

Why teach listening?

Why teach listening? seems an odd question. It is standard practice nowadays for language teachers to provide sessions that focus on this particular skill. There is a wide choice of listening materials available with accompanying CDs, and DVD or video is used in many classrooms.

Nevertheless, there is still plenty of evidence that listening is undervalued. When there is pressure on contact hours, it is often the listening session that is cut. Students are rarely assessed on their listening skills, and the problems of many weak listeners pass undiagnosed. The methodology of the listening lesson has been little discussed, researched or challenged; and there is a tendency for teachers to work through well-worn routines without entire conviction. Alternatively, a faddish commitment to an 'integrated skills' approach may result in listening being relegated to a hasty topic-driven session wedged between reading and writing, which tend to be regarded as more manageable skills.

Listening on the back burner

The reasons for this lack of priority are partly historical. There was a time when listening in the language classroom was almost entirely subordinated to the presentation of new items of language. Short dialogues on tape provided examples of structures to be learned (see, for example, Alexander, 1967), and this was the only type of listening practice that most learners received. It was not until the late 1960s that enlightened teachers began to practise listening as a skill in its own right – and even then the idea persisted for a while that an important function of the listening lesson was to reinforce recently taught grammar by exemplifying it in use.

Another reason for downgrading listening is, frankly, the difficulty of teaching it. It is widely seen as a 'passive' skill, one that takes place in the hidden reaches of the learner's mind. It is not tangible in the way that speaking and writing are, and a listening text is not easily manipulated like a reading one. Demonstrable results are difficult to achieve. Even after extensive practice, there may be little evidence of any improvement in performance. If teachers want to demonstrate a class's progress in knowledge of the target language, how much better to focus on grammar, vocabulary, speaking and writing. At best, this lack of measurable benefits makes teachers chary of spending too much time on the listening skill. At worst, it leads to a complacent (and perhaps defensive) claim that listening can be 'picked up' simply by exposure to the target language in a way that other skills cannot. Once the learner's ears have adjusted to the phonology of the target language (the argument goes), listening skills from the first language (L1) will transfer themselves to the second (L2) by some process of osmosis.

To this, a quasi-psychological justification is sometimes added. The process of listening to our native language demands little effort. As infants, we acquire listening skills without being conscious of any cognitive demands being made upon us. Surely, then, listening to a foreign language is something that learners will achieve sooner or later for themselves, without too much intervention by the teacher?

Given these received ideas, it is worth giving some thought to the role that listening plays in second language learning.

A rationale for teaching listening

A two-way traffic

Why bother about listening? If we asked the same question about speaking, the response would be one of incredulity. It has been taken as axiomatic for many years that the development of spoken fluency is one of the most important goals (if not *the* most important goal) of the language teacher. The view goes back to the assertion by Harold Palmer (1922) and others that speech is 'primary' because it antedates writing, or even further back to 1878 and Berlitz's claim that languages are best learnt by 'direct' methods involving the spoken word. Throughout the second half of the twentieth century, instructors placed great emphasis upon speaking, on the grounds that possession of this skill constituted the most important long-term need of the majority of language learners.

But there has perhaps been some rather muddled thinking here. The long-term needs of the learner do not, in fact, reside in speaking as such but in *interacting orally with other speakers of the target language*. Communication requires a two-way traffic, and unless the non-native speaker has a listening competence as developed as his/her command of speech, then it will simply not be possible to sustain a conversation. This may seem a blindingly obvious point. But the briefest review of listening proficiency in a language class will identify more than a few learners whose ability to interpret what is said to them lags well behind the level of language that they are capable of producing.

Fluency forms one side of the coin in developing speaking skills; the other being accuracy. But how often do teachers make a concerted effort to develop the equivalent competencies in listening? These might be regarded as (for fluency) the acquisition of patterns of listening which approximate to those of a native listener and (for accuracy) the possession of an ability to decode pieces of connected speech, word by word. The prevailing tendency in the teaching of listening is to provide practice and more practice without clearly defined goals. How comfortable would we feel about an approach to speaking which told learners simply to 'get on with the task' and provided no pronunciation teaching, no modelling, no controlled practice, no pragmatic input and little feedback?

The skewed priorities of educators

To make matters worse, the plight of the weak listener often goes unrecognised. This is partly because of the inaccessible nature of listening, which can only be tested indirectly, often by means of cumbersome comprehension questions. But it is also a reflection of the priorities adopted by language teaching professionals. Let us take a typical language school in the UK, USA, Australia, Canada or New Zealand. The school is very professionally run and has a sophisticated entry test for those who come from overseas to study there. The test consists of a battery of grammar exercises followed by a short composition and perhaps a hasty oral interview. Mainly on the basis of their knowledge of grammar, students are graded and allocated to a class at the appropriate level.

In syllabus design terms, the procedure appears to work well: the learner is slotted in to the system at the point where much of the grammatical information being presented will be new. But we should not lose sight of the fact that the incoming learner will now be required to learn entirely through the medium of the target language. Some of the information will be presented visually through coursebooks and on the whiteboard; but most will be presented through the voice of the teacher. A critical factor in the success or failure of the learners, and in how much they benefit from their course, is thus the ability to understand speech. This consideration should surely outweigh what the learners do or do not know of grammar. Yet listening ability is rarely taken into account during entry tests and, if it is, is accorded only minor importance. On my many visits to language schools as a listening researcher and as an inspector, I have come across disturbingly large numbers of learners who

3

have been graded as (say) 'intermediate' on the basis of a grammar test, yet whose listening skills are minimal. They sit in class day after day, comprehending little and often blaming themselves. But the fault lies with a system that does not accord sufficient attention to the skill that, above all others, is crucial to their learning.

Lest anyone should feel that I have unfairly singled out language schools for criticism, I should add that the same situation prevails in state systems where the teaching of modern foreign languages is carried out mainly through the medium of the target language. The policy of using L2 as widely as possible is a commendable one but is only valid if it is accompanied by adequate assistance in understanding L2 speech.

Learner concerns

In setting priorities for skills teaching, we also need to take account of learners' perceptions of their needs. Many of them, if asked to rate the relative difficulty of the four language skills, cite listening as the area about which they feel most insecure.[1] There are several possible explanations for this concern. One is the lack of tangible evidence that they are making progress in acquiring the skill. Another is the fact that listening takes place in real time. If a stretch of speech is not understood at the moment it is heard, it is extremely hard to relive it in memory. Failure at a basic level (matching speech to words under the pressure of time) often leads to a loss of confidence, and to the belief that listening is too difficult or that L2 speakers speak too fast. If teachers omit to address these and similar concerns, they create insecurity which may seriously affect learners' motivation for acquiring the second language.

Language learning for life

There is another, and equally compelling, argument for paying greater attention to listening as part of language learning. One of the central goals of the language teacher must be to provide for life after the classroom. Much has been written about the concept of autonomous learning, which is usually taken to refer to the sort of learner training (Ellis and Sinclair, 1989) that enables students to operate more effectively within the classroom and within a learning centre. However, there is another type of learner training which has not yet received the attention it deserves.

---

[1] See Graham, 2006, for evidence to this effect, drawn from British learners of French.

It involves preparing learners so that they can take full advantage of the sources of linguistic information that the real world provides. It offers a more exciting form of independence than autonomy within the learning environment: namely, the ability to continue learning when the course is over and the teacher is no longer there. Surely this, rather than successful mastery of the Third Conditional or the vocabulary of shopping, should be the stuff of language teaching. The reason is that it constitutes, to use a currently fashionable term, a transferable skill.

Once the classroom has been left behind, two channels of information enable learners to extend their knowledge of the target language. The first is exposure to the written word through reading. The second is exposure to the spoken word through listening – listening to videos, radio broadcasts, podcasts, talks and announcements, or to an interlocutor. Of the two, it is listening which is arguably the more important since it is listening which enriches the learner's *spoken* competence with new syntactic, lexical, phonological and pragmatic information. But this wealth of material is available only to those who are able to crack the code of speech with a fair degree of confidence. A strong case can therefore be made (Field, 2007) for training learners in listening, with a view to equipping them for independent learning in the outside world.

Rethinking our approach

In this introduction, several reasons have been cited for giving more prominence to second language listening than we currently do. We need to recognise that successful L2 communication demands listening in equal measure with speaking. We need to ensure that the words of teachers do not fall on stony ground because they have taken the comprehension of learners for granted. We need to address a major cause of anxiety among learners – especially those confronting oral exams. And we need to open up a rich source of new linguistic material for those who leave the classroom behind and enter the L2 environment.

But any change of priorities is pointless unless we also recognise the limitations of the methods that we currently use in the listening lesson. Part of the neglect of second language listening must be attributable to the rather sterile methodology that teachers have to rely upon. For many years, teachers have based their teaching and testing upon an approach which measures achievement in terms of the ability to provide answers to comprehension questions. No matter that those answers might be derived by a variety of means, including intelligent guesswork. No matter that they tend to be supplied by the more able listeners, while those who most need help simulate an understanding they have not achieved. The format is a well-established one and, though it may not lead demonstrably to better listening, it is easy to apply. Teachers and teacher trainers tend not to ask why this particular approach has become attached to the teaching of second language listening or to question whether it is the most effective way of developing the skill in learners.

A further indication that we have not given listening the attention it deserves can be found in the dearth of reliable background information about the skill. In order to teach listening effectively, it is important for teachers to have a clear picture of the end behaviour they are aiming to achieve in their learners. Yet teachers' manuals tend to be vague or sometimes inaccurate about the processes that make up listening, about the problems it poses for those acquiring a second language and about the precise nature of the input which novice listeners have to learn to handle. If teachers are to raise the profile of listening in the language classroom, they need to know considerably more about the skill and about how it operates. The information will help them to define their goals more clearly and to identify more closely with the challenges that learners face.

Here, then, are the concerns of the present book. It aims first and foremost to challenge the present orthodoxy so far as pedagogy is concerned. In doing so, it suggests ways in which our current methodology can be adapted to make it more viable. It also proposes some quite radical alternatives that enhance the support we give to learners. Secondly, it aims to provide the reader with a clear understanding of what second language listening entails: examining both the raw material which the listener has to make sense of and the processes which an expert listener brings to bear.

About this book

The book falls into six parts.

- *Background.* The first two chapters cover current approaches to the teaching of listening. Chapter 1 contains a brief history of the methodology of the listening lesson. It outlines how present-day instructors tend to design their lessons and considers the thinking that lies behind the procedures they adopt. In Chapter 2, there is a critical look at current practice. One problem is that our thinking about how to teach listening has been largely shaped by previously established methods for the teaching of second language reading. Another is that a routine based on asking learners questions about a series of recorded texts is not the most constructive way of improving L2 listening performance. Answers to comprehension tasks provide few, if any, insights into where learners' listening problems lie.

- *Rethinking the comprehension approach*. In the next part, I examine ways in which the current approach to teaching second language listening might be adapted so as to make it both more effective and more learner-friendly. The focus of Chapter 3 is upon practical innovations to change the dynamics of the listening classroom. I consider how the roles of both teacher and learner can be modified to ensure greater engagement. I then go on to examine how teachers can ensure more intensive listening practice by promoting listener autonomy. In Chapter 4, the view is expressed that current pedagogy limits the forms of listening that are practised in the classroom. Ideas are put forward for expanding the range of listening types and tasks that are featured, with a view to aligning them more closely with the listening experiences that a learner might have in the real world.

- *Process, not product*. The third part of the book presents two alternatives to current methodology. One, described in Chapter 5, entails treating the listening lesson as a diagnostic exercise, in which the teacher makes use of learner responses in order to detect areas of difficulty. The teacher can then devise small-scale tasks that provide remedial practice in the specific problems that have been identified. The other approach is prognostic, attempting to anticipate the problems that a second language listener is likely to encounter. It entails dividing listening into a set of components that can be practised intensively and individually. Proposals for a sub-skills approach similar to the one adopted in second language reading are discussed in Chapter 6. An alternative framework for deciding what is to be practised is then put forward in Chapter 7: a framework based not upon the intuitions of commentators but upon psychological models of how expert listeners actually perform. This is referred to as a process approach.

- *A process view of listening*. If, as advocated here, instructors are to base their programmes upon the behaviour of expert listeners, then it is clearly important for them to have a better understanding of (a) the nature of the signal that reaches the listener's ear and (b) the processes that the listener employs when making sense of it. The aim of the next part of the book is to provide a detailed account of these areas. Though the treatment is partly theoretical, implications are drawn for the practising teacher, and extensive examples are given of exercise types that enable the relevant processes to be practised.

Chapter 8 provides an introduction to the listening skill which distinguishes between two principal operations. One (known as **decoding**) broadly consists of the listener matching the signal to words, while the other consists of the listener constructing larger-scale meaning. We consider the ways in which these operations interact and which might be the more important to success in L2 listening.

The next two chapters focus upon decoding. Chapter 9 contains a detailed look at the many ways in which the speech signal deviates from standard forms and at the problems that this variation causes for the non-native listener. Chapter 10 describes how expert listeners succeed in identifying sounds, syllables, words and phrases in what they hear, despite its inconsistencies.

We then move on in Chapter 11 to consider the part played by larger units in the form of grammar and intonation. Each is examined first in terms of its role in decoding and then in terms of the contribution it makes to meaning.

Chapters 12 and 13 are concerned with meaning building. We consider how a listener enriches the bare meaning conveyed by a speaker's words. We then take note of the subsequent decisions that the listener has to make about the relevance and logic of the information that has been obtained. Suggestions are once again made for exercises which enable a learner to practise these processes in a second language context.

- *The challenge of the real world.* The types of listening practice illustrated so far have been developmental and likely to extend over a period of time. But while learners are in the process of acquiring listening competence, the teacher also needs to ensure that they are capable of coping with the everyday demands of real-world listening. In Chapter 14, I consider the use of authentic materials in the classroom, with an emphasis on their importance to the early stages of listening instruction. Chapter 15 concerns the compensatory strategies that learners use in order to extract meaning from partially understood pieces of everyday speech. In Chapter 16, I consider how effective it is to train learners to use these strategies.

- *Conclusion.* A final chapter brings together the various themes of the book and summarises the proposals that have been made.

English is used throughout the book as the language of exemplification, but the general comments made apply to the teaching of all foreign or second languages. Examples are sometimes cited from languages other than English and allowance is made for differences in pronunciation systems.

Certain chapters of the book (particularly Chapter 9) make use of phoneme characters to represent the sounds of English. For those who do not have a background in this area, Appendix 3 briefly explains the sound system of the language and how to interpret the non-alphabetic characters. Also to assist the reader, there is a glossary of listening-related terms at the end of the book, and there are suggestions for further reading after each chapter.

Anyone writing about human communication encounters a thorny problem in determining the gender of the two or more participants. An early draft of this book attempted even-handedness by making the listener male and female in alternate chapters. This created some confusion, and I have therefore settled for a consistently female listener – except, of course, where the text refers to a specific individual – and a male speaker. Lest this decision be misconstrued, I hasten to add that listening (the point is made many times in the book) is *not* by any means a passive skill.

Finally, a note on terminology. In discussions of second language listening, certain terms such as 'skill', 'process' and 'strategy' tend to be employed rather loosely. Attempts have been made here to use them with some degree of consistency, though I apologise in advance for any oversights. I have used the word 'skill' when referring to the four 'language skills' and to the 'listening skill'. The latter is represented as being divisible into 'sub-skills' or (in the approach preferred here) into a set of 'processes'. Throughout, the book attempts to sustain a distinction between 'processes' which are part of the expertise that we all need in order to listen and 'strategies' which are ways in which listeners (particularly L2 listeners) compensate for gaps in their understanding. All of this will, I hope, become plainer as the book proceeds.

Part I: Background

1 Listening then and now

*In order that all men may be taught to speak the truth, it is
necessary that all likewise should learn to hear it.*
Samuel Johnson (1709–1784), British lexicographer

1.1 Early days

In the early days of English Language Teaching (ELT), listening chiefly
served as a means of introducing new grammar through model dialogues. Commentators have sometimes implied that it was not until the
late 1970s and the advent of communicative approaches that the skill
was first taught in its own right. This version of events is not strictly
true. In language schools in Britain, listening practice featured quite regularly in course programmes from the late sixties onwards, though the
materials available were relatively few and on tape rather than cassette.
One of the first listening courses (Abbs, Cook and Underwood) came
out in 1968, and Mary Underwood's now-classic authentic interviews
and oral narratives date from 1971 and 1976 (though, admittedly, they
were ahead of their time in terms of recorded content). Still, it is sober-
ing to reflect that it was only from 1970 that a listening component
featured in the Cambridge First Certificate exam, and that until 1984
its listening texts consisted of passages of written prose which were read
aloud.[1]

The lesson format used by many teachers in those early days was a
relatively rigid one which reflected the structuralist orthodoxy of the
time (see Table 1.1).

Some features of this early lesson format are worth noting.

- *The three stages.* The lesson provided for a preliminary stage when
  teachers prepared learners for the listening exercise and for a final
  stage during which the listening experience was reviewed. During **pre-
  listening**, teachers traditionally presented the new items of vocabulary that learners were about to encounter in the recording. In **post-
  listening**, they checked the answers to comprehension questions and
  explored the language of the recording.

---

[1] Spolsky (1990) identifies the first-ever second language listening test as being the
Barnard–Yale Aural test, developed by Brooks in the early 1950s.

13

Table 1.1   *Early format for a listening lesson*

Pre-listening
   Pre-teach vocabulary 'to ensure maximum understanding'

Listening
   Extensive listening followed by general questions on context
   Intensive listening followed by detailed comprehension questions

Post-listening
   Teach any new vocabulary
   Analyse language (*Why did the speaker use the Present Perfect here?*)
   Paused play. Students listen and repeat

- *Listening at two levels.* A procedure developed whereby learners are first asked to listen to the recording generally, in order to gain some idea as to who the speakers are and what they are speaking about. This phase of **extensive listening** serves a similar purpose to skimming a reading text: it ensures some familiarity with the content and also allows the listener to establish the 'geography' of the recording in the form of what information is provided where. The kind of question that the teacher might ask at this stage is extremely general: *Who are the people? What are they talking about?* and (one I personally favour) *How are they feeling: angry? happy? disappointed?* During the second and subsequent plays, the listeners, now familiar with the general content of the text, are able to listen for detail and to respond to more focused questions. This central part of the listening exercise was traditionally referred to as **intensive listening**.

- *Multiple-play.* The format embraced the notion that the listeners might benefit from several plays of the listening passage during intensive listening. The thinking at the time (with its emphasis on form rather than meaning) was that repeated listening enabled the teacher to focus by degrees on the language of the recording and habituated the learner to the rhythms and intonation patterns of the target language.

These three characteristics have proved remarkably robust and continue to feature in present-day practice. The overall format of 'pre-listening – listening – post-listening' has formed the basis for many accounts of listening methodology (e.g. Underwood, 1989; Wilson, 2008), though there are serious questions to be addressed about the relative timing and importance accorded to each part, and about what constitutes appropriate 'preparation' and 'follow-up'.

The continued use of an 'extensive listening' phase might perhaps be questioned on the argument that, in real life, a listener does not have the opportunity to listen twice. That may be so, but in real life a listener usually has the advantage of visual cues which establish both the context of the conversation and the respective roles of the participants. In a hotel check-in encounter, we would see a hotel foyer, a guest with a suitcase standing on one side of a desk and a receptionist (possibly in uniform) standing on the other. Our understanding of the conversation might also be considerably assisted by facial expressions and gesture. None of this is available when a learner is listening to an audio recording.

Recognising the issue, listening teachers increasingly make use of visual material on DVD or video. One could argue that, when this kind of information is available, the case for an extensive listening phase is less convincing. But we also have to bear in mind that the situation of sitting and listening to a recording in a classroom is a highly artificial one. As Brown and Yule (1983b: 82) point out, eavesdropping on some-body else's dialogue rather than participating in it is not a conventional listening activity. It is all very well to aspire to real-life conditions, but a real-life conversation would provide the listener with the possibility of interrupting the speaker and asking for a clarification of anything that had not been understood.

On these grounds, most teachers continue to favour a first hearing which enables learners to establish a general idea of what is going on. In point of fact, the extensive listening phase does much more than compensate for the limitations of an audio recording. It also serves an important function for the weaker listeners in the class. They may have understood very little the first time round, but the answers given by their peers provide them with a few pegs upon which to hang ideas when they listen again.

Indeed, any rehearing of the recorded material assists all members of the class to extend their understanding of it. A case can be made not just for keeping the extensive/intensive tradition but also for employing multiple replays throughout the listening lesson. The original thinking was that replaying the recording allowed attention to be given to the forms of language, but it is now recognised that repeated listening enables the learner to build increasingly on the information that is extracted. A first hearing of a foreign-language passage may produce a partial understanding, which can be deepened only by subsequent exposure and by increasingly demanding questions on the part of the teacher.

The convention of multiple-play thus embodies a principle which shapes much text-based work in language teaching – the idea of

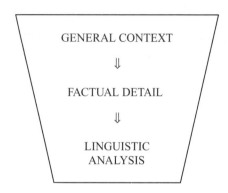

Figure 1.1   'Narrowing in'.

'narrowing in' (see Figure 1.1). The lesson starts with general notions and focuses on more detail as the learner becomes increasingly familiar with the text.

So much for the features of this early lesson format that have survived. But a general criticism of the format is that it was inflexible, and that the sequence of activities became highly predictable. Over time, a number of other aspects of the approach were also called into question.

- It was not correct (and smacked of 'nannying') to assume that students could handle a listening exercise only if they knew most or all of the vocabulary in it.
- Intensive listening took place without any clear aim. Students were not asked questions until after they had heard the passage, so they did not know what they were listening for. Their success in answering depended on memory as much as on listening skill.
- The convention of drawing attention to examples of grammar was a relic of the idea that the listening lesson should serve to demonstrate recently taught language in everyday use. In the end, lessons often focused more on discussing the language of the recording than on practising listening.
- Paused play could lead to 'parroting'. Its critics argued that students could repeat a stretch of sound without necessarily understanding what it meant.

1.2 Current practice

Over the years, the original model has been modified. The listening lesson that one encounters in good ELT practice today has a rather different

Table 1.2 *Current format for a listening lesson*

Pre-listening
 Establish context
 Create motivation for listening
 Pre-teach only critical vocabulary

Extensive listening
 General questions on context and attitude of speakers

Intensive listening
 Pre-set questions
 Intensive listening
 Checking answers to questions

Post listening (optional)
 Functional language in listening passage
 Learners infer the meaning of unknown words from the sentences
  in which they appear
 Final play; learners look at transcript

structure, which includes some or most of the elements shown in Table 1.2. Let us consider the rationale behind the changes.

1.2.1 Pre-listening

• *Pre-teaching vocabulary.* There are a number of reasons for not pre-teaching all the unknown vocabulary in a recording. It takes time – time which is much better spent listening. Very importantly, it also leaves students unprepared for what happens in a real-life listening encounter where, inevitably, there will be words which they do not know and have to work out for themselves. A third consideration is the effect upon the listening process. By pre-teaching all the new words in a recording, regardless of their importance, the teacher encourages the learner to listen out for those words. Result: the learner's attention is focused upon the language of the text rather than its meaning. It may also be misdirected to parts of the recording which are not strictly relevant to the main argument.

  The current policy is to pre-teach only **critical words**. 'Critical' is taken to mean those words without which the recording could not be understood (for example, in a passage about jogging, we would want to be sure that learners knew the verb *to jog*). In any given listening

17

text, there should be very few such critical items – at most, four or five.

• *Establishing context.* As already noted, it is important to compensate for the limitations of using an audio cassette by giving students a general idea of what they are going to hear. In a real-life situation, they would usually be aware of who the speakers were, where they were and so on. It is only fair to provide some of this information before the listening exercise.

  However, the information does not need to be extensive. In fact, there is considerable danger in expounding too much on the context of the listening passage. The more we tell the learners, the less they will need to listen to the recording to extract the answers they need. The criterion should be: *what would the listener already know in real life before the speech event began?*

Here are typical pieces of contextualisation from the Cambridge First Certificate (FCE) exam:

You will hear part of a radio programme in which two women, Mary and Pat, will talk about their interest in being an amateur radio operator, or radio 'ham'.
(Paper 103, Part 3)

You will hear a man talking about how he jogs – runs – in order to keep fit.
(Paper 103, Part 2)

These introductions serve three different pre-listening purposes:

a. They establish 'context': including the situation, the topic and the genre of the recording.
b. They introduce critical vocabulary.
c. They mention names which help the listener to 'label' the speakers. A teacher might also include other proper nouns (e.g. names of cities) which would not be regarded as 'fair game', i.e. as part of any learner's normal vocabulary base.

• *Creating motivation.* This is an important goal of pre-listening, and one that is sometimes neglected. We need to give listeners a purpose for listening. The quality and depth of listening is also enormously enhanced when the listener has the right **mental set** – in other words, when she has given some forethought to what the listening passage is likely to contain.

  How to create motivation? One way is to write a title for the listening passage on the board, and then to ask the learners to predict what they will hear (see panel below). Once they have created a set of expectations, the goal of the extensive listening phase is to check which of their predictions prove to be correct and which not. The process can even be competitive (*Anna thinks there will be something about noise pollution; Enrique doesn't agree. Let's see who is right.*). Note, by the way, that the interaction exemplified in the panel does more than just create mental set. It also performs the pre-listening functions of outlining context and introducing critical vocabulary.

Creating motivation for listening

T: You're going to hear somebody talking about camels. He's a zoologist who's studied them. What do you think he'll talk about?

S1: Desert.

T: Yes, he might mention deserts [*writes DESERT on board*]. Anything else?

S2: Water. Water on the camel's back.

T: He might mention what the camel has on its back. Its hump. The word is 'hump' [*writes HUMP*]. Any other ideas?

S3: Hot temperature.

S4: Walking. Long distance.

T: He might talk about the heat in the desert [*writes HEAT*]. How do we measure that?

S1: Degree.

T: Yes, in degrees. Anything else?

S4: Walking. Camels walk a long distance, carry people.

T: Yes, he might mention how far the camel walks [*writes DISTANCE*]. Or . . . ?

S3: Very slowly.

S5: How fast is the camel.

T: Yes, how fast the camel walks [*writes SPEED*]. [*Other possibilities explored*]

T: Well, some of you guessed correctly and some of you are wrong. Let's listen and see who was right.

A similar guessing activity takes advantage of the lack of real-life context in an audio recording by playing a short uncontextualised extract and asking learners to work out what is happening. This is done to great effect by Maley and Duff (1978) with passages such as the one below. Conflicting interpretations lead to animated discussion in the classroom and (most importantly) to some very careful listening and re-listening to justify the conclusions that have been reached.

Contextual ambiguity

A: You know what this is, I'm sure . . .
B: Um . . .
C: Oh, isn't it, er . . .
A: Yes, I thought you might like something familiar.
B: Oh, yes . . .
A: It's funny, it took me a long time to get to like it . . .
C: Oh?
A: But now I'm very fond of it . . . Of course, it's nothing special . . .
B: Oh no, it's . . . very good.
A: I thought you'd like it . . . (Maley and Duff, 1978: 82)[2]

1.2.2 During listening

The goals of extensive listening remain unchanged – for the reasons outlined above. However, the approach to intensive listening has been greatly restructured.

- *Pre-set questions.* If questions are not asked until after the recording has been heard, learners listen in a very untargeted way. They are unclear about where to direct their attention; and their ability to answer depends upon which parts of the recording they happen to have paid special heed to. Their responses also become heavily dependent upon memory – and their recall becomes unreliable as the teacher asks more and more questions and as time goes by.

  A policy of setting questions *before* the second play of the cassette ensures that learners know in advance what they are listening for. They can write notes of their answers during listening, and their ability to respond will not be dependent upon their ability to remember what was said. Note the convention in both teaching and testing (a convention that has rarely been questioned) whereby the questions follow the same order as the passage.

---

[2] Possible explanations: A has cooked a meal for two visitors from overseas. A has just played a recording of a rather heavy piece of classical music.

• *Checking answers.* The teacher allows learners time to write up their answers, and then checks them with the class as a whole. This is sometimes a difficult phase of the listening lesson. Learners may be slow to respond – partly because they need to switch psychologically from the receptive role of listener to the active one of class participant but often because of a lack of confidence in their replies. Some learners attribute their insecurity to the fact that they do not (as in reading) have the text before them in order to double-check before they commit themselves to an answer. One way of overcoming reluctance is for learners to compare answers in pairs before submitting them to the whole class.

1.2.3 Post-listening

• *Functional language.* The practice of replaying a listening passage in order to reinforce recently taught grammar has been abandoned, along with other structuralist notions. However, many of the dialogues which feature in published listening materials represent common types of human interaction. They therefore afford useful and well-contextualised examples of language **functions** such as refusing, apologising, threatening, offering, etc. These functions are relatively difficult to teach in isolation. It is worthwhile drawing attention to any which feature prominently in a listening passage, and even pausing briefly to practise them.

Drawing attention to functional language

T: What did George say about the damage?
S1: He wanted to pay.
T: Do you remember the words George used?
S2: 'I'll pay the damage.'
T: Yes. 'I'll pay for the damage.' So what was he doing?
S3: He promised.
T: Not quite promising . . .
S4: He offered.
T: That's right. He offered to pay for the damage. He *offered* . . . Offer to carry my bag.
S2: [*pause*] I'll carry your bag.
T: Offer to post the letter.
S5: I'll post the letter. *etc.*

- *Inferring vocabulary*. If only minimal vocabulary is pre-taught, listeners have to learn to cope with unknown words in the passage. Here, they are gaining experience of exactly the kind of process that occurs in a real-life encounter, where there is no teacher or dictionary on hand to explain every word in an utterance. It is usually assumed (perhaps by analogy with L2 reading) that the way in which an L2 listener deals with an unknown word is to work out its meaning from the context in which it occurs. If one accepts the assumption, it is appropriate to give listeners some controlled practice in the process of inferring word meaning, similar to the practice given to readers. The teacher identifies a number of useful words in the recording which may be new to the class and whose meanings are relatively clearly illustrated by the context (one or two sentences) within which they occur. The teacher then writes the words on the board, and replays the sections of the listening passage which contain them. Students suggest possible meanings.

  That is the principle; my experience is that it often does not find its way into practice. Although many teachers recognise the value of this kind of inferring activity, they are reluctant to engage in it. The reason is simple: even with a counter on the cassette or CD player, it can be quite complicated and time-consuming to locate a number of short pieces of text. In fact, the solution is simple as well. It is to pre-record the target sentences on to a separate cassette or CD so that they are easily retrieved for the inferring exercise.

- *Paused play*. Paused play has generally been dropped. It was often used as a way of practising intonation patterns – and was thus part of the unsatisfactory mixing of language and listening goals which has already been commented on. It was also criticised on the grounds that learners could repeat what they heard without necessarily understanding anything – the kind of parroting associated with behaviourist drilling. My personal belief is that paused play can still serve some purpose, as a way of checking whether learners can divide up short sections of connected speech into individual words. However, one has to recognise that it does not fit in well with current communicative approaches.

- *Final play*. There is sometimes a final play during which, for the first time, the students are given a transcript of the listening passage. This is a valuable activity, since it allows learners, on an individual basis, to clarify sections of the recording which they have not so far succeeded in decoding. It may also enable them to notice, for example, the presence of short weak-quality function words which they would otherwise have overlooked.

22

One of the strengths of early approaches to listening was the insistence on separating the spoken and the written word. However, there is no reason why the latter should not be introduced at a late stage in the lesson in the form of a transcript that assists word recognition. It is important that learners take away with them some kind of permanent record of what they have covered in the listening lesson – and not just an echo in their heads of the voices of the speakers.

In addition to the above, two other major developments have occurred. Firstly, it has been recognised that it is very difficult to check understanding accurately through the use of conventional comprehension questions. Answering such questions often involves a great deal of reading or writing; and if a learner gives a wrong answer, it may not be due to a failure of listening at all. It may be because he/she has not understood the question properly (a reading problem) or because he/she lacks the language to formulate a written answer (a writing problem). There has therefore been a move towards checking understanding by setting **tasks** rather than questions (see, e.g., Blundell and Stokes, 1981). These tasks can be quite simple. Many involve the completion of simple grids. Others involve filling in forms. If the listening passage is a dialogue between a customer and a travel agent, then the task might require the learner to complete the kind of form that the agent would be using (see Figure 1.2). The advantage of this kind of activity is not just that it reduces the amount and complexity of reading (and indeed writing) that has to be done. It also aligns the purposes and processes of listening more closely with what occurs in real-life encounters.

Task-based activities compare favourably with the practice of asking whole-class comprehension questions, where the strong listeners are often keen to respond while the weaker ones mask their failure of understanding behind bright smiles. All class members have to participate, and there is a tangible outcome in the form of a completed form or checklist which can be collected and marked.

Secondly, there has been a move towards using **authentic recordings** wherever possible. The term 'authentic' usually refers to listening items originally intended for the ears of a native listener rather than specially prepared for language learners. The arguments for using such materials are that they expose learners to the real sounds of the language (including the hesitations of spontaneous speech) and that they provide a listening experience more like that of real life, where students do not know every word and have to make guesses to fill in gaps in understanding. Authentic materials are discussed in Chapter 14 of this book.

To summarise, the changes that have taken place reflect three developments in the way listening is viewed. Firstly, there has been a shift

Lemming Travel Ltd

Holiday no:...

Client   Family name: ....*WILLIAMS*..........

Given names:..   Nationality:.................................

Address: ....

Telephone: Home:...........................Work...........................

Travel   [ ] ship   [ ] plane   [ ] train   [ ] coach

From:..   To: ....

Departure date: ....   Return date:....................................

Company/Airline:..

Outward flight no.:   _____

Accommodation   [ ] Hotel   [ ] Self-catering

No. of nights in hotel/apartment ....

Name of hotel/apartment ....

Resort (town and country)................*PATTAYA, THAILAND*

Room: [ ] Single   [ ] Double   [ ]Twin-bedded
            [ ] Without bathroom   [ ] With bath   [ ] With shower

Meals: [ ] None   [ ]Bed and breakfast
            [ ] Half-board   [ ] Full board

Special requirements (balcony, sea view etc)

Cost   [ ] low season   [ ] mid-season   [ ] high season

Cost of holiday   HK$ ....
Single room supplement   HK$ ....
Special requirements   HK$ ....
Insurance   HK$ ....

            Total cost   HK$

Payment by: [ ] cash   [ ] cheque   [ ] credit card

Figure 1.2   Example of a form-filling task (Field, 1983: 73).

in perspective so that listening as a skill takes priority over details of language content. Secondly, there has been a wish to relate the nature of listening practised in the classroom to the kind of listening that takes place in real life. This is reflected in the way the teacher provides contextual background, gives practice in inferring the meaning of new words, uses recordings which are 'authentic' in origin and uses simulated tasks rather than formal exercises. Thirdly, we have become aware of the importance of providing motivation and a focus for listening. The listener is encouraged to develop expectations as to what will be heard in the recording, then to check them against what is actually said. By pre-setting questions and tasks, we ensure that learners are clear from the start about the purpose of the listening exercise and will not have to rely heavily on memory.

1.3 Conclusion

The purpose behind this review of changing practice has been to highlight some of the principles which gave rise to present-day approaches to the teaching of listening. It may seem curious that the discussion should have covered these important ideas in the brief space of a single chapter rather than extending them over the major part of the book. But the overview presented here is intended to serve simply as a point of departure. My aim is not to provide a detailed exposition of current practice; other sources (Ur, 1984; Underwood, 1989; Wilson, 2008) already do that comprehensively, if in rather different ways from the historical angle adopted here. Instead, it is to challenge many of the received ideas which underlie our views of second language listening and the methods that we employ in practising it in the classroom. It will be argued that our present comprehension-based methodology is flawed. A case will be made for a radical rethinking of the way in which we approach listening in the second language classroom so that we can more closely address the needs and concerns of the learner.

2 The comprehension approach: pluses and minuses

He ne'er presumed to make an error clearer;
In short, there never was a better hearer.
Byron (1788–1824), British poet, *Don Juan*

In Chapter 1, we reviewed the changes that have taken place in the methodology of the listening lesson and the rationale behind them. The changes have been extensive, but it can be argued that they have not been extensive enough. We have made adjustments to the format of the listening lesson; but we have not addressed in any fundamental way the question of what it is that we aim to achieve in teaching listening. Nor have we taken adequate account of recent insights from research into the nature of listening processes. One has to conclude that the current approach does not serve our purpose adequately – indeed it misleads us dangerously into believing that we have dealt with the listening problems of our learners when we may barely have touched the surface.

What has survived intact from the original approach shown in Table 1.1 is a received view that the best way of developing listening skills entails presenting learners with a recorded passage of about three minutes, then checking their understanding of the passage by means of a comprehension exercise. If a right answer is given (at least by the more vocal members of the class), teachers assume that understanding has been achieved and move on. If a wrong answer is given, teachers replay the part of the text that has caused difficulty. The presentation can be made more learner-friendly by playing the recording in short sections; similarly, the comprehension exercise might take the form of a task rather than a set of questions. But the underlying supposition is that testing for understanding is the most appropriate form for the listening class to take. This supposition has rarely been questioned; so prevalent is it that teachers' manuals often use the term 'listening comprehension' to refer to all work on listening skills.

In this chapter, we take a critical look at the comprehension approach (CA), pointing out some of its weaknesses, but also acknowledging that it brings some benefits to the learner. The issues raised here are explored in greater depth in the remainder of the book.

2.1 Weaknesses of the comprehension approach

2.1.1 Reading versus listening

It seems reasonable to ask where the established view of how to teach listening originated. The most likely answer is that the approach, and the assumptions that go with it, was carried over from the teaching of reading. As noted in Chapter 1, the dedicated listening lesson came quite late, at a time when there was already a set of established methods for L2 reading. Small wonder if perceived similarities between the skills (especially the need to test performance indirectly) led to a transfer of methodology from one to the other. Today, we continue to apply to both listening and reading the assumption that correct answers to questions provide evidence of achievement, and we employ similar exercise types to check understanding in the two skills. But listening is in many ways a very different skill from reading; and we should not let conventions of methodology distract us from recognising the important differences between the two.

Consider first the differences in the raw material that readers and listeners have to handle. A reader has the advantage of a standardised spelling system. By contrast, a listener is exposed to speech sounds which vary considerably from one utterance to another, and from one speaker to another, and which even blend into each other. A reader benefits from blank spaces between each of the words in a written text. There are no such regular gaps separating words in connected speech; and the listener largely has to decide for herself where one word ends and the next begins. One might conclude from this that listening is a rather more demanding skill than reading. That is certainly my own view. But the main point at issue is that the signal which the listener has to deal with requires an entirely different kind of processing to that demanded by reading. Teaching programmes need to give much more attention than they do at present to the features that make listening distinctive.

A second important difference lies in how permanent the text is. The reader retains evidence on the page of the words that have been read, whereas listening relies upon information that is transient and unfolds in time. So reading can be **recursive**, with the reader going back to check word recognition and to check overall understanding in a way that the listener cannot. The transitory nature of listening appears to be a major cause of L2 **listener anxiety**, leading to the often-expressed conviction that native speakers 'speak too fast' or 'swallow their words'.

Of course, it cannot be denied that the two skills have certain meaning-building elements in common. They both draw upon the same comprehension processes (extracting ideas, relating the ideas to what has gone

before, interpreting what the speaker/reader has left unsaid, making connections to world knowledge). But this resemblance should not be over-
stated. Because of the temporary nature of the speech signal, a listener
has to carry forward in her memory all the ideas that have been expressed
so far if she wishes to build a complete account of a conversation. By
contrast, as we have just noted, a reader can always look back. So even
at the level of comprehension the processes are distinct.

Similarly, it could be argued that both skills demand the ability to
'bundle up' words into phrases and grammar structures. But there are
marked differences in the patterns of language that are involved. Consider the circumstances under which writing and speech are produced.
Most writers have time to plan what they say with some care, to pol-
ish their sentences, to choose exactly the right words and to structure
what they say in a tightly organised way. By contrast, speech has to be
assembled under the pressure of time. Speakers produce shortish clusters
of words, often loosely linked by *and*, *but* and *so*. They may mispro-
nounce, hesitate, rephrase, repeat and even lose track of what they are
saying. Clearly there is a gradient from very informal conversation at
one end to very precise and careful writing at the other. But in many
circumstances, the patterns which a listener is called upon to trace in a
speaker's words will be very different from the patterns which a reader
identifies in a piece of writing. Not least, the listener has to allow for possible repetition and has to supply some of her own connections between
ideas.

Yet another cause for concern lies in the methods used to check understanding, which have been adopted from reading but may not be suitable
for listening. Take the use of multiple-choice questions in listening exams
and published materials. It quite often happens that written multiple-
choice options are more difficult to interpret than the recording that is
supposed to be the focus of the exercise. If the learner fails to get the
right answer, it is as likely to be due to inadequate reading ability in
handling the questions as to inadequate listening ability in handling the
recording. Admittedly, this type of question represents an extreme case,
but teachers need to be cautious about relying too heavily upon exercises
in written form and upon test methods originally designed with reading
in mind.

To summarise, the present approach to teaching listening misleads us
by drawing close parallels between listening and reading on the grounds
that both result in something loosely termed 'comprehension'. It directs
the attention of the teacher away from many of the features which make
listening distinctive. These features are precisely the ones which cause
most difficulty for the learner and the ones that we need to focus on if
we wish to promote more effective listening.

2.1.2 More practice versus better listening

Our current pedagogy is also open to criticism for its lack of clarity about the goals of the listening lesson and its failure to consider whether the methods it prescribes are the best way of achieving those goals. A detached look at the comprehension approach suggests that it is founded upon some very questionable thinking.

The approach centres upon exposing learners to a series of spoken texts. The emphasis is on repeated encounters rather than on the quality of the listening that takes place. A large assumption is thus made: that learners become more competent listeners as the number of L2 listening experiences increases. With some learners, this may indeed happen, but there can be no guarantee that it will. Instead, somebody who is a weak listener at the outset might well become increasingly demoralised by their lack of perceptible progress.

The chief problem with an approach based upon 'one text after another' is that the learning that occurs is localised and may not extend to future listening experiences. Learners are given feedback on whether their answers are correct or not; they are sometimes allowed to hear problematic passages again. But that does not mean that they take away from the experience the kind of generalised technique that will enable them to avoid a similar problem of understanding if one occurs in future. A learner might come to realise that a sequence that sounds like *might-adun* in the voice of a male taxi driver corresponds to the grammatical pattern *might + have + done*. Learning has taken place in respect of this sample of speech, and the knowledge will assist the learner if she ever hears the same recording again. But it may not assist her in deconstructing *shouldadun* or *mightathought*, encountered in a different context and in the voice of a female academic.

Conventional listening courses often claim to be progressive; but they do not in fact develop learners' competence in any systematic way. They are progressive only in the sense that the passages are graded by linguistic difficulty or that the tasks are graded by the demands they are said to make of the learner. This smacks of an obstacle race in which the organiser keeps raising the height of the barriers without ever showing the runners how to get over them. As the barriers get higher, some listeners will find their own ways of dealing with the increased challenge; others will simply decide that what is being demanded of them is too difficult and withdraw their cooperation. It is very difficult to persuade somebody to lend attention to a piece of speech if they believe that they are incapable of making any sense of what is said.

Even the notion of 'comprehension' as the goal towards which listening strives is quite misleading. Comprehension is certainly the end product of listening, and achieved by an expert listener with minimal apparent effort. But the concern of a novice listener surely has to lie with the means as well as the end. To form another analogy, we might say that safe handling of a vehicle is the goal towards which driving instruction strives. But nobody would suggest that the learner driver can get by without a great deal of hands-on, step-by-step guidance along the way.

The emphasis on comprehension has had an unfortunate effect in that it has led many commentators to focus their attention on how listeners construct wider meaning and away from the nuts and bolts that enable the operation to take place. It has led to a received view that difficulties in recognising sounds and words in the input are of a lower order of importance, and that many of them can be resolved by the use of 'context'. This is demonstrably not the case. In fact, one could say that the opposite is true in that many problems of understanding have their origins in low-level mistakes of perception.

2.1.3 Answering questions versus showing understanding

Even the use of conventional comprehension questions does not achieve what it appears to. Here, the gross assumption is that right answers demonstrate a high level of listening competence, while wrong answers or silence show that the learners fall short of what was expected. But we must be very careful of jumping to easy conclusions. For a start, just because a learner succeeds in identifying isolated points in a recording, it does not mean that she understands how the points contribute to the overall message intended by the speaker (e.g. which are major topics and which are examples or explanations). In addition, learners often achieve correct answers by using **testwise strategies** that draw heavily upon the wording of the questions. As for the supposedly weaker listener, silence may not show incomprehension; it may just mean that the listener is not 100% certain about what she has heard.

Of particular concern is the way in which current practice fosters the idea that answers are necessarily 'right' or 'wrong'. What appears to be an incorrect answer might actually be supported by evidence which the listener has drawn upon but which the teacher or materials writer has overlooked. This happens more often than one might suppose.

Perhaps the greatest criticism of answers to comprehension questions is that they are *uninformative*. They enable us to pass a rather superficial judgement on a learner's listening proficiency, but they do not say what has enabled the learner to perform successfully or where her weaknesses lie. They enable us to say to the learner, 'Try harder next time' – or perhaps more realistically, given the serendipitous nature of the exercise,

'Better luck next time'. But they give no hard evidence as to why things went wrong – of the kind that might help us to assist learners to improve their listening. They enable us to judge but they do not enable us to remedy.

2.1.4 Comprehension approach versus communicative language teaching

Less fundamental, but nevertheless problematic, is the way in which the comprehension approach impacts upon the classroom. The teacher sets the questions; the teacher passes judgement on the correctness of learner responses; the teacher makes decisions about which parts of the recording to replay. The CA thus embodies a very teacher-centred methodology, of the kind that good practice in other areas has generally left behind.

It also fits rather oddly into a pedagogy that sets great store by communication in the classroom. Granted, listening is a very individual activity in terms of the processes employed and the interpretations reached; and we cannot change that. But, by emphasising methods associated with testing rather than teaching, and requiring each student to report her own set of answers, the CA tends to isolate learners. The atmosphere in a listening class often approximates more closely to that of an exam centre than to that of a forum for communicative practice of the second language.

2.1.5 Classroom versus outside world

A further weakness of the CA lies in the lack of fit between the types of activity that take place in the language classroom and the listening that a learner might expect to do in the real world.

One factor is the question-based format of the CA lesson. Pre-set questions provide the listener with more information in advance of hearing the speaker than she would normally possess in real life. The questions also restrict the tasks that are undertaken – with the result that certain important listening functions (e.g. deciding which pieces of information are important and which are not, or building information from the speaker into an overall line of argument) are rarely performed by the classroom listener.

It is sometimes argued in defence of comprehension questions that it is good listening behaviour to approach a speaker with a set of enquiries in mind. That may be true for a very limited number of real-life listening events. But, even so, the questions would be very different in form from those that feature in the CA. They would concern major ideas rather than details and certainly would not have been invented by the listener in exactly the same order as the speaker is going to mention them.

The CA also imposes restrictions on the relationship between listener and recording. Typically, listeners are asked to eavesdrop on a two- or three-way conversation. That type of listening happens in real life – but there will also be many situations where listeners are direct participants in a conversation and have to form an immediate response to what the speaker says. Practice in **interactive listening** is accorded relatively little importance in the comprehension classroom.

A further concern is that the CA does not provide learners with survival techniques that equip them for real-world encounters. Early language learners are quite heavily dependent upon their ability to compensate for gaps where they have been unable to recognise words in a piece of connected speech. The CA makes no effort to develop the use of listening **strategies** that enable them to deal with this situation. Indeed, it often does the opposite: reducing the extent to which strategies are required by simplifying the language of the passages that are used or using slow speech. Small wonder that some learners achieve quite a high level of listening success in the classroom but find that they are ill equipped for the demands of the outside world.

2.2 Benefits of the comprehension approach

Despite the many concerns which have been discussed, the comprehension approach still has a place in the teaching of listening – though, it will be suggested, a much more limited place than at present. It brings at least two major benefits to the trainee listener.

The first consists of *experience and exposure*: exposure to natural samples of the target language and experience of making sense of them in order to build a message. Whatever the drawbacks of the CA, the importance of these factors should be recognised. Listening, like speaking, improves through use: through encountering problems of recognition and understanding, forming hypotheses as to what was heard and storing the hypotheses for future use if they prove correct. One of the characteristics of an expert listener is the ability to process spoken input in a highly automatic way – one which does not make heavy demands upon the listener's attention. That kind of automaticity can be achieved only by extensive experience of actually using the skill.

Of course, the exposure needs to be brought about in a measured way. Here, we should not simply rely upon the old idea that language difficulty decides listening difficulty. An equally important consideration must be the nature of the input. Instructors need to expose learners over time to a wide range of voices, accents, text-types and degrees of 'authenticity', but they also need to remain sensitive to the challenges that such features pose and to grade them accordingly.

The second benefit of the comprehension approach is a rather more dubious one for an instructor concerned with long-term listening expertise. It enables students to *pass exams*. International tests of listening tend to adopt the assumptions of the CA as well as its methodology in the form of batteries of questions about short listening passages. The methods they employ satisfy the requirements of testers in terms of ease of marking and high **reliability** (i.e. they are likely to produce the same range of scores wherever and whenever they are applied). That is not the same thing, of course, as saying that they always tap in to underlying listening competence or succeed in distinguishing the able listener from the less able.

With these considerations in mind, the reader will not be urged to abandon the comprehension approach entirely. But it is very important to remain aware of its limitations. We may need to rethink quite radically some of the assumptions that the CA carries with it. We may also wish to fine-tune many aspects of the way in which the CA is applied in the classroom in order to ensure that it addresses the needs of the learner much more closely and effectively, and that it takes much greater account than at present of the nature and realities of L2 listening.

2.3 Goals of the book

The purpose of this book is to provide solutions to the failings of the comprehension approach in its present form. It has three broad goals. One is to ensure that the reader gains a better understanding of the listening skill; another is to suggest ways in which the comprehension approach might be modified to make it more effective; a third – and perhaps the most important – is to propose methods which might supplement or replace the approach. The sections described in the opening pages correspond closely to these goals:

- adapting the comprehension approach (Chapters 3 to 4)
- alternatives to the comprehension approach (Chapters 5 to 7)
- listening processes, with practice exercises (Chapters 8 to 13)
- adjusting to listening in the real world (Chapters 14 to 16)

Throughout, listening is treated not just as a means of obtaining answers to questions but as a form of **expertise** which an L1 listener possesses and which an L2 listener can be helped to acquire through targeted practice.

Further reading

Field, J. (2001a) 'The changing face of listening'. In J. C. Richards and W. A. Renandya (eds.), *Methodology in Language Teaching*. Cambridge: Cambridge University Press, pp. 242–7.

Part II: Rethinking the comprehension approach

3 Listening and the learner

Nature gave us one tongue and two ears so we could hear twice as much as we speak.
Epictetus (*c.*55–*c.*135), Greek Stoic philosopher

The purpose of this chapter is to consider the ways in which the comprehension approach affects the dynamics of the classroom and to put forward suggestions on how some of the teaching practices with which the approach is associated might be made more effective. We consider the impact of the CA upon the teacher and upon the learner before going on to explore ways in which second language listening can be made more individual.

3.1 The individual and the group

A major theme of the chapter is the tension between the nature of the listening skill, which is personal and internalised, and the whole-class teaching situation, where the teacher is obliged to consider the needs of a whole group and to pace the lesson accordingly.

In some respects, listening is a very individual activity. A speaker does not implant a message in the listener's mind. The listener has to remake the message: trying to gauge what the speaker's intentions are and extracting from the message whatever seems relevant to the listener's own goals. The message is a product of the individual listener, not something which a group of listeners hold identically in common. Second language listeners also vary in how they approach the challenge of making sense of input that has only been partly understood. Some are prepared to form hypotheses as to what the speaker said; others are more reluctant to do so and depend upon recognising as many words as possible. There is thus a tension between the personal nature of the skill and the pedagogical tradition of practising it in groups – a tension that is heightened by the fact that individual copies of the text to be studied are not available as they are in reading; there is one recording, which is played to the group as a whole.

Three specific aspects of classroom listening deserve mention because of their impact upon the learner. One derives directly from the tradition of the comprehension approach, the other two from the very nature of listening.

(a) *The listening class is teacher-centred.* The comprehension approach does not fit comfortably into a teaching culture which favours communicative methodology, in that its procedures are very much under the control of the teacher. It is the teacher who operates the button on the CD or cassette player, predicts where problems are likely to occur, asks relevant questions, replays certain passages and decides how much time is spent on each breakdown of understanding.

(b) *Playing a recording to a group of learners has an isolating effect.* Most teachers have at some time had the experience of a lively, interactive class becoming withdrawn and non-committal after a period of listening. It may be that the learners are reluctant to contribute because they are uncertain about whether they have fully understood the recording; here, the CA can partly be blamed for fostering the notion that listening is about achieving a right answer rather than discussing what has been heard. A second explanation is a social-psychological one: the experience of silent listening fragments an established group into a set of individuals and they find it difficult to revert to the normal dynamics of the communicative classroom.

It could be said that classroom listening is, of its very nature, isolating. Of the four skills, it is the most internalised. At least with reading, we can see the reader's eyes moving down the page. But we cannot force learners to listen if they do not want to, and we cannot be sure whether they are listening at all or whether their minds are elsewhere. Here is a problem that current practice rarely addresses: how can we ensure that the weaker listeners do not simply give up and daydream instead of attempting to impose meaning on what they hear?

(c) *Listening takes place in **real time**.* The cassette moves on, and the learner's mind has to keep up with it. There are really two issues here. Firstly, listening is not under the control of the listener: the speaker decides how much to say, how fast to speak and so on. It is even less under the control of the listener if the speaker's voice is on a CD and cannot be interrupted with a request for an explanation. The second point is that listening is not recursive like reading. The learner cannot look back to check a word or words that they have only partially recognised or to resolve ambiguities in their understanding. Returning to the earlier point about teacher control, in a whole-class situation it is the teacher who identifies actual or potential problems of understanding and rewinds the cassette to enable learners to listen again. An individual listener may need more time to listen and re-listen than the group as a whole is allowed.

The three factors identified contribute to learner anxiety and provide a reason for learners citing listening as a difficult skill to acquire. There is a clear need to revise the current approach in ways that increase the level of interaction and give learners greater control over the listening processes.

3.2 The role of the teacher: a non-interventionist approach

Transcript 3.1 is my own recording of a listening class which adheres quite closely to CA principles. The teacher played a short section of a listening passage, asked comprehension questions to the class as a whole, then replayed the relevant part of the text so that those who did not understand the first time could check the facts.

Transcript 3.1

Teacher plays 60 seconds of a narrative (Underwood, 1976: 133).

T: so what was in + in the folder
Ss: silence
T: the folder + do you understand the word + it's a piece of card-board + like this [*demonstrates with hands*] + what was in the folder
S1: passport
T: yes their passports + anything else
S2: tickets
T: what kind of tickets
S2: ticket for a car
S3: tickets for a boat
T: that's right + they were tickets for the boat + anything else
S4: money
T: how much + does anyone know
S2: hundred pounds
T: not a hundred pounds + it was hundreds of pounds + hundreds + was that in money
[Ss: *silence*]
T: it was in traveller's cheques + you know cheques that you change into foreign money + let's listen again

---

The teacher is doing quite a competent job in testing comprehension at a very local level and in supplying what is missing. But the exchanges are characterised by the relatively limited contribution made by the students. This is partly because the culture of the CA marks out the student's role as being to answer questions. It is partly because of the teacher's desire to be helpful and to fill gaps – though note that no distinction is made between gaps that are due to lack of vocabulary knowledge and gaps that are due to failure to recognise a known word. Note too that the subsequent replay does not challenge the learners' listening skills any further but just gives them the chance to check the truth of what they have been told.

It is the teacher who controls the agenda – in ways that would be unacceptable if this were a lesson to practise speaking. He perceives his role as being to determine, on the basis of his own knowledge and experience, where potential problems might occur and to intervene as often as necessary to provide correct answers to assist the listeners. It is the teacher, in short, who does most of the work.

The CA was founded on the premise that there is a 'right' answer to each question that is asked. Tradition thus places the teacher in the role of sage, the person who holds the keys to understanding. If a learner's response is deemed accurate by the teacher, the lesson moves on; if it is not, the teacher takes responsibility for giving and explaining the correct answer and replays the relevant section of the listening passage by way of justification.

The single-interpretation assumption is very much open to challenge. As Brown (1995: Chap. 1) points out, there may be two or more possible answers to a comprehension question, depending upon how the individual listener has interpreted the information. The issue is not whether an answer is correct but whether it conforms to the evidence. Yet CA methodology remains heavily dependent upon right and wrong, upon ticks and crosses.

Teachers are sensitive to the fact that L2 listeners differ widely, not simply in how much they know but also in how they approach the listening task. Yet underlying the CA is the implicit premise that learners listen in ways that are broadly similar. Standard practice obliges the teacher to make decisions for a class as a whole:

- *How much of the text should I play at a time? Should I stop if there are signs that some class members do not understand?*
- *Do I ask questions of the whole class or nominate? If I nominate a weak listener, will it slow things down and possibly embarrass the individual?*
- *If Student A gives the right answer, can I take it for granted that everyone understands?*

- *How serious was that last breakdown of understanding? How widespread? Do I briefly explain it or do I replay the relevant part of the recording?*
- *How long should I spend on reworking a part of the text, given the danger of losing the attention of those who understood it from the start?*

The methodology thus places heavy demands upon the teacher in terms of moment-to-moment decision-making, since any decision runs the risk of either boring the better listeners or demoralising the weaker ones. Even the most committed teacher sometimes feels the need to take an easy course in order to keep a listening lesson moving. There is a temptation to accept that understanding has been achieved once one or two class members have given the target response proposed by the materials writer.

What of the learners? The notion of a single 'correct' answer influences their behaviour, too. Because the pace is set by the better and more outspoken listeners, those who are defeatist about listening do not focus effort on the input when it is first heard. Instead, they monitor it at a low level of attention, listening out for the odd familiar word, until such time as the 'official' answer is established. It is at this point that their attention becomes fully engaged: for them, listening practice consists chiefly of checking the answer given against a subsequent replay.

The solution to this situation is relatively simple. It requires teachers to change the persona they adopt in relation to the listening exercise. They need to suppress their instinct to assist; instead, what is needed is *a deliberate policy of non-intervention*. Instead of assuming that their role is to explain/paraphrase/target, teachers should ensure that the learners do much more of the listening work for themselves. It is by listening and re-listening and by testing hypotheses for themselves that learners progress; not by having the answers handed to them.

To give an idea of how this works in practice, Transcript 3.2 comes from a lesson in which a group of learners was presented with an authentic text somewhat beyond their lexical level and encouraged to mine it for words, phrases and information.

This teacher provides minimal assistance. Instead of giving answers, he is simply acting as a facilitator: encouraging the class to compare the pieces of information they have extracted for themselves from the passage. Listening becomes a problem-solving exercise which engages the attention of the class to a much greater degree. It is the class who, between them, construct a provisional meaning representation and revise it as more is heard.

Transcript 3.2

Teacher plays a short extract (30 seconds) from a recording about international relations after the Second World War and about the then US Secretary of State.

T:	right + how much have you understood so far
S1:	two or three years ago before the + no two or three years before the second war
T:	two or three years before the second world war + does everybody agree that's
S2:	after after
S3:	after
T:	two or three years after the second world war
S1:	ah
S2:	yes after
T:	well what do you think + before or after
Various Ss:	after
T:	after + what did he say about two or three years after
S1:	the president of North America + I don't know + what country he is president
T:	the president of somewhere [...] + does everybody agree + are we talking about the president
Various Ss:	yes
T:	ok anything else + any other words you picked up [...]
S4:	er finish + America was the only one superpower
T:	America was the only superpower + do you agree that's what he said
S3:	super?
T:	superpower + can you tell me what does superpower mean
S4:	wars [*laughter*] + strong
S3:	oh yes
T:	the superpowers are the most important countries in the world + so he was saying that America was the only superpower
S5:	and the Soviet Union
T:	you think that the Soviet Union was also a superpower
S5:	he said something but
T:	he mentioned the Soviet Union
S6:	he said something from + but er England
S3:	Spanish

T:	you heard something about Spanish + and you heard England
S1:	Britain
T:	is it Britain [. . .] + talking about Britain
S3:	he also said a moustache
T:	he mentioned a man's moustache [. . .] + do you think the moustache was important
S3:	no
T:	I'm not going to tell you any more + listen to a little more and see if you change your minds

[*Plays another 15 seconds ending in the sentence 'America was now top nation'*]

T:	anything you want to add
S7:	he says that America wasn't top nation
Various Ss:	was was
S1:	was now
S3:	was now was not
T:	you think America was top nation or wasn't
Various Ss:	was
T:	was

In this particular case, the passage was a demanding one in relation to the language level of the students. The main focus of attention was therefore at the level of the word and the information that could be generated from it. In a more advanced class, the teacher might have asked students to compare their different interpretations of the speaker's main points or to make decisions as to which ideas were most central. He would then have replayed the passage without passing judgement, to see if the class members changed their minds or not. The important principle is that the views of the teacher and the teacher's ability to match input to words should be called upon only as a last resort.

3.3 The role of the listener: an interactive approach

It has been suggested that listening activities tend to have an isolating effect, breaking up a class into individuals operating on their own. But, if listening is isolating, surely the same can be said for reading and writing, which are also solitary pursuits.

Compare the handling of listening in the communicative classroom with the treatment of these other skills. Today's learners are asked to write with a clearly defined goal and reader in view; they are encouraged to work together to compose texts and sometimes to write and reply to other class members. In other words, what is potentially an isolating skill has become, in the language classroom, an interactive one. Something similar happens in reading lessons. Teachers feature activities that externalise what is normally a silent process: pair reading, the use of Big Books with young learners, jigsaw reading, analysing text structure. By contrast, classroom listening appears to have been left behind. Methodologists have not shown the same concern about ensuring that it is interactive. A possible reason can be found in the availability of the comfortable routines offered by the comprehension approach.

A second way of improving the quality of comprehension work is therefore to ensure that learners work together rather than in isolation. Even within larger classes, learners can be encouraged to share their interpretations of a listening passage with those next to them. The teacher no longer starts off by eliciting answers from the class as a whole to the questions that have been set, but instead gets students to work in pairs or small groups, discussing and comparing their versions of what they have heard. They try to achieve agreement on the correct answers, then listen again to check their decisions before the matter is settled.

The advantage of this is that it enables weak listeners to confess to, and to share, their problems of understanding. It brings the benefit of all pair work: namely, that two minds are usually better than one (in this case, four ears are better than two). It can also be used to foster a degree of competition, with listeners vying with each other to see who manages to come up with the correct answer. At the very least, each member of a pair feels a compulsion to try to contribute something to the joint interpretation. The attention of every learner is thus engaged – a very different situation from what commonly happens when individuals listen in isolation. When listening alone (especially in large classes), a learner who lacks confidence in her listening skills is free to withdraw cooperation: it is all too easy for her to direct her attention elsewhere if the passage appears impenetrable and to shelter behind nods and a facial expression that suggest complete understanding.

What kind of revised methodology can one construct around these two principles of low teacher engagement and high learner interaction? Table 3.1 gives an idea of what a reshaped comprehension lesson might look like. To some readers, it might seem that replaying a passage five times is excessive, but a great deal will obviously depend upon the level of the learners and the demands of the passage. The two factors of *teacher intervention* and *number of replays* should be treated as continua and adjusted according to the needs of the class. A high-level class might

Table 3.1 *Non-interventionist format for a listening lesson (intensive listening phase)*

- **Pre-set questions**
- **First play**
  Learners note down what they understand.
- **Second play**
  Learners check their understanding. They discuss it in pairs.
  Where pairs disagree, they try to reach agreement.
  Teacher: no comment except where widespread and serious misunderstanding.
- **Third play**
  Pairs check to see who is right.
  Pairs present their understanding to the whole class.
  Teacher summarises, without commenting on correctness.
- **Fourth play**
  Class checks to see who is right.
  Teacher comments.
- **Fifth play**
  Class listens with a transcript.
  Teacher answers any questions.

---

reach an agreed interpretation of a piece of speech after only three plays, while classes at the most basic levels might find an enigmatic approach by the teacher frustrating if it were sustained too long.

That said, trials by teachers have shown that L2 listeners generally respond well to this methodology: they welcome the opportunity to hear a piece of input several times and to form their own conclusions without undue intervention by the teacher.

3.4 Listener independence

The third issue to be considered relates to the listener's lack of control over the input. As already noted, in a whole-class situation it is the teacher who determines which parts of a recording to focus on. At times, the teacher may dwell overlong on sections of the recording that the individual learner has been able to match and interpret accurately; at other times, the teacher may take for granted areas that the learner finds problematic. The process would clearly be more focused if listeners could control the pace of the operation for themselves. This would permit them to regress and to check and re-check areas which they had failed to understand, thus compensating for the fact that listening does not normally permit recursion.

3.4.1 Group listening

A suggestion occasionally made is that the teacher should hand over control of the CD or cassette player to a student. That, frankly, is not very practical: it simply transfers to a learner the difficult whole-class decisions that the teacher has to make. A more viable alternative along the same lines is to provide the class with several players and to ask them to work in small groups on the same recording. There are certain practical needs that have to be met: among them, the availability of sockets, the size of the room(s) and the level of noise. Clearly, it is an option that is only open to small or medium-sized classes (up to, say, four or five groups of four). But my own experience suggests that group listening of this kind can be a very productive activity: one in which loyalty to the group fosters patient and persistent listening and where learners respond well to the challenge of assisting each other's listening skills.

As with any group-work activity, a class needs to be prepared for a session of this kind. The teacher should first play the recording to the whole class for general understanding and then introduce and explain the questions or task. The learners move into groups to carry out the exercise, each group with its own copy of the recording. One member of the group takes responsibility for replaying short sections of the recording on demand, as the group seeks to locate the information it needs, while another serves as secretary and records the answers. There can then be a final whole-class phase where answers are reported back and compared.

3.4.2 Listening homework

There are clearly limits to how much can be achieved through whole-class listening practice. Teachers therefore need to supplement class work by seeking ways of promoting independent listening. Encouraging a learner to listen on her own carries the same benefits as other types of learner autonomy. It ensures that she:

- demonstrates the ability to accomplish a listening task without reliance on the contributions of others;
- has ample time to achieve the task without having to proceed at the pace of the class;

- can replay the recording as often as she needs (achieving the kind of recursion that reading offers) and can focus upon specific stretches of the input which are difficult for her personally rather than for the class as a whole.

It is possible today to give learners much greater access to listening resources than they previously had. CD and cassette players are widely available and relatively inexpensive. In many parts of the world, every learner can be assumed to have one at home, or at the very least to be able to borrow one. It thus seems a practical proposition to provide listeners with individual copies of listening material for personal practice. CDs are cheap to produce, and, thanks to modern technology, multiple copying is no longer as cumbersome as it once was. In addition, copyright holders (publishers, radio and TV companies) are more willing to tolerate multiple copies of their material than they were in the past.

If teachers have reservations about copying commercially produced material, they can always make use of their own off-air recordings or download recorded material from the Internet. They can even use their own voices. Where there are sufficient computer facilities in the school or in the students' homes, the possibilities become even greater. Teachers can record sound files from radio to computer and then upload them to students as email attachments. Alternatively, they can give students a set of questions in class, with directions to a website from which a chosen podcast can be downloaded.

One of the best ways of fostering independent listening (and indeed of increasing the time which learners give to this critical skill) is to set listening homework. Each learner is given a copy of the recording on which the homework is based, and allocated a period of (say) seven days to complete the task or exercise that is set. With smaller classes (especially in language schools), teachers can assemble a whole term's homework on a single CD. In circumstances where some or all students possess MP3 players, the teacher might select a weekly podcast for intensive study. All students can be asked to download the podcast at the beginning of the week, to listen to it as often as they feel they need to, then to give feedback on it at the end of the week.

This recommendation might seem to be possible only with small classes and in countries with considerable financial and technical resources. In fact, with a little administrative skill, it is also possible to provide listening homework in parts of the world that are less well equipped. If the school's resources run to a small number of cassettes, the solution is to produce a limited number of copies – say, eight for a class of forty. Each class member keeps the cassette for long enough to achieve the task (say, three days), after which it is passed on to another.

Of course, this assumes that at least some of the pupils will have access to a cassette player.

Even where the opportunities for receiving broadcasts in the target language are limited or the reception is of poor quality, teachers can still record samples of the target language in their own voices, telling a story, recounting an incident in their lives or conversing with colleagues.

Listening homework requires a degree of preparation. The teacher might play a recording for general understanding, then introduce the task that is to be accomplished or the questions that are to be answered, and check that they have been fully understood. When the homework has been done, answers should be collected in and checked. They may be found to include acceptable alternatives to the 'official' answers. They also provide valuable evidence about the listening skills of individual class members, enabling the teacher to offer support where needed. Some of the results may come as a surprise: it is by no means always the case that a student with a sound basis of spoken grammar and vocabulary possesses listening skills to match.

The discussion so far has implied that the chief benefit of setting listening homework is to improve the learner's ability to match the input to words. It gives the individual more opportunity to mine a recording for information, adjusting her ears to the sounds, rhythms and intonation patterns of the target language. But, as these skills improve, more varied types of homework can be considered, which draw upon general comprehension skills. For those studying in an English as a Second Language (ESL) context, the teacher might ask the whole class to tune in to a particular TV programme, radio broadcast or podcast and to report back (perhaps in the form of a summary). Those studying in an English as a Foreign Language (EFL) context might be asked to find a source of the target language (world service radio or TV or the Internet), to make a short recording of their own and then to present the text to other class members. For some inventive outside-class projects, see White, 1998.

3.4.3 Listening centres

Another possibility is to establish a **listening centre** within a school. Many of the routine drilling activities associated with language laboratories were discontinued in the 1970s as early behaviourist views of language learning became discredited. But the disused labs found a new life in the following decade as centres where learners could practise listening independently. The labs, in turn, have now been supplemented by computer facilities which enable learners to download listening material from the Internet. In some institutions, sophisticated language centres have been set up, which give access to video recordings of L2 TV programmes and news broadcasts that are received daily by satellite.

For secondary schools with limited resources, a listening centre may seem an extravagance that cannot be afforded. But this perception derives in part from unrealistic ideas as to what a centre requires by way of equipment. Language labs were expensive. They required sound-proofed booths, microphones, twin-track tapes and a central console, because drilling and pronunciation practice required participants to speak aloud and to record their voices. Equipment of this kind is not necessary in a listening centre. All that is needed is a properly ventilated room with space for learners to sit a short distance apart from each other, an adequate number of players on desks, headphones for the players to reduce noise levels and an ample supply of recordings in the target language, classified by level of difficulty. Granted, a considerable amount of work is involved in setting up such a centre, particularly in copying and classifying the recordings and in devising tasks, but the costs are not nearly as great as is sometimes assumed.

Listening centres need the backing of clear policy decisions; they quickly become white elephants if they are not sufficiently incorporated into the learning programmes of the school. First of all, the class teacher needs to establish what might be termed a *listening culture*, reversing the neglect which sometimes attends the skill. The value of acquiring listening competence should be stressed: not least, the way in which a listener with good word-recognition skills is able to acquire new grammar, vocabulary and idiom from exposure to target language speech. A brief beginning-of-course diagnostic test might indicate to learners how strong their listening skills are, and which areas of listening would benefit from independent practice.

A clear bridge needs to be built between whole-class listening practice and work in the listening centre. At the very least, learners should be familiarised with the centre on their arrival in the school or college and shown its resources. Some teachers choose to transfer some or all of their listening classes to the centre, with learners working in pairs if there are limited places. Others set listening homework which requires learners to use the centre (and incidentally avoids the need to make multiple individual copies of cassettes).

Some institutions leave it entirely up to the learner to decide whether and how to use the listening centre. This is not entirely satisfactory: there is a danger that the learner will waste time with recordings at an inappropriate level or with activities that are unproductive. The effectiveness of independent work done in a listening centre often depends critically upon the quality of assistance which a learner receives (Holec, 1985). There are two general policies. One is a *consultancy approach*, with an informed adviser available in the centre at certain set times of the day. Alternatively, one can adopt a *prescriptive approach*, where the class teacher provides a listening programme for the individual learner, taking full account of the learner's listening needs and personal interests. It is easy to design a form, on the lines of a doctor's prescription, which recommends certain recordings, certain listening activities and even how long to spend in the centre at any one time.

When advising learners how to listen independently, it is important to recognise that they come with their own, sometimes poorly informed, ideas about what L2 listening entails and about how to improve their own skills. A serious oversight of many listening centres is that they do not ask learners about these beliefs and suggest alternative paths where appropriate. As a result, some listeners spend a great deal of time in fruitless dictionary work while others try to answer a battery of questions after a single hearing, then fall back on the tapescript. Others never get further than following a tapescript word by word. Listeners should be clearly briefed as to how to make the best of their time in the centre; alternatively, the type of exercise set (and in particular the type of rubric used) should be designed so as to enable them to extract the maximum benefit from the text that they are studying.[1]

3.4.4 Adapting materials for self-study

Some comprehension exercises and tasks designed for use in the class-room adapt well to independent use (whether as homework or in listening centres). Imaginative activities such as those in Doff and Becket (1991) are as productive when used by the single listener as when used by the teacher with a class. Certain exercise types seem particularly suited to independent listening. They include:

- form-filling and labelling;
- completing a grid;
- comparing and contrasting;
- putting events in order of occurrence or facts in order of mention;
- making notes on specific topics;
- filling in gaps in a paraphrase summary or in a paraphrase set of notes
- explaining connections between topics or completing a mind-map.

Not so suitable are conventional multiple-choice and true/false ques-tions, where independent listeners sometimes devote excessive amounts

---

[1] However, this recommendation comes with the rider that advisers must take care not to be over-directive (see the Hong Kong studies of self-access support under-taken by Voller, Martyn and Pickard, 1999, and Pemberton *et al.*, 2001).

of time to trying to establish why a particular proposition is wrong rather than focusing on those that are right. They might be replaced by more productive exercises where listeners have to read a text and then correct it in the light of the information in the recording. Also useful are exercises where listeners have to decide which topics or points on a list are mentioned in the recording, and then (on a replay) to note briefly what is said about each one. Exercises that ask listeners to anticipate what comes next have their purposes, in that they oblige the listener to summon up a meaning representation of what has been heard so far.

Some classroom material may need to be adapted quite radically. Most obviously, the teacher in the classroom usually provides pre-listening contextual information, whereas, in a self-study context, the same information (including any critical items of vocabulary) has to be given in the rubrics. One also has to bear in mind that more can be demanded of the independent listener: she has more time to listen to the recording and the opportunity to handle it recursively. In addition, the listener's attention can be directed towards specific areas of difficulty where intensive and repeated listening will assist in the development of word-recognition skills. The aim of self-study work should be to encourage the learner to listen more effectively and not simply to test general understanding.

One way of achieving this in a listening centre session is to design exercises and tasks that require listeners to 'narrow in' on a listening passage along the lines described in Chapter 1; then finally to consider global meaning and the argument structure of the text as a whole. The panel below provides an example of the kind of worksheet that is appropriate for listening centre work (adapted from classroom materials in Field, 1983, Unit 24). It indicates the type and extent of rubric that needs to be provided, and illustrates a relatively comprehensive sequence of activities. Note the simple and user-friendly language.

Sample worksheet for a self-study listening activity

- *Stage 1*. Play the whole recording. You will hear two people talking about a journey. Where do you think they are? What is the purpose of the journey? Which of the two people is going on the journey? Who is the other person?
- *Stage 2*. Below you will see a form about two hotels, which has been partly completed [*Task sheet taken from coursebook*]. Study the form carefully. Make sure you know what goes on each line and where to put each piece of information. Listen carefully to the recording. When you come to an important piece of information,

---

stop the recording and fill in the form. Note that the information in the recording may not be in the same order as it is on the form.

- *Stage 3*. Replay the recording and check what you have written.
- *Stage 4*. Play the first part of the recording as far as *afraid*. Listen carefully when you come to the following words and fill in the gaps.

A: I want to _____ a short holiday.

B: _____ you want to go?

A: I _____. _____ sun.

B: And _____ you want to go?

A: _____, if possible.

B: Well, you've _____ late. We haven't _____, I'm afraid.

- *Stage 5*. Listen carefully to the next part of the recording, as far as *swimming pool*. Can you guess the meaning of these words? *brochure vacancies southern fancy well placed*
- *Stage 6*. What does the female speaker seem most concerned about?
  a. Comfort   b. Price   c. Size of hotel   d. Time   e. Number of stars
  List the similarities and differences between the two hotels.
- *Stage 7*. Turn this worksheet over and check your answers. Replay any sections of the listening passage where your answer seems to be wrong.
- *Stage 8*. Listen to the recording again. This time, listen with the tapescript. Listen carefully (two or three times) to any parts that you find difficult to follow.

Stage 1 corresponds to the extensive listening phase of a classroom listening session, enabling the listener to sample the gist of the recording. *Stage 2* constitutes the 'intensive' information-gathering task. Note that the listener is free to stop if she wishes to. There is no reason why, under self-study conditions, the listener should have to operate under the time constraints of a test or have to deal with the difficult cognitive demands of writing and listening at the same time.[2] While the rubric does not say as much, the listener should feel free to replay and check information that is being written down. Note too that, in these conditions, one can dispense with the tradition of always asking comprehension questions in the same order as the information occurs in the passage. The great advantage is that, if the listener misses a piece of information, she can

[2] Unless, of course, the listener is training for a particular exam.

roam at will throughout the recording, seeking it. She can handle the text just as she would a book.

Stage 4 targets a small section of the recording, giving practice in word-recognition skills. The pieces omitted in the exercise are not very prominent (and thus quite difficult to identify) or are idiomatic. They represent, in short, the kinds of word cluster that real-life L2 listeners might have trouble in processing or might need to respond to.

> A: *I want to **get away for** a short holiday.*
> B: ***Where did** you want to go?*
> A: *I **don't really mind. Somewhere in the** sun.*
> B: *And **when did** you want to go?*
> A: ***The week after next,** if possible.*
> B: *Well, you've **left it rather** late. We haven't **got a lot left,** I'm afraid.*

Stage 5 operates at a similar level of detail, asking the listener to infer the meaning of new words from context. A later chapter will suggest that vocabulary inferencing is not as common in real-life listening as we tend to assume. But it is still a useful skill for an L2 listener to practise, since it offers a means of acquiring new vocabulary. It also obliges the listener to think quite carefully about the significance of the sentence in which the word appears.

Stage 6 asks the listener to collate the information gathered from the entire passage. With a more academic text, one might ask the listener to summarise the speaker's main points and/or to cite the speaker's final conclusions and the reasons given for them.

As for the checking of work (*Stage 7*), it is important to ensure that the answers appear on the reverse of the worksheet, so that the listener's eye resists the temptation to wander. Alternatively, they might appear on a separate sheet, which the listener has to collect from the supervisor of the listening centre once the task has been completed. The same is true of the transcript. Early use of the transcript should be discouraged in this type of exercise; the issue of the uneasy relationship between spoken and visual input is discussed more fully in the following section. But it is extremely valuable for the listener to hear the recording one last time with the transcript available – thus enabling her to recognise any sections of the recording that have proved especially intractable.

The example we have just examined is designed for a single level of L2 competence. An alternative approach sometimes adopted by listening centres (especially those which are short of recorded material) is to provide four or five groups of exercises for each recording, grading and colour-coding them according to the complexity of the tasks they require learners to perform. Learners can either attempt the tasks which are marked as appropriate to their current level or work through all the tasks until they feel that they have reached a ceiling of difficulty.

3.4.5 'Extensive listening'

A further means of fostering listener autonomy is through what is sometimes referred to as 'extensive listening'. This recent use of the term (Prowse, 2001) came about by analogy with 'extensive reading' programmes such as the one designed by Edinburgh University. It should be distinguished from the more traditional type of extensive listening, i.e. listening to a recording for general understanding (Chapter 1).

The principle is to encourage listening for pleasure and without obliging the listener to keep demonstrating a satisfactory level of understanding. At its broadest, this might entail encouraging learners to exploit the opportunities afforded by sources of the target language in their everyday environment: international radio and TV programmes, podcasts, films with L2 soundtracks, the lyrics of popular music. But one can also set up, within a listening centre, a library of audio and video materials which offer the opportunity of listening for pleasure. There is no shortage of such materials: audio books are available in most languages, and feature films and other forms of entertainment can be purchased on DVD.

The key lies in preparing the listener. Any preconceptions that the listener may have about what listening demands (particularly about the necessity of achieving accurate word recognition throughout) need to be carefully discussed. It has to be made clear that the goal of this activity is to gain general understanding; if some of what is said is unclear, it should not unduly worry the listener or impair the enjoyment of listening. In an instructional programme, this message may not always be an easy one to get across. In addition, a great deal may depend upon the listening style of the individual. 'Holistic' listeners will adapt readily to the experience of listening for overall understanding; others who are more dependent upon making accurate word matches may find the experience frustrating and may even end up asking for a script.

The most important consideration is that the listener should choose materials which fit her own interests or which relate to areas in which she has sound background knowledge. Learners sometimes come to 'extensive listening' with unrealistic expectations; so, to avoid disappointment, it is a good idea to give the listener some idea of her level and limitations. It is also advisable to grade the materials very loosely by difficulty (easy – average – demanding). Here, conceptual difficulty, cognitive demands and (in the case of video) level of visual support should perhaps weigh more heavily than linguistic difficulty. Much of the material available as audio books or on DVD is in narrative form, requiring the listener simply to follow the stages of a plot. In the case of feature films, the narrative is usually well supported with visual cues. So, if processing difficulty rather than linguistic difficulty is adopted as the chief criterion, quite a large number of recordings can be classed as falling at the easy-to-average end.

When watching second language video material, subtitles in L1 provide a useful prop for understanding. Subtitles greatly increase ease of comprehension and viewing pleasure. But they also raise an important issue, which merits more consideration than it often receives. The cinema or video viewer seems remarkably adept at combining reading with listening. Nevertheless, there are clearly increased cognitive demands when one operates in speech and writing at the same time (consider the difficulty which we would all experience in following a radio programme at the same time as reading a novel). It thus seems probable that, over an extended period of viewing, the viewer will come to rely more heavily on one source than the other. In the case of L2 listeners (apart perhaps from the most advanced), we should assume a bias in favour of the written source.[3] Subtitles may display only a truncated version of what a speaker says, but they constitute a more reliable form of input for the non-native speaker in that every word is encoded with equal clarity, and word boundaries are clearly marked. This suggests that the chief locus of attention for the learner in following the plot is likely to be the visual record of the dialogue, *which is in L1*, rather than the spoken form. The degree of exposure to L2 oral input may thus not be as deep as we might assume.

This is certainly not a reason for dispensing with subtitled films. But, for the purposes of listening practice, it would seem to be better for the learner to watch for short periods, or alternatively to watch L2 films with subtitles in L2. A range of such films are available, produced with L2 listeners and hearing-impaired L1 listeners in mind.

A similar reservation applies to the practice of learners listening to audio recordings with the original book in their hands. The most obvious problem with this approach is that the recordings are sometimes abridged versions, with the result that much of the listener's attention becomes preoccupied with matching or failing to match the written form to the spoken. But, even where a one-to-one text of the recording is available (as might happen in the case of short stories), there is no escaping the

---

[3] This remains an assumption based upon what we know of human attention limitations. We have little evidence in this area relating to the L2 user. But the assumption is supported by the author's own experience as a competent listener to French and an above-average listener to Spanish. When watching French and Spanish films, he becomes very aware that his reliance upon the English subtitles (if they are available) increases over a period of time.

'divided attention' issue just raised. For the reasons given, a sound-plus-script activity would seem likely to direct attention much more upon the written word than upon the spoken. It certainly provides assistance in building links between written forms and their spoken correlates; but that is not the same as providing listening practice. If the listening session extended over a period of time, one might predict an even greater bias towards the written input, to the extent that the oral might become little more than background noise.

An easy solution is for the learner to listen to the audio recording once without the support of a book or script, and then to listen again with it. Better still, the listener might tackle the recording in relatively short sections, first listening 'blind', then listening with the support of the text. This should not detract unduly from the enjoyment of the material: on the contrary, the listener can relax in the knowledge that, if an important point is missed on the first hearing, it will be possible to retrieve it on the second.

3.5 Conclusion

Listening is a skill which impacts in specific ways upon the classroom context in general and upon the individual learner in particular. If these effects have not been fully discussed by methodologists, one important reason may be the availability of an established pedagogical model in the comprehension approach. Despite concerns expressed by some practitioners and commentators, there has been widespread acceptance of the notion that listening is best taught by means of playing medium-length recordings and requiring learners either to answer questions on them or to recode information in diagrammatic form. The side effects of this approach have not received the attention they deserve. It sits uneasily with current communicative priorities in language teaching methodology, in that it (a) places the teacher at the centre of all activity as controller and interpreter of the input and arbiter of the correctness of answers, and (b) has an isolating effect upon the learner.

Two important methodological solutions were proposed here. Firstly, the teacher needs to resist the professional impulse to assist, and instead needs to pass much more of the initiative over to the learners. He/she needs to adopt what has been described as a non-interventionist stance. Secondly (an expedient towards which many practitioners are already moving), there needs to be far greater emphasis on learners sharing the outcomes of listening: thus ensuring a higher degree of engagement in the listening task and sustaining the kind of interactive imperative which informs other areas of language teaching.

Consideration was also given to the nature of listening itself, which is personal, internalised and time-constrained, and to the difficulty of practising such a skill in a whole-class context. The recommendation was that practitioners should explore ways in which practising the skill can be individualised, enabling learners to play and replay specific pieces of text which cause them difficulty and to work at their own pace. The goal is to introduce an element of recursion into listening, but recursion which is driven by individual needs rather than the prescriptions of the teacher. The activities proposed included autonomous listening centre work, listening homework and the provision of material which facilitates extensive listening.

Further reading

Gardner, D. and Miller, L. (1999) *Establishing Self-Access: From Theory to Practice*. Cambridge: Cambridge University Press.
Prowse, P. (2001) 'Success with extensive listening'. Cambridge University Press website: www.cambridge.org/elt/readers/teacher/articles/current4.htm.
Sheerin, S. (1989) *Self-Access*. Oxford: Oxford University Press.
White, G. (1998) *Listening*. Oxford: Oxford University Press.

4 Types of listening

Listening to someone talk isn't at all like listening to their words played over on a machine. What you hear when you have a face before you is never what you hear when you have before you a winding tape.

Oriana Fallaci (b. 1930), Italian writer and journalist, *The Egotists*

The main theme of this chapter is that the types of listening which feature in the language classroom are limited by comparison with those that occur outside. The demands of the comprehension approach place certain constraints upon the choices of listening passage made by teachers, while the tasks that are set tend to follow orthodox patterns of answering discrete questions or of filling in information. A case will be made for greater variety, both in the recordings used and in the responses demanded. Teachers are also urged to attempt to reproduce more closely the relationships between the two that occur in real-life contexts.[1]

4.1 Constraints of the comprehension approach: text and task

The requirements of the comprehension approach favour a particular type of *listening text*.

- It has to be long enough to permit around eight comprehension items; and the items need to be quite widely spaced so that two do not occur too closely together. This indicates a medium-length recording (say, around three minutes) – ideally, one which can be divided into shorter subsections for more intensive listening if necessary.
- The recording needs to be information-rich.
- Because of potential problems in distinguishing voices, the recording is most likely to feature a single speaker or two speakers of different sexes.
- The listener's role is usually as a non-participant, whose goal is to extract meaning rather than to respond in any way.

[1] However, issues associated with the use of 'authentic' texts (i.e. texts not primarily designed for language teaching purposes) are reserved for Chapter 14.

In real life, input is much more various. Much listening involves face-to-face events when we listen for shorter periods of time. Some of these exchanges have very little informational content: they are social and even phatic in intention (Brown and Yule (1983a: 1) term them 'interactional'). Conversely, many situations where the listener is a non-participant (radio programmes, lectures) involve a much more extended period of listening than three or four minutes. Here, the information is sometimes more dispersed and there is the opportunity to retrieve points that have been missed, when the speaker repeats or reformulates a remark.

The comprehension approach also favours a single type of *listening task*.

- The listener has to identify various points of information within the text.
- Listening therefore demands a high level of attention throughout the passage.
- The points that are targeted are selected by the teacher or materials writer, not by the listener.
- The listener is often required to focus upon micro-points rather than macro- ones.

Enlightened materials writers and testers sometimes extend the scope of their tasks by featuring questions which demand global information alongside those which demand local. But the point remains that **auditory scanning** is the major type of listening practised in the listening classroom. It is also practised in a way that differs markedly from real-life conditions, since there is an unspoken agreement between teachers/testers and learners that questions will follow the same order as the points in the text to which they refer.

Outside the classroom, a much greater range of listening types occurs, and much greater flexibility is demanded of the listener. Indeed, the mark of a competent listener is the ability to *select a listening type that is appropriate to the input being processed and the task in hand*. We might choose to listen for gist, listen for a single piece of information, listen in depth. We would listen very differently to somebody giving life-saving instructions, to a radio programme on a familiar topic or to an extremely boring guest at a party. There is also a close relationship between the listener's goals and the type of listening in which she engages. Even within a single utterance, we might vary the depth of attention that we bring to bear, homing in on points that we regard as important and sidelining others.

In sum, it is important for skills practice to take greater account both of the varied nature of the listening situation and of the listener's need to respond appropriately to a particular type of input.

4.2 Constraints of the comprehension approach: the listener's role

The CA restricts the role which the listener is called upon to perform. Most activities require learners to listen to and report on a recorded passage. The content of the passage may be a monologue, or it may be an exchange between two or more speakers; but the listener's role is **non-participatory**.

It can be argued that this is not at all representative of the type of listening which the learner is most likely to experience in real life, and that, in L2 contexts, the learner's most pressing need will be to communicate with others (see Underwood, 1989: 5 for just such a claim). The type of listening demanded by an *interactive* situation (Lynch, 1995: 166–68; Buck, 2001: 12–14) is very different from listening to a recording, since an important part of the process is the listener's need to formulate, within a tight time frame, an appropriate response to what is heard. The listener must achieve an understanding of a comparatively brief piece of input and be ready with a reply when a change of turn is signalled by the speaker. This contrasts markedly with the non-participatory situation where the input may, as already noted, last for much longer, and where there is more time for the listener to monitor what has been understood and to test out hypotheses as to the speaker's intended meaning.

The relevance of the classroom experience can also be questioned when the recorded material takes the form of an exchange between two or more speakers. Critics have argued that this kind of activity is inauthentic: to what extent, in real life, do L1 listeners need to eavesdrop upon the conversations of others?

On the strength of the points just made, an extreme conclusion might be that teachers should abandon any approach to listening that is based upon non-participatory responses to recorded material. In its place, they might feature, for example, carefully graded communication tasks, in which learners are monitored separately for their listening and speaking skills. This solution runs the risk of throwing out the baby with the bathwater, principally to satisfy considerations of 'authenticity'. The fact is that authenticity (see Chapter 14) is a notoriously slippery concept. Much as teachers may aspire to reproducing the circumstances of real life, their efforts to do so are inevitably limited by the demands of the classroom and the expectations which are associated with it.

One should also be wary of the assertion that interactive listening is overwhelmingly the most common type that the learner is likely to engage in, and that therefore non-participatory practice is largely irrelevant. A great deal depends upon the needs of the learners and the contexts in which they are most likely to encounter the target language. Potentially, much L2 listening (to instructions, announcements, tourist information, films, radio and TV, talks) is mainly or wholly one-way. This is especially so in foreign language, as against second language, situations. Furthermore, however important it is for most L2 listeners to participate in conversations, there is every reason to regard listening to extended input, with its redundancies and the greater opportunity for monitoring comprehension, as an easier option. One might wish to defer interactive listening, with its heightened time pressures, until such time as the listener has demonstrated a basic level of expertise in handling one-way material.

The 'eavesdropping' criticism can also be countered. Most obviously, hearing native speakers participating in dialogues provides practice in listening to short utterances and changes of turn, in a way that hearing monologues does not. Dialogues supply models of L2 discourse, showing learners how to interact with others, both as speakers and as listeners. Furthermore, it is not true that listeners do not eavesdrop in real life. L1 listeners do monitor the conversations of those around them, though they are capable of doing so at such a low level of attention that they are barely aware that they are processing the input at all. Nor is it correct to assume that all conversations consist of two partners making equal contributions. Gillian Brown (personal communication) points out that in an exchange involving a group of four or five people, any one of them may be 'eavesdropping' for 70% or more of the time, without necessarily feeling any pressure to respond every time a turn ends.

As for L2 listeners, eavesdropping is an activity in which they engage quite frequently when in a target language setting. It provides them with many more opportunities for noticing and acquiring new language than are possible in face-to-face encounters, where they have to be ready at any moment to reply. So 'eavesdropping practice' in the classroom is certainly relevant to the development of listening skills in real-life situations.

There thus appear to be two possible directions available if one wishes to expand the types of listening material that are employed in the classroom. We should not abandon non-participatory forms of listening practice. Rather, we need to look critically at the types of text and task that the comprehension approach gives rise to, with a view to expanding the range of experience available to the learner. On the other hand, it is clear that interactive listening is very different from non-participatory in terms of the processes involved, and that learners may require specific practice in it. It features relatively rarely in dedicated listening lessons; and we need to consider in some detail how it can be practised and developed in a targeted way.

4.3 Listening event and appropriate response

The limited nature of the text-types traditionally used in listening classes becomes apparent if one brainstorms the wide range of listening events that occur regularly in everyday life. Many types of utterance are distinctive in that they require their information to be structured in a particular way, while some (e.g. answerphone recordings) are delivered in a specific format. Table 4.1 suggests some of the more obvious listening events that provide potential teaching material. If you consider these utterance types from the point of view of how the listener handles them, it is clear that they vary enormously in the processing demands that they make. Some types of input require more careful attention than others, and some demand more complex storage of information than others.

This raises quite important questions for the listening instructor. If we aim to prepare the learner adequately for real-life listening encounters, we need to assess the extent to which the listening task demands the sort of processing that would occur outside the classroom. Whatever the conventions of the comprehension approach might dictate, the most appropriate process may not be auditory scanning, and the most appropriate response may not entail answering questions or form-filling.

To give a simple example, a listener does not respond to an airport announcement by filling in a grid with the times, gates, numbers and destinations of the flights that are called. Instead, what she actually does is:

- monitor the announcements at a low level of attention until her own destination is mentioned;
- focus attention on the announcement of this particular flight and especially the gate number;
- tune out for the remainder of the announcement since it is not relevant to her needs.

The type of behaviour just described rarely features in the classroom for the simple reason that it does not exploit a three-minute cassette recording intensively enough. But it is clearly the way in which the material in question would be handled by the listener in real life and consequently demands practice. Listeners might perhaps be asked at an initial stage of a lesson to monitor a recording for a particular flight or flights before later filling in the inevitable grid. In the same way,

Table 4.1 *Some genres of listening event*

- *Face-to-face*: Conversation   Obtaining and giving information
  Negotiation
- *Distant, but two-way*: Phone conversations   Taking a message
- *External to listener*: Announcements   Instructions
  Answerphone messages
- *Listening for pleasure*: Drama excerpts   Film clips   Jokes
  Extended anecdotes   Songs
- *Informative*: News headlines   News items   Documentaries
  Interviews   Discussions   Sports commentaries
- *Instructional*: English lessons   English-medium lessons
  Lectures
- *Persuasive*: TV ads

it makes sense to provide 'listen and do' activities to accompany oral instructions and to provide an auditory skimming task ('which items are interesting/relevant?') to accompany radio news headlines. The key is to make the task as appropriate as possible to the text, with real-life processing needs in mind.

This line of argument does not rely upon any narrow criterion of 'authenticity'. It is not an attempt to rigidly reproduce real-life circumstances in the unavoidably artificial context of the classroom. It simply recognises the need to provide training in specific types of process that are required for listening in the real world and that are not elicited by a Q and A format.

So far, two proposals have been put forward for expanding the traditional content of listening programmes:

(a) that we should introduce greater variety in the types of input offered to the L2 listener;
(b) that we should match the type of listening required of the listener as closely as is practical to what would be expected in a real communicative context.

One possible approach is to identify as wide a range of everyday listening events as we can, and then consider how the listener would be most likely to handle the input and how she would be most likely to respond. Table 4.2 illustrates how this might work. It lists a number of listening events, including some of those mentioned earlier, and suggests the types of listener behaviour that are most appropriate to each.

Table 4.2 *Listener response appropriate to type of input*

Genre	Listener response
Conversation	Listen and respond
	Eavesdrop (see previous discussion)
Negotiation	Listen and respond or challenge. Retain detailed meaning representation
Transmission of information	Locate and retain main points
Announcement	Monitor for one item
News headlines (radio/TV)	Monitor for interesting items
News (radio/TV)	Monitor for previously identified item Listen for main points in item
Sports/outside broadcast	Construct spatio-visual representation
Song	Gist; listen for words
Personal narrative	Listen for plot essentials
Film/TV drama	Listen for plot essentials
Instruction	Listen and do
	Listen; retain details and their order
Form-filling	Scan and locate relevant points
Phoning	Listen and respond. Allow for minimal context
Taking a message	Close listening for details
Lesson	Listen for main points – show understanding
Lecture	Listen for main points and relative importance. Take notes
Tour guide	Listen for main points
Translation	Listen for meaning; rephrase

4.4 Listening types

An alternative line of attack proceeds in the other direction. We attempt to list the various types of listening that a real-world listener engages in (low-level monitoring, listening for detail, auditory scanning, etc.) and then go on to practise them by linking them to the types of situation in which they occur. To take examples from Table 4.2, we might decide that one type of listening that needs practice is monitoring what is heard for pieces of information that are of interest or relevance. Learners are then asked to apply that process to the types of input that would normally require it: namely, news headlines, airport announcements, etc. Similarly, listening for details might be practised in situations where messages or instructions are being given, while listening for main points would be relevant with complete news items and with the output of lecturers and tour guides.

There is nothing very revolutionary about this idea. Indeed, current L2 listening materials quite often pay lip service to it, marking out certain passages and the tasks that accompany them as practising 'listening for main ideas', 'listening for gist', etc. However, only a limited range of '*listening for*' categories are usually featured and the way in which the materials match utterance type to listening type is not always consistent. So far, no system seems to have been devised of grading the types of listening in terms of the demands that they make of the learner or of organising them so that one type leads on to another.

A useful way of thinking about types of listening is suggested by Urquhart and Weir's (1998) account of the reading skill. They regard a competent reader as one who commands a range of different reading processes and is capable of matching the appropriate process to the text provided. They suggest (p. 123) that reading types vary in two main ways. One relates to how much attention the reading requires (on a gradient from *expeditious* to *careful*); the other relates to the level of detail that the reader aims to acquire (whether it is *local* or *global*).

If we attempt to apply the same criteria to listening, the 'expeditious'/'careful' distinction does not seem to form quite such a neat dichotomy. The listener appears to have much greater scope for varying the level of attention that she gives to the input – and even for 'tuning out' altogether. Table 4.3 represents a tentative proposal on my part. It follows Urquhart and Weir in distinguishing whether the listener's focus of interest is local or global; but it recognises four levels of attention that might be brought to bear according to the nature of the task. The relevance of this model to a teaching programme is that instructors should ideally try to ensure that learners are given practice in as wide a range of these listening types as possible: taking due account of whether the locus of interest is local or global and of the closeness of listening demanded by the type.

Clearly, that will not always be a practical proposition, as a great deal will depend upon the level of language and the listening expertise of the learners in question. Generalising somewhat, one might suggest a gradual progression. Listening types that demand a low focus of attention or

Table 4.3 *Types of listening as determined by listener's goals*

	Global	Local
Shallow attentional focus	**Skimming** (listening generally) to establish discourse topic and main ideas. *'What is it about?'* e.g. TV channel hopping, TV advertisements, eavesdropping **Phatic communion** *'What are the speaker's intentions?'* e.g. greetings	**Unfocused scanning** to locate information relevant to the listener. *'Does the speaker mention anything of interest to me?'* e.g. news headlines
Medium attentional focus	**Listening for plot; listening to commentary** *'What happened next?'* e.g. film/TV drama, TV/radio interview **Conversational listening** *'What is the speaker's message?'* e.g. everyday chat **Information exchange** *'How much do I need to know?'* e.g. tour guide	**Focused scanning** to locate one area of information needed by the listener. *'When will the speaker mention X?'* e.g. airport announcement, weather forecast **Search listening** to locate and understand information relevant to predetermined needs. *'What is the answer to these questions?'* e.g. hotel/travel information **Message listening** *'How many details do I need to retain?'* e.g. answerphone
Deep attentional focus	**Close listening** to establish the speaker's main points and to trace connections between them. *'What is important?'* e.g. lecture listening	**Close listening** to record in depth the speaker's main points and supporting detail. *'I assume that everything is relevant.'* e.g. negotiation
Very deep attentional focus	**Listening to check critical facts** *'Is this consistent?'* e.g. witness evidence	**Listening to vital instructions** *'I assume that everything is important.'* e.g. street directions **Listening to the form of words** *'What precisely did he say?'* e.g. listening to quote somebody

require chiefly local information are likely to prove easier for less experienced L2 listeners to handle. It is only when listeners have achieved the ability to recognise the majority of the words in the input that we can expect them to extract multiple facts from a listening passage and to register the complex relationships between them. Similarly, it is only when listeners are able to divert some of their efforts from word recognition that they are able to allocate resources to building the kind of detailed representation that enables them to report on global meaning.

The principal point remains that instructors should aim to ensure that type and depth of listening are appropriate to the text that is being used. The panel below provides some concrete examples of tasks which could be applied to the kind of recorded material that is generally available from listening courses, off-air and internet sources. It will be noted that the tasks described are rather more demanding than those associated with the comprehension approach in that the listener has to seek out information for herself rather than simply locating information which the teacher has targeted. The tasks are loosely organised by depth of listening; some have both global and local components.

Of course, one cannot be too dogmatic in insisting upon a close text–task match. On their own, the exercises exemplified in the panel may not provide enough work for a full listening lesson – in which case, the teacher will need to supplement them with traditional CA classroom tasks based upon 'local' details. But a principal consideration should be the need to model the types of listener response that are likely to occur, rather than simply mining a text for general and specific information.

Sample tasks based on listening type

'You are a radio listener interested in ecology and psychology; but not politics. You are going to switch quite quickly between five different programmes. Find one or two which might interest you.'

'You will hear five sports commentaries. Identify the sports involved.'

'Your partner works in Cardiff and is late home. Listen to the traffic news for the whole area and try to work out why.'

'Listen to part of this soap opera episode. Say what has happened. What is the "cliff-hanger"? Say what you expect to happen next. Then listen and decide if you were right or not.'

'You are in southern Europe. What will the weather be like tomorrow?'

'You are waiting for a train to London and hear a number of announcements. What do you find out about *your* train?'

'You have gone to a tourist information office to find out about hotel accommodation in Cambridge. You are standing in a queue behind a fellow visitor who seems to be asking about hotels. What can you find out?'

'You are hoping to be interviewed for a job. Listen to your answerphone messages to see if the employer has phoned and what the arrangements are.'

'You will hear part of a rather chatty lecture. What is the speaker's main point?'

'You will hear a man and a woman discussing a contract to provide food at a party. What terms and conditions do they agree on?'

'You are a juror in a court case. Listen to the defendant's statement. Do you believe it?'

'The map shows where you went after leaving the railway station. Listen to the instructions and work out where you went wrong.'

'What positive and what negative words did the critic use about the film she was discussing?'

4.5 Task difficulty

We should not leave the topic of listening type and task without a brief mention of the vexed issue of task difficulty. It has often been suggested (see Anderson and Lynch, 1988: 80–96) that an alternative to grading a listening passage in terms of its linguistic content is to grade the demands placed upon the learner by the task. This is an attractive solution to the question of grading which works well with weak or very experienced listeners. There might, for example, be no problem in using an authentic recording with a novice listener if the only task were to report on how many times colour words occurred, what the roles of the speakers were or what the general context was. Conversely, even a recording at an elementary level of vocabulary might be demanding to an experienced listener if she had to infer the pragmatic intentions of the speakers or compare the facts with those in another recording.

But it has by no means proved easy to grade tasks with confidence across the entire range of listening competence. Firstly, it is extremely difficult to assess the cognitive and linguistic demands that a particular task makes. Secondly, even if course designers decide not to grade text content on the basis of narrow linguistic considerations (frequency of vocabulary and complexity of syntax), they still need to consider how dense the ideas are in the text and how complex the relationships are that link them. There is also the issue of whether certain texts impose heavier demands because of the type of content they include (narrative vs discursive, instruction vs exposition). In a listening context, we cannot consider the 'text' in isolation from the familiarity of the voices and the varieties of L2 employed, or from factors such as the speaker's fluency and the rate at which he speaks. We also need to recognise that listeners are individuals, each with their own L2 listening experience. A task that is easy for one listener who has engaged in a number of similar listening activities might be difficult for another who has not.

This is a complex area, and the only (very tentative) suggestion made here is that the depth of attention which a task requires might provide some very general indications as to the demands which it imposes upon the listener. Table 4.3 might thus provide some broad guidelines to assist grading decisions.

4.6 Interactive listening

We now consider how the range of listening types might be expanded by providing classroom activities that promote interactive listening. Interactive listening will be discussed as a general concept, but we should not lose sight of the fact that, in real-life contexts, the degree of interaction varies considerably from one listening encounter to another.

Let us assume that the listener is adequately equipped to participate and feels a pressure to do so. In this case, a two-way exchange entails a very different listening process from a non-participatory one. It is in many ways a more threatening and more challenging experience for the L2 listener than listening to a CD recording. It is certainly not an easier option – though it evidently needs to be practised from the earliest stages of learning a second language.

Consider the differences in the listening process when participation is involved:[2]

- The input is often very short, making a single point.
- The input may be oriented towards the listener or closely connected to the listener's own last utterance.
- The listener is under time pressure to extract at least the gist of what is being said. The shortness of the turns does not allow many opportunities for the listener to store alternative meanings in cases of uncertainty.

---

[2] This expands considerably upon the account given by Ur (1984: Chap. 1). She singles out three features as chiefly characterising what she terms 'real-life listening': namely, access to environmental cues, input in the form of short chunks and the need for reciprocity and response from the listener.

The listener cannot wait until such time as the speaker's intentions become transparent or the speaker repeats or rephrases a point.

- The listener has little time to monitor her own understanding. But, more positively, the listener can have recourse to a **repair strategy** if she feels that understanding has broken down. This might consist of a formula such as *Sorry?* or an appeal for the speaker to repeat or to rephrase.
- The listener has to listen not simply for meaning but also for signals indicating that the turn has shifted and that an immediate response is required.
- The listener has to interact with the speaker by shaping her responses to the way in which the speaker's last turn was expressed. In L1 contexts, it often happens that the listener **accommodates** to the speaker by echoing the speaker's words or grammatical patterns. In other words, the language processed by the listener-as-receiver plays an important part in the way in which the listener-as-respondent constructs her next utterance.

Four characteristics emerge from the outline above: the listener is under time pressure; the listener needs to make links between short turns; the listener needs to pay greater heed to the speaker's form of words; and the listener has the possibility of seeking clarification. Within the conventions of the comprehension approach, there is little scope for practising the kind of processing that is required. Teachers need to consider alternative exercise types, which can take a number of forms. Some suggestions follow, which might be applied to either scripted or authentic materials.

- *Modelling.* Dialogue material for non-participatory listening provides the teacher with useful models of conversation structure, especially where the recordings are authentic. After checking understanding in the traditional way, the teacher might go on to draw attention to some of the following, with interactive situations in mind:
  - how changes of turn are signalled;
  - the links between one turn and another; how changes of topic are marked;
  - any examples of repair strategies;
  - any examples of **back-channelling** where the listener signals that she has understood and is still listening;
  - any examples of accommodation, where the listener echoes the vocabulary or grammar of the speaker;
  - any examples of pauses in the conversation where the listener can gain processing time.

- *Paused practice.* Instead of presenting a listening dialogue for overall comprehension, the teacher pauses the recording after each turn of the first speaker and asks learners to anticipate the response of the second. The technique is especially apt where the dialogue follows a consistent pattern of 'question–answer' or 'initiate–respond'. A gentler version of the exercise simply uses the pause to give learners time to work out what was said and to reflect individually upon how they themselves might have replied. They then hear the second speaker's actual words. A more demanding version attempts to replicate some of the time pressures of a real-life encounter, giving learners a narrow window within which to respond. Clearly, in the early stages there are bound to be long delays while learners construct their replies. It thus makes sense to develop the exercise in a graded way: with listeners first learning to interpret short turns quite rapidly, later going on to discuss possible responses and finally formulating their own responses under time pressure. As learners become more proficient, they should be encouraged to compare their responses critically with those that occur in the recording, checking both for appropriacy and for accuracy.

  This type of exercise is especially suitable for listening centre work. A small amount of editing is required, with the teacher re-recording the text and inserting timed pauses after each turn that is targeted. Typically, pauses should be about one and a half times the length of the recorded response, allowing the learner rather longer to match the input to words and respond than would a real-life encounter. Learners should be asked to check their responses carefully against the recording, and to repeat the exercise if they are not satisfied with their performance. It should be made clear, of course, that there is no single 'accurate' response and that a range of variation is to be expected. A rather more behaviourist format might, following language laboratory tradition, insert a second pause after the target response in which learners repeat the exact words they heard.

- *Quick-fire questions.* The recording consists of a series of interview questions (possibly about the learner's own life and interests), to which the learner has to give short and immediate replies within a tightly controlled time frame. This exercise is especially suitable for intensive practice in a listening centre, where the learner can record, check and revise responses.

- *Rehearsal.* Successful L2 learners often anticipate encounters in L2 by constructing in their minds a range of possible sentences that they might need. The process, known as **rehearsal**, involves a kind of 'voice in the head'. It can be used to predict both questions and responses, thus improving performance in person-to-person exchanges. Learners might be given a topic such as 'your hobbies', 'your family' or 'travel'. Working in pairs, they are asked to predict the questions that might be asked about the topic and to formulate possible spoken answers. The teacher then poses a series of such questions, nominating individual learners, who have to respond rapidly and appropriately. Since this is a listening task, speed and relevance are the criteria by which the answers are judged rather than strict grammatical accuracy. A different version of the same task provides learners with a set of written questions to which they have to rehearse oral responses. The questions are then played to them in random order in a recording, and they have to muster the appropriate response.

- *Jigsaw listening.* A simple listening exercise scrambles the turns in a recorded dialogue. Those of the first speaker are grouped together in random order and tagged *a, b, c, d*; those of the second speaker are similarly randomised and tagged *1, 2, 3, 4*. Learners listen several times. They first match each initiating turn with its response; they then decide on a likely order for the pairs of utterances they have identified. This exercise works well in sensitising learners to the relationship between turns; but, because the medium is purely an oral one, the number of turns has to be limited to (say) a maximum of ten to avoid excessive demands on memory.

- *Recording.* Video recording is used very frequently to monitor the performance of teachers, but rather less to monitor that of learners. Any type of language lesson which uses L2 as the medium of instruction provides a good example of the kind of short-turn interaction that the listening teacher needs to practise. It is thus worthwhile recording learners' performance in a class and replaying short sections for them to discuss (a) moments where their understanding broke down and why; and (b) responses which were inappropriate and why.

- *Communicative tasks.* All too often, the outcomes of communicative tasks are evaluated in terms of either the effectiveness of oral production or the achievement of a particular target. Too little attention is given to the role of listening, though it is clearly an equal partner with speaking in this type of activity. From time to time, it is worthwhile to set up an information gap task in the listening classroom and (either through video recording or through observation) to monitor:
  - the extent to which listening skills are successfully used;
  - the use made by learners of repair and back-channelling;
  - the causes and effects of misunderstanding.

An important consideration is to choose a task (for example, one involving times, prices or location) where there is little scope for a failure of oral production and the chief onus is on the listener. There is a strong precedent for this type of activity: Brown (1995) used a 'map task' as the basis for a large-scale and illuminating research project into L1 classroom listening.

4.7 The 'integrated skills' option

In examining listening texts, types and tasks, we should not overlook a development in skills teaching as a whole that has constituted one of the few attempts to deal with the dissatisfaction expressed by teachers about current methodology. The proposal is that the four language skills should not be taught in isolation but should be closely linked to each other in what is termed an **integrated skills** approach. In its strongest form, this might entail switching quite frequently from one skill to another: dedicating, for example, 15 minutes of a one-hour lesson to each of the four skills in turn. At the very least, it requires learners to employ two or more of the skills in activities that share a single topic or similar features of language. After hearing a recorded passage about global warming, learners might be asked to discuss what they have heard, then to write it up as a short essay.

The precise rationale behind this approach is unclear, but it perhaps stems from a view that skills are rarely used in isolation in real life, and that one skill is very often used to support or complement another (see McDonough and Shaw, 1993: 202 for reasoning of this kind). In the case of listening, the example has already been given of conversational exchanges which require a listener to operate as a speaker as well. Likewise, in academic contexts, listening is usually accompanied by writing in the form of note-taking or reading that follows up what has been learned orally.

The integrated skills approach has obvious benefits in that it restricts the amount of new language that a learner needs to use. Vocabulary in particular can be transferred from one skill to another and from spoken to written form. Formulaic sequences picked up in listening and reading might be echoed when the learner comes to report back in the form of speaking or writing. Newly acquired language is thus reinforced by being used more than once.

These are appealing arguments, but they miss the point somewhat. First of all, it is not at all true to say that listening is always or necessarily closely linked to other skills. This chapter has given many examples of real-life listening types that are non-participatory. But let us take the clearest example of listening dovetailing with another skill: namely, its use in conversation. Enough was said in Section 4.4 to make it clear that the type of listening involved in conversational exchanges is entirely *different in kind* from the type that is involved in one-way situations. It is time-constrained; it involves a degree of accommodation to the speaker; and the speaking element has to be constructed while listening and not afterwards. An integrated approach in which learners listen to a recording on a particular topic and then go on to discuss the topic does not in any way model the way in which the two skills interact in real-life contexts. Rather than this, we need activities such as those just proposed which aim to replicate the circumstances of conversation.

If anything, the 'integrated skills' concept has put back the clock in skills teaching. Its chief benefit appears to lie in the way in which the learner carries forward language from an activity involving one skill to an activity involving another. The value of this kind of reinforcement is undeniable – but there is an ever-present danger that the approach will deflect attention away from the skill being practised and on to the language that is to be taught (Byrne, 1981). It takes us back to the 1960s view of the four skills as sources of new language, rather than as processes to be developed in their own right.

The tendency is reinforced by the fact that, at least in its strong form, the approach does not allow for extended attention to be given to any of the skills. Focusing upon a single skill for (say) 15 or 20 minutes gives the learner little more than a taster. It gives no opportunity to explore the skill in depth – for example, to attempt to cover a range of types of reading or listening, along the lines suggested earlier.

The assumption that a spell of practice, short or long, is all that is needed reflects a very traditional line of thought, at least so far as listening is concerned. It reinforces what is argued here to be one of the greatest weaknesses of the comprehension approach: the view that L2 listening competence can be developed simply by providing learners with occasions to use the skill. The form taken by integrated skills work and the assumptions that lie behind it are thus strongly at variance with the view of listening that is presented in these pages. A constant theme of this book is the need to spend time on the listening skill. We need to look systematically and in detail at the problems which listening in a second language can cause, and to tackle them in a way that reflects an understanding of the skill and in some cases an understanding of the individual listener.

Listening consists of a set of interacting processes. Some of the most challenging of these processes (for example, the need to identify words in connected speech) are only used in conjunction with this particular skill. From this, it seems reasonable to conclude that teachers can only do the skill justice if at some point they examine it in isolation from other skills and focus on the operations which are essential to it. Leaving aside any arguments about analogies with real life, the best way of achieving this aim in the classroom is through intensive training based upon recorded material that permits multiple replays, not through brief periods of token practice before moving on to another skill.

4.8 Summary

It has been argued in this chapter that listening texts and listening tasks are sometimes quite severely limited by the requirements of the comprehension approach. The case has been put for an expansion of the types of text that are employed, to reflect the different types of listening encounter that a learner is likely to experience, rather than simply providing an information-rich source.

Perhaps the most important recommendation is that teachers should aim to ensure a closer match between the type of text and the way in which learners are asked to handle it. One of the marks of a competent listener is the ability to match listening type to current demands. A good listener varies the depth of attention (shallow vs deep) and the locus of attention (micro- vs macro- ideas) according to her current goals, to the text genre and to online decisions about which information is important and which is not. It is clearly important that this shifting of attention, and the decision-making process which underlies it, should be practised in the classroom. They are not encompassed by the standard comprehension approach, which demands auditory scanning at local level, a consistently high level of attention and responses to questions that closely follow the order of the text.

It was recognised that at least some of the L2 listening that learners do outside the learning environment is likely to be participatory and therefore very different in kind from the non-participatory work which forms the core of classroom practice. Teachers need to make use of one-way listening exercises because of the opportunities they afford for multiple-plays and intensive listening within a classroom setting. But they also need to make provision for practising interactive listening, with activities that take due account of the distinctive characteristics of the type – time pressure, the need to trace connections between turns, greater attention to the speaker's form of words, the use of appropriate repair and back-channelling formulae.

Further reading

Anderson, A. and Lynch, T. (1988) *Listening*. Oxford: Oxford University Press, pp. 54–60, Chap. 6.

Brown, G. and Yule, G. (1983b) *Teaching the Spoken Language*. Cambridge: Cambridge University Press, Chaps. 1 and 3.

Lynch, T. (1995) 'The development of interactive listening strategies in second language academic situations'. In D. Mendelsohn and J. Rubin (eds.), *A Guide to the Teaching of Second Language Listening*. San Diego, CA: Dominie Press, pp. 166–85.

Rost, M. (1992) *Listening in Language Learning*. Harlow: Longman, Chap. 4.

Ur, P. (1984) *Teaching Listening Comprehension*. Cambridge: Cambridge University Press, Chaps. 1 and 5.

Part III: Process, not product

5 A diagnostic approach to L2 listening

When I am getting ready to reason with a man, I spend one-third of my time thinking about myself and what I am going to say and two-thirds about him and what he is going to say.
Abraham Lincoln (1809–1865), US President

Our current approach to the teaching of second language listening places faith in extended practice. It embodies a belief that learners' listening skills improve if they are exposed over time to a large number of spoken texts in the target language. Attempts are made to grade the texts in terms of the frequency and complexity of the language they employ; and progress is judged by the learner's ability to handle texts of increasing linguistic difficulty.

The fallacy in this version of events lies in the assumption that extended exposure to L2 speech necessarily leads to better listening skills. This may well be the case when learners are living in a target language environment. Under such conditions, they have a high level of exposure, a strong motivation for teasing out meaning from the speech that is going on around them, and the possibility of negotiating meaning and repairing breakdowns by means of face-to-face encounters. But the situation of those who are acquiring L2 in a classroom is very different. It certainly happens that some learners' skills do improve over time by dint of answering comprehension questions on a series of recordings, but those of many others do not. These weaker listeners do not succeed in recognising enough of the input to feel capable of extracting meaning from it. As the texts employed become more challenging, they either adopt a defeatist attitude and give up listening altogether, or fall back increasingly on loose compensatory strategies based upon contextual information.

There is, of course, some limited value in the truism that 'practice makes perfect'. The chief benefit of repeated exposure to L2 speech lies in the way it reinforces connections between groups of sounds on the one hand and items in the learner's vocabulary on the other. Sound–word links become increasingly automatic the more often they are made. What is more, the listener keeps expanding her experience of the various forms that a given word or lexical chunk might take when it occurs in connected speech. But the fact is that these connections cannot be made unless the listener first has confidence in her ability to process what she hears.

It is not stretching the argument too far to trace parallels with the acquisition of skills such as driving a car or playing tennis. The operations which these activities demand become increasingly efficient and automatic as a result of extended practice. But a driver or tennis player still needs initial training and demonstration in order to acquire the basic techniques. Otherwise, practice simply serves to fossilise bad or inefficient ones.

Instead of assuming that 'more = better', the language teacher needs to establish precisely what techniques and strategies the successful L2 listener employs and the unsuccessful one does not. An understanding of the nature of listening permits teachers to instruct weaker listeners in routines appropriate to the target language, and thus to ensure that exposure to L2 recordings offers an opportunity rather than a threat.

This chapter proposes a way of revising the goals of the comprehension approach, so as to develop learners as listeners rather than simply providing more and more practice in listening.

5.1 Process versus product

Practitioners and methodologists have often expressed reservations about the effectiveness of the comprehension approach. Perhaps the most frequently aired criticism (Brown, 1986; Sheerin, 1987) is the view that the CA tests listening but does little or nothing to teach it. This is a serious charge: it is an educational axiom that an instructor should not test a skill or a body of knowledge unless it has first been taught.

But the 'testing not teaching' assertion does not entirely address the point. The fact is that listening and reading are internalised skills: they take place in the mind of the learner and cannot be studied directly. The only evidence available as to whether listeners are operating successfully is *indirect* and takes the form of responses to exercises and tasks similar to those that testers favour. One can hold strong reservations about the validity of certain methods adopted from testing contexts (particularly true/false and multiple-choice questions, which demand sophisticated *reading* skills), but teachers cannot avoid asking questions of some kind if they wish to check understanding.

The problem, it will be suggested, lies not so much in the approach to obtaining information as in the use we make of the answers. Consider this extract from an imaginary L2 listening class employing multiple-choice questions:

> T: So ... what answer did you get to Question 3? Marta?
> S1: C.
> T: Alfonso – did you get the same answer?
> S2: Yes: C.
> T: Well done. That's right. Who else got C? ... Most of you? Good
> ... Now what about Question 4? Dmitri?
> S3: A.
> T: Er ... What did you get, Leila?
> S4: D.
> T: Paolo? Was it A or D?
> S5: D.
> T: Well done. D's the right answer. Did most of you get it?
> [*students nod*]

The teacher has established that, in each case, two members of the class managed to achieve the right answer. It is not entirely clear that others have done so (even if they put up their hands to claim success). But what is regrettable is that the teacher has learnt nothing about the means by which the students achieved the answer and thus nothing about their listening processes. Did Marta understand all the words in the relevant part of the listening text? Did she choose the correct answer on the basis of an overall understanding of the text? Or did she make an informed, or even an uninformed, guess? It may be that she managed to match words to 90% of the listening passage; or it may be that she only decoded 10% and relied upon contextual information for support. Nor does the teacher learn anything about the specific problems encountered by those such as Dmitri who had the wrong answer. Without establishing why the errors occurred, we have no means of assisting learners to get it right next time.

This exchange illustrates the most fundamental flaw of the CA. The approach focuses attention upon the *product* of listening in the form of answers to questions or responses in a task, and fails to provide insights into the *process* by which the product is derived. It also, of course, adopts the assumption that there is a single correct answer to each question. As we have seen, that belief is very much open to challenge: the listener does not just 'receive' the speaker's message but has to actively reconstruct it. There may well be information in the listening passage, unnoticed by the materials writer, which partly or wholly supports Dmitri's choice of option A. Or the problem may lie not in his listening skills at all, but in certain ambiguities of the multiple-choice question.

The solution is simple. It is to ask learners to justify their choice of answer. After encouraging a class to explore possible interpretations of a section of a recording, a listening teacher might then go on to ask the simple question *Why?* The learners' explanations for their choice of answers are informative, whether the answers themselves are correct or not.

- In the case of a *correct answer*, the teacher finds out how the answer was arrived at, and thus establishes the extent to which it was based upon information from the text as against external contextual information. The teacher also gains possible insights into the learner's listening style. Comparisons can be made between the techniques used by this successful listener and those of others who did not answer correctly.

- In the case of a *wrong answer*, the teacher gains an indication of where the learner's listening difficulties originate. This opens up the possibility of a later session in which these problem areas are practised intensively. A further benefit of following up a 'wrong' answer is that the conclusion reached by the learner may sometimes prove to be well founded. She may have drawn upon evidence which the teacher or the materials writer overlooked. In this way, one takes on board Brown's argument (1995: Chap. 1; Brown and Yule, 1983b: 57) that listening demands 'adequate' answers to questions, not answers deemed 'correct' by a single listener.

This discussion is edging the reader towards a view of the comprehension approach not as an end in itself but as the means to an end. The teacher's goal should not be to obtain correct answers to questions but to discover more about the techniques and strategies employed by the respondents. By establishing how answers to comprehension tasks are arrived at, we build up a picture of the strengths and weaknesses of a group of learners – one which enables us to contribute constructively to their development as listeners. On this analysis, the principal aim of a full-length listening session is **diagnostic**. It affords insights into where understanding has broken down, which can then be followed up with small-scale remedial exercises that aim to prevent these errors from occurring again.

This approach accords very much with a view expressed by Brown (1986: 286): 'Until we have some diagnostic procedures, the teacher [of L2 listening] can only continue to test comprehension, not to teach it. We need to move into a position where the teacher is able to recognise particular patterns of behaviour in listening manifested by an unsuccessful listener and to provide exercises for the student which will promote superior patterns of behaviour (superior strategies).'

5.2 The format of the listening lesson

The addition of a diagnostic dimension to the listening lesson fits naturally with the less interventionist approach which was recommended in Chapter 3. Together, they entail an important shift in the way we perceive the role of the listening instructor. At present, much of the activity in which teachers engage involves providing and checking answers. An alternative is to oblige learners to take more responsibility for making sense of the recording, and to move much of the burden of instruction on to examining their answers and trying to repair gaps in their listening competence.

This change of emphasis has implications for the way in which a listening lesson is designed. As already noted, commentators (e.g. Underwood, 1989) tend to regard the standard lesson as falling into three stages: pre-listening, listening and post-listening. There is a tendency by practitioners to over-extend the first of these. They naturally feel, as teachers, that they wish to prepare learners adequately for a listening session; as a result they sometimes pre-teach more new vocabulary than is strictly necessary to ensure understanding. The notion of activating background information is also sometimes misapplied, leading to an extended discussion of the topic of the session, which may even anticipate much of the information contained in the listening passage. The writers of listening materials are also responsible in that they often introduce a great deal of superfluous scene-setting prior to listening.

The result is to reduce the time available for the 'listening' phase, and thus the possibility of multiple replays or of investigating learner responses. In these circumstances, the teacher is likely to adopt a more interventionist stance: proffering correct answers rather than requiring learners to re-listen. The final post-listening phase is often cursory, focusing mainly on new vocabulary or on checking answers.

Figure 5.1 roughly represents the format of a listening lesson of this kind. Its principal features are the emphasis on preparation (usually involving not listening but speaking and/or the teaching of new language) and the limited opportunities for revisiting the text, or for remedial work on learners' problems. In my long experience as an inspector of language programmes, this was by far the most prevalent pattern I observed.

The format is clearly not compatible with the type of approach that has been advocated here: one that allows for multiple replays with learners forced to form conclusions of their own, and one that provides for post-listening remedial work that tackles problems that may have arisen during the session. The distribution of such a lesson shifts the balance

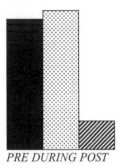

PRE DURING POST

Figure 5.1 A conventional listening lesson format.

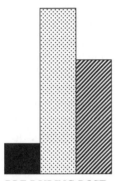

PRE DURING POST

Figure 5.2 A diagnostic format.

much more towards the 'listening' and 'post-listening' phases, as shown in Figure 5.2.

An alternative format might feature a rather shorter post-listening phase, with the teacher noting the problems manifested by learners as they arise, but dealing with them in a subsequent lesson. This allows time for remedial materials to be prepared. There are several ways of recording information about learners' difficulties that support this more extended approach. They include:

- *Field notes.* The teacher keeps records during and after listening classes about where breakdowns of understanding occurred and about the parts of a recording which caused most difficulty.
- *Video recordings.* The teacher views a video recording of a listening class to identify where major problems arose, and which learners were most affected.
- *Listener diaries.* The learners note down problems of understanding which they encountered.

- *Verbal report.* The learners view a video recording of a listening class and report what was in their minds at the points where understanding broke down.

But, however short or long the post-listening phase, the point remains that there is little justification for spending too much time on pre-listening activities, which often involve skills other than the target one and which may distort the listening experience by giving away too much information in advance. The more time spent listening and re-listening, the better.

5.3 Decoding and meaning building

Before we go on to look at some concrete suggestions for classifying and dealing with listener problems, an important distinction needs to be made. A listener (whether in L1 or L2) engages in two different types of listening behaviour. Firstly, she has to deal with the signal that reaches her ear. It comes in the form of a set of acoustic cues which have to be translated first into the sounds of the target language and then into words and phrases in the listener's vocabulary and then into an abstract idea. The operation is basically one of changing information from one form into another; and it is therefore often referred to as **decoding**.

What the listener derives from the decoding operation is just the literal meaning of what the speaker has said. Clearly, this is not enough. If the speaker says *Fair enough* or *What a pity!* the sentence is meaningless without some kind of earlier context. So the listener then has to bring external information to bear on what she has heard. She might draw upon her knowledge of the world or upon her recall of what has been said so far in the conversation. She also has to make important decisions as to the importance and relevance of the sentences she has just heard. This whole operation will be referred to as **meaning building**.

Decoding and meaning building will be discussed in more detail when we come to look at the entire listening process. But it is clear that the two operations give rise to two very different types of difficulty. A problem of decoding is likely to be very closely related to the unfamiliar nature of the spoken language. It might be caused by a gap in the learner's knowledge of vocabulary or grammar. Or it might be caused by a weakness in the learner's listening skills. In the latter case, the learner might hear a word or grammar pattern that she knew but might not recognise it when it occurred in natural continuous speech.

By contrast, problems of meaning building relate to how efficiently the learner handles the information she has extracted from the text. Many meaning-building processes will certainly be fully established in the learner's native language, but they may not be applied in L2 listening because of the additional attention that has to be given to decoding unfamiliar sounds and words. Other processes may founder because they are dependent upon the learner taking account of words and phrases in the second language (*but, or, on the other hand, what's more*) which mark the relationship between different pieces of information.

It also makes sense to separate decoding and meaning building when considering how to remedy learners' problems. Problems of decoding are often generalisable. To give a very simple example, if a learner has difficulty in noticing the *-ed* ending in *walked* in one listening encounter, then it is quite likely that the problem will occur across all instances of the word, and even across all instances of *-ed* when it is pronounced /t/. This is the kind of area that can be tackled by means of practice exercises. By contrast, problems of meaning building are often closely related to an individual utterance or an individual context and might not occur elsewhere – though (as we shall see) some do indeed lend themselves to sustained practice.

5.4 A diagnostic approach to decoding

Problems of decoding are in many ways familiar territory to a teacher with experience of using the comprehension approach. It is common practice to focus on parts of the recording that the learners have incorrectly matched to words or failed to recognise. The teacher might replay the problematic section, explain it and ask the class if they now understand it better.

The drawback with this approach is that it draws attention to a single instance of the problem. But the feature in question might well take a different form the next time the learner hears it. The CA assists the listener in decoding the present listening passage; but that does not guarantee that the learning experience will transfer to other encounters.

If we are to handle decoding problems diagnostically, we need some broad means of classifying error types that enables us to provide remedial practice that is not just linked to one example. The best procedure is for teachers to build up their own field notes of frequent breakdowns of understanding that have been observed. They might group them according to the level of language where the error occurred – i.e. by whether the problem related to the recognition of sounds, syllables, words, grammatical patterns or features of intonation.

The 'levels of language' approach provides a useful general framework, but unfortunately the levels are not as watertight as they might seem at first glance. Suppose, for example, that a learner has difficulty with one of the sounds of the language. What originates as a wrong phoneme might be taken as a word-level error if it leads to the learner not recognising the whole word.

Even when the level of breakdown is correctly identified, there may be more than one reason for it. For example, when a problem of understanding is caused by a single word, teachers tend to assume that the listener does not know the word, and teach it as a new item of vocabulary. However, a listening problem at word level has at least six possible causes:

- the learner does not know the word;
- the learner knows the written form of the word but has not encountered the spoken form;
- the learner confused the word with a phonologically similar one;
- the learner knows the spoken form of the word but does not recognise it in connected speech generally or in this utterance in particular;
- the learner recognised the spoken form of the word but failed to match it to any meaning;
- the learner recognised the spoken form of the word but matched it to the wrong meaning.

What this illustrates is that, in diagnosing problems of word recognition, the instructor needs to be very persistent in establishing precisely where and how the breakdown of understanding occurred.

A similar situation exists with errors that appear to involve grammar. Some may not relate to grammatical knowledge at all but may be simple errors of perception. Suppose that a learner hears the sentence *I've lived in Italy for ten years* and fails to understand that it implies that the speaker still lives in Italy. The easy assumption is that the learner does not understand this 'durational' use of the Present Perfect (a state that continues through and beyond the present moment). In this case, an explanation may be needed. But it might simply be that she has not heard the sound /v/ (in connected speech, often reduced to little more than a token narrowing of the gap between upper teeth and lower lip). In this case, the teacher would take a very different course. It would make sense to expose the learner to a set of similar examples so as to develop her ability to discriminate between *I've lived* and *I lived*.

The examples just given quite neatly illustrate the difference between two types of problem:

- a *text problem* of decoding, relating to knowledge of the language and dealt with by providing information;
- a *process problem* of decoding, relating to a gap in the learner's listening competence.

My impression as a frequent observer of listening classes is that teachers tend to fall back on the former as a default assumption; whereas what learners very often need is not an explanation but some kind of practice in a specific aspect of L2 listening that is causing them difficulty.

How do we provide practice once a process problem has been identified? The answer is to expose learners to spoken material that contains multiple examples of the feature they have trouble with. There is absolutely no reason why a remedial exercise of this kind should involve a lengthy listening passage; instead, it might take the form of a **micro-listening task** lasting as little as five or ten minutes. It might involve a set of (say) ten sentences, all of them exemplifying the problem in question.

The best resource at the teacher's disposal is dictation. By this, I mean not the notorious *dictée* that once featured in secondary-school language teaching, where short sections of a text (usually literary) were read aloud twice, with pauses for learners to write and instructions on punctuation. Instead, the teacher reads aloud naturalistic spoken sentences as informally as possible, or plays sentences which have been excised from a naturalistic or authentic recording. Learners are asked to write down what they hear or to respond to it in some other way that demonstrates understanding. Spelling is not an issue: the important thing is for learners to demonstrate their ability to recognise words. The sentences employed should share a single listening problem that has been diagnosed in a preceding comprehension session. For example, if learners have problems in identifying the weak forms of function words like *of* or *for*, they might be asked to transcribe a series of sentences containing such forms.

Models of the many types of exercise that can be used appear in later chapters. Let us for the moment consider a single example based on a problem of grammar similar to the one described above. Assume a teacher discovers during a listening comprehension session that learners have problems in handling indirect speech. This is not uncommon in L2 listening because of changes in the time frame to which the quoted speaker refers (the speaker says *'I'm waiting'* but is quoted in the form *He said he was waiting*). In addition, in English, the single phoneme /d/ can represent both *had* (*he said he'd gone*) and *would* (*he said he'd go*). So we need to train learners to draw their time reference from the form of the main verb (*gone* vs *go*) rather than expecting a reliable clue in the auxiliary verb *'d*.

A solution is for the teacher to devise a set of short sentences to be read aloud along the lines of those in Table 5.1. The pairs of items are arranged in a rough order of *perceptual* difficulty. Learners might then be asked to listen to the sentences and to transcribe what they

Table 5.1 *Exercise to practise processing of indirect speech*

a) He said he'd write to John.
b) He said he'd written to John.
c) She said she'd found the keys.
d) She said she'd find the keys.
e) He said he'd meet them.
f) He said they'd be angry.
g) They said they'd repair the car.
h) They said they'd repaired the car.
i) She said she'd phone Peter.
j) She said she'd phoned Peter.
(Field, 1983: 82)

hear. Alternatively, a rather more sophisticated approach might not involve transcription at all. Instead, the teacher could give the following rubric:

You will hear some sentences which report what somebody said. When the person was talking about something in the future, write F. When the person was talking about something in the past, write P. For example, if you hear: *He said he'd wait*, you write F. If you hear: *He said he'd waited*, you write P.

This then becomes purely a listening exercise, in which the learner has to form a direct link between recognising a syntactic pattern and the meaning that the pattern carries.

The important point to note about these types of remedial dictation exercise, whether they involve transcription or some other type of response, is that they are small-scale. They enable the teacher to focus, over a short period of only five minutes or so, upon a specific listening problem that has been identified. That problem might often be one of perception or it might, as here, relate to the interpretation of what has been perceived.

If, over the years, the teacher has developed a portfolio of pre-prepared exercises to deal with the most common decoding problems, then it makes sense to use them during the post-listening phase in order to give immediate remedial practice when necessary. But very often the teacher may need to prepare new exercises – in which case, notes of learners' difficulties can be taken during a listening lesson with a view to dealing with them later. Short sessions of intensive listening practice can then be designed, which provide useful five-minute 'fillers' at the end of the teaching day.

5.5 A diagnostic approach to meaning building

The learner problems discussed so far have been associated with decoding and constitute the type of difficulty that lends itself most easily to micro-listening practice. Many breakdowns of understanding that derive from problems of meaning building are specific to a particular text and are best dealt with by the traditional means of replay and explanation. However, the instructor will also come across instances where a failure of understanding might benefit from more extended remedial practice.

These more general meaning-building processes fall into four groups, depending on whether they are broadly connected to:

- *text-so-far*: what the listener has heard up to now;
- *context*: outside information which the listener has to bring to bear;
- *pragmatics*: the listener's understanding of what the speaker intends at any given point;
- *global understanding*: the direction taken by the speech event as a whole.

Self-evidently, the difficulties associated with meaning building are less tangible than those associated with decoding. It is harder for the teacher to devise examples for practice because (with a few exceptions) the processes to be modelled are not associated with specific words, inflections or grammatical patterns. But that does not mean that focused practice is impossible. One can certainly design remedial tasks and exercises for short micro-listening activities. As before, they ideally feature single sentences, pairs of sentences or very short sections of text, drawn from published, off-air or internet recordings. Teachers need to avoid questions that simply require general comprehension. Instead, they might feature tasks where learners:

- sum up what they have heard so far and say what they expect to hear next;
- have to use world knowledge to establish a context or to expand upon what is said;
- use the speaker's opening sentences to identify the situation;
- listen out for certain pronouns and say what they relate to;
- paraphrase an ambiguous piece of text, or a set of ideas that are linked by the speaker in a way that is not very clear;
- simply identify the main point or the speaker's attitude or role;

and so on.

Here is an example. Let us say that a group of L2 learners tends to process meaning at quite a shallow level, in that they are capable of matching a written sentence to what they hear if it is expressed in similar words to those used by the speaker, but not if it is expressed in terms that are very different. This might seem rather a fine point, but it is not, since much of the testing of listening (especially in the form of multiple-choice, true/false and 'fill the gap' exercises) is heavily dependent upon the candidate's ability to match a point made in the recording to a paraphrased version on the page.

In this situation, the teacher might design an exercise based upon a set of individual sentences from a listening passage. The sentences can be excised from the passage and presented on a new CD, or read aloud by the teacher. Learners are given written paraphrases of the sentences and have to decide if they accurately represent what was heard. There is nothing very novel about the approach – it is simply an elaboration of the traditional true/false test method. But the point here is that it is directed specifically towards correcting an observed problem. It also requires learners to respond under the pressure of time, since the matching is on a sentence-by-sentence basis. Table 5.2 shows an example of such an exercise. It was designed for advanced learners; the first items might tax even a native listener.

Many more examples of exercises that tap into meaning-building processes are provided in Chapter 12.

Table 5.2 *Paraphrase exercise to practise inferencing*

Exercise
Read these sentences carefully. Pay careful attention to the meaning.
1. The planet Mars is sometimes as near to the earth as Mercury.
2. Venus is not hot enough to produce life.
3. You can only see Mercury as the sun rises and sets.
4. The moon's gravity is six per cent of the earth's.
5. Mars is the least likely planet to have life on it.
6. Jupiter is probably completely gas, without a solid centre.

Now you will hear six sentences, numbered 1 to 6. Some will mean the same as those you have just read; others will have a different meaning. Write √ if the meaning is the same and × if it is not.

(cont.)

Table 5.2 *(cont.)*

Listening material
1. *At certain times, the planet Mars is no further from the earth than Mercury.*
2. *The temperatures on Venus are too high for it to be able to support life.*
3. *Mercury is only visible in the opening and closing minutes of daylight.*
4. *The gravity of the earth, as compared with that of the moon, is about six times greater.*
5. *If life is found on any planet, it would be Mars.*
6. *Far from being entirely gas, Jupiter may well have a solid centre.*

(abridged from Field and Wiseman, 1994)

5.6 Individualising a diagnostic approach

It has to be conceded that an exclusively diagnostic approach faces problems in the fact that listeners (especially L2 listeners) are very various. One listener's processing difficulty may not be that of another. This is less of an issue with a smaller single-nationality class, but certainly becomes one with a large class of students with different first languages and different degrees of exposure to L2.

The obvious solution lies in providing supplementary materials, for use at home or in a listening centre, which enable learners to self-diagnose – perhaps along the lines of Wilson's (2003) Discovery Listening. They might take the form of computer materials that encourage listeners to think about their own strengths and weaknesses. For example, an interesting initiative by CRAPEL at the University of Nancy in France asks learners to reflect on their listening needs and difficulties and upon the listening style that they feel is best suited to them (Debaisieux and Régent, 1999).

An avenue yet to be explored is the extent to which L2 listeners are capable of assessing their own performance in terms of phoneme and syllable recognition, grammar analysis, strategy use and meaning building. It is sometimes worthwhile ensuring that listening sessions include a brief **reflective phase** in which learners consider individual problems that may have arisen and their likely causes. This serves to heighten awareness of difficulties (especially difficulties of perception), to mark them out for future practice and perhaps to give learners a sense that L2 listening is rather more manageable than it sometimes appears. Learners might then go on to do individual self-study practice based upon the kinds of remedial exercise that have been proposed in this chapter.

To encourage self-diagnosis, a post-listening feedback sheet like the one in Table 5.3 can be useful. It encourages learners to classify the problems that have been experienced (admittedly, this is not always an easy thing for them to do). It asks them (assisted by the tapescript) to provide concrete examples of breakdowns of decoding or understanding,

Table 5.3   *Sample feedback sheet for reflective self-study*

- **Overall recognition**
  1. *Roughly how many of the words in the whole passage did you recognise*
     a. the first time you listened to it? . . . . . . %
     b. after listening to it several times? . . . . . . %
     c. when listening with the help of the tapescript? . . . . . . %

- **Problems in recognising words**
  2. *Using the tapescript, write down some of the words that you*
     a. did not recognise at the beginning but recognised after listening several times.
     b. did not recognise until you had the help of the tapescript.
     c. found difficult to recognise even when you had the tapescript.
  3. *Now look at each of the words and try to say why you had difficulty in recognising it.*
     I did not recognise the sounds.   I got the syllables wrong.
     The word was not said in a standard way.
     The word was not easy to hear.
     I confused it with another word.   Other reason
  4. *Using the typescript, write some new words that you heard. What did you do when you heard each one?*
     I ignored it.
     I guessed its meaning by comparing it to words in my own language.
     I guessed its meaning by comparing it to other words I know in English.
     I guessed its meaning from the words before and after.
     I misheard it as a similar word in English.   Other response

(cont.)

Table 5.3 *(cont.)*

- **Problems in recognising grammar**
  5. *Using the tapescript, write down any groups of words that you did not recognise.*
  6. *Now try to say why you did not recognise the structure.*
     I misunderstood or did not hear important words.
     I did not notice inflections (*-ed*, *-s*, etc.).
     I was misled by the word order.
     I heard all the words but did not connect them to the grammar.
     I was misled by the grammar of my own language.
     I did not know the grammar.   Other reason

- **Problems with meaning**
  7. *Using the tapescript, write down groups of words where you recognised most of the words but did not understand the meaning.*
  8. *Now try to say why you misunderstood.*
     There were problems with pronouns (*it, her, him, this*, etc.).
     I had made a wrong guess earlier in the recording.
     I was expecting the speaker to say something different.
     I did not understand what topic the speaker was talking about.
     I could not connect it to what I had heard before.
     I did not understand the comprehension question.
     I looked for the wrong key words from the question.
     Other reason
  9. *In what ways do you think your listening has improved as a result of this practice?*
     Recognising sounds   Recognising words
     Guessing word meaning
     Recognising grammar patterns
     Working out what the speaker means

thus increasing their awareness of where their weaknesses lie. It also draws their attention to the various compensatory strategies that they use where decoding has failed. The other value of such feedback sheets is that they provide a further source of information for the instructor, who can then design remedial exercises in a more targeted way.

5.7 Conclusion

It was acknowledged in Chapter 2 that the comprehension approach has its benefits: it exposes learners to extended pieces of connected speech in L2 and it provides opportunities for some limited skills practice. However, the principal weaknesses of the CA as at present applied are that:

- it does not practise listening processes in any targeted way;
- it draws attention to the products of listening in the form of answers, but tells the instructor nothing about the processes which have given rise to them.

In this chapter, I have proposed treating the CA not as the centrepiece of listening practice but as the means to an end. Instead of simply checking answers, the instructor operates diagnostically, establishing precisely why certain answers (correct or incorrect) have been given. In this way, insights can be obtained into the problems that are being experienced by the learners – insights which enable remedial steps to be taken. Instead of simply providing more and more practice, instructors direct their attention to improving the quality of listening that takes place in their classrooms and in the world beyond. A question posed by Richards (1983: 233) sums up the situation neatly: 'Does the activity or set of procedures assume that a set of skills is already acquired and simply provide opportunities for the learner to practise them, or does it assume that the skills are not known and try to help the learner acquire them?'

Further reading

Brown, G. (1986) 'Investigating listening comprehension in context'. *Applied Linguistics*, 7/3: 284–302.
Sheerin, S. (1987) 'Listening comprehension: teaching or testing?' *ELT Journal*, 41/2: 126–31.
Wilson, M. (2003) 'Discovery listening – improving perceptual processing'. *ELT Journal*, 57/4: 335–43.

6   Dividing listening into its components

*Know how to listen, and you will profit even from
those who talk badly.*
Plutarch (46–127? CE), Greek biographer

In the last chapter, a diagnostic approach was outlined, where we treat the answers to questions as a source of information about learner behaviour rather than a means of judging performance. One drawback was briefly considered: the fact that, with a large class, it may not be possible to discover every individual's concerns and problems. Another limitation is that a diagnostic approach depends upon a constant and reliable supply of feedback from learners. It constitutes a response by the teacher to the somewhat unpredictable outcomes of the listening class rather than providing a basis for an extended and systematic programme of listening training.

A possible alternative is to practise the relevant processing routines *before* exposing listeners to longer stretches of the second language. Instead of providing targeted practice at a point where unproductive patterns of behaviour may have become quite strongly entrenched in the learners, the teacher employs exactly the same kind of micro-listening activities as part of an extended programme of listening development.

This is an attractive idea because it deals with the criticism that the comprehension approach provides practice and more practice but does little in any systematic way to ensure that learners' listening skills improve. The goal is to guide learners from the outset into acquiring behaviour that is appropriate to listening to a second language generally and listening to the target language in particular. It is also to assist them, especially in the early stages of L2 acquisition, in cracking the code of connected speech so that their confidence is boosted and the defeatism that often afflicts the weaker L2 listener is minimised.

What this approach entails is that teachers offer a pre-planned programme of practice exercises. As in Chapter 5, the exercises should be small-scale; they might take only five to ten minutes. Typically, an exercise would be based upon a group of sentences illustrating a single aspect of second language listening that is likely to cause learners problems. The sentences would be dictated by the teacher or extracted from longer recordings for learners to transcribe.

A redesigned listening lesson might feature two or three of these pieces of micro-listening practice followed by discussion and feedback. Or an exercise might form the introductory stage of a lesson before learners move on to listen to a longer passage. Or it might, as suggested in Chapter 5, provide a 'filler' for the end of a session. The purpose is both to raise awareness of the problem and to expose learners to several examples of it in one concentrated task.

Teachers and materials designers have been slow to explore the possibilities of this more structured type of programme. An obvious disincentive has been the availability of an easy and established formula in the form of the comprehension approach. But perhaps a greater obstacle has lain in deciding exactly how to choose a set of appropriate targets for the kind of focused practice that is envisaged. We will examine two possible ways of making such a choice. The first involves a **prognostic approach** based upon the teacher's previous experience of listening instruction. The second divides the listening skill into a set of component parts which are capable of being practised individually. We will recognise the strengths of the componential approach, and the evidence that it feeds into larger-scale performance. But we will also have to admit some problems, not in the basic principle of dividing up the skill for localised practice but in how commentators have visualised the kind of unit that we might work with.

6.1 A prognostic approach

One way in which teachers can design a programme of listening practice is by drawing upon their own experience of where learners' listening problems lie. A conscientious listening instructor might keep detailed notes of the difficulties that have led to breakdowns of understanding – difficulties which recur quite commonly in applying the kind of diagnostic approach described in Chapter 5. The result would be the reverse side of the diagnostic coin: a prognostic programme which predicts where difficulties are likely to occur and deals with them in advance. The advantage of this kind of programme, of course, is that it derives from hands-on experience at the chalk-face and relates to a specific group of learners, with specific listening needs and studying within a specific context.

The areas chosen need to be those which are most likely to contribute to breakdowns of understanding on the part of the learners. They might reflect:

* the nature of the target language (especially its phonetics);
* possible mismatches between L1 and L2;

- the different experience of listening to a foreign language as compared to a native one (not least, the higher level of uncertainty about the accuracy with which words and phrases have been identified).

They also need to be:

- specific enough for the instructor to be able to provide concrete examples;
- frequent enough to make an important contribution to the message that the learner derives from a recording.

A quick glance at the listening processes cited in Appendices 1 and 2 will suggest areas where difficulty might occur.

6.2 A sub-skills approach

6.2.1 Skill training

An alternative approach draws upon a procedure that is standard in many kinds of *skill training*. It examines the final goal that one wants a trainee to achieve (i.e. expert use of the skill) and attempts to divide that target behaviour into a number of smaller actions that contribute to it. It then provides practice in each of the actions in turn, before the trainee goes on to combine them. Thus, in training somebody to drive a car, one might demonstrate and practise pedal control, gear changes and mirror routines, before combining them into more dedicated routines that relate to starting off, turning corners, reversing, etc. In guiding a karate novice, the trainer demonstrates each of the movements independently and asks the learner to copy them, before linking them into a larger sequence of gradually increasing fluency.

This is sometimes represented as a move from what is called **declarative knowledge** (information stored in the mind) to **procedural knowledge** (the ability to perform a sequence of actions, with minimal attention given to setting up the sequence). In point of fact, in the case of many skills it does not begin with novices thinking intellectually about the skill but with them imitating and practising a single part of the skill, which later becomes absorbed into a larger operation.

Applying a similar principle to listening, some commentators have chosen to regard it not as a monolithic skill but as a complex of many contributory abilities or **sub-skills**. They suggest that a language learner wishing to develop listening competence needs to acquire a command of as many of these abilities as possible. Following the classic skill-training model, the trainer focuses on one sub-skill at a time: enabling the learner to build up local routines first, before using the sub-skills in conjunction with each other. An approach of this kind to L2 listening makes three important assumptions: that sub-skills can be identified; that they are capable of being practised independently; and that, once practised, they can be recombined in a way that enhances overall performance in the target skill.

The potential value to the instructor is obvious. By providing practice in individual components of the skill, the approach takes an important step towards *teaching* L2 listening rather than simply providing opportunities for practice. It thus addresses the principal criticism levelled against our current methodology: that it provides a variety of recorded material but does nothing to ensure progress over time in the way in which learners process the material.

The skill-training solution also goes some way to resolving a further weakness of the comprehension approach that has so far been little commented on. The CA makes no real provision for *development*. It marks progress in listening competence purely in terms of the ability to understand recordings that gradually become more and more complex in their language and content. The assumption is that simple exposure to the language will enable the learner to advance in this way.

By contrast, identifying a set of discrete abilities that the novice listener needs to acquire enables an instructor to devise a programme that is structured and progressive. Admittedly, it is difficult to grade sub-skills in relation to each other, to the demands they make or to their importance to the learner. But using them as the basis for a point-by-point syllabus introduces an element of development into listening training. It even allows the teacher to set targeted progress tests to establish how well learners have mastered the particular operations that featured in their most recent period of instruction.

What the approach demands of a programme designer is to find a systematic way of dividing listening into smaller components, each of them capable of being practised on its own. This requires some thought: as we shall see in due course, it is not quite as easy as it might seem.

6.2.2 A precedent in L2 reading

The idea of teaching listening as a set of sub-skills finds a strong precedent in current approaches to the teaching of second language reading. Reading methodology has moved on from a tradition based solely upon asking and answering comprehension questions in a way that listening has not. For some 25 years, and thanks to the influential work of, among others, Françoise Grellet (1981) and Christine Nuttall (1996) in the UK, and Carr and Levy (1990) in the USA, reading in the second language classroom has been treated as comprising a set of distinct sub-components, which can be practised separately and intensively. Reading materials commonly feature tasks which provide experience in skimming, scanning, making anaphoric connections, inferring word meaning from context and so on. It is generally recognised that some of these sub-skills are already employed by the learner in first language contexts; but the goal is to ensure their transfer to the novel circumstances of reading in a second language. The L2 reader is said to need assistance in (a) acquiring a new set of skills that are appropriate to the target language and (b) applying existing skills to new conditions.

It is evident that a number of the sub-skills which feature in L2 reading materials (e.g. developing expectations, recognising words, using word order, understanding pronoun reference, recognising patterns of argument) have equivalents in the demands imposed by L2 listening. Given this and given the historic links between the way in which the two skills are practised, it seems surprising that teachers and materials writers have been so slow to extend the skills approach to the teaching of listening.[1] One reason may perhaps be the difference of form. Spoken material lacks the tangibility of written; so there is a perception that it is more difficult to design listening exercises along sub-skills lines.

6.2.3 Identifying sub-skills

Though instructors have been slow to accept sub-skills into listening methodology, commentators have argued for some while (see, e.g., Field, 1998) that this kind of componential approach offers the best prospect of teaching listening in a structured way rather than relying entirely upon comprehension work. Some have attempted to list the components that make up listening expertise. Their aim has been to provide a framework for teaching, even if not necessarily a programme for instructors to follow. The reader will find examples in Munby, 1978: 123–31; Richards, 1983: 228–30; Lund, 1990; Rost, 1992: 152–3; Weir, 1993: 98; and Rost, 1994: 142–4.

One of the most detailed of these lists is also one of the earliest. Richards (1983) produced two sets of sub-skills, one relating to conversational listening and one to academic listening, but with the proviso that they should be treated as examples and not as a definitive list. The first group, which appears in Table 6.1, has been widely quoted. It consists

---

[1] It may be significant that, in discussing language skills training, writers tend to refer to reading *skills* but to listening *comprehension*.

Table 6.1 *Sub-skills of general listening*

1. ability to retain chunks of language of different lengths for short periods
2. ability to discriminate between the distinctive sounds of the target language
3. ability to recognise the stress patterns of words
4. ability to recognise the rhythmic structure of English
5. ability to recognise the functions of stress and intonation to signal the information structure of utterances
6. ability to identify words in stressed and unstressed situations
7. ability to recognise reduced forms of words
8. ability to distinguish word boundaries
9. ability to recognise typical word-order patterns in the target language
10. ability to recognise vocabulary use in core conversational topics
11. ability to detect key words (i.e. those which identify topics and propositions)
12. ability to guess the meaning of words from the contexts in which they appear
13. ability to recognise grammatical word classes
14. ability to recognise major syntactic patterns and devices
15. ability to recognise cohesive devices in spoken discourse
16. ability to recognise elliptical forms of grammatical units and sentences
17. ability to detect sentence constituents
18. ability to distinguish between major and minor constituents
19. ability to detect meaning expressed in different grammatical forms / sentence types
20. ability to recognise the communicative function of utterances, according to situations, participants, goals
21. ability to reconstruct or infer situations, goals, participants, procedures
22. ability to use real-world knowledge and experience to work out purpose, goals, settings, procedures
23. ability to predict outcomes from events described
24. ability to infer links and connections between events

(cont.)

Table 6.1 *(cont.)*

25. ability to detect causes and effects from events
26. ability to distinguish between literal and applied meanings
27. ability to identify and reconstruct topics and coherent structure from ongoing discourse involving two or more speakers
28. ability to recognise coherence in discourse, and detect such relations as main idea, supporting idea, given information, new information, generalisation, exemplification
29. ability to process speech at different rates
30. ability to process speech containing pauses, errors, corrections
31. ability to make use of facial, paralinguistic and other clues to work out meaning
32. ability to adjust listening strategies to different kinds of listener purposes or goals
33. ability to signal comprehension or lack of comprehension, verbally and non-verbally

(Richards, 1983)

of 33 items covering a range of levels of processing (phoneme, word, syntax, etc.). The list has two entries (at 32 and 33) which might be described in the present book as strategies rather than skills (see Chapter 15). But, as we shall see, Richards' suggestions conform quite closely to what we have learnt over the past 25 years about the nature of skilled listening. The only entry which might no longer be categorised as amenable to training is the first one. Our current state of knowledge suggests that the capacity of an individual's phonological working memory is not easy to extend.

Some commentators have expressed reservations about the prospect of basing listening programmes upon lists like these. Rost (1992: 150–1) is concerned that it might lead to fragmentation, with instructors spending too much time practising individual sub-skills. It would certainly be pointless to move from one type of product-led approach, based on answers to questions, to another, based on a checklist of isolated targets for practice.

It is here that the conventional comprehension approach has a part to play. Listening instructors adopting a sub-skills approach need to support focused small-scale practice with general comprehension work involving longer recordings and featuring more global demands. By combining the two, the teacher helps the learner to integrate newly acquired behaviour into a larger set of routines.[2] The comprehension work itself might perhaps be made more focused than it usually is. In designing it, the instructor can include items which elicit the most recently practised sub-skills.

6.3 Evidence supporting a componential approach

Despite the apparent benefits of a sub-skills approach, a number of concerns have to be addressed. The most important is: can we necessarily assume that small-scale practice in individual sub-skills will transfer into learner performance in real-life contexts or when listening to longer 'comprehension' passages? There has been disappointingly little research into this question. The reasons are understandable. It is very difficult to demonstrate progress in listening, especially over a relatively short period of time. If we want to measure the effects of a period of training, how can we be sure that the text, tasks and items in the post-training test are at the same level of difficulty as those in the test that the learners took before training? How can we monitor the exposure that learners might have to L2 outside the classroom, and that might contribute to their listening development independently of any training we give?

Considerations such as these have historically discouraged research into the impact of micro-listening practice on performance. Nevertheless, there are recent signs of a new interest in investigating the effectiveness of sub-skills training. Among recent submissions for a special edition of the academic journal *System*, around a fifth tackled precisely this issue. The evidence so far suggests that small-scale practice does indeed have positive effects upon overall listening competence.

An encouraging development is the growing interest by practising teachers in carrying out classroom research projects into the effects of sub-skills training. One such was undertaken by Dawn Daly (2006) as part of a diploma course at Sheffield Hallam University in the UK. Daly chose to avoid the complications associated with pre-testing and post-testing; instead, she relied upon reports by students in the form

---

[2] It should also be said that Richards did not design his taxonomy as a simple checklist. He makes clear that he envisages it being used in conjunction with a needs analysis of the learners and with the kind of diagnostic approach to determining problems of performance that was proposed in Chapter 5.

of course feedback and listening diaries. Her study therefore provides insights not into whether sub-skills teaching leads to improvements in test performance but into how its benefits are viewed by the trainee listener.

The final questionnaire in particular testifies to the positive effect of the training upon the confidence of the group. For example:

> H: *I do feel more confident to listen to the radio and watch TV.*
> K: *At first, I had to concentrate a lot, but now it's very easy to listen to English natives.*

This positive outcome might, of course, have been achieved by any long-term exposure to L2, but the students are explicit about the perceived benefits of the training that they were given:

> A: *When I'm having a conversation I don't have to ask them to repeat lots of time. When we are listening to something I can understand quicker and better.*
> E: *I am better in identifying missing words and whether or not individual words are used . . .*
> H: *My eavesdropping is better than before.*
> K: *I have noticed a change in my listening. It has become [sic] for me to listen to people at first chance. Earlier I was struggling with it!*
> M: *I surely can see the difference of listening other people.*
> R: *My ability of identifying stress and chunking has fairly improved. I can now understand what I can't understand in the listening before.*

It is worth observing that the programme concerned itself mainly with decoding. Following suggestions made in Field (1998), it targeted specific features of spoken English input that can prove problematic and made use of dictation exercises based on short samples of text. The students' reports of improved listening competence thus lend support to the view that practice in word recognition feeds into wider understanding. Asked to cite the aspects of the programme which they found most helpful, most or all of the group mentioned the use of transcription, locating key words, identifying stressed words, replacing omitted words and recognising groups of words that often occur together.

As with much classroom research, the group investigated by Daly was a small one. We must be cautious about generalising her findings to all learners and all listening styles. Nevertheless, it is evident that the sub-skills programme she administered had a considerable impact upon the morale of her students and upon their assessment of their own listening ability. Another perceived benefit of the training programme was an awareness-raising one. The students felt that post-listening discussions had helped them to understand better what L2 listening is, where their problems lay and how they might deal with them.

6.4 Some reservations about 'sub-skills'

It seems, then, that there is growing evidence that small-scale training makes a positive contribution to listening performance. However, we must also take account of other concerns that have been raised about the sub-skills approach. One line of argument questions whether we should be trying to develop skills in this way at all; another draws attention to the very miscellaneous nature of what are called 'sub-skills'; a third challenges the validity of dividing up a language skill along the lines suggested.

6.4.1 Teaching listening or teaching language?

The first position is neatly summed up in the title of a 1984 article on L2 reading by Charles Alderson: 'Reading in a Foreign Language: a Reading Problem or a Language Problem?' In it, Alderson tentatively raises the question of whether it is the responsibility of second language teachers to train learners in language skills such as reading. He cites commentators who argue that many aspects of L1 reading competence should readily transfer to second language reading. In their view, the single most important factor impeding the transfer of L1 skills is the learner's lack of vocabulary and grammar in the target language. They therefore conclude that a language teacher's time is better spent in teaching new language than in attempting to practise reading as a skill. Alderson's article generated much discussion about whether there is a **Threshold Level** for vocabulary, beyond which the transfer of L1 skills becomes possible because a sufficient proportion of a reading text (or for that matter a listening text) is understood. A number of writers have suggested a vocabulary level of 3,000 words as a basic requirement for L2 reading or alternatively a level of vocabulary knowledge which enables the reader to recognise a high proportion of the text (estimates range around the 95% to 97% level). These figures are rather speculative, but a body of opinion has emerged which holds that a language-based programme might be more effective in improving L2 reading (at least in the early stages) than a sub-skills one.

Let us bring the discussion back to listening. The question we must consider here is whether the 'language not skills' argument might suggest that a sub-skills approach to listening is not the best use of class time. Some commentators (e.g. Kelly, 1991) have suggested, along 'Threshold' lines, that building up a learner's oral vocabulary is the most reliable way of ensuring better listening. But they tend to overlook the fact that many gaps of understanding in L2 listening relate not to unknown words but to *known words that have not been recognised*.

It is clearly important to build up the learner's oral vocabulary by teaching words in their standard **citation forms** – but that by no means ensures that the learner will identify them successfully when they occur in connected speech. As we shall see when we look at the input that a listener receives, words often deviate greatly from their standard forms when they are combined with others. In this respect, there is no substitute for exposing the learner to samples of natural speech – and it is especially useful if they are short samples of the kind that feature in micro-listening tasks.

It is also dangerous to assume that the listening we engage in when exposed to a second language is closely similar to listening in a native language apart from some gaps in vocabulary and grammar. The processes employed by less experienced L2 listeners are heavily marked by uncertainty. Much of what they elicit from the input is based upon approximation or upon a principle of finding the best match. There are inevitable moments where they understand nothing. Unlike a native listener, they need to pay much greater attention to the simple business of decoding, since they do not have an expert's ability to make automatic word matches. If, in these unfamiliar conditions, they fail to apply well-established listening behaviour from L1, it should not be surprising. The root of the problem lies not in their limited knowledge of L2 but in the strangeness of a listening event where they have to handle information that is not easily accessed and is sometimes unreliable. The solution is not just to improve their vocabulary but also to improve the efficiency and accuracy of the listening processes they employ in relation to the target language.

If one accepts this version of events, then something like a sub-skills methodology would seem to be what is needed. We need some kind of approach that compares the *performance* of a novice L2 listener with that of an expert L1 listener, and tries to bridge the gap between them.

6.4.2 The fuzzy term 'sub-skill'

A more serious concern is the vagueness of the term 'sub-skill'. It can be traced back to an early piece of brainstorming by Munby (1978), who attempted to provide a comprehensive list of sub-skills for all four language skills. Influenced by Munby's suggestions, second language reading materials have come to target areas which are very miscellaneous in terms of the processes involved. Typically, 'sub-skills' practice might include *skimming* (a technique for handling a text), *word recognition* (an automatic decoding operation), *using linkers* (a way of tracing a writer's arguments) and *inferring vocabulary from context* (a compensatory strategy). Of course, all of them require practice if a learner is to become a competent reader, but throwing them together obscures the fact that they contribute to the reading skill in very different ways and fulfil very different types of purpose so far as the reader is concerned.

A similar comment applies to listening. At the very least, we need a system that classes together what we hope will become automatic processes relating to sound and word recognition (here, we have called them 'decoding') – and that distinguishes them sharply from processes where a learner brings in outside knowledge to enrich her understanding of the bare words of the message (here called 'meaning building'). Clearly, the first set of processes has to be acquired anew for the target language, while at least some of the second set can be carried over from the first language.

We need to relate the notion of 'sub-skills' more closely to the type of listening that the situation demands. More attentive listening (Chapter 4) clearly demands a different set of processes from monitoring what a speaker says to see if any of it is relevant. Similarly, a great deal will depend upon the content of what is being listened to. If we are concerned with academic listening, then we might indeed train learners to listen out for the kinds of signpost that a lecturer provides in order to mark a new topic or the relationship between two points (Lynch, 2004). But many of these markers are absent from informal conversational speech, where they are often replaced by *and* or *but*, used very loosely. It is thus incorrect to suggest that identifying markers is a generalised 'sub-skill' of the listening construct as a whole, regardless of the type of listening and the type of listening event. For precisely this reason, Richards provided not one but two lists in his 1983 proposal and stressed that the lists were only broadly indicative.

Does it make sense to bring together so many different types of operation without distinguishing more carefully between them? Either we need to divide the concept of a 'sub-skill' into more precise categories, or we need to fit the different types of 'sub-skill' that we teach into a wider framework that clearly defines the relationships between them.

6.4.3 How psychologically real are sub-skills?

A third set of concerns is more abstract, but still needs to be addressed. They relate to what part a sub-skill plays in the larger skill and to how commentators manage to identify sub-skills for practice. Here are some of the issues that writers such as Gary Buck (2001: 59) and Michael Rost (1992: 150–1) have raised:

- Sub-skills like those listed in Table 6.1 carry the ring of truth; however, they are based upon the intuition and experience of expert commentators rather than on hard evidence.
- The notion of a 'sub-skill' is a very hypothetical one. Strictly speaking, it does not refer to what a listener or reader actually does, but to *the abilities that they need to possess in order to carry out that activity*. We can only guess what those abilities might be. Sub-skills might offer areas for practice, but we cannot necessarily assume that they correspond to actual processes that take place in the mind of the skilled listener.
- It may be that sub-skills do not really exist independently but are always employed in combinations where each is dependent upon the others. If that is the case, what is the point of practising them on their own? We already have considerable evidence from brain imaging that a language skill such as listening is supported by a large number of interconnected processes, and that the areas responsible for them are very widely distributed across the brain.

These concerns, and those in the preceding section, are quite difficult to respond to. However, it is important to note that the questions they raise are specifically directed at the viability of sub-skills as a concept: whether the category is too loose, whether there are such phenomena and whether we can confidently identify them. *They do not invalidate the wider argument – which was for a developmental approach to second language listening based on the skill-training model.* If we persist with the idea that it is useful to break listening into its component parts for localised practice, then it may just be that we need to find a more convincing way of identifying what those sub-components are. The next chapter proposes one possible solution.

Further reading

Buck, G. (2001) *Assessing Listening*. Cambridge: Cambridge University Press, Chap. 2.

Field, J. (1998) 'Skills and strategies: towards a new methodology for listening'. *ELT Journal*, 54/2: 110–18.

Nuttall, C. (1996) *Teaching Reading Skills in a Foreign Language.* Oxford: Heinemann, 2nd edn.

Richards, J. C. (1983) 'Listening comprehension: approach, design, procedure'. *TESOL Quarterly*, 17: 219–39.

Rost, M. (1992) *Listening in Language Learning.* Harlow: Longman, Chap. 6.

7 A process approach

*I have often lamented that we cannot close our ears with as much
ease as we can our eyes.*
Sir Richard Steele (1672–1729), Irish politician, writer and editor

7.1 A process approach

Sub-skills are generally defined as a set of abilities that enable a listener to
achieve understanding. However, it is difficult to show that such abilities
exist, and that they correspond to what actually goes on in the mind of
a language user. There exists an alternative and more concrete way of
identifying targets for listening practice. It is to base the choice upon *the
target behaviour towards which the L2 listener aims*: upon the processes
which have been shown to contribute to successful L1 listening.

Note that the word 'processes' is used here in preference to 'sub-skills'.
This marks a shift of focus away from the assumption that there are
underlying abilities which enable us to perform as listeners, and towards
aspects of listener behaviour that have been observed and investigated.
The strength of this alternative is that it can draw upon a body of evidence
about what those processes are, underpinned by extensive research and
worked into comprehensive models of the listening skill.

This approach to the teaching of listening will be referred to as a
process approach. It clearly has something in common with the sub-
skills approach. It still adheres to the skill-training principle of dividing
a macro-skill into its component parts. But an approach based on process
differs in a number of significant ways, which will be considered below.

The change of focus fits in well with a recent movement towards associating the goals of L2 skills training more closely with the processes that
underlie first language performance. Specialists within language testing
in particular have shown increasing interest in the idea of **cognitive** (or
theory-based) **validity** (Weir, 2005). They are concerned to establish the
extent to which a candidate's performance in a test of L2 reading, writing, speaking or listening can be measured against the processes which a
native speaker would bring to bear in applying the skill.

Any attempt to align L2 performance with that of a 'native speaker'
may meet with distrust in certain parts of the English-language teaching
community, on the argument that today English operates as a lingua
franca and is no longer the exclusive property of those for whom it is a

first language. So it is important to point out that this proposal does not in any way concern the *forms* of language that are used by native users. It relates to the *processes* which underpin native-speaker performance. These processes have been acquired as a result of many years' experience of using the target language, during which the most efficient routines for handling the language have become established. It is in this respect that the native performer provides a model for the non-native: as the possessor of **expertise** in the form of tried, rapid and efficient systems for processing connected speech. Indeed, it may be more precise to refer to an 'expert' listener in the target language rather than a native one. An equally good example would be a non-native listener who had achieved a high degree of listening competence. However, we have a great deal of evidence as to how native listeners perform, but much less on what distinguishes a proficient non-native listener from a novice.

7.2 A rationale

The proposal, then, is that we keep to the principle of dividing listening into a number of contributory elements that can be practised intensively, but modify the criteria that we use in selecting them. This change of perspective deals with some of the objections that were raised in Chapter 6 to the notion of 'sub-skills'. We noted there that the term 'sub-skill' has come to be used very loosely. The advantage of taking processes as our guiding principle is that they are part of a wider framework of theory and not just items on a list. They fit into detailed descriptions of listening behaviour, which indicate the functions that individual processes perform and the ways in which they relate to each other. Within the descriptions, a clear distinction is made between the processes connected with analysing what is in the speech signal (decoding) and those which serve to build meaning by bringing in outside knowledge.

A second point, made earlier, is that a process approach is concrete. Instructors can base their teaching on hard evidence of how skilled listeners behave; they can even model certain aspects of expert listening (for example, the way English listeners use stress to recognise words) in a way that learners can imitate. By contrast, sub-skills are hypothetical: based on the assumption that there are certain distinct and separable abilities that enable learners to perform well. It is hard to demonstrate whether they do or do not exist.

As for the argument that sub-skills may only operate in clusters rather than individually – the same issue does not arise if we focus on processes. All we need to know is that they are aspects of behaviour that have been observed in expert listeners. It matters little whether a process represents a single unit of behaviour or whether it represents a more complex operation with several strands in it – though (as we have seen) the neurological evidence strongly indicates that the latter is the case.

Perhaps the major strength of choosing processes rather than sub-skills as our criterion is that, instead of relying upon intuition, we can draw upon the insights that are provided by listening research. We may well end up with categories which resemble those proposed by Richards and others, but we can add the justification that we are basing them on established sources of evidence. Psychologists have studied the operations which go to make up expert listening and the ways in which they interact. Phoneticians have studied the nature of the input that reaches the listener's ear and the accommodations that the listener needs to make in order to interpret them. Neurologists have studied the ways in which the brain responds to the demands of listening. Together, their findings over the past 30 years have taught us a great deal about the listening skill that we did not know before.

Adopting a process approach also means that one takes a rather different view of the task that faces the learner. Much of what has been written about sub-skills seems to assume that the learner has to construct an entirely new set of capabilities specific to the L2. By contrast, a process approach recognises that the L2 listener already possesses a fully formed listening competence in L1, in which the interactions between the different processes are well established. The function of targeted practice in L2 is not to add completely new components but *to adapt existing ones to make them relevant to the different circumstances of a second language*. To give an example, the beginnings and endings of words are marked in different ways across languages, and a learner will have a well-established procedure for recognising them which is appropriate to the first language. Second language listening does not require this function to be learned again from zero. The need to locate word boundaries remains the same whatever the language; it is just the means by which it is achieved that has to be modified. The challenge confronting the novice listener is not to acquire an entirely new type of skill but to add new routines to existing ones. Compare a driver who has to switch from a left-hand-drive car to a right-hand-drive one.

That is not to suggest that the task is undemanding. On the contrary: the learner has to suppress some highly automatic routines which she uses in the first language and which her established listening patterns incline her to apply to L2. She also has to learn to apply some unfamiliar new routines. At first, her performance will be slow and subject to quite careful control. It will take time and practice for her to achieve a more rapid and more automatic command of processes that are generally effortless for the native listener.

The need to suppress a process familiar in L1 is greatly assisted by intensive practice. So too is the need to make a new process automatic rather than laboured and attention-demanding. In this respect, a programme that relies upon focused small-scale exercises is exactly what a process approach requires. The chief concern is to add new routines little by little: to modify behaviour by degrees instead of attempting to change it at many different levels.

7.3 Decoding processes

Decoding turns the acoustic input that the listener receives into what we think of as the standard forms of language. One way of representing what happens is through an **information-processing** model that shows the listener reshaping a piece of speech into ever-larger units of language. Figure 7.1 provides a picture of this sequence, showing how a listener might build up the sentence *Do you speak English?* The listener's ear receives a series of acoustic sensations, which have to be matched to the sounds (**phonemes**) of the target language. The phonemes are grouped into syllables and the syllables into words. Often the words fall into familiar clusters corresponding to frequently encountered **chunks** of language. At another level still, the listener has to recognise two types of larger pattern. One is the grammatical structure of the utterance; the other is its intonation, which binds together a group of words. Often, the two coincide.

It has to be stressed that this is a very simplified account. To give just one reason: it is unlikely that the listener uses these levels of analysis one after the other; she might use two or more together. For example, she might use her familiarity with frequently occurring groups of words (*Doyouspeak*) at the same time as making matches to individual ones (*Do + you + speak*). However, the information-processing model provides quite a neat way of classifying the various decoding processes by relating them to the units of language that they serve to identify.

Table 7.1 suggests some of the processes that an L2 listener might need to master at each level. It should be stressed that they are examples and not intended to form a comprehensive list. A more extensive set (see Appendix 1) will be considered at a later stage. In putting together the table, attempts have been made to represent the items as processes rather than sub-skills; but there remains considerable overlap with the list proposed by Richards. Any similarities should not surprise us. Richards was no doubt influenced by current thinking in L1 speech processing (then in its early days) when putting together his list.

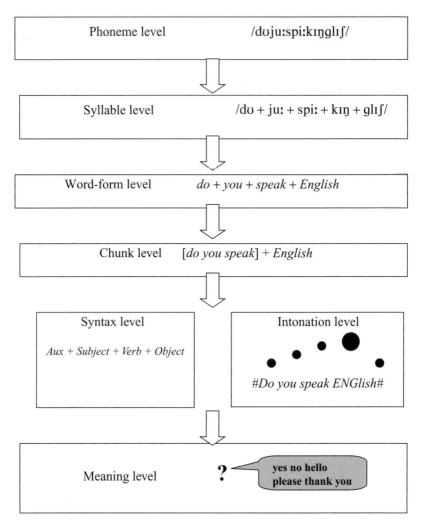

Figure 7.1   Levels of representation of a simple utterance.

What most if not all of these decoding processes have in common is that they reflect a need for the learner to adapt to the unfamiliar characteristics of the L2 (its phonology, function words, words forms, grammar structures and patterns of intonation). This means that the processes listed are all capable of being practised in micro-listening sessions where the teacher provides examples of specific aspects of language or pronunciation.

Table 7.1 *Examples of important L1 decoding processes*

- **Phoneme level**
  Identifying consonants and vowels
  Adjusting to speakers' voices

- **Syllable level**
  Recognising syllable structure
  Matching weak syllables and function words

- **Word level**
  Working out where words begin and end in connected speech
  Matching sequences of sounds to words
  Identifying words which are not in their standard forms
  Dealing with unknown words

- **Syntax level**
  Recognising where clauses and phrases end
  Anticipating syntactic patterns
  Checking hypotheses

- **Intonation group level**
  Making use of sentence stress
  Recognising chunks of language
  Using intonation to support syntax
  Reviewing decoding at intonation group level

The practice provided in some of the areas may need to be quite intensive. A major difference between the novice listener and the expert is (as noted above) that the expert commands a set of decoding routines that are highly **automatic**. By this, we understand that the expert makes matches between groups of sounds in the input and words in her vocabulary that are

- *accurate*. Except possibly in conditions of high noise, she usually has a fair degree of confidence that she has made a correct match.
- *rapid*. The listener does not have to try to recall a group of sounds several seconds after they have passed.
- *effortless*. The matching process demands minimal mental attention.

She differs in this respect from the novice decoder, who may have to lend considerable effort to the word-matching process – effort which is therefore not available for thinking about wider meaning. An important goal for decoding practice is thus to achieve greater automaticity in the way in which the L2 listener handles what is heard. It is to move her from processing that is controlled and demanding to processing where the recognition of words and chunks comes easily.

7.4 Meaning-building processes

Meaning building is markedly different. To arrive at a full understanding of the speaker's message, the listener has to draw upon a range of contextual information that is independent of the actual words that are used. It includes the listener's knowledge of the world, the speaker and what has been said so far. Clearly, the relevant information varies enormously from one listening encounter to another, with the result that meaning building cannot rely upon the kind of generalised recognition processes that decoding uses.

Whereas decoding at the level of sounds, words and grammar has to come to terms with the spoken forms of the language being learned, meaning building draws upon processes that are already employed in the native language. Whether for the L1 or for the L2 listener, it has two main goals:

- *Meaning enrichment.* The listener uses her knowledge of the world, the speaker, etc. to add to the raw message conveyed by the words that have been said.
- *Information handling.* The listener has to decide whether an incoming piece of information is important or not, how it relates to previous pieces of information and how it relates to what seem to be the intentions of the speaker.

It might seem that there is no need to practise meaning building in the classroom. But the learner's inclination to transfer processes from L1 to L2 is inhibited by the unfamiliar nature of the L2 listening experience. Firstly, the listener has to lend much greater effort to decoding, which diverts attention that would normally be given to meaning building. Secondly, the limited listening expertise of the learner means that the amount of information derived from decoding is likely to be much less than it is in the first language. The learner therefore has to commit at least part of her thinking to trying to fill gaps in understanding. These two factors lead the novice listener to feel that the experience of L2 listening demands a very different type of processing from first language listening.

Meaning building thus needs to be practised just as decoding does. Micro-listening exercises can help learners adjust to the circumstances

Table 7.2 *Examples of important L1 meaning-building processes*

- **'Context': using knowledge sources**
  Drawing upon: world knowledge – topic knowledge – cultural knowledge
  Analogy with other similar listening encounters

- **Deriving meaning**
  Storing the literal meaning of an utterance
  Accepting an approximate meaning
  Checking understanding

- **Adding to the meaning**
  Making inferences
  Dealing with pronouns
  Dealing with ambiguity

- **Selecting information**
  Selecting relevant information
  Recognising redundant information

- **Integrating information**
  Carrying forward what has been said so far
  Connecting ideas
  Self-monitoring for consistency

- **Recognising the overall argument structure**
  Noticing connecting words used by the speaker (*On the other hand...*)

---

of an L2 listening event and encourage them to carry over established routines from L1. Table 7.2 indicates the kinds of process that can be targeted. Again, the list is provided by way of example; a more comprehensive one appears in Appendix 2.

The processes listed are all ones that a first language user employs. They form part of standard listening behaviour – the kind of behaviour that a learner aims to acquire in L2. They do not include the techniques that language learners rely upon when trying to compensate for gaps in understanding caused by their limited knowledge of language or their limited L2 listening experience. These learner strategies are a very different phenomenon, one that is connected to the special circumstances of L2 listening. They are dealt with separately in Chapter 15.

Practice exercises for meaning-building processes are more difficult to design than is the case with decoding. One reason is that they are not so closely associated with the forms of words used by the speaker (an exception being the use of connecting words). Some practice may thus need to be embedded in larger-scale comprehension sessions, where the questions that are asked require the use of a particular meaning-building process. But it is also possible to identify and excise short sections from recordings, in order to illustrate and provide practice in individual processes.

7.5 Which processes to prioritise?

A question quite often asked about sub-skills is how they can be graded to form a progressive syllabus. Part of the problem lies in the very miscellaneous nature of what are classed as sub-skills. But, even allowing for this, it is not easy to decide what an instructor should prioritise. The same difficulty arises even if we switch to an approach based on processes. Should precedence be given to processes that assist the listener early on or to those that make fewest mental demands? Should the instructor begin with the smallest units, practising phoneme recognition first and gradually working up to processing at the level of the intonation group? Should we work on decoding first or on meaning building? To what extent can we group processes so that one potentially feeds into another? A few general guidelines will be attempted here.

7.5.1 Decoding processes

So far as decoding is concerned, there is emerging evidence that less experienced listeners rely heavily upon processing at word level as their point of entry to second language speech. Instead of drawing upon the general context to provide them with clues to what is being said, they often seem (Field, 2004, 2007a) to construct a hypothesis on the basis of a number of dislocated words that they have succeeded – or think they have succeeded – in identifying. This would suggest that training learners to recognise words accurately is time well spent in the early stages of listening. Rather than proceeding in the most obvious way from smaller units (phonemes) to larger (intonation groups), we should perhaps focus our attention first on practice at word level and at the level of the recurrent lexical chunk. This would enable even the weakest listeners to gain a few footholds.

Alternatively, instead of trying to grade the processes, it may be more appropriate to grade the recorded material that is employed when practising them (and indeed that is employed in the larger-scale comprehension sessions that follow). Because the focus is on decoding, the criteria used should reflect the phonetic content of the recordings. Considerations might include:

- *speech rate*: slow careful → rapid relaxed
- *adjustment to speaker*: one familiar speaker → many unknown speakers
- *variety*: one familiar accent → many accents, potentially unknown
- *speaker fluency*: fluent and planned → dysfluent and spontaneous

By varying the difficulty of the input along these gradients, one can offer decoding practice at most levels of L2 competence, and still ensure that it is challenging.

As for signs of progress in L2 decoding skills, it is not very useful to think in terms of a progression from 'less difficult' processes to 'more difficult'. The principal criterion should be evidence of an increasing degree of automaticity. This shows itself in more accurate and more rapid processing at word, chunk and clause level – whether the text concerned is a micro- one for transcription or a longer one used for comprehension. The acquisition of automatic decoding processes is a slow affair, which needs to be supported by a great deal of intensive practice. So it makes sense to persist with decoding work even when a learner appears to have achieved quite a high level of L2 proficiency in the language as a whole.

7.5.2 Meaning-building processes

Table 7.2 lists processes in the order in which they might occur during the building of meaning; it does not provide a sequence for a possible syllabus. So how can we establish the relative difficulty of a meaning-building task? One way might be, as with decoding, to recognise that it is difficult to grade processes in terms of how challenging they are, and to concentrate instead on the characteristics of the recording that is used. What particularly affects meaning building is not so much the recording's language as the density and complexity of the ideas that it contains (Bachman, 1990: 131–9). The more ideas there are in a short space of time and the more intricate the links between the ideas, the greater the demands made upon the listener.

Another possible criterion is the demands made by the task – especially the extent to which a listener is required to manipulate and reshape the information provided by the speaker. There is obviously a great deal of difference between an exercise type that demands simple note-taking to

119

record what was heard and one that asks the listener to compare and contrast information obtained from three different speakers.

In addition, the question of what to prioritise in meaning building may to some extent be resolved by reference to learners' needs. Some of the processes are particularly important to a student preparing for academic listening, where the speaker has prepared what to say and is likely to have organised his ideas coherently. Others are more appropriate to listeners who have to function in everyday contexts, where the language is less structured and there are fewer signposts to change of topic.

7.5.3 Decoding versus meaning building

The few suggestions made so far have not fully addressed the issue of where the instructor should start. Is it better to focus on decoding before moving on to meaning building or the reverse? Should one combine the two? The questions tap into a long-running discussion as to which is more fundamental to the needs of the novice second language listener: the ability to recognise words and familiar chunks or the ability to draw upon features of the context to support understanding. We will return to this issue in Chapter 8.

7.6 The need for information

The arguments that have been put forward here carry important implications for the content of teacher training and development. If instructors are to teach listening along the lines suggested, they need to be very aware of what the skill demands of the user. Such knowledge will undoubtedly pay dividends. One of the characteristics of our present methodology is its lack of clearly specified outcomes. We ask novice listeners to engage in practice activities without a clear view of the behaviour that we want them to achieve by the end of the programme. An increased understanding of what is involved in listening (and particularly L2 listening) will equip teachers better for developing the skill in the classroom, whatever methodology they employ. It will also make them better able to understand the challenges that learners face.

Unfortunately, much of the recent discussion of listening theory has taken place in academic journals. Manuals for teachers tend to cover listening in a rather cursory way and rarely examine it as a complex set of processes. To overcome this shortage of accessible information, the chapters that follow provide a detailed picture of the listening skill as we currently understand it and point out the implications for the classroom teacher. They compare the observed behaviour of expert listeners with the likely behaviour of inexperienced ones, taking account of the different circumstances of performing as an L2 listener, and the specific demands and problems imposed by the target language.

We will first examine listening as a combination of decoding and meaning building, and consider the relationship between them. This may lead us to question the notion that 'comprehension', loosely conceived, provides the best line of attack when developing listening skills. There then follows a more detailed examination of the processes that contribute to listening in the form of two whole chapters focusing on decoding and two focusing on meaning building.

Throughout, we will consider the implications for the listening instructor – taking account of the nature of the input and of the types of process that we need to develop in learners. Suggestions will be made as to how we can reduce the challenges posed by second language listening. Most important of all, concrete examples will be provided of practice exercises that might contribute to the proposed process approach.

Further reading

Brown, G. (1990) *Listening to Spoken English*. Harlow: Longman, 2nd edn, Chap. 7.

Rost, M. (1994) *Introducing Listening*. Harmondsworth: Penguin.

Part IV: A process view of listening

8 Input and context

*So when you are listening to somebody completely, attentively, then
you are listening not only to the words, but also to the feeling of
what is being conveyed, to the whole of it not part of it.*
Jiddu Krishnamurti (1895–1986), Indian theosophist

8.1 Some terms defined

8.1.1 Decoding and meaning building

My aim in the present chapter is to provide a framework for thinking
about the processes involved in listening. Much of the discussion will be
shaped by the important distinction that was made in Chapters 5 and 7
between the two major operations that make up the skill:

- *decoding*: translating the speech signal into speech sounds, words and
  clauses, and finally into a literal meaning;
- *meaning building*: adding to the bare meaning provided by decoding
  and relating it to what has been said before.

We need to understand the relationship between these two operations
if we are to achieve a clear picture of listening. The parts they play
also have relevance to decisions made by the listening teacher. Which
should we give priority to in a process approach? Which of the two –
decoding or meaning building – is likely to prove the more critical in
assisting an L2 listener at an early stage to crack the code of speech?

In decoding (dealt with in Chapters 9 to 11), the listener has to make
sense of the speech signal. The main goal is to identify words. As soon
as a native listener has formed a word match, it triggers a rapid and
automatic link to the word's meaning. However, that is not the end of
decoding, as the listener then has to go on to trace a grammatical pattern
in the words that she has assembled.

What I have called 'meaning building' (Chapters 12 and 13) covers two
general functions. The listener (a) expands on the meaning of what the
speaker says, and (b) adds incoming pieces of information to her overall
picture of the talk or conversation. The first function operates at both
word and sentence level. The listener has to relate the speaker's words
to the context and situation in which they occur. Say the listener hears
the word *turn*. It will not open up a single specific meaning but a range
of possibilities: one can turn a corner, turn a handle, turn over a page.

One can even turn pale or turn thirty. The precise sense of *turn* that the speaker intended will only be recognised once the listener has taken full account of the words that surround it. A similar process operates at sentence level. What the listener extracts from an utterance is a bare and literal meaning. It needs to be enriched by using knowledge of the world (*what do I know about this topic?*), and by deciding its relevance to the present situation (*why did the speaker say this at this point?*).

The second function of meaning building entails making decisions about which pieces of information are important and which are not. The listener then uses the relevant ones to construct a record of the whole listening encounter.

The decoding/meaning-building distinction helps us to separate the hard evidence of the speaker's words from the conclusions that the listener forms about them. It makes sense to examine them separately because of the different processes they demand (highly automatic ones in the case of decoding and more rational ones in the case of meaning building). But we should not lose sight of the fact that they are very closely interconnected. A good example has just been given in word meaning. It is retrieved automatically as part of decoding, but the general range of meanings which the listener obtains then has to be refined according to the context in which the word occurs.

8.1.2 'Input' and 'context'

Let us now consider the types of information that supply the material for decoding and meaning building. There are three:

- **input** (also referred to here as the **speech stream** or the **signal**): the sounds reaching the ear of the listener; and the syllables, words and clauses that those sounds represent;
- **linguistic knowledge**: knowledge of the sounds, vocabulary and grammar of the language (including knowledge of word meanings);
- **context**: which includes (a) general knowledge and personal experience which the listener provides; (b) knowledge of what has been said so far in the conversation.

Decoding is closely associated with the first and the second: the listener has to use knowledge of the language, whether L1 or L2, to turn the speech stream into words, phrases and sentences. Meaning building is especially reliant upon the third, though it also draws upon linguistic knowledge in the form of word meaning (see the example above of the word *turn*).

In the rest of this chapter, we will examine the contribution that input (and with it decoding) makes to the message that the listener derives, and compare it with the contribution made by context (and with it meaning building). The topic has quite important implications for how we view the methodology of the listening lesson. There is general agreement that listeners need to draw upon both input and context. But the heavy emphasis placed by current methodology upon 'comprehension' as the target of listening practice seems to have contributed to a perception that using contextual information is more central to successful L2 listening than recognising words and phrases accurately. The impression has perhaps been bolstered by experience of listening in a first language, where our recognition of words is apparently effortless, as compared with the attention which we need to devote to working out the speaker's intended meaning.

A belief in the power of context appears to be quite deeply established. Language teachers sometimes prove quite resistant to the idea of training learners in speech perception on the grounds that if there are local difficulties in matching sounds to words, the listener's knowledge of the topic, the world or the prevailing circumstances will surely be sufficient to resolve any ambiguities. Similarly, any review of research into second language listening will show that, until recently, interest in how learners make use of various aspects of context (knowledge of the topic, the world, the conversation so far) greatly outweighed any work that was done on how learners handle the speech signal.

The notion that 'context saves the day' will be subjected to quite careful examination here in the light of what we know about first language listening. If it proves to be soundly based, then it will confirm that a process approach to listening should focus first and foremost upon meaning building. If it does not, then we might need to consider giving considerably more time than at present to training the L2 listener to identify sounds and words with confidence.

8.2 Input

Let us first examine what we mean by 'input'. What reaches our ears is not a string of words or phrases or even a sequence of phonemes. It is a group of **acoustic features**. Clusters of these features occur together, providing evidence of the speech sounds that the speaker has made. We must not think of the words or phonemes of connected speech as transmitted from speaker to listener. It is the listener who has to turn the signal into units of language.

Decoding takes the form of a matching process. On one side of the process is the group of acoustic cues which have reached the listener's ear; on the other is the listener's knowledge of the language being used.

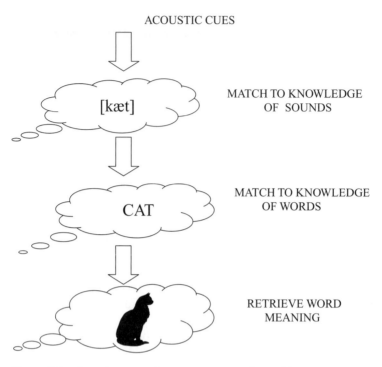

Figure 8.1   Speech perception as a process of matching.

That knowledge is stored long term in the listener's mind and consists of the spoken forms of words and maybe the individual sounds of the language as well. It seems likely that it also includes chunks of language in the form of familiar and recurrent sequences of words (*just about, do you know, should have done, anything else*). The matching process, very simplified, is represented in Figure 8.1. The thought bubbles serve as a reminder that the process is taking place *in the mind of the listener*.

It is important not to lose sight of the concept of matching. It is easy to slip into the assumption that sounds and words are present as independent units in the speech stream. They are not: it is the listener who brings form and meaning to the input by drawing upon her knowledge and experience of the language being used. In the case of the inexperienced L2 listener, the operation is complicated by the listener's limited ability to recognise the sounds of the target language or limited vocabulary against which to make a match. It may also be complicated by the listener's lack of confidence in the matches she makes.

Decoding, of course, extends beyond simple matching. The outcome of the identification process is a string of words, with meanings and intonation attached; but the listener then has to impose a grammatical pattern upon the string. The final product of decoding is a piece of information which is no longer in the form of language but has been turned into an abstract idea.

One way of representing the whole decoding operation is in terms of the kind of sequential process shown in Figure 7.1 (p. 114): a series of stages in which smaller units are progressively built into bigger ones with the help of knowledge of the language. From bundles of acoustic cues in the speech signal, the listener manages to identify phonemes, the sounds of the language. Then the phonemes are built into syllables, the syllables into words, the words into phrases and the phrases into clauses or sentences. Finally, the sentences have to be converted from language into ideas.

This analysis seems plausible at first glance, but there are a number of problems with it. Firstly, it is by no means sure that listeners do employ all these **levels of representation**. For example, the sounds of a language vary greatly according to the syllable in which they appear, so they are a very unreliable unit to make a match to. Commentators have suggested that listeners may not use phonemes at all when analysing the speech signal. They might use syllables instead, or might go straight to a match with a word.

Most importantly, it has been shown that a listener does not wait until the end of a clause or a sentence before deciding what a speaker is saying. Listening seems to be very much an **online** activity, with the listener decoding the sounds of speech at a delay behind the speaker of as little as a quarter of a second. A quarter of a second is about the length of a syllable, so this adds support to the idea that the syllable is an important unit of processing.

If listening is so immediate, then it cannot proceed in neat steps (syllables into words, words into phrases and so on). It seems likely that the listener forms an idea about what the speaker is saying quite early on in the utterance, but constantly revises it as she hears more and more. So decoding is not the simple sequential operation that it is sometimes said to be.

8.3 Context

The final outcome of decoding is no longer in word form but is an abstract idea (sometimes called a **proposition**) which contains the literal meaning of what has been decoded. But a proposition does not mark the end of the listening process. Consider the literal meaning that a listener might extract from the sentence *It's going to rain*. We could represent it like this (bearing in mind that it is no longer in the form of words):

That is the literal meaning. But the final message that the listener derives will vary enormously depending upon the situation in which the sentence has occurred. Consider the different responses that would be called for if:

a. the speaker is a keen gardener and there has been a drought;
b. the speaker has tickets to watch some open-air tennis;
c. the speaker and listener are having a picnic;
d. the speaker points at some dark clouds;
e. the listener knows that British people often make relatively meaningless statements about the weather;
f. the comment happens during a conversation about climate change.

Whereas in the case of (a), the listener might respond *Great!*, an appropriate response in the case of (b) would be *Oh dear!*. In both instances, the listener's understanding of the message is enriched by personal knowledge about the speaker. Examples (c) to (f) suggest other possible sources of evidence: (c) draws upon the immediate situation, (d) upon world knowledge that is shared by speaker and listener (dark clouds presage rain), (e) upon cultural knowledge, and (f) upon knowledge of the topic (the likelihood that future climate change will reduce rainfall). All of these tend to be referred to very generally as constituting 'context'. However, the word has become rather a catch-all, and it is greatly preferable to specify exactly what kind of information the listener is bringing to bear.

We might envisage a further situation in which the utterance *It's going to rain* occurs during a conversation about a current water shortage. Here, the comment draws its relevance from what has been said earlier. This, too, is sometimes loosely referred to as 'context', but it is a very different type in that the information comes not from the listener's long-term knowledge but from short-term recall of this particular conversation. It is useful to distinguish this type of information by calling it 'co-text' (Brown and Yule, 1983a: 46) or 'text-so-far'.

The main point illustrated by the examples just discussed is that a listener draws upon multiple sources of evidence, which go beyond the raw information in the speech input and give depth and relevance to the message that is finally extracted. We have treated this evidence as instrumental in meaning building. But it does, in fact, contribute to decoding as well. A listener might need to draw upon co-text in order to select the appropriate sense for a word: compare *right* in *Turn right at the traffic lights* with *right* in *She got three questions right*. In addition, co-text and context assist in correcting possible misperceptions. A listener who identifies the word *knickers* during a radio discussion about the Church might conclude that the word she heard was actually *vicars*. A listener who hears the word *dessert* in a talk about camels might assume that the speaker mispronounced *desert*.

So we should note that context and co-text fulfil two distinct functions, which are sometimes confused by commentators on L2 listening:

• They enrich the raw meaning of the utterance and make it relevant to the current situation.
• They provide extra evidence that assists the decoding process.

8.4 Context and the less skilled listener

There has been disagreement about the extent to which language learners with limited vocabulary and grammar are able to make use of context and co-text. One well-established view (Oakeshott-Taylor, 1977; Osada, 2001) has it that their attention is so focused upon the effort of decoding unfamiliar sounds and words that they have little left to spare for wider considerations. Evidence from language testing (Hansen and Jensen, 1994: 265) shows that lower-level learners report much less successfully on the global meaning of a listening text than do more advanced ones.

However, contradictory findings have been reported in relation to unskilled L1 *readers*. They have been shown to make quite heavy use of context because they find it easier than decoding what is on the page. In a much-quoted experiment, Perfetti and Roth (1981) showed that it is weak readers, not good ones, whose ability to recognise words is most assisted by a clear context. There are similar findings within L2 listening. The most extensive investigation of the 'input/context' issue to date was undertaken by Tsui and Fullilove (1998), who analysed answers given by 20,000 Hong Kong examination candidates to different types of listening question. The difference between successful and less successful listeners was found to be that the successful ones were much better at answering test items where the candidates could not fall back on world knowledge for support. They could get by without it because their decoding skills were so good. This suggested that it is the *un*skilled listener who is more dependent upon context.

So there is evidence supporting the view that less experienced second language listeners rely heavily upon contextual and co-textual information. Yet a contrary view persists that the need to focus upon decoding the input distracts these individuals from using context/co-text to build larger patterns of meaning.

There is an easy way to resolve this apparent contradiction. The truth is that both unskilled and skilled listeners make use of context, but that they do so for different purposes.

- Skilled listeners and readers (whether in L1 or L2) make use of context to *enrich their understanding of the message*. Less skilled listeners are not always able to achieve this wider understanding because their attention is so heavily focused upon details of the signal.
- Less skilled listeners and readers (whether in L1 or L2) make greater use of context and co-text to *compensate for parts of the message that they have not understood*. In second language listening, the failure might be due to problems of decoding, problems of word and grammar knowledge or problems in recognising the relationships that link ideas.

8.5 'Bottom-up' and 'top-down'

It may seem strange that we have so far avoided the terms 'bottom-up' and 'top-down', which are very often used in discussions of second language listening. This is intentional because they have come to be used rather confusingly. Strictly speaking, the terms refer to *directions of processing*: distinguishing between, on the one hand, building phonemes into words and words into phrases and, on the other, using context and co-text to help identify words that are unclear (Field, 1999). It is in this sense that they will be used in this book: 'bottom-up' referring to building small units into larger and 'top down' to the influence of larger units when identifying smaller ones. Even here, as we have seen, there are complications. Because listening is online, we cannot assume that there is an easy 'bottom-up' progression from sounds to syllables to words to phrases. And the 'top-down' uses of context can serve two very different purposes: to compensate for gaps in understanding or to enrich a fully decoded message.

It is when we move on to consider how a listener manages to combine information from the input with information from context that the terms 'bottom-up' and 'top-down' cause particular problems. They are sometimes associated loosely with 'decoding' and 'meaning building'; they are also sometimes treated as if they were synonyms of 'input' and 'context'. Commentators might contrast a 'bottom-up view' of processing (meaning a view that listening relies upon input) with a 'top-down view' (a view that listening relies upon context).

This is unhelpful for two reasons. Firstly, when terms such as 'view' or 'model' are used, the impression is given that we are dealing with contrasting theories of listening. But it should be obvious that a listener has need of both. We could not identify the topic of an utterance without some minimal decoding, and we could not appreciate the relevance of the utterance without some minimal use of context and co-text. For this reason, psychological descriptions of listening assume that the processes involved are highly interdependent.

Secondly, if we think of 'bottom-up' and 'top-down' as representing types of processing (one small-to-large, one large-to-small), it is misleading to imply that top-down processes involve only context and co-text. Here is an example. Let us suppose that you hear somebody say the word *veshtables* ['veʃtəblz] and succeed in matching it to a word in your vocabulary. How did you do it? If you had proceeded in a bottom-up way, you would have been fazed by the presence of the unexpected sound [ʃ]. To resolve the issue, you might have drawn upon co-text, for example: *cabbages, carrots and other*.... Or you might have drawn upon context (the fact that you are in a greengrocer's or ordering a meal in a restaurant). But you might equally well have drawn upon your knowledge of a familiar chunk of language (*fruit and vegetables*) or just of the word *vegetables*. You might even have drawn upon the knowledge that the syllable *vesh* is not used in English. The point at issue is that all of these are examples of top-down processing in that all of them involve using larger units to resolve a decoding problem that concerns a smaller one in the form of the unorthodox sound [ʃ]. As well as context and co-text, the listener has other (linguistic) means available for resolving decoding problems in a top-down way.

This account of the listening process is important to bear in mind. It illustrates how we deal with the issues that arise when we decode the input of a non-native speaker or of somebody with an unfamiliar accent. Above all, it illustrates the way in which a second language listener behaves when confronted with input that is difficult to follow, reminding us that multiple sources of top-down information (not all of them contextual) are available to assist her.

So, modern interactive accounts of decoding see it as a kind of negotiation, where the listener weighs a number of pieces of evidence in order to decide what is in the input. The issues that concern researchers today are not whether listening is 'bottom-up' or 'top-down' – since it is clearly both – but which source of knowledge an unskilled listener is most reliant upon. Which source prevails if information from 'bottom-up' processing conflicts with information from 'top-down'?

133

8.6 Compensatory processing

A tentative answer to these last questions will now be suggested. Let us consider the case of a native listener. For such a listener, input is decoded in a way that is highly automatic. Decoding is fast and accurate and makes few demands upon the listener's mind. By comparison, having to draw upon the evidence provided by context or co-text is much slower. So it makes sense in L1 to rely upon input, and to use other sources of information as a fallback in cases of ambiguity, inconsistency or lack of clarity in the signal.

Now compare the case of somebody listening in a foreign language, especially a less experienced listener. She is likely quite often to feel the need to make checks upon the accuracy of her decoding. We can represent the situation in terms of her *level of confidence*. If a listener feels that she (a) has succeeded in decoding a sufficiently large proportion of the input and (b) is confident about the accuracy of what has been decoded, then there will be less need to rely compensatorily upon information provided by context and co-text. On the other hand, if the listener feels unsure of what she has made of the input, then she will rely more heavily on external information.

This perspective owes much to Stanovich's (1980) **Interactive Compensatory Hypothesis**, which aims to account for the way in which weak L1 readers handle text. The trade-off is shown in Figure 8.2. Where confidence in the input is high, the role of compensatory 'top-down' information (the dark part of the column) is relatively small. But, where confidence is low, 'top-down' information makes a much greater contribution.

HIGH CONFIDENCE IN INPUT   LOW CONFIDENCE IN INPUT

Figure 8.2   Stanovich's Interactive Compensatory Hypothesis.

Although we have assumed that first language listeners can generally rely upon their decoding skills, the model also accounts for situations in L1 listening. Compare the kind of listening that takes place in a lecture theatre with the kind that takes place in a crowded pub. The absence of noise in the first situation allows listeners to feel a high level of confidence in their ability to decode what is said. Though external evidence will be used to enrich meaning, there will be little need to rely compensatorily upon it to supply missing words – except perhaps when an unknown piece of terminology occurs. By contrast, the high level of noise in the pub situation means that listeners cannot trust the input so completely; they need to draw much more heavily upon context and co-text.

This suggests that there is no constant relationship between input and context but that the way in which they influence each other varies from one situation to another. It also suggests that listeners approaching a second language are already well practised in the compensatory process. Of course, the 'noise' in an L2 context is rather different: it is created by sections of the text that the listener cannot decode because of problems of recognition or lack of linguistic knowledge. But the process still involves striking a fine balance between confidence in the input and the need to draw upon external information. If the use of context to plug gaps in understanding is such a feature of second language listening, it must be because it is already a familiar experience in L1 situations.

8.7 The importance of decoding

Listening teachers might interpret the Stanovich model in one of two ways. They might conclude that L2 listeners are not at all dependent upon their decoding skills because they have another resource to hand in the availability of contextual and co-textual knowledge. Or they might conclude that L2 listeners need to give priority to developing their decoding skills so as to reduce their dependence upon outside information.

As noted at the outset, there has been a tendency in recent years to downgrade the part played by input in L2 listening, and to assume that, if a listener has perceptual problems, they can readily be resolved by drawing upon contextual evidence. From a pedagogical perspective, the tendency has been reinforced by the high importance which the comprehension approach gives to the outcomes of listening rather than to the processes which give rise to them. As a result, much recent research and comment on L2 listening has focused upon the contribution made by world knowledge (e.g. Long, 1989) or topic knowledge (Long, 1990).

However, the evidence from Tsui and Fullilove (1998) cited above paints a very different picture. It suggests that what differentiates skilled from unskilled listeners is that the latter have to rely more heavily upon contextual and co-textual evidence to supplement their decoding. They need to compensate for gaps in their understanding where decoding has failed and for their lack of confidence in the accuracy of the word matches they have made. If a teacher asks what characterises a skilled listener, the answer would seem to be *accurate and automatic decoding*, not the ability to make use of context.

Alongside the research evidence, there are other objections to the notion of 'context saves the day'. We need to look closely at what commentators mean when they mention 'context' in this way. There is no doubt that world knowledge and knowledge of topic, situation and speaker provide useful support to a decoding process that is running into trouble. But much of the discussion of compensatory processing in L2 assumes that listeners draw heavily upon co-text, i.e. upon their recall of what the conversation has been about so far. This leads to a very circular argument. The recall can only be of value *if the listener was able to decode accurately what the speaker said previously*. Far from offering an alternative to poor decoding, co-text depends entirely for its reliability upon whether the listener's decoding skills are adequate or not!

To make this clearer, consider what happens when decoding fails the L2 listener. At one extreme, the listener might have such a lack of decoded information that it is impossible to construct any clear notion of what the utterance is about. There would then be no co-text available to help resolve later problems of decoding. Alternatively, and perhaps worse, inaccurate decoding at an early stage of listening might have a 'knock-on' effect as far as later understanding was concerned. A listener who mis-segmented a sequence like *I went to assist her* might come to assume that the remainder of the text would be about a female sibling or a nun (*I went to a sister*).

A further reason for stressing the importance of input draws upon what we know about memory. There are two major components in our memory store: one that holds long-term knowledge and one that holds and operates upon short-term information. What is clear about the latter, termed **working memory**, is that it is very limited in what it can contain. This has important implications for listening. If a listener is able to decode the input effortlessly, the result is to leave a great deal of working memory free for thinking about larger issues such as the overall meaning of the text. If (as with a novice L2 listener) decoding is uncertain and makes heavy demands upon attention, then it leaves no memory resources spare for interpreting what has been heard or carrying forward a recall of what was said earlier.

The wrong message thus seems to have been getting through to practitioners. If early learners emerge as too dependent upon bottom-up processing, teachers should not conclude that the solution is to switch the focus mainly or entirely to top-down alternatives. Instead, they need to direct their efforts towards ensuring that learners' decoding becomes more expert and thus demands less effort.[1] In this way, they ensure that there are fewer demands upon the learners' attention, enabling them to devote some of that attention to wider meaning rather than to compensating for understanding.

Quite apart from the freeing of working memory, there are also benefits so far as confidence is concerned. It is no coincidence that, when questioned on their concerns about listening, language learners frequently cite decoding difficulties. Evidence that phoneme and word recognition are a major source of concern for low-level L2 listeners comes from a study by Goh (2000). Of ten problems reported by second-language listeners in interviews, five were connected with perceptual processing. Low-level learners were found to have markedly more difficulties of this type than more advanced ones. Here is an explanation for the listening anxiety that often arises as a result of the transitory nature of the speech signal.

8.8 Some implications for the teacher

The main argument of this chapter has been that both input and context play an important part in second language listening, regardless of the level of the learner. The important difference is that a novice listener is likely to make use of context to compensate for inadequate decoding skills, while a more experienced one employs context to enrich understanding of a message. The argument has been put that expertise in listening is assisted by the ability to decode connected speech in a way that is automatic and accurate. This (a) gives the listener confidence in her ability to shape sounds into words and (b) releases attention that can be switched from basic processing to deeper issues of meaning.

There are clear implications for the listening teacher wishing to adopt a process approach to the skill. Firstly, it is useful in the early stages of listening instruction to dedicate time and effort to building up the learners' decoding processes. The goal is to ensure that their listening comes to approximate more closely that of a native listener who enjoys the benefit of being able to decode automatically. Secondly, the way in which 'context' is treated by the teacher needs to vary according to the level of the learners. At lower levels of English, the emphasis will be on

---

[1] Though this should by no means rule out a parallel 'top-down' approach by the teacher, which equips learners with strategies that enable them to make the most of the little they succeed in decoding.

encouraging learners to make use of world knowledge, topic knowledge, etc. to compensate for gaps in understanding. At higher levels, learners can be encouraged to expand on what they hear by relating it to background knowledge just as they would in L1.

This raises issues about the convention of a pre-listening phase in a lesson, when learners reflect on the topic of the recording. At either level, it makes perfect sense; but the purposes for which it is employed should differ significantly. For the novice, it provides a framework which may assist in interpreting some imperfectly grasped fragments of speech; it also alerts the learner to certain words associated with the topic which may occur in the listening passage. In other words, it assists in decoding. For the more advanced listener, it creates a mindset which brings forward knowledge of the topic available from L1 and possibly raises questions and expectations about the content to be heard. In other words, it assists in building meaning.

When thinking about the less skilled listener, it is worth bearing in mind the distinction made between context (= external knowledge) and co-text (= 'text-so-far'). Teachers need to recognise that the latter only slowly becomes a resource on which the L2 listener can depend, since its reliability depends upon how much of the input the listener is able to decode. This means that there will be a progression from a situation where the learner supports decoding almost entirely with outside knowledge to one where co-textual information can increasingly be relied upon.

For the process teacher, then, the relationship between input and context/co-text is not a constant one, but one that evolves. This has consequences for the types of task that are set within the listening lesson, and in particular for the ways in which the teacher encourages the learner to make sense of what has been heard. Early work on compensatory strategies should first draw on *con*textual cues and only gradually involve the use of *co*-textual ones.

We should also consider moderating the meaning-building demands imposed upon learners in the early stages of listening. Here, two considerations come together: the limited attention that the novice listener can allocate to wider meaning and the unreliability of the listener's understanding of 'co-text'. It is wise to restrict the number of questions which require the listener to report on the meaning of the recording as a whole, or to interpret or evaluate it. It is also wise to employ texts which are narrative or instructional, and where one assertion leads to another chronologically ('then') or in an additive way ('and'). This spares listeners from having to build complicated meaning relationships at the same time as dealing with the problems posed by inexperienced decoding.

We have now identified some very general guidelines for a developmental element in a process-based programme:

- early priority accorded to decoding skills;
- early attention to the development of strategies that make use of context;
- a carefully moderated increase in reliance upon co-text;
- minimal use in the early stages of questions relating to wider meaning or interpretation of what has been heard;
- a shift over time in the purposes for which we use the pre-listening stage;
- an early preference for texts where the meaning construction is additive or chronological rather than entailing more complex meaning structures.

Further reading

Field, J. (2004) 'An insight into listeners' problems: too much bottom-up or too much top-down?' *System*, 32: 363–77.

Field, J. (1999) 'Key concepts in ELT: bottom up and top down'. *ELT Journal*, 53/4: 338–9.

Lynch, T. (2006) 'Academic listening: marrying top and bottom'. In A. Martinez-Flor and E. Usó-Juan (eds.), *Current Trends in Learning and Teaching the Four Skills within a Communicative Framework*. Amsterdam: Mouton, pp. 99–101.

Tsui, A. and Fullilove, J. (1998) 'Bottom-up or top-down processing as a discriminator of L2 listening performance'. *Applied Linguistics*, 19: 432–51.

9 Decoding and the inconsistent signal

Vox nihil aliud quam ictus aer. (The voice is nothing but beaten air.)
Seneca (*c.* 4 BC – 65 CE), Roman philosopher and politician

The last chapter suggested that decoding skills should play a larger part than at present in L2 listening programmes, and certainly a larger part than the comprehension approach normally provides for. Focusing on decoding skills rather than general comprehension is probably the most effective means of improving a novice listener's performance. This is not on the grounds that decoding is in some way 'simpler' than extracting information from a recording, but on the grounds that efficiency in the fundamental process of matching strings of phonemes to words and phrases allows the listener greater opportunity to focus on wider issues of meaning.

This chapter and the one that follows therefore take a close look at the way in which sounds reaching the listener's ear are turned into words. Here, we examine the raw material that the listener has to analyse and consider how informative it is. How consistent is the input received from a speaker and what difficulties do its inconsistencies present to the less experienced listener? Many of the characteristics to be discussed are common to all spoken production: for example, the tendency of the speaker to take short cuts between one sound and the next or the foregrounding of important words. But they are realised in different ways in different languages – thus posing challenges to the novice L2 listener.

By noting where the challenges lie, we can identify a set of targets for small-scale practice exercises like those recommended in Chapter 5. The teacher can play or dictate multiple examples of a single feature, in order to raise learner awareness of it or to ensure that learners are able to handle it more adequately next time they encounter it. With the needs of the classroom in mind, the chapter will illustrate in detail the aspects of connected speech that are discussed, using examples from English. There will be concrete suggestions for exercises that practise specific features.

9.1 Introduction

If decoding is central to the acquisition of L2 listening competence, it is important for teachers to achieve a greater understanding of the nature of the speech signal and of the potential problems that it poses for the listener. There is already, in Brown, 1990, an authoritative and wide-ranging account of this area. The outline that will be given here covers some of the same ground, but inevitably in a more abbreviated way. The goal is to inform the teacher about the problems which lie in wait for those learning to recognise speech in a foreign language: problems which often arise not from the learners' unfamiliarity with the sounds, grammar or vocabulary of the L2 but from the very nature of spoken language. The information provides the basis for a programme of practice in this area.

We will focus on a single major source of difficulty: the variability of spoken language. It is easy to think of the units of language (phonemes, words, set phrases) as constants, and to teach them as such; but the fact is that, in their spoken forms, they differ quite widely from one utterance to another. What affords a major stumbling block for the language learner is the considerable divergence between the **citation form**, which a word has when spoken in isolation by a careful speaker, and the various forms which the same word assumes when it occurs in connected speech. It is the citation form that a language learner encounters and masters when a teacher introduces a new item of vocabulary. We tend to make a gross assumption that, once a word has been presented like this, the learner will have no trouble in recognising the very different shape that the word might take when occurring in a natural utterance.

We will consider two main types of variation: those affecting the sounds of the language and those affecting whole words. We will then, in a third section, look at the ways in which different speakers vary, not just in their accents but also in their voices. Inevitably, the chapter contains quite a lot of detail. The purpose is not just to provide an overview of the issues, but to equip teachers of listening with sufficient information for them to be able to identify the areas which are most likely to give rise to decoding problems. Phonemic notation is used when illustrating the points made; readers who are not entirely familiar with English phonology are referred to the brief introduction provided in Appendix 3.

9.2 Phoneme variation

One of the many simplifications of Figure 7.1 (levels of representation) is that it shows the input to the listener as a string of precisely formed and neatly sequenced phonemes. This is certainly not the case. The raw material that a listener works with is not in a neat standard form. It consists of clusters of acoustic cues; and it is the listener herself who has to match these cues to phonemes, syllables and words.

How she does so is somewhat of a mystery. Speech science researchers have tried for many years to find a one-to-one relationship between acoustic features and individual phonemes as reported by listeners. They have not succeeded – indeed, they have found that the same acoustic features may be interpreted differently according to where they occur. For example, the same input is taken to be [wɑ] when a speaker has a slow rate of speech but [bɑ] when the speaker has a faster rate.

Secondly, it is often impossible to identify a point at which one phoneme ends and the next begins. Phonemes blend into each other. One linguist (Hockett, 1955: 210) famously commented that phonemes in natural speech are not like beads on a necklace but more like Easter eggs of various sizes and colours that have been put through a wringer and become hopelessly intermixed. This effect, known as **co-articulation**, results from the way in which a speaker takes short cuts when moving the **articulators** (tongue, teeth, lips, jaw) from one position to another. A consonant at the beginning of a syllable is shaped by the vowel that follows it and vice versa. To give a very simple example, the nasalisation associated with the sound /n/ extends to the following vowel. This means that the [iː] in *need* is quite different from the [iː] in *feed*.

Thirdly, the segments of the signal that indicate the presence of a given phoneme vary in duration. A well-known example of this in English is the lengthening of vowels before voiced consonants (compare the timing of [iː] in *feed* and in *feet*). But less recognised is the fact that phoneme timing also varies according to the type of syllable. The more consonants a syllable possesses, the more the vowel of the syllable is likely to be compressed.

What does this mean for the teacher? Well, firstly and most obviously, the sounds of speech cannot be presented and practised in isolation. This does not just apply to plosives such as /p/ or /k/, which cannot be produced without adding schwa (the sound /ə/) to them; it applies to all sounds. Because sounds vary so much from one context to another, there is a lot of sense behind the established practice of presenting them in minimal pairs (*ship/sheep*, *right/ride*, etc.). But, of course, learning to distinguish one pair is not enough. If the novice listener is to build up a clear mental representation of the sound /k/, then she needs to hear it in not one but a number of contexts (*kill, cut, cart, kerb, back*). This is particularly true in the case of vowels, which are heavily influenced by the characteristics of the consonants that precede and follow them.

Information at phoneme level plays an important part in distinguishing closely similar words, as evidenced by the existence of so many minimal pairs. But teachers should beware of giving too much importance to sound discrimination in any listening programme. A listener has multiple sources of evidence available; and (see Chapter 8) many perceptual problems at phoneme level can be resolved by lexical knowledge.

9.3 Word variation

Words often differ markedly in connected speech from the forms they take when said in isolation. This poses a serious problem for a second language listener. Instead of matching a group of phonemes to a model of how a word sounds, she must either make an approximate match that allows for the kinds of modification that may have taken place, or must keep adding to her stored memories of a word to allow for different variants of it.

Some of the ways in which words vary in form are relatively systematic, and it is helpful for the listening instructor to have an understanding of the factors involved. Systematic variation might occur due to:

- phonological rules which *regularise* connected speech by attaching words to each other and by reshaping syllables (Section 9.3.1);
- *alternative weak forms* for function words (Section 9.3.2);
- the tendency of speakers to cut corners in the way they form sounds so as to *make articulation easier* (Section 9.3.3);
- the way in which words become *reduced* when they occur within a larger group (Section 9.3.4).

9.3.1 Redistribution

Connected speech sometimes slips into regular rhythmic patterns, which affect the apparent shapes of the words within it. Two of these effects are worth noting: they are taken for granted by the L1 listener, whose ear has become habituated to them, but can complicate word recognition for somebody listening to a second language. Examples are given from English, but similar regularising influences apply in other languages.

Cliticisation

English has a liking for a strong–weak (SW) rhythmic pattern, an alternation of stressed and unstressed syllables, as in:

```
W  S W  S   W  S  W
a  very big  adventure
```

Clearly, by no means all spoken English falls into this pattern, but studies have shown that the language has a marked tendency towards it. Speakers find themselves slipping into an SW rhythm; and listeners seem to listen out for this pattern. A second, less common, pattern is SWW (*bicycle, kind of you*).

The effect is to group syllables together. Unstressed syllables become attached to preceding stressed ones; but of course this happens according to rhythm and without regard for where words begin and end. Figure 9.1 indicates what can occur. Syllables become grouped in ways that do not necessarily fit word boundaries or the syntax of the sentence.

1.	S	W	S	W	⟹	S W	+	S W		
	'tʊk	ɪz	'hæt	ɒf		'tʊkɪz		'hætɒf		
	took	his	hat	off		tookhis		hatoff		
2.	S	W S W			⟹	S W	+	S W		
	get	ɪk'saɪtɪd				getɪk		'saɪtɪd		
	get	excited				getik		sited		
3.	S	W S W S	W		⟹	S W +	S W +	S W		
	'lɪz	bɪ'keɪm ə	'stɑː [*pause*]			'lɪzbɪ	'keɪmə	'stɑː [*pause*]		
	Liz	became a	star			Lizbe	camer	star		

Figure 9.1 The effects of cliticisation.

Resyllabification

A second type of redistribution affects the ends of syllables and thus potentially also the ends of words. English speakers try to steer clear of syllables that begin with a vowel. They do so by transferring a consonant from the previous syllable, a process known as **resyllabification**:

went in → when tin   *made out* → may doubt

can't help it → (carn) tell pit   *great ape* → grey tape

a boat I saw → a bow tie saw

Similarly, consonants are sometimes reattached to form a cluster:

need rain → knee drain   *keep late hours* → key plate hours

let's leave → let sleeve   *place no bets* → play snow bets

Table 9.1 *Exercises in redistributed word forms*

- *Cliticisation.* Learners transcribe short extracts from authentic recordings. Choose especially clips with many instances of schwa (/ə/) and clusters of weak syllables.

  > *There was another factory on the other side of quite a narrow road. And this happened in the early hours of the morning.* (Underwood, 1975: 146)
  > *It isn't as if they don't have the money.*

- *Resyllabification.* Teacher designs simple sentences with resyllabified words in them (see examples above) or uses sentences from a naturalistic recording. Look especially for instances where the second word begins with a vowel. The sentences should give very little contextual information.

  > *The children went in* → when tin
  > *The customer made out a cheque* → may doubt
  > *I can't help it if the bus is always late.* → (carn) tell pit
  > *This great ape is found in several countries* → grey tape
  > *I described the boat I saw* → the bow tie saw

The two features that have been discussed in this section can lead to considerable confusion. A strong case can be made for exposing students to multiple examples of them. In Table 9.1 there are suggestions on how teachers can design simple, small-scale exercises.

9.3.2 Function words

In many languages, function words such as *the, it, of* or *with* are down-graded in prominence when they occur in connected speech. This seems to reflect a general pattern of behaviour among speakers and listeners, who pay greater attention to meaning-bearing bricks in the form of content words than to the mortar which joins those bricks together.

The low perceptibility of function words serves the purpose of fore-grounding important parts of the message, but it also makes function words much more difficult for the L2 listener to decode. Context and co-text often help, but getting by without function words is not always easy. They are sometimes critical to syntactic distinctions: compare *I've driven home* and *I was driven home*, or *I've been followed* and *I'm being followed*, or *discover a planet* and *discover the Planet*. They can also mark important differences of meaning: compare *I'm looking at the photos* and *I'm looking for the photos*.

English reduces the prominence of function words in connected speech by making use of a set of **weak forms**. At least 50 function words in English possess such forms,[1] which may differ from the full forms in four ways: weak vowel quality, loss of phonemes, lack of stress and short duration. Some teachers characterise the full form in English as the default one and the weak one as a substitute. This seems unrealistic, since the weak one occurs much more frequently. The full one is mainly restricted to marking emphasis or contrast, or to a position at the end of a question (*What are you waiting FOR?*). So it makes sense to treat the weak form as the standard one and the full one as the exception (Gimson, 1994: 230). The benefit of this approach is that it encourages the listener to store the most frequent form in her mind. Even so, learners' expectations of what they will hear are sometimes unduly influenced by exposure to the written language.

Function words present an interesting case. On the one hand, they are very frequent in everyday speech. Of the 100 most frequent spoken items in the British National Corpus, a 100-million-word corpus of speech and writing, about 80 are function words. Surely, by dint of constant exposure, the listener must learn to identify them with a considerable degree of accuracy. On the other hand, function words are difficult to hear in many languages because they are short and unstressed and contain weak vowels. Evidence from my own research (Field, 2008b) suggests that the second factor has the most impact upon learners of English. At most levels of proficiency, they have much more trouble identifying function words accurately than they do content words – no matter what the phonology of their first language has accustomed them to.

Function word recognition, then, is another area where intensive practice will pay dividends. For reference, Table 9.2 shows a list of weak forms, mainly drawn from Gimson, 1994: 228–9. The items included are those where there is a change of vowel quality and/or the loss of a sound. Other items such as *it* do not have a distinct 'weak form' as such; though their status as function words is still marked by their low prominence, so they too can be difficult to detect. Note that the spoken forms shown here are simply representative: there are other possible forms, and realisations differ between varieties of English.

The list in Table 9.2 can provide a basis for a programme in which learners are given systematic and targeted practice in recognising function words when they occur in connected speech. Choosing from the list,

---

[1] Plus two anomalies in the titles *Saint* and *Sir* which possess weak forms in some varieties of English: /sənt/ and /sə/ respectively.

Table 9.2 *Weak forms grouped by word class*

word	weak form	word	weak form
a	ə	am	əm
an	ən	are	ə
any	nɪ	be	bɪ
some	səm sm	been	bɪn
the	ðə	was	wəz
		were	wə
at	ət	can	kən kn
for	fə	could	kəd kd
from	frəm	do	dʊ də
of	əv ə	does	dəz dz
to	tə	had	həd hd
		has	həz hz əz
he	ɪ hɪ	have	həv hv əv
her	ə hə	must	məst
him	ɪm	shall	ʃəl ʃl
his	ɪz	should	ʃəd ʃd
I	ʌ	will	wəl əl
me	mɪ	would	wʊd wəd
we	wɪ	-n't	n
she	ʃɪ		
them	ðəm m	and	ənd ən nd n
us	əs	but	bət
you	jə	as	əz
your	jə	than	ðən ðn
our	ɑː ʌ	that	ðət
		there	ðə ðə(+r)
who	ʊ hʊ		
where	we wə		

(after Gimson, 1994: 228–9)

the teacher might dictate a series of simple sentences for transcription, such as:

I'm paying for a ([frə]) holiday.

It's at the top of the ([əðə]) building.

I'm waiting at a ([ətə]) bus stop.

I went to the shops and ([ən]) the bank.

It is worth stressing that in any exercises of this kind the material must be presented from the point of view of the *listener* and not of the speaker. If one ignores the written form and takes as one's point of departure the spoken form of the 50 items in the table, an additional problem of identification becomes apparent. Several of the forms listed (see Table 9.3) are indistinguishable; the listener (whether native or non-native) has to use syntactic context to distinguish them from each other.

Some confusion between forms (particularly *have/of*) even affects native listeners, as is demonstrated in the spelling errors of primary school children, not to mention some adults (*should of done, would of done*, etc.).

Table 9.3 *Homophonous weak forms*

ə	a	əv	of	ən	an	əz	as	jə	you
	are		have		and		has		your
	of								
	er								

9.3.3 Transitions between words

Producing speech is a demanding operation. It is done under pressure of time and it requires some complex and rapid movements from one setting of the articulators (the lips, the tongue, the jaw, the soft palate) to another. Small wonder if speakers take short cuts. The next two sections consider ways in which words become altered in form when a speaker adopts more convenient ways of producing them. A rather arbitrary distinction will be made between the changes that occur when moving between adjacent words (discussed here) and similar changes which result from words becoming combined into larger units (discussed in Section 9.3.4). The latter situation affects words internally as well as at their boundaries.

In connected speech, a speaker often has to make a difficult transition between the consonant at the end of one word and the consonant that begins the next. The movement is especially demanding if it involves switching between consonants that involve different parts of the mouth. A speaker often responds by changing the way a word-final consonant is pronounced so as to anticipate the consonant that follows it. To give an example, it is quite difficult to move from the position for /n/ to the position for /p/. To sidestep the problem, a speaker might adjust the /n/ in a sequence like *green paint* so that it becomes /m/ (*greem paint*). The resulting transition is easier because /m/, like /p/, is a sound that involves the two lips.[2]

In English, these processes usually involve modifying the sound at the *end* of a word in anticipation of the sound that follows. Broadly they take two forms. The speaker might adjust a sound to the following one (**assimilation**) or might omit a sound (**elision**). The message for the language learner is: trust the beginnings of English words rather than the ends.

Assimilation

English teachers tend to assume that assimilation at word boundaries is highly complicated and rather unpredictable. In fact, the type that is likely to cause most problems for the L2 listener is limited to five word-final consonants ([n, t, d, s, z]). It is very systematic and can be reduced to a few basic rules, as shown in Table 9.4.

Does assimilation affect the ability of the second language listener to identify whole words? Commentators (Brown, 1990: 60; Gimson, 1994: 281) tend to assume that it does. But there is no reason why that should necessarily be the case. Less experienced listeners do not have fully established phoneme values for L2 and are therefore inclined to be cautious about the evidence of their ears. They are aware that their decoding process is an approximate one. Their decisions are more likely to be made at word level than at phoneme level, and they may not be unduly fazed if the input does not concur 100% with what they might have expected. On the other hand, some confusion might be expected when assimilation produces a form that is identical to an actual word: examples might be *light grey* → *like grey* or *white board* → *wipe board*.

In fact, a study by Koster (1987) found that assimilation caused an increased number of word-recognition errors by non-native listeners, even when it did not give rise to an existing word. The findings confirm that assimilation is a factor in failures of decoding, and something that the listening teacher needs to take into account.[3] Once again, the solution is to devise simple exercises for transcription practice, to enable students to adjust to this phenomenon.

---

[2] Compare the way the prefix *in-* (*inefficient*) has mutated to *im-* before adjectives beginning with a *p* (*impossible, imperfect*).

[3] Tauroza (1993) reported the opposite: that word recognition did not suffer when the final consonant of a word was imprecise. However, he examined how his students processed words within sentences that provided a clear context. The possibility remains that the assimilated forms did cause problems of recognition but that they were resolved by means of contextual cues. Furthermore, the words used by Tauroza were quite mixed in kind and length.

Table 9.4 *Consonant change in assimilation*

Before these sounds Y	the sound	becomes sound Z	Example
/p,b,m/	/n/	→ [m]	*ten people → tem people*
	/t/	→ [p] or [ʔ]	*hot bath → hop bath*
	/d/	→ [b] or [ʔ]	*good play → goob play*
/k,g/	/n/	→ [ŋ]	*ten cars → teng cars*
	/t/	→ [k] or [ʔ]	*that gun → thak gun*
	/d/	→ [g] or [ʔ]	*good cause → goog cause*
/j/	/t/	→ [ʧ]	*Right you are → rye chew are*
	/d/	→ [ʤ]	*Did you go? → di due go*
/ʃ/	/s/	→ [ʃ] or [-]	*this shirt → thi shirt*
	/z/	→ [ʃ] or [-]	*those shoes → tho shoes*

Note: [ʔ] indicates a glottal stop, a brief constriction in the throat; [-] means the phoneme is omitted.

Elision

Elision is much more frequent than is sometimes assumed. It most commonly affects instances of /t/ and /d/ at the ends of words. Brown (1990: 69) even concludes from her samples of English speech that 'it is more common for /t/ and /d/ to be elided between consonants than it is for them to be pronounced'. Unfortunately, these are also the sounds that provide the inflectional endings in English, not to mention the contracted forms of auxiliary verbs. There is a chastening message here for grammar teachers: they cannot assume that learners will pick up and internalise these endings through real-life encounters, since the endings may well be absent or modified in spontaneous speech.

Other sounds that are sometimes elided include /v, ð, l, r, n, k/. The inclusion of /ð/ in this list might seem surprising given its importance in items such as *there, they, the*. Brown (1990: 69) reports some interesting examples in her data where the definite article *the* is realised as /ə/ (i.e. is indistinguishable from the indefinite article *a*). There is also a tendency to weaken *there* in sentences like *There's a bird on the roof* (*there's* → [ez] or [əz]).[4]

When seeking examples to present to language learners, it is useful to distinguish two conditions under which elision occurs. The first is a matter of chance; it depends partly upon how fast the speaker is speaking, how informally and so on. This is quite difficult to demonstrate to learners because it varies from one utterance to another. Table 9.5 provides some examples (my own data, supplemented by examples from Brown, 1990).

Table 9.5 *Examples of sequences where elision is likely*

nex(t) spring → [nek'sprɪŋ]	*studen(t) card* → ['stʃuːdnkɑːd]
nigh(t)club → ['naɪklʌb]	*Eas(t) Coast* → [iːs'kəʊst]
firs(t) three → [fɜːs'θriː]	*cou(ld) take* → [kʊ'teɪk]
arm(ed) guard → [ɑːm'gɑːd]	*blin(d) man* → ['blaɪmæn]
ol(d) people → [əʊl'piːpl]	*fi(ve) pm* → [faɪpiː'em]
lea(ve) school → [liː'skuːl]	*back t(o) London* → [bæk'tlʌndən]

However, not all elisions are one-off examples like this, and it is possible to trace others that occur quite consistently. It is especially worth paying attention to elisions involving inflections. The superlatives of adjectives very commonly lose their final /t/ when the next word begins with a consonant: *bigges(t)*, *fastes(t)*, *oldes(t)*. The suffixes /t/ and /d/ in regular past forms of verbs are likewise dropped quite regularly before consonants: *walk(ed) past*, *help(ed) customers*, *look(ed) nice*, *begg(ed) money*, *robb(ed) banks*, *prepare(d) to pay*. Sometimes it is the consonant before the inflection that is affected. Examples are:

cos(t)s fac(t)s frien(d)s fin(d)s clo(th)es as(k)ed
sixths (= [sɪkθs])

A good example of a high-frequency item that is subject to very consistent elision in connected speech is *'nt*, the English marker of negation. Except before a vowel, the final /t/ is often omitted:

isn't → [ɪzn]   *hasn't* → [(h)æzn]   *doesn't* → [dʌzn]

However, matters are then complicated further by the [n] sometimes adjusting to the first consonant of the following verb:

isn't coming → [ɪzŋ'kʌmɪŋ]   *hasn't paid* → [(h)æzm'peɪd]

---

[4] Shockey (2003: 43) provides other examples of '/ð/ reduction'.

It is clearly important for learners to familiarise themselves with the variants of high-frequency words such as these, and it is a task that the teacher can and should assist them with. At an early stage, the teacher might provide transcription practice by dictating sets of common words that are often elided (see the many examples of consistent elision that are provided above). There might be a progression from single words to word pairs such as compound nouns. At a later stage, the teacher might wish to use extracts from scripted or authentic recordings that provide one-off examples of elision.

A similar approach can be adopted to assimilation, with the teacher first dictating examples of word pairs that are very likely to give rise to between-word changes (the *greem paint* syndrome). One might wish to focus in turn on each of the assimilation patterns identified in Table 9.4. At a later stage, it is worthwhile listening out for examples of assimilation that occur in scripted or natural recordings and excising them for transcription practice.

9.3.4 Reduction

Words also become reduced in form when they are part of a larger group. One or more of their standard phonemes might be dropped and syllables might be shortened or weakened. This often happens because a word is of low importance within the group. Alternatively, it might be that a frequent and familiar group of words has become stored in the minds of speaker and listener as a single simplified chunk.

Importance within an intonation group

In natural speech, words combine to form an **intonation group**. The group exerts certain pressures upon the words within it. If it contains many syllables, the speed at which the speaker produces them is likely to increase, and individual words of low importance may become shorter or get modified. The consequence is that many words possess several different forms to fit different circumstances. Some of these forms might be reduced relatively little by comparison with the citation form, while others might be reduced a great deal.

An extreme case of variation is represented by the very frequent word *actually*. Laver (1994: 67) cites the seven forms shown in Table 9.6. This example gives an idea of how many variants a single frequent word can possess in natural speech, and thus the challenge faced by the second language listener in recognising the word when it occurs. Nor is it only the commonest words in the language that are affected. Laver estimates

Table 9.6 *Progressively more casual versions of the word 'actually'*

Maximally careful	[æktjʊəlɪ]	[*citation form*]
	[æktʃʊəlɪ]	
	[æktʃʊlɪ]	
	[æktʃəlɪ]	
	[æktʃlɪ]	
	[ækʃlɪ]	
Maximally casual	[æʃlɪ]	

that on average each polysyllabic word in English has two or three reduced pronunciations that are used in contexts where careful speech is not called for.

The best way for language teachers to deal with this type of variation is by dividing recordings of natural speech into small sections in order to raise awareness among second language listeners of the patterns of reduction that occur within intonation groups. The type of approach that can be adopted is illustrated in Figure 9.2, taken from the online materials produced by Cauldwell, 2003.

Within a recording of (say) two to three minutes, the teacher identifies clusters of two, three or four words that have been compressed by the speaker. The best approach is a staged one. For the purposes of awareness raising, it might proceed as follows:

a. Teacher plays the whole recording for extensive listening, thus establishing a context.
b. Teacher plays an intonation group and asks learners if they can report or transcribe the actual words used. No comment on whether learners are correct or not.
c. Teacher plays compressed words within the group and asks learners to transcribe them. Several replays might be necessary.

Once learners become used to the idea that words are often distorted by their co-text, the teacher might reverse this sequence: first asking them

Click ...   Click the speaker icon to hear these speech units.
            Click each line to hear it on its own.

<table>
<tr><td>These numbers
refer to the
Speech Units
transcript.</td><td>014 // and we set up</td><td>// 233</td><td></td></tr>
</table>

```
                  014 // and we set up                    // 233
These numbers     015 // a whole lot of evening classes   // 258    These numbers
refer to the      016 // in                               // 153 ·  give the speed
Speech Units      017 // pottery and                      // 181    in words per
transcript.       018 // woodwork and                     // 127 ·  minute.
                  019 // drama and that kind of thing      // 281
                  020 // erm                               // 047
                  021 // and i got very involved in those  // 194
```

Circle the words you did not hear clearly, and listen to them again.

3.1 Notice the missing and linked sounds

Say the words of 019 slowly and carefully; click on the first speaker icon to hear a slow paused version.

```
019 // drama and that kind of thing        //
```

Listen to how Corony says this speech unit (Click on the second speaker icon). Pay attention to the sounds at the ends of the words 'drama', 'and', & 'that'.

Click on the words in both the slow version, and Corony's version. You will hear the difference between the fast and the slow forms.

```
019 // (drama) and that kind of thing // [slow version]

Click here

019 // (drama) and that kind of thing // 282 wpm [original]
```

3.2 Notice the missing and linked sounds

Click on the speaker icon, and on the words in green to notice what happens between the words.

drama and	– there is a slight suggestion of an r between the two words
and that	– the d and the end of **and** does not occur
that kind	– the t at the end of **that** does not occur
kind of	– the two words are run together
of thing	– the f is extremely difficult to hear

Corony's speech flows in such a way that there are no gaps between the words: and because the words are streamed together, sounds which would be there in the paused pronunciation disappear or change. This illustrates the fact that people speak in streamed, flowing units (we call them speech units) which, most often, are larger than a single word.

Figure 9.2   Adapted from Richard Cauldwell, *Streaming Speech: Listening and Pronunciation for Advanced Learners of English* (Student Workbook), Speechinaction 2003 © Richard Cauldwell.

to identify a highly compressed cluster, then playing the intonation group and finally playing the sentences that precede and follow it.

Formulaic chunks

Many groups of words are stored in the mind in the form of **chunks** of language. They include not only **lexical phrases** such as *in front of* but also frequently recurring sequences such as *I don't know* or *[ten] years ago*. They play an important part in assisting speakers to construct utterances rapidly, because they circumvent the need to assemble a common phrase afresh every time it is used (Pawley and Syder, 1983). Speakers work on the assumption that listeners also have these chunks in their mental store and can be relied on to process a frequent string of words as a whole. Consequently, they give rather less prominence to the components of a chunk than they might if they had had to assemble it word by word. In any frequently heard string, some of the words are likely to be reduced through elision, assimilation or both. The sequence *do you know what I mean?* used by British speakers as a conversation filler can be reduced to as little as *narpMEAN* ([nɑːpˈmiːn]).

Among these formulaic chunks, a number represent common syntactic relationships. One can identify:

- a distinct *to* group:

    want to [ˈwɒnə] *going to* [ˈgənə] *have to* [ˈhæftə] *got to* [ˈgɒdə]

    need to [ˈniːtə] *ought to* [ˈɔːtə] etc.

- a *have* (= /əv/) group:

    must have (been) [ˈmʌstə]   *might have (been)* [ˈmaɪtə]

    should have (done) [ˈʃʊdə]   *needn't have (done)* [ˈniːntə] etc.

Table 9.7 provides examples of other common chunks that I have observed. The transcriptions should not be taken to represent realisations that are in any way 'standard', since formulae of this kind usually have a number of different realisations. Lists of similar frequent formulae are provided in Gimson, 1994: 261–2 and in Ur, 1984: 46.

Because the pressures of the intonation group so often make less important words difficult to recognise, learners do better to listen out for familiar chunks rather than attempting word-by-word processing. It is useful, from quite an early stage, to draw their attention to the role that chunks play in everyday speech. Table 9.8 gives examples of some simple exercises which move from awareness raising to the practising and internalising of recurrent chunks.

155

Table 9.7 *Frequent formulaic chunks*

Standard	Reduced	Standard	Reduced
Do you like	[dʒəˈlaɪk]	*Would you like*	[dʒəˈlaɪk]
There isn't any	[ˈðɪznenɪ]	*how much*	[hʌˈmʌtʃ]
got any	[ˈɡɒtnɪ]	*How are you?*	[hɑːˈjuː]
I've already	[vɔːˈredɪ]	*more and more*	[mɔːˈmɔː]
I don't know	[dəˈnəʊ]	*Just a moment*	[dʒəsˈməʊmənt]
I'll be	[ˈʌbɪ]	*in a week or two*	[nəˈwiːkətuː]
half-past	[hʌˈpɑːs]	*Let's see*	[leˈsiː]
pair of	[ˈpeərə]	*If I were you*	[faɪwəˈjuː]
this morning	[ˈsmɔːnɪŋ]	*Never mind!*	[neˈmaɪn]
What do you mean?	[wɒdʒəˈmiːn]	*Are you all right?*	[jəʊˈraɪʔ]

Table 9.8 *Exercises in recognising chunks*

- *Isolated groups.* Teacher uses a tapescript of authentic speech to select groups of words which occur frequently in everyday speech with a relatively consistent intonation pattern. Examples: fixed formulae (*You all right?*), longer fillers (*do you know what I mean?*), syntactic patterns (*I should have done*) Teacher plays them; learners report what they hear. Learners then practise producing them.
- *Focus on chunks.* After playing an authentic text for comprehension, teacher replays sections of the recording representing chunks that occur frequently in natural speech. Learners transcribe.
- *Locating chunks.* During an extensive listening phase, the teacher asks learners to listen not for general meaning but for groups of words that they have often heard together. Class discusses and listens again.
- *Reduced forms in larger chunks.* Teacher identifies formulaic chunks in authentic recordings, and asks learners to transcribe

(cont.)

Table 9.8 *(cont.)*

them. The most useful are noted down by learners and practised orally as items of vocabulary. Examples from English:

- syntactic chunks (*wanna go, must've done*)
- fillers (*do you know what I mean?*)
- frequent sentences (*Where are you from? Any idea of the time?*)
- strings with a pragmatic purpose: (*Do you mind if I...? Why don't we ...? Sorry about the... Any chance of a ...?*)

9.4 Speaker variation

In the interests of presenting a complete picture of variation, this section considers the way in which spoken input varies from speaker to speaker. The discussion will be relatively brief – not because this is an unimportant area of listening, but because the points raised have fewer implications for the process approach that is recommended in this book.

In L2 contexts, any discussion of differences between speakers tends to focus quite heavily on *accent*. But a point that is often overlooked is that accent is not an all-or-nothing feature. Within the county of Yorkshire in the UK, for example, there are fine gradations of accent from one town to another. Other gradations reflect the life and experience of the individual speaker. The English of somebody from Western Australia who went to school in New York is likely to show traces of both locations; alternatively, the speaker might well command two accents and choose between them according to location and listener. Similarly, the speech of somebody who has acquired English as a second language is likely to reflect not only their first language but also what national or local varieties of English they have encountered and the extent to which they have been exposed to them. Accent, then, is a more complex and more individual factor than is sometimes admitted.

Nor should we overlook the other important features that distinguish speakers. *Physiological characteristics* cause speech to differ markedly from speaker to speaker. Every mouth has a different shape, as does every palate, every tongue, every set of teeth. Variations in these articulators produce marked differences in voices and in the sounds they produce. Similarly, variations in vocal-cord length result in most women's voices being at a higher pitch than men's. It is a matter of wonder that an infant acquiring its first language manages to detect any consistent patterns at all in the range of adult voices to which it is exposed.

There are also personal variations in *style of delivery*. Some people adopt a typical speech rate that strikes us as fast; others speak overall more slowly. Some speak loudly under normal circumstances; others speak more quietly. Some pause at consistent points such as syntactic boundaries; some pause frequently; some make use of long pauses.

These considerations are not trivial. In a first language context, an extraordinary achievement occurs whenever we meet or just hear somebody new. Within a matter of seconds, we adjust (or **normalise**[5]) to the speaker's voice and are able to follow what he or she is saying. Encountering a voice for the first time, we succeed very rapidly in establishing a set of baseline values for it. We form an idea of the speaker's speech rate, loudness and pitch setting under normal conditions (see Brown, 1990: Chap. 6 for an interesting discussion of these features). This enables us to recognise shifts of mood, when the speaker, for one reason or another, speaks faster, more loudly or within a higher range. The judgements we make about a speaker's emotional state at a particular moment are to some extent relative. If somebody raises their voice in anger, we notice not necessarily that the voice is loud by universal standards, but that it is louder than it usually is. The same is true of changes in speed, which we might attribute to excitement, or changes in pitch, perhaps due to fear.

Language learning specialists take too little account of individual characteristics such as those just described when considering the challenges that face the second language listener. Aside from the problems posed by regional accents, they tend to assume that learners can normalise to voices speaking in L2 as rapidly as to those in L1. But it seems probable that it requires a much higher level of attention (and a longer stretch of time) to get used to a voice that employs the unfamiliar sounds, rhythm patterns and intonation of a foreign language. The characteristics of individual voices even vary to some extent according to the language being spoken. Thus, Greek tends to be spoken louder than English, French with tenser articulation, Japanese and Chinese with higher ranges of pitch. Anyone acquiring the languages mentioned has to adjust their expectations in relation to these features.

There are implications here for teachers and testers of listening. The issue of normalisation provides support for the widely expressed view

---

[5] The terms *normalise/normalisation* tend to be used in two slightly different ways: (a) to refer to the way in which the listener adjusts to the individual features of a speaker's voice; (b) to refer to the way in which (according to some commentators) the listener edits out features such as voice pitch and quality in order to arrive at a standard form for what is being said. Here the term is used in sense (a).

(Brown and Yule, 1983b: 80) that the more voices there are in a recording, the more difficult a listening task becomes. It is not just a matter of distinguishing one voice from another (an unfortunate by-product of audio recording); it is also a matter of establishing baseline characteristics for each one.

A second conclusion to be drawn is that language learners should be allowed sufficient time to normalise to the recorded voices of L2 speakers. One way of achieving this is to ensure that comprehension questions do not target the first 10–15 seconds of a recording, to ensure that listeners have time to accustom their ears to the speaker (perhaps longer if there is more than one speaker). Another is to adhere to the tradition of playing a text at least twice, the first time for very general understanding. There has been much discussion amongst L2 testing specialists as to whether a double play is acceptable, on the argument that we usually hear an utterance only once in real life. But here is a persuasive reason for adhering to the established practice.[6]

It is also worthwhile employing exercises which focus specifically on normalisation and give learners practice in adjusting to the voices of L2 speakers. It is curious how rarely this aspect of listening is targeted by instructors – especially when one considers that rapid normalisation may make the difference between success and failure on the first item in an exam. Table 9.9 provides some suggestions for exercise types.

The issue of normalisation also serves to draw attention to an under-valued resource in the voice of the teacher. In our enthusiasm for lively cassette recordings of a range of native speakers, we tend to overlook the benefits of familiarity – of a voice which learners encounter on a regular basis and do not need to adjust to. Where teaching takes place through the medium of the second language, much unscheduled listening practice already takes place in the form of information, instructions and feedback. In addition, a strong case can be made, in the earliest stages of listening practice, for using simple factual passages read aloud by the teacher, as a way of building listening confidence. The voice is familiar and (especially for young learners) has none of the daunting effect of being asked to understand unseen adult actors from a distant land.

Finally, any consideration of the many variables involved in adjusting to the voice of an L2 speaker must raise concerns about the current fad among both testers and materials writers for exposing listeners at all levels to a mixture of varieties of the target language. It can be argued that, at least in the early stages, listeners already face a formidable enough

---

[6] There are, of course, a number of others, in particular the way in which an audio recording disadvantages the listener by providing no visual or paralinguistic cues.

Table 9.9 *Examples of normalisation exercises*

- *Comparing speakers.* Teacher plays a recorded natural dialogue. Learners do not listen for detailed understanding but comment on differences between speakers in terms of speech rate, accent, fluency, etc. Learners speculate on the age of each.
- *Same text, different voices.* Teacher gets two or three colleagues to record the same set of four sentences. Learners compare voice pitch, speech rate, pausing, etc. Teacher plays two or three words said by each speaker; learners match them to the speaker.
- *Distinguishing voices.* Teacher plays samples of four voices (ideally two male and two female) excised from an authentic recording. Voices are identified as A, B, C and D. Learners listen and compare voices. Teacher plays further extracts; learners say who is speaking in each one. In a later exercise, teacher chooses four female or four male voices.
- *Speaker stance.* Teacher plays short samples of sentences that are neutral in terms of context, but where the speakers are speaking angrily, happily, thoughtfully, etc. Learners try to describe the mood conveyed.

---

challenge in simply tuning in to a number of voices within one variety without the added complication of switching from one accent to another. If one takes adequate account of normalisation as an issue in L2 listening, a more gradual progression would seem to be desirable:

1. an emphasis on the voice of the teacher, supported by occasional recordings;
2. a range of voices (male and female) in one standard national variety; initially, older speakers, who tend to speak more slowly; later more rapid speakers;
3. the gradual introduction of one or two other varieties, ideally widespread or standard ones; each exemplified in a range of voices;
4. an expansion of the range of accents covered to include a greater number of native-speaker varieties;
5. exposure to a range of non-native speaker varieties – recognising that a great deal of communication today takes place between individuals who speak the target language as a lingua franca.

In this, the programme designer should not lose sight of the point made above: that there is no such thing as a 'model' accent, since all of us speak with personal characteristics which reflect our experience and upbringing. To represent a listening course as containing examples of 'the Australian accent' is a considerable simplification: what it actually contains will be examples of individuals speaking with Australian phoneme values, but with personal variations resulting from residence in difference parts of the country, the influence of peers versus the influence of family, the influence of education, and so on. Achieving familiarity with a new accent thus entails distinguishing the features which are common to all speakers of the group from those which are specific to an individual.

9.5 Conclusion

The purpose of this chapter has been to add to the reader's understanding of the perceptual difficulties faced by the L2 listener. It has challenged a widely accepted view that the goal of the teacher in vocabulary or pronunciation teaching is to instil in the mind of the learner a set of citation forms or perfect phonemes, against which spoken input can be matched. The only way in which this assumption can be sustained is if the listener is capable of somehow converting the many variations of a word that occur in real speech into a single standard version that exactly matches a model form stored in the mind. Alternatively, the listener has to be willing to accept some highly approximate matches, and to be quite heavily reliant upon cues provided by co-text.

The chapter has given a full account of the unreliable nature of the input to which the listener is exposed. Among the issues that have been identified are:

- the lack of any set of signals that uniquely identifies a given phoneme wherever it occurs;
- the large amount of variation that occurs when the same word is produced in different contexts;
- the need to normalise to different voices, even within the same variety of L2.

The point should be made that the discussion has been conducted from the perspective of the L2 *listener*, who needs to make sense of stretches of connected speech which contain variant features. No position has been taken on whether the learner needs to acquire the same features when operating as an L2 speaker.

The principal conclusion drawn has concerned the need for focused small-scale practice in decoding samples of connected speech. This, it has been argued, is likely to increase the speed and accuracy of processing, boost listener confidence and leave a more systematic set of traces than simple exposure to extended passages. A second conclusion, which has featured less, is that cracking the code of connected speech may demand some intensive individual work on the part of the learner. The learning process partly entails playing and replaying problematic passages to resolve particular perceptual difficulties so that they can be overcome the next time they are encountered. It may often be better for the listener to decide for herself where such passages occur.

Further reading

Brown, G. (1990) *Listening to Spoken English*. Harlow: Longman, 2nd edn, Chaps. 2 and 4.

Field, J. (2003) 'Promoting perception: lexical segmentation in L2 listening'. *ELT Journal*, 57/4: 325–34.

Shockey, L. (2003) *Sound Patterns of Spoken English*. Oxford: Blackwell.

10 Decoding: sounds, syllables and words

If you wish to know the mind of a man, listen to his words.
Chinese proverb

We have seen that the information provided by the speech signal is at best inconsistent and at worst misleading. So how does a first language listener succeed in making sense of the input that meets her ear? And in what ways is the decoding technique of a second language listener likely to differ from that of the first? Our exploration of decoding now moves from the raw material that reaches the listener's ear to the processes that an expert listener employs in order to make sense of it.

It is worth recalling that an important part of the decoding operation entails *matching*: making a connection between clusters of acoustic cues and the listener's knowledge of units (phonemes, words and grammatical patterns) of the language being heard. How that matching operation takes place will be the main theme of the present chapter. We start by trying to answer the crucial question of how a listener manages to connect speech that is so variable with the standard forms of words. We consider some explanations that have been proposed and their implications for the listening teacher. We then go on to examine the matching process in relation to units of various sizes: beginning with phonemes and moving on to syllables and words.

Throughout, the behaviour of an expert listener is treated as the goal towards which a teacher might wish to lead an L2 listener and as a benchmark against which the performance of an L2 listener can be measured. The aim is to identify the processes that a skilled listener uses and an unskilled one does not, so that an instructor can provide systematic practice in them. As before, the type of practice proposed takes the form of intensive, small-scale exercises. The difference here, however, is that the exercises are designed to develop and modify the learner's listening behaviour.

There are some who might dispute the usefulness of providing intensive practice that aims to change learner behaviour. Does it perhaps smack of the kind of discredited approach favoured by **behaviourist** views of language learning (most notoriously the suggestion that children acquire their first language in a way that resembles Pavlov's training of his dogs)? The answer lies in a point made in Chapter 8. An important difference between an expert and a novice listener is the fact that the expert can achieve decoding with a high degree of automaticity. In L1 listening,

163

the matching process takes place without demanding huge resources of attention and thus leaves the listener free to focus upon aspects of wider meaning. One of the chief goals of decoding practice must therefore be to induce this kind of automatic matching facility in the L2 learner.

It is a well-established principle that automaticity is achieved by repeated use of the same process until it becomes second nature. How much better, then, to focus on a single process and to practise it intensively with a view to enhancing performance in it, than to rely solely upon the chance of the learner needing to employ the process from time to time during traditional comprehension work.

10.1 Finding matches for inconsistent input

Let us first consider a major question left unanswered in Chapter 9. If the input to listeners is so variable, how on earth do they succeed in matching it to their knowledge of the sounds and words of the language?

10.1.1 Listening as a tentative process

One possible conclusion from the evidence is that much listening, whether in L1 or L2, is *approximate*. If the input is so variable, then listeners may need to form tentative matches on the basis of the available evidence and to confirm or change them as they hear more and more of the utterance. The idea that listening is based upon forming and testing hypotheses will recur at many points throughout this chapter and the next.

It accords well with the **interactive** account given in Chapter 8, which holds that the matching process does not rely upon a single source of evidence (e.g. just a series of phonemes). Instead, the listener is seen as constantly weighing many different pieces of information against each other in order to establish what has been heard. To repeat the *veshtables* example, the listener might draw not only upon matches made at the level of the phoneme but also upon matches made at the level of the syllable (*vesh?*) and the word (*vegetables*) and upon clues provided by the surrounding text (*fruit and...*). The goal is to find the 'best fit' rather than a fit that necessarily forms a 100% match with what was heard. In this way, the listener is able to overcome the many variations acquired by the citation forms of words when they occur in connected speech.

Psychologists often portray this weighing of evidence in terms of **activation**. Think of activation as a kind of electric current that has to reach a certain strength in order to light up a light bulb. Let us assume that a listener hears the sequence [maɪ'treɪn] and is unsure whether to match it to *my train* or *might rain* or even *might train*. All three would be activated in her mind, i.e. would receive a certain level of electrical current. As the sentence proceeds, the current for one or more might be boosted by subsequent evidence (e.g. if the next word was *came, heavily* or *students*) and the current for others would weaken. When there was sufficient evidence for one interpretation, its light bulb would turn on and the listener would be satisfied that a match had been achieved.

If listening is such a tentative operation, it requires us to keep quite a precise trace of the sounds that reach our ears, in case we have to go back and reinterpret them. It also means that we have to be very flexible in our ongoing interpretation of what we hear. There are difficulties here for the L2 listener. She may find it harder to store a temporary record of the sounds that were uttered because her knowledge of the L2 sound system is so much more limited. She also has to lend much greater attention to decoding, which must limit her scope for rethinking her early matches. Furthermore, the process of weighing evidence is complicated by her limited vocabulary, which may mean that she is not aware of all the possibilities that need to be considered, and by her uncertainty about how accurately she can apply the phoneme values of L2.

Small wonder if, instead of forming several hypotheses, a less experienced L2 listener often chooses one and clings to it, ignoring subsequent evidence that is inconsistent. The light bulb for *might rain* might light up prematurely and cause the listener to ignore the disambiguation provided by *leaves at six*.

10.1.2 The question of how we store language

Another explanation considers not what the listener does but how she stores sounds, words and grammar patterns in her mind. It should be noted that this explanation is not necessarily an alternative to the one just given; we might choose to treat it as complementary.

It seems to be taken for granted by some commentators on second language learning that a listener carries a 'pure' version of a phoneme or a citation form of a word in her mind, against which she matches what she hears. The problem with this assumption is that one then has to assume that the listener possesses some means of editing out all the variation that occurs in natural speech, in order to make the match. She needs to edit out not only the voice and accent of the speaker but also features described in Chapter 9 such as assimilation, reduction, etc. This would appear to be a very complex operation.

A more recent view is that we retain multiple records of the sounds and words of a language in our memory, and match new instances against them. To give the example of the word *actually*, a native English listener would have at least the seven different versions of it shown in Table 9.6, all linked together in the mind as representing the same word. The listener would also have records of the word said in a range of different voices and different accents. Hearing a sequence of sounds, she would make a direct link to one of these stored memories without having to edit anything.

This account of how we store sounds and words might seem implausible and wasteful. But it is a solution to which speech scientists are increasingly turning.[1] It agrees with evidence that the brain is capable of holding much more information than we ever suspected. It explains how a listener is able to make allowances for the enormous variations between speakers' voices. It also suggests how, over a period of time, we come to understand those who speak with different accents from our own. We do so by a process of laying down more and more traces of voices speaking in those accents until we have sufficient points of reference to be able to understand them.

If an **exemplar view** of this kind becomes widely accepted, there are implications for L2 listening instruction. Teachers will need to rethink the received wisdom that learners must spend a lot of time internalising the sound system of the target language in some kind of abstract form. They will also need to recognise the limitations of learning and storing words in their citation forms. A primary requirement will be for the listener to encounter the same words in a wide range of contexts and voices.

We can then conclude that exposure to lengthy listening passages (as in the comprehension approach) does assist the listener in that it establishes multiple traces of particular words and patterns. But, given the limited amount of time available to the instructor, we should also conclude that it is important to support this extended approach with more focused practice activities. One useful innovation in the early stages of L2 listening might be to assemble examples of the same groups of words uttered in different circumstances and at different speeds by a number of different speakers.

Having discussed some general principles in this section, we now move on to look more concretely at how listeners make matches at several different levels. We will consider matching at phoneme level (Section 10.2), syllable level (Section 10.3) and word level (Section 10.4). The format in each case will be the same. There will first be an outline of some current ideas about the processes that a skilled listener employs. We will then consider the ways in which they might pose a challenge for the second language listener. There will be suggestions as to the implications

---

[1] Usually in conjunction with an interactive view of how a final match is made.

for the classroom and concrete examples of exercise types that a teacher might use.

10.2 Processing phonemes

10.2.1 Recognising phonemes

First language processing

Chapter 9 drew attention to the lack of a clear one-to-one connection between the sounds that are present in the speech stream and the phonemes that a listener perceives. So how does a listener recognise the phonemes of her native language?

Given that the phoneme varies so much in the way it is realised, there is a possibility that we do not use it as a unit at all when processing speech. The view is supported by evidence (Morais *et al.*, 1979) suggesting that illiterate people have difficulty in recognising separate sounds within words (for example, in saying what is left if you take the /g/ out of *gold*). Some commentators have argued that maybe we map straight from the speech signal to the word. Others have suggested that we analyse spoken input syllable by syllable. The advantage here is that syllables are much more consistent than individual sounds because most co-articulation takes place *within* the syllable. Furthermore, there is a limited number of syllables in any language, and the commonest words make use of a relatively small set of them.

Other solutions to the problem of phoneme variation were mentioned in the previous section. Firstly, it is clear that listeners are not solely dependent upon phoneme-based evidence but draw also upon their vocabulary store, their ability to recognise recurrent chunks of language, their understanding of the context – and even upon their recall of a word that was heard recently. Secondly, the idea that expert users of a language develop a 'pure' version of a phoneme in their minds against which to match all possible variations can only be sustained if we also believe that these users develop a complex set of editing operations that eliminate all the possible deviations from the norm that might occur. We need to give serious consideration to the alternative likelihood that a phoneme in the mind of a listener (if there is such a thing) is a generalisation based upon many different stored memories.

Second language practice

So where does this leave the instructor? Given the current understanding of how decoding occurs, we might wonder about the function of the kind of low-level ear-training exercises favoured by pronunciation teachers, in which learners are taught to distinguish between single-syllable **minimal pairs** such as *pack/back, ship/sheep* or *leaf/leave*. Clearly, perceiving the differences between phonemes is a useful first step towards producing them. But does it bring any long-term benefits in terms of *listening* development? Does class time allocated to discriminating between phonemes constitute time well spent, so far as the listening teacher is concerned?

We should not overstate the usefulness of ear-training of this kind, but it certainly has a part to play in a process approach to listening. It serves to practise the distinctions that experience has taught an L1 listener to make between words that are closely similar. It is even possible that a record of the confusability of certain words forms part of the L1 listener's lexical knowledge.

There is a great deal of evidence that L2 listeners tend to analyse input in terms of word-sized units. But many of the matches they make are rough approximations that do not correspond exactly to the sounds that the listener heard. To reduce the prevalence of this kind of guesswork (which may have knock-on effects for an understanding of the recording as a whole), we need to take steps to ensure that the matches made are based on accurate perception. As the listener becomes more confident of her phoneme values, she becomes less inclined to make rash leaps in the dark at word level.

The minimal pairs tradition provides a starting point, but we need to extend it to take account of recent insights into how learners internalise phoneme values. The experience of academics training students in L1 phonetics suggests that, to fully master an unfamiliar sound, a learner needs to be able to identify it within individual words as well as between minimally different pairs. Teachers thus need to expand the range of ear-training exercise types that they use. Table 10.1 proposes several different formats, graded by difficulty, which draw upon the methods that speech scientists employ when researching L1 phoneme perception.

Lists of minimal pairs for a programme of discrimination exercises can be found in Gimson (1994) and Baker (2006). But, in designing exercises, the following considerations should be taken into account:

- The words used should be relatively frequent and roughly equivalent in terms of frequency.
- When practising consonants, a range of different vowels should be featured; when practising vowels a range of adjacent consonants should be featured. This allows for the way in which phonemes vary according to the context in which they occur.

Table 10.2 suggests various types of phoneme discrimination exercise. The examples that are given practise the /p–b/ contrast.

168

Table 10.1 *Graded ear-training tasks*

a. *Minimal pair discrimination between spoken words (A/B).*
Given a choice in writing, listener decides if she heard A or B.
Given two choices in writing, listener matches one to A and one
to B.
b. *Say whether what is on the page matches A or B. (A/B – X)*
Listener hears two spoken words A and B, then one of them is
repeated.
c. *Transcribe one member of a minimal pair. (A or B?)*
Listener hears a word that is readily confused with another.
d. *Repeat spoken non-words which comply with the phonology
of L2.*

Table 10.2 *Phoneme discrimination exercises*

- *Contrast response (A/B)*: 'Put up your left hand when you hear
the sound represented by P and your right hand when you hear
the sound represented by B.'

  pack   pack   pack   back – bill   bill   pill –
  bush   bush   push   push –
  pea   bee   pea   bee   bee

- *Matching exercise (A/B – X)*: 'You will hear two words. Then
you will hear one of them again. Write A if it was the first word
and B if it was the second.'

  back – pack   back   bill – pill   pill   bush – push   push
  bee – pea   bee

- *Contrast dictation*: 'On your worksheet, you will see pairs of
words: BACK/PACK, BILL/PILL, BUSH/PUSH, etc. Decide
which one I say'.

- *Transcription*: 'Write down the word you hear.'

  pack   bill   bush   pea   bought

- *Unknown word repetition*: 'You will hear a word that you do
not know. Repeat it.'

  balm   perk   pent   batch

10.2.2 Extrapolating written forms from spoken ones

First language processing

As well as acquiring experience of the multiple forms a phoneme might take, a literate first language listener has also built up a set of **phoneme– grapheme correspondences**. These rules link the sounds of a language to the letters and pairs of letters (*sh-*, *th-*, *-ea-*, *-ay*, etc.) that represent them in writing; they also associate sound sequences with letter sequences (/aɪt/ to *-ight*, /aʊnd/ to *-ound*, /aɪv/ to *-ive*, /ʃn/ to *-tion*, etc.).

A knowledge of sound–spelling relationships is more important than commentators often realise. It has obvious applications when a native speaker is *producing* language in that it enables him to work out how to say a word of low frequency that has only ever been encountered in reading. But it also has a part to play in listening. A listener might need to record in written form something that has occurred in speech; an example might be when a note-taker has to represent unfamiliar technical terms heard in a lecture. A more everyday type of sound–spelling matching is required when one hears an unfamiliar place name and has to locate it on a map.[2]

Second language practice

For the second language listener, there are additional uses. Because of the primacy given to the spoken word in language teaching methodology in many parts of the world, the likelihood is that a learner will first encounter a word in its spoken form. In that case, she will need to work out how it is written, for the purposes of:

- making a note of a new item of vocabulary;
- 'fixing' a mental representation of the word (written representations in the mind are much more robust than spoken ones);
- looking the word up in a dictionary.

Even when not acquiring new words, L2 users have to engage quite frequently in sound–spelling matching. The linking of spoken words to written forms occurs frequently in academic contexts, in business meetings and in social interaction (*I'll meet you in Waterstone's*). Personal names are an especially treacherous area (*This is Geraldine Frobisher, your new manager*). They may have to be retrieved later, and memories stored in phonological form tend to be unreliable. The listener may feel the need to picture the name in terms of its spelling even if she does not write it down.

[2] Not always easy to do with British place names.

Spelling extrapolation is an area that currently receives little attention in listening instruction. It deserves to form part of a process approach in that it is important both to learning a second language (enabling dictionary skills to be acquired) and to using it. Exercises should aim to create awareness of the underlying spelling system, not to teach individual word forms. They should thus feature words which are as regular as possible in terms of the spelling system, and exemplify particular sound–spelling relationships (see Kenworthy, 1987: 94–112 for examples). Table 10.3 suggests some exercise types that an instructor might wish to use.

Table 10.3 *Examples of extrapolation exercises*

- *Transcription of unknown words.* 'Write down the words you hear. Each word will be said twice.' Teacher dictates infrequent words.

  butcher panic robbery sceptical cherub turnip simper camber bristle pristine

- *Dictionary practice.* 'Listen to these words; then look up their meaning in your dictionary.'

  quibble pheasant stretcher limb alight despite freight innate grain cane slovenly breath relief fraud

- *Vocabulary strings.* 'Look at these words, which rhyme. Write down other words that rhyme with each one. Be careful with the spelling.' Teacher uses a homophone pair like *pane/pain* or a common word ending like *-ight* in *light*.

- *Cognates.* Teacher dictates words with cognates in L1. Learners spell them using L2 spelling rules.

- *Non-word dictation.* 'Listen and write down these trade names.' Teacher dictates non-words which conform to L2 phonology.

- *Proper name dictation.* 'Listen and write down the name of the city.' Teacher chooses cities with regular spellings.

  Cardiff – Vancouver – Nottingham – Darwin – Wellington – Madison

  (*cont.*)

Table 10.3 *(cont.)*

- *Note-taking.* 'Listen to these answerphone messages. Write down the names of the people who left them and where they are from.'

    Hello. My name's Harper. I'm ringing from the Grove Corporation in Darwin.

- *Locating words on a map by approximate matching.* 'Follow the journey on a map, marking the stations that are mentioned.'

    Here is a map of the London Underground / New York subway / Sydney City Circle. Let me tell you how to get to where I live. The nearest station to you is [A]. Can you find it? Now, get the northbound train as far as [B]. When you get to [B], you have to change to the [X] line and get the train going towards [C]. You get off at [D]...

10.3 Processing syllables

As we have seen, the syllable is a more consistent unit than the phoneme, so in some ways it forms a more useful target for second language practice. First language listeners might well divide what they hear into syllables rather than into phonemes. Even if they do not, they certainly possess a close familiarity with all the syllables of their language. This does not demand an enormous feat of memory: there is a fixed number of syllables in any language, of which relatively few (around 500) are usually enough to form all the most frequent words.

Syllable-level information contributes more than is sometimes realised to the processing of an expert listener. Many words are monosyllables. In addition, as we shall see, single stressed syllables provide cues to the identity of longer words, cues to the function of words (content versus functor) and cues to where word boundaries fall.

Another important consideration is the fact that the rhythm of a language is largely shaped by what happens at syllable level. There is a long-standing myth that languages divide into those whose rhythm is **stress-timed** (i.e. characterised by roughly equal periods of time between stressed syllables) and those whose rhythm is **syllable-timed** (characterised by syllables of roughly equal length). Attempts to prove this theory scientifically have failed, and it seems more likely that a listener's impression of a language's rhythm is formed by one or more of the following:

- the *structure* of the syllable (basically, the number of consonants that a language permits within a syllable);
- the *frequency of weak syllables* like those in English containing schwa (/ə/);
- the ratio between *the time taken by weak and by strong syllables.*

An unfamiliar rhythm can interfere significantly with a listener's ability to recognise known words in connected speech. So here is another reason for a language instructor to give adequate time to syllable-level processing.

10.3.1 Syllable structure

First language processing

The first factor mentioned, the structure of the syllable, demands particular attention. It varies greatly from one language to another, and a listener's expectations are inevitably shaped by what she is familiar with in L1. It would seem that that by far the most common syllable forms across languages are CV (consonant–vowel) and CVC (consonant–vowel–consonant). Some languages such as Spanish or Italian rely heavily upon an open CV syllable consisting of a consonant and vowel, while others allow much greater variety. English represents an extreme case in the number and complexity of its syllable types. It even permits a CCCVCCCC syllable in the word *strengths* (/streŋkθs/ in its citation form).

Native listeners are also attuned to processing the specific **consonant clusters** that exist in their language: combinations such as /kl/ or /pr/ or /spl/ that occur at the beginnings of syllables and others such as /ŋk/ or /ntʃ/ that occur at the ends. These clusters are usually discussed in terms of how they are produced: native speakers are said to have no difficulty in making the /s/–/p/ transition at the beginning of a word like *sport*, whereas non-native speakers sometimes employ **epenthesis,** producing [e'spɔːt] (Spanish speakers) or [sɪ'pɔːt] (some varieties of Arabic). However, recent evidence has suggested that this may be a problem of listening as well as of speaking. While expert listeners hear the /sp/ as a cluster, less experienced ones hear the consonant sequence the way they pronounce it.

Second language practice

Listening instructors should introduce learners at an early stage to the range of syllable types in the target language. Simple transcription exercises can be used over a period of time in order to ensure that the L2 listener can reproduce the more complex syllables accurately. Given the

173

epenthesis finding, there should also be practice in detecting consonant clusters in words. Table 10.4 provides some examples.

Table 10.4 *Exercises in syllable structure*

- *Syllable recognition* (an alternative to phoneme recognition). 'Listen and write down the syllables you hear. Some may be whole words; some may not.' Teacher reads aloud the most frequent syllable strings of the target language, based on a word frequency ranking.

- *Matching exercise.* 'Listen to the words on your worksheet. Identify the syllables which occur in more than one word.'

  consum*ption* ex*citing* *reckon* *somebody* Egyp*tian* phys*ics* *tinkle*

- *Consonant clusters.* 'Write down the words you hear. They may be words you do not know.' Teacher dictates infrequent words beginning or ending with common consonant clusters of the language. Learners are encouraged to recognise clusters by analogy with known words. Teacher checks to see if learners have inserted additional vowels.

  blank bracken plight prickle clench crackle glimpse grind speckle spasm spray strangle slacken scribble

- *Graded syllables.* Teacher dictates monosyllabic words representing all possible L2 syllable patterns: starting with V, CV and VC and going on to complex patterns. Repeat with infrequent words that the learners do not know. For guidance on syllable types in English, see Roach, 2000: Chap. 8.

  A ray pray spray sprain strained
  E fee eat east beast cream creased screen screamed
  rang rank crank length strength

10.3.2 Syllable stress

First language processing

In many languages, there is a clearly marked distinction between syllables that are given prominence and those that are not. This contributes to the characteristic rhythm of a language and serves to highlight certain parts of the input that are especially informative. It has been suggested (Grosjean and Gee, 1987) that the stressed syllable of a word might provide an **access code** for the skilled listener – a way of locating the word when searching through one's mental vocabulary. An important key to recognising the word *phoTOGraphy* would lie in the stressed sequence /tɒg/ and the key to *magaZINE* would lie in /ziːn/.

Whether this is the case or not, stressed syllables are of considerable help to the listener. They tend to be reliable and easier to perceive since they are usually louder and more clearly produced than unstressed ones. There is much evidence (Bond, 1999) that first language listeners rely much more heavily on the phonetic information in stressed syllables than on the information in unstressed ones, treating the former as 'islands of reliability' in a speech stream that is sometimes muddy and fast-flowing.

Unstressed syllables also play a part in the decoding of connected speech. In many languages, they are associated with function words such as *the, it, for, of,* etc. – words, usually of one syllable, which contribute to the grammatical structure of the sentences rather than bearing the kind of meaning we associate with items of vocabulary. There is considerable evidence from English that first language listeners exploit this association in order to identify possible function words at an early stage of decoding. There are advantages attached to this procedure in that it enables a listener to process function words separately from content words and more rapidly. With a content word, one needs to retrieve a meaning; but with a functor, all that is required is for the listener to match the weak syllable against a small set of around 100 to 150 highly frequent items.

Second language practice

The way in which prominence is marked varies from language to language, and in some cases listening instructors may need to ensure that their learners are capable of distinguishing syllables that have been foregrounded (usually those that have been stressed) from those that have not. Pronunciation handbooks (e.g. Dalton and Seidlhofer, 1994: 97–9) often provide useful examples of ear-training exercises which require learners to distinguish stressed from unstressed syllables in lists of words.[3]

---

[3] Recognising stress in words may not be a serious problem for many listeners. Archibald (1998: 184) records a much lower rate of error in perceiving stressed syllables than in producing correctly stressed words.

It is quite easy to design exercises that encourage learners firstly to pay special heed to stressed syllables and secondly to use them as guides to the presence of a particular word. Table 10.5 provides some examples. Note that one can apply a minimal pair approach to syllables as well as to whole words.

Table 10.5 *Exercises using syllable cues*

- *Faint speech*. 'You will hear some sentences in L1 played very quietly. You may not be able to hear all of the words. Try to write down the stressed syllables. Then try to guess which words they come from.'
- *Strong syllables as access cues*. 'Sometimes a stressed syllable is the only part of a word that you hear clearly. Listen to these stressed syllables. Can you guess what the whole word is?'

[*initial syllable*] /twen/ (twenty)   /mɔːn/ (morning)
/brek/ (breakfast)   /nʌm/ (number)   /nʌθ/ (nothing)
/nʌð/ (another)   /dɪf/ (different/difficult)   /dɪs/ (distant/distance)
/prɒb/ (problem/probably)   /prɒp/ (proper/property)
/weð/ (whether/weather)   /kwes/ (question)   /sɜːf/ (surface)
/sɜːv/ (service)   /sɜːt/ (certain)   /mʌn/ (money)   /mʌŋ/ (monkey)
/mɪn/ (minute/minimum)   /mɪs/ (Mr/Mrs)   /pɒs/ (possible)
/pɒz/ (positive)   /bɪz/ (business)   /bɪs/ (biscuit)

[*internal or final syllable*] /mem/ (remember)   /hæps/ (perhaps)
/pəʊz/ (suppose)   /saɪd/ (beside/decide)   /pɔːt/ (important)
/meɪʃ/ (information)   /næʃ/ (international)   /twiːn/ (between)
/nʌf/ (enough)

It is also relatively easy to design exercises which make learners aware of the connection between weak syllables and function words in the language they are studying. A teacher might, for example, play groups of words such as the following which contain combinations of stressed and unstressed syllables. Learners would be asked to transcribe the stressed words on a first play of the recording and the others on a second play. They would then be asked to comment on the fact that many of the unstressed words play a grammatical role rather than contributing to lexical meaning.

> THIS *is the* DOG *that* CHASED *the* CAT *that* KILLED *the* RAT
>   *that* LIVED *in the* HOUSE *that* JACK BUILT.
> BOX *of* MATCHes   WAITed *at* HOME   WENT *to the* BANK
> LOOKING *at the* SKY   GUESSes *the* TIME   PLACes *in* SPAIN
> WANTed *to* KNOW   PIECes *of* CAKE   RULES *for* DRIVers
> *The* GLASS *is* BROKen.

10.4 Processing words

We tend to assume rather too readily that an L2 listener's problems in decoding words derive mainly from vocabulary limitations. In fact, there are several possible causes. Learners do not always have full confidence that they have heard a particular group of phonemes correctly, and have to allow for a degree of approximation. Their representation of what a word sounds like may be imprecise. And because the vocabulary in their mental store is much more limited than that of a first language listener, they have to decide whether a group of phonemes represents a known word or whether it potentially represents one that they do not know. The seeds are sown for considerable uncertainty.

Even for native listeners, processing at word level is quite a complex operation. Firstly, they have to determine where in a piece of connected speech each word begins and ends (Section 10.4.1). In this, they may be assisted by phonological cues. They then have to match a group of sounds in the input to a stored model of what a particular word sounds like – or to many stored examples of the word. In this, they are assisted by automatic processes (Section 10.4.2) that a less experienced listener does not possess because she does not have a sufficiently well-established vocabulary base. And they, too, have to recognise and deal with new words, misheard words or words that they have not heard before in spoken form (Section 10.4.3).

10.4.1 Lexical segmentation

First language processing

We saw in Chapter 9 that spoken word forms are often subject to variation when they are produced in a sentence. Another complication is that there are no consistent gaps between words in connected speech as there are in most writing systems. The speaker pauses occasionally to plan what comes next, but not after each word. *It is the listener who has to determine where in a piece of continuous speech one word ends and the next begins.*

The operation, known as **lexical segmentation**, might seem a straightforward task if one has the vocabulary knowledge. Surely all a listener has to do is to match a group of sounds to a word. Once the match has been made, she can locate the end of the word and go on to seek a match for the next group of sounds. In fact, the process is not so easy. Suppose an L1 listener hears the word *catalogue*. The simplest matching routine would suggest that it consists of not one word but three: *cat + a + log.* Or consider a longer sequence such as *The captain's in cabin eight.* Possible matches that a listener might make include (beside the correct ones): *cap, capped, tins, zinc, cab, in, innate.*

One easy solution to this question suggests that the listener is capable of making use of context and co-text (including grammar) to resolve any ambiguities of the type described. Yes, indeed; but as we saw in Chapter 8, employing contextual and co-textual cues is both slow and demanding upon mental resources. The listener needs some other, more automatic, routine which enables her to make rapid matches with a low likelihood of failure.

Several theories have been put forward about the techniques that L1 listeners employ to locate word boundaries. The most convincing holds that listeners exploit the phonology of the language in question. For English, it appears that native listeners employ a *metrical segmentation strategy* (Cutler, 1990). In segmenting the speech stream into possible words, they are guided by the assumption that each stressed[4] syllable marks a likely beginning for a word. The strategy makes sense because it has been calculated that somebody listening to English has a 90.2% chance of being right if she operates on the basis that each **stressed** syllable marks the beginning of a new content word.[5]

Another way of locating word boundaries lies in detecting frequently occurring syllables in the form of prefixes (marking the beginning of a word) and suffixes (marking the end). Prefixes and suffixes, like function words, are often of very low prominence; but it seems likely that

---

[4] The terms *stressed* and *unstressed* are used here, but this involves a deliberate simplification. Cutler (1990) refers to a **strong syllable**, meaning one with a full-quality vowel as against a **weak syllable** with a weak-quality vowel. Other commentators on segmentation, however, make the distinction on the basis of stress.

[5] This figure allows for the fact that many content words consist of one syllable. It also allows for the relative frequency of words in a typical piece of connected speech.

L1 listeners become adept at recognising them because they are so frequent.

Second language practice

Evidence exists (Field, 2001b) of French intermediate learners adopting an English-like segmentation strategy when transcribing short pieces of speech recorded by an English speaker. Nobody had trained these learners in segmenting speech; they just showed themselves sensitive to rhythmic regularities in the target language. They had learnt from experience the value of inserting word boundaries before stressed syllables, without realising that learning had taken place. This strongly suggests that training learners in segmentation would pay dividends. It might ensure that they acquire the requisite techniques more rapidly than if left to their own devices. It might also alleviate some of the early frustration of the novice listener at the apparent impenetrability of connected speech. Table 10.6 gives examples of the kinds of exercise that can be used to practise stressed-based lexical segmentation like that of English.

It has to be said that, for certain languages, segmentation does not pose a major problem. These are languages where the words carry a regular stress (on the first, penultimate or final syllable), providing the listener with a reliable and consistent guide to where each one begins or ends. Nevertheless, it still makes sense to demonstrate to learners how to use the appropriate cues when locating word boundaries.

With languages that do not have this kind of fixed stress, teachers should bear in mind that a lexical segmentation strategy represents a rule-of-thumb technique: one that succeeds in many instances but that may not always do so. A first attempt may have to be revised if it does not give rise to a group of phonemes that match a word. So, while it is important to ensure that L2 listeners are given practice in the strategy appropriate to the language being acquired, it is also important to ensure that they treat segmentation outcomes as provisional and are prepared to adjust their first hypotheses.

A second type of segmentation practice relevant to many languages draws attention to weak syllables that potentially represent common prefixes or suffixes. It is necessary to train the L2 listener to recognise them as word-boundary markers because of their low prominence in connected speech. The exercise carries an additional benefit when L2 listeners encounter an unknown word in a piece of spoken input. While they may find it difficult to recall the phonological form of the word or to work out its meaning, they will at least be able to identify its word class from the presence of a familiar suffix. This may help in fitting the unknown word into a larger grammatical structure. See Table 10.7.

Table 10.6   *Lexical segmentation exercises*

- *Standard segmentation practice.* Teacher plays a sentence excised from a piece of natural speech. Learners transcribe the words they understand. Teacher replays, learners add more words to their transcriptions. Learners compare answers, teacher replays. Repeat with several sentences. Ideal also for self-study.

- *Gap filling.* 'Listen and fill in the missing words.' Teacher gives learners a transcript, in which groups of words (not just single words) have been omitted.

- *Awareness raising.* 'Write what you hear.' Teacher dictates ambiguous sequences to the learners; then adds an unexpected ending.

  a nice cream ... dress   [learner writes 'an ice cream', then has to revise it]
  The way to cut it ... is like this.   ['the waiter cut it' → 'the way to cut it']
  Some boxes have ... arrived.   ['some boxes of' → 'some boxes have']
  I want to drive a ... train.   ['a driver' → 'to drive a']

- *Ear-training.* Practice in recognising the specific feature in L2 that assists lexical segmentation. If the feature is word stress, the teacher dictates short sentences and learners mark on a transcript the syllables which carry stress. Teacher draws attention to the role stress plays, e.g. in English, the fact that most words are monosyllabic or carry stress on the first syllable.

- *Segmentation of strings.* 'You will hear one, two or three new words. Try to write them down.' Teacher dictates sequences containing non-words whose boundaries are marked by the segmentation system used in L2. Teacher reviews answers and explains the L2 segmentation system. Examples for the English strategy might be:

  TANdion HEAKal   LECKnif KEDGern   PIFEtal KIFFnoke
  SAMPren TINGlort

- *Sample sentences.* 'You will not understand everything. But try to guess how many words there are.' Teacher reads aloud a sequence containing unfamiliar words whose boundaries are marked by the segmentation system used in L2. Teacher replays and learners attempt to write them down. Teacher explains the L2 segmentation system. For English, take examples of the rhythmic pattern from poetry:

  Dirty British coaster with a salt-caked smokestack.
  Every tiger madness muzzled, every serpent passion killed.

Table 10.7 *Prefix and suffix exercises*

- *Affix spotting.* 'What is a prefix? What is a suffix? Give examples. You will not understand many of the words in this recording. Just write down each prefix or suffix that you hear.' Teacher plays a short section of authentic speech beyond the learners' language level. Teacher later replays the text, pointing out the value of affixes as word-boundary markers.

- *Suffix awareness.* 'Listen to the words I say. Then listen again and write down any syllable which occurs twice.'

    government, happiness, disappear, careless, excitement, revisit, blindness, disappointed, rebuild, hopeless

- *Cued affixes.* 'Read aloud the prefixes and suffixes written on the board. Listen to the recording and count how often each one occurs.' A useful source of material is *Longman Dictionary of Contemporary English*, Appendix B7.

- *Affix segmentation.* Teacher plays a short extract (three or four sentences) from an authentic recording beyond the level of the learners. Learners are asked to listen for prefixes and suffixes. Teacher replays the recording, and learners try to transcribe only the words beginning with prefixes or ending with suffixes.

- *Suffixes and word class.* 'Listen and write down these words. Guess their meanings, then write a sentence containing them.' Teacher dictates unknown words which contain known words as their stems.

    washable postage imagination musical strongly ending smoker modernise replacement mountainous loudness sleepy warmth

10.4.2 Activation and automatic processes

First language processing

A picture was painted in Section 10.1 above of a listening process that draws upon multiple pieces of information, including evidence from the speech signal (the sounds and syllables that have been detected), vocabulary knowledge of the existence of a range of words, and evidence from co-text and context. In making a word match, the listener draws upon all these sources, weighing one against another. But the weighing

181

of evidence also receives support from other processes that are so well established that a competent listener is not even fully aware of them. They derive from the wide vocabulary base that a native speaker possesses, and from many years' experience of hearing the spoken forms of words used in everyday encounters. The most important are:

- *Frequency.* Associated with the vocabulary store is an internalised knowledge of how frequent different words are. This affects the way in which an experienced listener processes the input, lending extra weight to interpretations that favour common words.
- *Current activation.* When a word has been heard quite recently, it remains partly activated in the mind of the listener, assisting her if and when she hears it again.
- *Spreading activation.* The vocabulary of somebody who knows a language well draws upon elaborate connections between word meanings as well as word forms. When a listener hears a word that is part of one of these networks, it activates a number of other words that are closely associated with it. On hearing DOCTOR, the words *patient, hospital,* etc. become foregrounded, so that the listener recognises them more easily if and when they occur.

Second language practice

These three sources of support are available to most second language listeners only to a limited degree. An awareness of the relative frequency of words develops only through extended exposure to a language. It represents one of the obvious benefits of the comprehension approach and of the kind of individualised practice recommended in Chapter 4, but it is clearly a gradual process. Current activation depends critically upon the listener's ability to recognise examples of individual words with a fair degree of confidence. The novice second language listener is acutely aware of the approximate nature of the matches that she makes at phoneme and word level, which does not provide a very strong basis for identifying a word that might recur.

Most limiting of all is the fact that most L2 listeners have a much more rudimentary knowledge of vocabulary than their L1 listener counterparts. Their word store is in a transitional state, with gaps for words not yet acquired and with connections between words still in the process of being established (Meara, 1997). In the early stages of acquiring a second language, this situation denies the listener much of the support that an L1 listener draws from spreading activation. Part of the solution is provided, of course, by the vocabulary teacher – and in particular by the tradition of introducing words in lexical sets which emphasise the conceptual links between them. But the listening teacher also has a technique available in the long-established practice of asking learners to predict the vocabulary content of a passage that they are about to hear and then to check which of the items actually occur. This exercise demands a much more conscious process than spreading activation, but nevertheless one that introduces word association into the way the target language is handled. Other possible exercise types are shown in Table 10.8.

Table 10.8 *Exercises to promote spreading activation*

- *Word association.* 'I will say a word and point to one of you. As fast as possible, say a word that is connected to it in meaning.' Teacher calls out a range of words (nouns, verbs, adjectives) within the learner's vocabulary.
- *Anticipating words.* 'You are going to hear a recording about X. What words do you expect to hear?' Teacher writes the words on the board. Teacher plays the recording and learners put up their hands every time they hear one of the predicted words.
- *Online activation.* 'You have just heard part of a recording. What were the important words? Think of other words that you might expect to hear in the next part of the recording. Now listen to see if you were right.'

10.4.3 A note on meaning

A perceptive reader may have noticed that the account given here has steered round the question of word meaning. One reason is that the emphasis in this chapter has been upon how listeners manage to form auditory matches. Most current accounts of listening assume a very close connection between recognising a spoken word and gaining access to its meaning. In a process known as **lexical access**, a listener opens up a mental record of a word as soon as the word has been identified as a possible match for what has been heard. But the exact sense of the word cannot be fully ascertained without taking account of the context within which it occurs. We will therefore look in detail at issues of word meaning in Chapter 12.

10.5 Conclusion

Two areas have been identified here that are of particular importance. Firstly, it has been suggested that language instructors need to give greater attention to information at syllable level. It is much more productive to attune the ears of a second language listener to syllable shape and to syllable prominence and length than it is to persist with attempts to discriminate between so-called stress-timed and syllable-timed languages. Secondly, attention has been drawn to lexical segmentation as a major factor in decoding difficulty, and to the importance of learners' practising the segmentation routines that are appropriate to the language being acquired.

More generally, the chapter has presented decoding as an operation in which tentative matches are made – matches which may have to be revised in due course. This is partly because the input to the listener is so subject to variation and partly because of the way information from the speaker unfolds over time.

Although listening is tentative, it can draw upon multiple sources of evidence. The evidence employed by the listener consists of her interpretation of the input at three different levels (phoneme, syllable and word), but she also makes use of her vocabulary repertoire and of the cues that are provided by context and co-text. The relevant processes, described in this chapter and the last, are listed in Appendix 1.

In the next chapter, we move on to look at larger units of decoding in the form of syntactic patterns and intonation groups. We will again conclude that decoding, whether in L1 or L2, must be a provisional process. We will also find again that it relies not just on the listener's familiarity with the sound system of the target language, but on the listener's ability to recognise a variety of other cues that are present in the input.

Further reading

Brown, G. (1990) *Listening to Spoken English*. Harlow: Longman, 2nd edn, Chap. 3.
Cutler, A. (1997) 'The comparative perspective on spoken-language processing'. *Speech Communication*, 21: 3–15.

11   Using grammar and intonation

Gentlemen, listen to me slowly.
Samuel Goldwyn (1882–1974), Polish-American film mogul

We now turn our attention to larger units of speech. We consider how an expert listener manages to identify grammatical patterns in the words that have been decoded. We also consider what information a listener obtains from the way in which intonation shapes the speech signal. There is logic in discussing syntax and intonation together, because, as will become clear, they are quite closely interconnected.

These two systems play a part in decoding but also contribute to meaning building. To give a simple example, if a speaker says *we're leaving*, the listener recognises the grammatical pattern that has been used (a matter of decoding) but can only fully understand it by relating it to context and co-text (does it refer to now or to the future?). Similarly, features connected with intonation often assist decoding by marking the end of an 'idea unit', but they also add to overall meaning by highlighting the most important element in the unit or by indicating the mood or attitude of the speaker. We will consider both types of function in the present chapter.

11.1 Syntax and decoding

11.1.1 Recognising syntactic units

First language processing

Having found matches for a group of words, a listener has to trace the grammatical structure that binds them together. This operation is known as **parsing.** It depends partly upon the listener's ability to monitor a structure as it develops and partly upon her ability to recognise when it is complete. Once she realises that the structure has come to an end, she turns the group of words into an abstract idea. From this point onwards, she may or may not be able to recall the exact words that the speaker used, but she can still report the information that the speaker conveyed.

How does a listener recognise the point where a syntactic unit (a clause or sentence) finishes? Clearly, L1 listeners draw upon their knowledge of the grammar of the language and of the most frequent syntactic patterns.

185

They know, for example, that a particular verb requires an object and that the sentence will not be complete until the object has been mentioned. However, equally important are the cues that the speech signal provides.

One such cue is found at the points where a speaker pauses to plan what to say next. We tend to assume that informal everyday speech is totally unplanned, but that is not the case. A sentence has to be assembled, using the speaker's knowledge of vocabulary and organising the words to conform to the rules of grammar. Speech thus consists of alternate spells of planning and uttering. Speakers usually plan their utterances as complete phrases or clauses, so a short pause in connected speech often signals the beginning of a new grammar structure. Alternatively, the speaker may use a meaningless **filler** (*I mean, as I was saying, so to speak*) in order to buy time for planning. Pausing and these fillers thus offer the kind of marker that commas, semicolons and full stops provide for the reader. Both carry an advantage for the listener in that they provide a brief remission from decoding, during which she can rapidly review what has been said.

However, some caution is needed here. Pauses for planning need to be distinguished from **hesitation pauses** where the speaker has forgotten or changed his mind about what he intended to say, or is having trouble in retrieving a word. Hesitation pauses are quite distinct. They are much less consistent in length than planning pauses, often occur in the middle of an incomplete intonation pattern and sometimes include fillers such as *erm* or *er*. A skilled listener distinguishes them from pauses that mark syntactic boundaries and edits them out.

Assistance in locating syntactic boundaries also comes from *intonation*. Natural speech falls into small groups of words which are linked together by the movement of the speaker's voice.[1] An **intonation group** of this kind often corresponds to a grammatical unit – a phrase, a clause or a sentence. It thus indicates to the listener that certain words are connected syntactically. One count (reported in Cruttenden, 1986: 75) suggested that about 40% of groups correspond to clauses, though this may depend very much on the speaker and the level of formality. Intonation groups also serve to mark out longer adverbial expressions (*at ten o'clock on MONday, in front of the SUpermarket*) or to divide a sentence into subject and predicate.

Sometimes intonation groups are clearly demarcated. For example, the end of the group might be indicated by a fall in **pitch**, a downwards movement of the speaker's voice. But when these cues are not present,

---

[1] In fact, the group might be as small as a single word.

the listener can usually identify the group by reference to its focal point, a stressed syllable which often occurs at or near the end.

Second language practice

It is helpful to give learners practice in identifying syntactic patterns that are characteristic of the language they are acquiring. Table 11.1 gives examples of possible exercise types. Learners can be told that pausing assists them to decide where one syntactic pattern ends and another begins, though it should be pointed out that pausing may not always be present. Intonation is more problematic to demonstrate, as intonation groups vary greatly both in their length and in the 'tunes' they adopt.

Table 11.1   *Exercises in recognising syntactic units*

- *Awareness raising.* Class listens for focal syllables and for pauses in a short authentic recording (30 secs). They listen again, and mark the stressed words and the pauses on a transcript. Class discusses the role of stress and pausing in marking out phrases and clauses.
- *Hesitation and juncture pauses.* 'Mark the pauses.' Class listens to a short authentic recording, then marks pauses on a transcript. Class decides which are hesitation pauses and which indicate syntactic boundaries.
- *Phrase patterns.* Class listens to a short recording for general understanding. Teacher plays a second version with pauses or bleeps inserted at phrase boundaries (i.e. after subject, after verb, after object, etc.). Class reports on improvement in understanding.
- *Dividing into phrases.* Class listens to a short recording. They listen again with a transcript and divide the sentences into phrase and clause groups.

11.1.2 Online parsing

First language processing

The parsing operation is rather more complicated than the account so far has suggested. There is evidence that listeners do not wait until the end of a sentence in order to start working out what a speaker is saying, but decode speech at a delay of as little as a quarter of a second after it has been uttered. (A quarter of a second is about the length of a syllable in many languages, suggesting a special role for the syllable in decoding.)

This means that listeners have to trace grammatical patterns in running speech *while the patterns are still unfolding*. They can form expectations about the shape a sentence will take; but they may have to revise them as they hear more and more, and they cannot be satisfied that they have achieved a final version until the sentence is complete.

So, for example, a listener might start off with the assumption that the first noun phrase she hears (e.g. *the hardened criminal*) is the initiator of an action; but when she goes on to encounter a passive verb (*was arrested*), she has to reverse this assumption. This view of parsing conforms very much to the picture of listening painted in Chapter 10: a process in which listeners constantly form and revise hypotheses until sufficient evidence has accumulated for them to be certain about what the speaker intends.

When parsing in this online fashion, an expert listener makes use of certain cues in the input, which help her to narrow down the possible options. Among them are:

- *Probability.* Long experience of listening to the language makes an L1 listener highly sensitive to the way in which certain word forms occur together or signal what is to come. Thus, the presence of *the* or *a* indicates that the speaker is beginning a noun phrase like *the fast train*, and that either an adjective or a noun is likely to come next. If that noun phrase occurs at the beginning of an utterance, experience dictates that it is probably the subject of the sentence; following the verb, it is most probably a direct object. While listening, the L1 listener is thus capable of forming cautious hypotheses as to what will come next and as to what the overall structure of the utterance will prove to be.

- *Chunks.* Also of assistance are clusters which speakers store and produce as pre-assembled chunks. These include collocations (*heavy smoker, light rain*) or short question initiators such as *do you* ([ʤə]) or *is it* ([zɪt]); but they also consist of complete syntactic structures (. . . *can't have done, I don't mind, I couldn't agree more, what I'm trying to say is*) which the listener does not need to divide into constituents because they can be recognised as a single unit.

- *The verb.* The structure of a sentence is often decided by the verb that is chosen. If a speaker elects to construct a sentence around the word PUT, then she has to follow the pattern

  PUT + [thing that is placed] + [where the thing is placed]

  The last element cannot be omitted (**Please put the money* is unacceptable). From the point of view of the listener, knowing the pattern associated with a particular verb thus serves as a forewarning of what to expect next.

Second language practice

What these three cues have in common is that they derive from knowledge not so much of grammar in the abstract as of how certain words combine with each other to form a phrase or clause. Language knowledge is not enough; also required is a level of processing expertise. Table 11.2 presents some exercises that provide focused practice in recognising syntactic cues. The first is based upon the 'gating' method used by researchers when investigating how listeners construct the overall meaning of an utterance little by little while it is still being heard.

Table 11.2 *Exercises in online parsing*

- *'Gating'*. Teacher gives the first word of a sentence and asks class to predict what will come next. Teacher gives the first two words; class predict again. Teacher gives first three words, and so on. Example: *The old woman in the green dress was eating a very large cake in the Italian restaurant.* Teacher draws attention to the most common phrase patterns in L2. Examples for English (square brackets show optional element):

  Noun Phrase: [article] + [adjective] + noun or pronoun
  Verb Phrase: [modal verb] + [aux. verb] + main verb
  Adjective Phrase: [adverb such as *very, quite*] + adjective
  Preposition Phrase: prep. + [article] + [adjective] + noun

- *Recall*. After a conventional comprehension activity, teacher replays a section, pausing halfway through each sentence and asking learners to try to recall the words that come next. This is a behaviourist exercise from the early days of listening teaching, but has value in fostering a more active approach to syntactic anticipation. Later, teacher employs it with passages that have not been heard.

- *Pausing to anticipate*. 'What word will you hear next?' Teacher plays the first two or three sentences of a recording, then pauses after every two or three words. Learners guess what word comes next (or just its word class) and check their guesses.

- *Complete the sentence*. Teacher dictates the first part of a sentence, stopping before a highly predictable word. Learners say or write a suggested ending.

(*cont.*)

Table 11.2 *(cont.)*

> *I'm waiting* * *[for]*   *I'm listening* * *[to]*   *We live at the top* * *[of]*
> *He was very proud* * *[of]*   *My daughter's very good* * *[at]*
> *She made a suggestion* *[that]*   *I didn't like the idea* * *[of]*

- *Recognising common groups of words.* Teacher plays a recording but pauses occasionally during a group of words that occurs very frequently. Learners suggest the words that follow.

- *Verb patterns.* Teacher dictates a set of sentences with verbs or verb forms which go with certain grammatical structures. Teacher pauses after each verb and learners complete the sentence – possibly in writing.

> *I'm going to put* [+ object] [+ destination]
> *I found* [+ object] [+ location]
> *I want my children* [+ *to* infinitive]
> *I remember my children* [+ *ing* form]
> *This bridge was built* [*by* or *in*]
> *I'll have finished the work* [*by* or *in*]

When engaged in online parsing, second language listeners may tend to draw upon cues that are appropriate to their native language but not to L2. Languages are said to vary greatly in the importance that they attach to four important features:[2]

- word order: SVO (Subject–Verb–Object) versus SOV (Subject–Object–Verb) versus VSO (Verb–Subject–Object);
- inflection (e.g. marking the verb for person and number);
- animacy (does the verb need a subject that is animate and/or human?);
- world knowledge.

The strength of one of these cues in a listener's L1 may determine the way she handles an utterance in L2. For example, there is evidence that English speakers find it hard to make sense of an Italian sentence like *La matita guarda il cane* (The pencil + looks at + the dog) because they are strongly influenced by the more rigid word order of their native language. Italian has a more flexible word order, and so Italian listeners would rely upon animacy here as a cue.

---

[2] These categories are drawn from MacWhinney's Competition Model (Bates and MacWhinney, 1987).

It is a good idea to raise awareness of the criteria which most influence parsing in the target language. There are some suggestions in Table 11.3.

Table 11.3 *Exercises in recognising L2 syntactic cues*

- *Anticipating word order.* For Subject–Verb–Object languages, teacher plays a recording, pausing each sentence after the subject and asking learners to suggest what words come next. Repeat with verb, with object and with any adverbial element. Later, do this on a word-by-word basis.
- *Flexible word order.* Where L2 has flexible word order, teacher devises a set of sentences which differ from the word order learners expect in their first language. Teacher dictates them and asks learners to explain them (possibly using L1). Learners may use world knowledge or syntax to work out meaning. Alternatively, teacher excises examples of flexible word order from available recordings.
- *Location of syntactic information.* Examples: in English, the inflection of the verb often tells us more than the auxiliary, which may be weak or elided. Teacher dictates pairs of sentences which contrast: *I flew* and *I('ve) flown, I('m) making* and *I make.* In spoken French, the pronoun is more informative than the inflection of the verb. Teacher dictates sentences contrasting: *je pense / il pense,* or *il pensait* and *ils pensaient* to point out that the spoken verb forms are identical. In Italian and Spanish, teacher dictates pairs of sentences with contrasting word-final inflections: *la signora / le signore, entiendo / entiendes.*

11.2 Syntax and meaning building

As soon as parsing is complete, the listener turns what she has heard into an abstract idea. However, that idea then has to be extended to cover not just what the grammar of the sentence has told her – but also what the grammar *implies.* We will consider two areas where extra meaning has to be added to the bare message: the speaker's use of functional language; and the implications that certain grammatical patterns (especially verb forms) carry.

191

11.2.1 Functional language

Imagine a speaker says: *Can you open the door?* Taking the question literally, the listener could reply: *Yes, I'm perfectly capable of doing it.* But the speaker is not using the sequence *can you?* in its literal sense but as the means for making a request. In order to respond appropriately, the listener needs to be able to recognise this pragmatic use of the sequence *can you?*, and to relate it to the present situation (the fact that the speaker has his hands full of books).

Teachers normally introduce learners to functional expressions as part of their general language syllabus. But (see Chapter 1) it is also good practice to take account of functional language when replaying a piece of listening. Here the listening teacher performs a double role: making sure that the learner understands the full intentions of the speaker, but also providing examples from the recording of how a listener replies. A useful exercise consists of the teacher pausing after each piece of functional language and pointing to a learner, who has to respond appropriately. Table 11.4 lists examples of some everyday functions to listen out for. This list of functional expressions is based upon my own variety of English and is given purely by way of example. Appropriate expressions will differ from one variety to another and from one speaker–listener relationship to another. They form part of the cultural understanding that an L2 listener has to acquire.

It is important for the listening instructor to draw attention to the expressions *within a context* (for example, after listening to a conventional recording of three to five minutes). This is partly because, as just mentioned, they may reflect the formality of the situation or the relationship between listener and speaker. But it is also because, in some cases, the listener cannot interpret the functional value of an expression without relating it to the accompanying co-text and the situation within which it occurs. The word *will* (or its contracted form *'ll*) is especially problematic: it can represent a prediction, a threat, an order, an offer or (in the form *won't*) a refusal, depending upon context.

11.2.2 Syntactic inferencing

Grammatical contrasts sometimes supply important information which the speaker takes it for granted the listener will infer. To give a simple example: if an experienced listener hears the English sentence *I'm living in Paris*, she concludes that the situation is a temporary one (by contrast with the more usual *I live in Paris*).

Table 11.4 *Some common functions in everyday listening*

- Asking a favour: *Can you...? Could you...? Could you possibly...? Would you mind...? I wonder if you could...?*
  Agreeing: *Of course. No problem. Certainly. By all means.*
- Asking permission: *Could I...? I wonder if I could...? Would you mind if I...?*
  Giving permission: *Of course. Please do. By all means.*
- Offering: *Shall I...? I'll... Would you like me to...?*
  Accepting: *Thanks a lot. That's good of you. If you could.*
- Suggesting a joint activity: *Let's... Shall we...? Why don't we...? How about...?*
  Refusing a suggestion: *Let's not. I'd rather not. Would you mind if we didn't?*
- Suggesting a course of action: *Why not...? Why don't you...?*
  Accepting the suggestion: *Yes, I just might. That's a good idea.*
  Rejecting it: *I'm not sure about that.*
- Inviting: *Would you like to...? I was wondering if you'd like to...*
  Accepting: *I'd love to. That would be great.*
- Apologising: *I'm very sorry about... I do apologise for... Please forgive me for...*
  Accepting an apology: *That's all right. Never mind. It doesn't matter.*
- Putting forward a view: *It seems to me... I'd say... If you want my opinion...*
  Disagreeing: *I'm not sure I agree. I don't quite agree.*
  Agreeing with a view: *I quite agree. I see your point.*
- Threatening: *I'll... If you don't (pay up), I'll (call the police).*

Here are just a few examples of sentences where a change in the grammar marks a significant change in the circumstances that apply. These are minimal pairs of a different kind – ones that are differentiated by grammar.

I live in Paris.	*I'm living in Paris.* (temporarily)
I worked there for ten years.	*I've worked there for ten years.* (and still do)
I won a prize.	*I've won a prize.* (hot news)
She's phoning Kate.	*She's to phone Kate.* (instruction)
We heard him cough.	*We heard him coughing.* (repeatedly)
He said he found it.	*He said he'd find it.* (future)

A second language listener benefits from practice in this area, particularly where the words which distinguish the two sentences are difficult to perceive. An example of the type of exercise that can be employed has already been given in Chapter 5 (Table 5.2).

11.3 The intonation group

We now turn to intonation and the way in which it contributes to listening. Here, a little background will be useful. A speaker assembles speech in short manageable pieces which (as already mentioned) often correspond to syntactic units in the form of phrases or clauses. They are produced in a single burst, held together by the movement of the speaker's voice. Figure 11.1 shows how an utterance might consist of several of these groups of words.

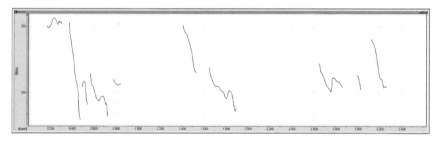

'I'll THINK about it   THANKS very much'   and left the SHOP

Figure 11.1 Pitch contours, based upon part of the recorded utterance *and eventually I said to the shopkeeper:' I'll think about it. Thanks very much' and left the shop* (Lynch 2004:143). Note how the extract falls into three separate intonation groups, corresponding to syntactic patterns. Note too how each group clusters around one syllable bearing focal stress, here marked by a sharp fall in pitch. [The graphic only represents voiced sounds, so sounds such as /θ/ and /ks/ in the second group show up as short gaps]. Many thanks to phonetician Jane Setter for advice and assistance.

Within a group of this kind, a speaker selects the word that he deems to be the most central to his message. The word or (if it has more than one syllable) the stressed syllable of the word is given prominence, so that it forms the focus of the group. In English, it might be marked by a sharp fall in the pitch of the speaker's voice.

*I think I'd rather go by **TRAIN**.*
*He said he was coming on **SATurday**.*

The intonation group has an important impact on the words within it. It highlights the syllable that carries focal stress but does so at the expense of the adjoining ones. So a group tends to consist of one syllable that is clearly articulated, surrounded by others that are squeezed in duration or reduced in form.

11.3.1 Decoding and the intonation group

First language processing

It will be clear that the intonation group brings both costs and benefits so far as the expert listener is concerned. The benefits are as follows:

a. As already noted, an intonation group often serves to mark out syntactic patterns.
b. It provides the listener with one syllable that is clearly articulated and more reliable than those surrounding it.
c. That syllable draws attention to the word that is most closely identified with the speaker's intentions in forming the clause or sentence.

Function (c) is especially important. It provides the listener with a handle upon which to hang the idea that the speaker is putting across. It strongly supports the parsing process by drawing attention to the element that is most important to the message.

But there are also costs in that many syllables of lesser importance become so reduced that they can be difficult to identify. An early piece of listening research discovered that, if a single monosyllabic word is excised out of an intonation group, listeners are very often unable to identify it. Here again, there is a conflict between evidence that listeners process what they hear online, at a short delay behind the speaker, and the fact that some of what they hear may not be clear enough at the time to be matched to words.

What seems likely is that listeners first process the input purely in terms of what they think they hear, making provisional decisions about possible word matches. But they reserve final judgement until the end of the intonation group makes everything clear. The all-important syllable that carries focal stress often comes at the end of the group, giving the listener time to assemble information and providing a reference point when the information in the group is nearly complete. In addition, as we have noted, an intonation group often corresponds to a phrase or clause, so that a final decision on syntactic structure can be made at the same time. This version of events once again lends support to the view that listening, in L1 as in L2, is a tentative operation, with listeners creating and revising hypotheses as they go.

Second language practice

The intonation group can be a means of support to the second language listener, especially the listener with limited decoding skills. Though the pressures of the group may lead to some words becoming reduced in form and thus more difficult to identify, there is a compensating benefit in that focal stress serves to foreground the most important piece of information. For the L2 listener, it provides a basis for forming hypotheses about what a speaker said when very little else may have been understood.

There is also a benefit in terms of perception. The syllable in each intonation group that carries focal stress is more reliable and more precisely articulated than the rest. For the L1 listener, this directs processing effort to the area where decoding brings the greatest rewards in terms of the information derived. For the L2 listener, it is even more critical. It marks the part of the group where the form of a word is not subject to reduction and is most to be trusted. In the early stages of L2 listening, this may be the only part that can be matched to the citation form of a word.

So the well-established teaching technique of telling second language listeners to listen out for 'key words' is justified. Even where listeners understand very little of the surrounding co-text, focally stressed words form a basis for constructing hypotheses about what the speaker is saying. What is more, this kind of activity is not just a remedial technique. In employing it, the teacher can also claim to be emulating (for slightly different purposes) the process that would be adopted by a more expert listener.

As ever, there are implications for practice. It is important to use chunks based on intonation groups for demonstration purposes and for small-scale listening tasks. Instructors should develop tasks which recognise that words take their shapes from the intonation group as a whole and may not be identifiable until the whole group has been heard. It is also important to raise learner awareness of how to make the most of the salient and reliable focal syllable. Table 11.5 has some suggestions.

Table 11.5 *Exercises in using focal syllables*

- *Identifying focal syllables.* Learners listen to a short recording (20 sec.) and underline the prominent syllables on a tapescript.
- *Key word gap-filling.* 'The important words are missing on your tapescript. Listen and fill them in.'

(cont.)

Table 11.5 *(cont.)*

- *Key word recognition.* Teacher plays a short recording (approx. 30 sec.) and asks learners to listen out for what they think are the most prominent (key) words. Teacher replays; learners write down the words and then compare notes. Learners listen again for general understanding.
- *Key word hypotheses.* Teacher writes on the board the key words from a short recording (30 sec.) and learners predict from them what the recording will say. Learners listen solely for the key words; then they listen again for general understanding.
- *Key word prediction.* On a transcript, learners mark what they guess will be the key words in a short recording (30 sec.). They listen to the recording and check. They then listen again and mark the boundaries of each intonation group.
- *Key word cues.* Teacher excises a number of intonation groups from a piece of authentic speech produced by a single speaker. Teacher plays them; learners note down the word carrying focal stress in each one. Teacher replays; learners try to decode the remainder of each extract. (There is a useful source in Cauldwell, 2003.)
- *Dealing with reduced sequences.* Teacher gives learners a tapescript of a short recording (30 sec.). It contains only the words bearing focal stress, with gaps between them. Learners guess what words are missing. Learners listen to the recording, paying attention to the stressed words. Teacher then replays the recording in short sections. Learners fill in the reduced words.

11.3.2 Intonation groups as chunks

First language processing

A different take on the account just given is that the intonation group itself might in many cases be stored in the speaker's mind as a ready-made unit (Wray, 2002). The patterns in question are not just lexical and idiomatic groupings like *on the other hand* or *It's beyond me*; they also include examples of syntactic structures (*should have done, have been waiting*). If chunks of speech are indeed stored in this way (perhaps with basic intonation patterns attached to them), then it would provide an extra source of evidence for the listener, and one explanation for the mystery of how we are able to decode speech as rapidly as we do.

197

Second language practice

Because of the integrative pressures of the intonation group, it is sometimes easier for a listener to recognise a group of words as a complete
unit rather than processing them individually. Practice in recognising
frequent and recurrent chunks of language (Table 11.6) can be very supportive to learners who find it difficult to deconstruct intonation groups.

Table 11.6 *Exercises in recognising chunks*

- *Isolated groups.* Teacher uses a tapescript of a piece of relatively
  rapid authentic speech to select groups of words which occur
  frequently in everyday speech and which have a relatively
  consistent intonation pattern. Examples: fixed formulae (*You
  all right?*), longer fillers (*Do you know what I mean?*), syntactic
  patterns (*I should have done*). Teacher plays them; learners
  report what they hear. Learners then practise producing
  them.
- *Focus on chunks.* After a general listening lesson using an
  authentic text, teacher replays sections of the recording which
  contain chunks that occur frequently in natural speech.
  Learners transcribe.

11.4 Interpreting intonation

We have concentrated so far on how the intonation group assists decoding and have yet to consider what intonation contributes to meaning.
This is a difficult area to present to learners. Pronunciation teaching traditionally gives detailed attention to the pitch movements of the speaker's
voice, especially rises and falls on the focal syllable. The movements are
classified into high fall, high rise, fall-rise, etc., but, for the teacher of
listening, this results in rather complex systems and in generalisations
about meaning that are sometimes difficult to sustain. The problem lies
partly in the difficulty of obtaining consistent reports from native listeners. Intonation varies greatly from speaker to speaker and from context
to context. It is difficult to make reliable one-to-one matches between
particular patterns and the interpretations placed upon them by listeners
when the cues that are provided by the context have been discounted.

So far as learners of English are concerned, there is also the consideration (Brown, 1990: 104; Cruttenden, 1986: 96) that pitch movement
is one of the features which varies most markedly between different

varieties (British, North American, South African, Australasian); it even varies greatly between one British city and another. So trying to get to grips with the falls and rises of a speaker of one particular variety may not be time well spent for a student who plans to use the language in international contexts.

With the listening teacher in mind, we will take a very broad brush approach here and focus upon the general impressions that an expert listener receives. The discussion will firstly, in Section 11.5, touch briefly upon the familiar area of how intonation reflects co-text and context. But in the main it will take a different angle and will explore the way in which cues from intonation might shape the listener's response to what the speaker has said. The emphasis will be upon a listener engaging in a conversation.

11.5 Information focus

First language processing

Focal stress chiefly serves to draw attention to something that is introduced into a listening event for the first time. Sentences like the following are often used to illustrate this point in language teachers' manuals:

> [*What did you give your grandson?*] – *We gave him some MONey.*
> [*When did you give your grandson the money?*] – *We gave it to him on his BIRTHday.*
> [*Who did you give the money to?*] – *We gave it to our GRANDson.*

As mentioned earlier, the focal syllable usually comes towards the end of an intonation group. This benefits the listener: she encounters what is familiar (or **given**) in the early part of the sentence, before going on to encounter what is **new**. It enables her to make a connection between new information and what went before.

The focal syllable sometimes occurs elsewhere, for example when the focus is on the subject of the sentence.

> [*Who gave the money to your grandson?*] – **WE** *gave it to him.*

This earlier placing also happens quite often in order to mark contrast or emphasis or what Cruttenden (1986) calls *insists*:

> *We didn't* **LEND** *the money to our grandson* + *we* **GAVE** *it to him.*
> *We didn't give him the money* **ON** *his birthday* + *but two days be*FORE *it.*
> *We were un*SURE *about giving him money* + *but we* **HAVE** *given him some.*

Notice that, in these circumstances, even function words (*we, on, before, have*) can be given focus.

It is also worth noting that these contrastive and emphatic uses of intonation have to be processed rather differently from the given/new ones. A listener often has to make a connection between the emphasised word and another one (stressed or unstressed) in an earlier part of the utterance:

We didn't give him the money ON his birthday + but two days beFORE it.

You forgot to post the LETter, didn't you? – No, I reMEMbered to post it.

In other cases, the contrast may not be expressed in words. It may lie not with co-text but with the prevailing situation. Compare:

> *Can you open the DOOR?* (normal 'given/new' focus)
> *Can you Open the door?* (to somebody who is shutting it)
> *Can YOU open the door?* (selecting a volunteer – or a speaker struggling with a door that is jammed)
> *Can you open THIS door?* (not the one you are opening)

Second language practice

The acoustic cues that mark focal stress differ between languages. In addition, languages vary in how consistently the focal syllable occurs towards the end of the group. So it is worthwhile checking that learners are able to identify the stressed syllable and the word that it forms part of. It is also useful to give some limited practice in showing the relationship between given and new elements in a piece of speech. It makes sense to treat contrastive and emphatic uses of stress as a special case, given the need to link them closely to co-text or to the current situation. Table 11.7 contains some exercises.

11.6 Speaker–listener interaction

First language processing

Intonation can also provide an indication of the attitude of the speaker to what is being said. We will not consider the fine distinctions that are sometimes made between different intonation tunes (high rise, fall-rise, etc.), but instead will focus on a limited number of general pitch movements which provide indications to a listener as to how to respond to the speaker.

Table 11.7 *Exercises in intonation focus*

- *Locating focal stress*. Teacher copies a number of intonation groups from a recording on to a separate CD. Learners identify and write down the word in each that bears focal stress. They comment on the position of the word in the group.

- *Given/new*. 'On your worksheet there is a word from each sentence you will hear. Listen carefully to the sentence and decide if the word refers to something that has been mentioned earlier by the speaker or something new that the speaker is introducing for the first time.' Teacher reads aloud sentences or (at a higher level) plays a short extract from a recording.

- *Speaker purpose*. After a conventional listening lesson, the teacher gives learners a transcript of part of the recording. Learners listen and mark on the transcript the words carrying sentence stress. They then listen again and (using their L1) say why the speaker chose these words to stress.

- *Contrastive/emphatic stress: co-text*. The teacher excises utterances from a recording in which there is contrastive or emphatic stress. Learners listen, write down the stressed words and explain how they are linked. Alternative: teacher dictates contrastive sentences such as:

  1. *They intended to FLY; but they went by TRAIN instead.*
  2. *They think I don't understand but I DO.*
  3. *Her birthday isn't on FRIday; it's on MONday.*
  4. *I made a mistake; I AM free on Tuesday.*
  5. *Her birthday isn't in JUNE; it's in SepTEMber. Her BROther's is in June.*
  6. *It isn't my BIRTHday today; it's our WEDding anniversary.*

- *Contrastive/emphatic stress: context 1*. Teacher dictates several variants of the same sentence, in which the focal stress is moved from one word to another (see the *Can you open the door?* example above). Learners are given a set of possible scenarios on a worksheet and have to link the situation to the intonation pattern.

- *Contrastive/emphatic stress: context 2*. Teacher pauses a video recording whenever examples of contrastive/emphatic stress occur. Learners relate the use of focal stress to visual components of the situation.

As noted, the syllable bearing focal stress often occurs towards the end of an intonation group. Across languages, the most common way in which stress in this position is signalled is by a fall in the pitch of the speaker's voice. The fall is likely to be especially marked if the end of the intonation group coincides with the end of a syntactic structure. So we can say that it brings to the listener an impression of *finality*, by contrast with rises or more modest falls that may have occurred earlier. In terms of listener–speaker interaction, it provides a signal to the listener that, if she wishes to interrupt the speaker, this is an appropriate point at which to do so. It might also suggest – especially if accompanied by a lengthening of the final syllable in the intonation group – that the speaker has finished what he wants to say and is handing over the turn to the listener.

Conversely, if a speaker maintains his pitch level at the end of an intonation group or if the pitch rises, the expert listener might often be left with a sense of *incompleteness* (hence the tradition of using a rising pitch on a comma when reading aloud). We assume that the speaker may have more to say.

There is a belief, widely expressed in teaching materials, that a rise at the end of an intonation group serves to distinguish 'yes/no' questions (*Are you reading the PAper?*) from *wh-* ones (*What are you READing?*). This may be the case with some languages, but studies by specialists (Brown, 1990: 122–3; Cruttenden, 1986: 96–7) have suggested that it does not happen consistently enough in English to be relied upon. Even where a statement is being used as a question, it is by no means always sure that the interrogative will be distinguished by rising pitch. Much depends upon whether the speaker is seeking confirmation or is unclear as to the likely answer.

a. *You're coming on* ↓*SATurday?* [expecting confirmation]
b. *You're coming on* ↑*SATurday?* [unsure]

So instead of asking what a rise in pitch signals in terms of grammar, it is perhaps more relevant to ask once again what it indicates to the listener in terms of her response. Similar examples to the ones just given can be found in tag questions, where there is a contrast between a rising tune spread over the tag part and a falling tune:

a. *You like British food,* ↓*DON'T you?*
b. *You like British food,* ↑*DON'T you?*

In (a), the speaker anticipates a positive response. The listener is faced with a choice of a token agreement (*Mhm, yes, I do*) or of contradicting the speaker in a way that may have to be hedged so as not to be confrontational (*Well, actually, I'm NOT too keen; Not REAlly*). By contrast, (b) shows a degree of uncertainty on the part of the speaker and leaves the listener rather more freedom in responding.

Leaving aside the special case of English, it is certainly worthwhile to practise the question/statement distinction in languages where intonation rather than syntax marks it. Examples are French, where the most frequently employed question form is a statement with a rising intonation (*Nous allons au théâtre?*), and Spanish and Italian, where (in the absence of a pronoun) statements and questions are identical apart from their intonation (*Vamos al teatro?/Vamos al teatro*).

Two other important, and rather contradictory, ways in which a rising intonation conveys a message to the listener are when it is used for *echoing* (usually quite a gentle rise) and for *challenging* (often a much more marked one). Compare these two examples.

a. Speaker B: *The concert's at seven-THIRty.*
   Speaker A: ↑SEVen-thirty? [just checking]
   Speaker B: *That's right.* [token confirmation]
b. Speaker B: *It's snowing in CaliFORnia.*
   Speaker A: ↑SNOWing? *[I don't believe it]*
   Speaker B: *Yes, honestly + I heard it on the NEWS.* [defends truth]

Again, the way in which a listener responds is influenced by the construction that is placed upon the intonation pattern.

Second language practice

We have now identified several general indications provided by intonation which might form part of second language listening practice:

- question type (especially where intonation serves to distinguish a statement from a question);
- degree of finality;
- expectation of confirmation vs more open-ended question;
- echoing to check;
- challenging.

So far as English is concerned, it is not a good use of time to practise recognising rising pitch as a characteristic of 'yes/no' questions. However, the ability to distinguish rapidly between 'yes/no' and *wh-* questions is useful, since it enables the listener to anticipate her response while still listening. If the teacher feels the need to assist learners in this regard, it is more constructive to direct attention to the opening words of the two types. Those in 'yes/no' questions constitute a limited set of operators (*do you, have you, are you,* etc.); and the L2 listener can be taught to recognise them as chunks ([ʤə], [əvjə], [əjə]). The activity provides

203

A *process view of listening*

an important corrective for a listener who is used to relying wholly or exclusively upon intonation to mark out the two question types.

We should bear in mind that many second language listeners are exposed to more examples of rising pitch at the ends of sentences than would normally occur in the L2. When using 'foreigner speak' or just trying to assist a non-native listener, speakers often introduce a questioning intonation to show they are checking understanding at word level or at utterance level. This is also the model that learners encounter very frequently in teaching contexts.[3]

Table 11.8 suggests some exercises in the areas discussed, which attempt to model listener responses as well as helping learners to recognise general pitch movements. Good sources for intonation exercises which consider listening alongside pronunciation are Bradford (1988) and Cauldwell (2003).

Table 11.8 *Appropriate responses to pitch movements*

- *Degree of finality.* Teacher records a sample of natural speech which contains long sentences (interviews are a good source). Teacher divides it into short sections corresponding to intonation groups. The sections are played to learners (either in order of occurrence or randomly). Learners indicate whether they think the extract marks the end of what a speaker has to say (a tick for a good place to interrupt) or not (a cross).

- *Statement and question 1.* In languages where questions are only differentiated from statements by intonation, teacher dictates pairs of sentences, one a question and one a statement.

  Vous fumez. / Vous fumez?
  C'est à trois heures. / C'est à trois heures?
  Le gusta el cine. / Le gusta el cine?
  Necesitas descansarte. / Necesitas descansarte?

  Learners mark (.) for statement, (?) for question.

- *Statement and question 2.* Teacher pauses a recording of a natural dialogue after statements and questions. Learners say if the listener needs to respond or not, then anticipate the response where one is necessary.

  (*cont.*)

[3] In addition, General American is said to use rising pitch that is more marked than that of British RP, while a much discussed feature of current Australian English is a 'tentative' rising tone at the end of many sentences that are not, in fact, questions.

Table 11.8 *(cont.)*

- *Noticing yes/no operators.* Teacher dictates the operators that mark 'yes/no' questions: in English, [ʤə], [əvjə], [əjə], etc. Learners transcribe. Teacher later dictates first words of questions mixed with first words of statements: [əvðeɪ] versus [ðeɪv]. Teacher presents them very quickly; learners write (.) or (?).

- *Question type marked by operators not intonation.* Teacher plays mixed *wh-* and 'yes/no' questions taken from a piece of naturalistic speech (e.g. a radio interview). Learners respond under time pressure (giving a likely answer for *wh-* questions and 'yes/no' for others). Alternative: teacher plays only the first three or four words of each question.

- *Tag questions 1.* Teacher dictates pairs of sentences ending in tag questions, some with rising intonation on the tag and some with falling. Learners categorise as C (confirm) or A (answer).

- *Tag questions 2.* Teacher pre-records a set of tag questions, with falling intonation on the tag followed by the words 'Yes' or 'No'. Learners have to give an immediate appropriate answer (*mhm* for agreement, but a defensive reply for disagreement).

- *Echoing to check versus challenging.* Teacher records simple dialogues with a colleague like those above, mixing echoing with challenging. Teacher plays the first two turns in each dialogue; learners then have to anticipate the third.

- *Confirmation checks 1.* Teacher records his/her own confirmation checks while doing vocabulary or grammar teaching (especially those which consist of statements that end in a rising intonation). Teacher then plays them to the class to raise awareness.

- *Confirmation checks 2.* Teacher records a piece of TV footage in which a member of the public is speaking to a non-native speaker with a limited command of the target language. Teacher plays it turn by turn. Learners identify moments where they think the native speaker is checking listener understanding.

11.7 Intonation and emotion

First language processing

Intonation also provides the listener with information about the emotions and feelings of the speaker. Is he happy, angry, bored, excited? This is perhaps the most difficult area of all in which to trace some kind of system. When researchers simulate emotion using synthetic speech, they find huge variations in the interpretations they get from native speakers. One study examined six emotional intonations that seemed very distinct from each other: *angry, disgusted, glad, sad, scared, surprised.* Recognition by L1 judges ranged from 91% accurate with *sad* to only 42% with *disgusted.* A similar study in Dutch obtained 94% accuracy for *boredom* but only 41% for *fear.* It would seem that the cues provided by intonation are often interpreted in relation to the prevailing situation: we know that somebody is expressing anger partly because we see that they are in a complaining context. It would also seem that the cues we draw upon are not simple but consist of a whole complex of features occurring at the same time.

Brown (1990: Chap. 6) provides interesting insights into what some of those features are. The ones that are most accessible and easy for the non-specialist ear to detect concern the pitch range covered by the speaker's voice: where in the range he chooses to place his voice ('squeak' – 'normal' – 'growl') and how much of the range he uses. However, these signals must be interpreted in conjunction with other cues. A voice that starts high and covers a lot of the range shows emotional engagement but might be interpreted as *happy* or *excited* if accompanied by a smile and a breathy quality in the voice, or *surprised* if accompanied by raised eyebrows and wide eyes (1990: 116).

Second language practice

Emotional interpretations are difficult to teach to L2 listeners. Despite this, testers of L2 listening began during the early 1990s to include questions that require candidates to report a speaker's mood. In our present state of knowledge about how emotion is recognised, one wonders if such questions are entirely fair. Anyone who has tried them out in the classroom can attest to the difficulty of getting learners to match a voice's intonation confidently to a particular label – and also of getting them to interpret the labels themselves (the difference between *content* and *happy*, between *calm* and *quiet*). If we do make use of this type of question, we should perhaps restrict it to moods that can be deduced by relating intonation to the situation that features in the recording.

So far as teaching is concerned, Brown (1990: 115–19) recommends a limited approach in which we alert learners to a broad set of contrasts based upon three possibilities:

- a medium pitch span (mainly within the normal speaking range) = *neutral*;
- an extended pitch span (often associated with increased loudness) = *emotional*;
- a restricted pitch span = *caution, detachment, timidity*.

This can be done by pausing selectively during a conventional listening session or by excising intonation groups (ideally all in the voice of the same speaker) for learners to compare.

Given the limitations of space, this has had to be a brief introduction to the role of intonation. Those who wish to follow up the subject in more depth should consult Dalton and Seidlhofer (1994: 43–64), Cruttenden (1986) or Brown (1990).[4]

11.8 Conclusion

Two important points have recurred throughout this chapter and the last. Firstly, listening has been shown to be an approximate process, and not one which relies upon exact matches. It is approximate in that the listener does not make identification decisions at phoneme or word level on the basis of a single piece of evidence but has to trade a range of cues against each other. It is also approximate in that the decisions made (especially those relating to syntax) have to be treated as tentative and may need to be adjusted as more of the utterance is heard and more evidence becomes available. Integrative pressures at the level of the intonation group may well mean that it is not possible to identify certain words in the group with full confidence until the group is complete.

A second recurrent point has been that listening expertise is not founded on linguistic knowledge alone but requires extensive experience of using the skill. It is misleading to claim (see, e.g., Kelly, 1991) that an expansion of the learner's vocabulary and/or grammar base offers the principal solution to problems of listening. This argument entirely overlooks a critical component of expert listening – namely the processes involved. Clearly, knowledge of the target language (especially its vocabulary) has a part to play, but it is as true in listening as it is in speaking that possessing linguistic knowledge is not the same as being able to use it.

---

[4] Brown in particular considers an area not discussed here: the way in which intonation differs between careful and more casual speech.

The point was first made in relation to the recognition of known words, but grammar provides an equally clear example. It is not enough to have mastered a particular syntactic structure; the listener also needs experience of recognising the structure from information which is being processed syllable by syllable or word by word. She may also have to adjust the habit of using certain syntactic or intonational cues which serve her well in L1 but are not appropriate to L2.

Further reading

Brown, G. (1990) *Listening to Spoken English*. Harlow: Longman, 2nd edn., Chap. 5.
Cruttenden, A. (1986) *Intonation*. Cambridge: Cambridge University Press.
Wray, A. (2002) *Formulaic Language and the Lexicon*. Cambridge: Cambridge University Press.

12 Amplifying what the speaker says

It requires a singular power to bear
with each one according to his understanding.
Benedict de Spinoza (1632–1677), *Ethics IV*, Appendix

The theme that runs through this chapter and the next is that listening is not the 'passive' skill it was once said to be. The listener does not meekly receive a ready-made message transmitted by a speaker. Far from it: the listener has to remake the message (Brown, 1995: Chap. 1). The end product may be something that is markedly different from what the speaker intended; it may even be something that reflects the goals of the listener rather than those of the speaker.

Meaning building can be thought of as broadly fulfilling two important functions. One is to *amplify what the speaker says* by adding in information that the speaker has taken for granted. The other is to *organise the information* that has been received. The listener has to decide which pieces are important, trace connections between them, build them into a coherent line of argument and check that they are consistent with what has gone before. We will consider the two functions separately, looking at the first in this chapter and the second in Chapter 13. But it is important to realise that this is just a matter of convenience. The functions are very closely interlinked and certain meaning-building processes (such as recognising the links between sentences) serve both purposes.

12.1 Background

12.1.1 Three levels of meaning

In considering how a listener expands on what the speaker says, we can think of meaning building as operating at three different levels.

Retaining large numbers of words in the mind makes heavy and unnecessary demands upon memory, so listeners rapidly turn what they have heard into a **proposition**, an abstract representation of a single idea. This seems to happen at the end of each clause or intonation unit. The listener stores the idea, but not the language that was used by the speaker, and may be unable to recall the exact form of words later on.

A proposition represents the literal meaning of the clause, without regard to its context. So the listener needs to draw upon information

---

PROPOSITION (bare meaning)

MEANING REPRESENTATION (enriched meaning)

DISCOURSE REPRESENTATION (overall meaning so far)

Figure 12.1   Three levels of meaning.

provided by world knowledge, topic knowledge, speaker knowledge, etc. in order to understand the proposition's relevance to the immediate situation. This results in a **meaning representation**, an enriched version of the original piece of information.

Finally, the meaning representation has to be added to the listener's memory of everything that has been said so far in the conversation, lecture or recording. It should be remembered, however, that the listener does not carry in her mind what the speaker actually said but only *her own version of it*. Much depends upon how much she has recalled and how she has interpreted the speaker's words. So rather than calling this information 'co-text' or 'text-so-far', I shall refer to it as the listener's **discourse representation** (the term is taken from Brown and Yule, 1983a: 206). A discourse representation is not fixed but keeps growing as the encounter continues. As each new meaning representation is established, the listener has to add it in.

The relationship between the three levels of meaning is expressed quite simply in Figure 12.1.

12.1.2 Knowledge and inference

Figure 12.2 provides a model of the way in which the simple meaning taken from a speaker's words is expanded by a listener. It is important to point out that the figure shows only part of the meaning-building process. We will add to it in the next chapter when we come to consider how the listener organises the information she obtains.

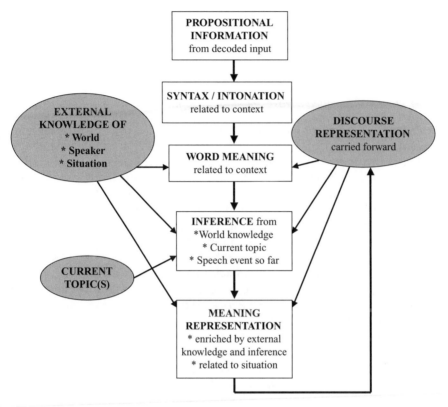

Figure 12.2 Building a meaning representation.

The figure illustrates the parts played by outside knowledge and by the listener's understanding of what has been said so far. In addition to reminding us of the need to relate syntax and intonation to the context in which they occur (see Chapter 11), it suggests that two further stages of meaning building contribute to the final idea formed by the listener.

- *Word meaning.* We tend to treat words in the mind as if they had very specific meanings attached to them like the ones you would see in a dictionary. But that is not quite the case. When a word is decoded, the listener usually retrieves not a single precise meaning but a range of possibilities. She has to make use of the co-text (the words occurring before and afterwards) and of her knowledge of the world in order to relate the word more closely to what the speaker is saying.

211

A classic example is the word TOMATO. A listener knows a lot about tomatoes, but she has to foreground a different aspect in each of the contexts below:

It looked like a squashed tomato. (softness)
His face was like a tomato. (redness)
The tomato rolled across the plate. (roundness)

• *Inference.* A listener has to form **inferences** about the raw information in the proposition in order to arrive at the speaker's intended meaning. Speakers often utter sentences without feeling the need to spell out the links between them. It is the listener who has to provide these links. A speaker might say, for example: *I'm sorry I'm late. The traffic was awful.* The speaker does not bother to make the connection between the sentences explicit. He relies upon the listener to work out for herself that the second sentence represents an excuse for the first.

A similar process occurs when the listener hears a pronoun such as *it, she* or *he* and has to track it back to a previously mentioned person or thing. As we shall see, the process is not always an easy one in listening – partly because speakers tend to use pronouns quite loosely. It is also difficult because the listener cannot explain *it, she* or *he* by referring to the general discourse representation that she has built up, which might be very complex by now and have a great many people or objects in it. *Alongside her large-scale discourse representation, she has to carry a more localised recall of what the current topic is that the speaker is talking about.* That way, if she hears a pronoun, she can work out what it is most likely to refer to. So one of the difficulties of meaning building is that the listener has to operate at two different levels. She has to keep track of the current topic in case a word such as *they* or *that* occurs which needs to be matched to something that has recently been mentioned. But at the same time, she has to carry forward a discourse representation of what has occurred in the whole of the listening event so far.

In the account that follows, we will first look at the nature of outside knowledge and how it affects the listener's interpretation of what she hears. We will then go on to examine how the meaning of a word is shaped to fit the context in which it occurs. Finally, we will consider inferencing and what it achieves.

12.1.3 Meaning building and the L2 listener

It might seem that the processes that have been described are less of an issue for second language listeners than decoding. After all, they are not dependent upon the phonetics and phonology of the language being learned. Meaning building relies upon processes which should already be well established in the first language. Can we not assume that they will transfer effortlessly to the L2 context? In that case, should meaning building be a concern of the listening instructor at all?

My own view is that it should. We cannot take it for granted that meaning-related processes familiar in L1 will be applied in the unfamiliar circumstances of L2 listening. Though the processes may not be affected by differences of phonology, listeners might well have to face differences in the ways in which speakers of the L2 organise and present their ideas. They might have to face cultural differences – affecting both their ability to draw upon shared world knowledge and their ability to interpret the pragmatic intentions of speakers (offering, threatening, apologising, etc.).

In addition, we must not forget that the conditions attached to processing a second language are very different from those that apply in L1. To start with, decoding is unlikely to be automatic until the learner has reached quite a high level of expertise. This means that it makes much greater demands upon the listener's attention than normal – limiting the amount of attention that can be given to meaning building. A heavy focus on literal information at the level of the single utterance (or even at word level) may impede the listener's ability to draw connections between sentences and to construct an enhanced idea of what the speaker intends.

We also have to bear in mind that limitations to the listener's decoding ability might result in there being much less raw material for her to draw upon than she is used to in L1. Building L2 meaning differs significantly if the language that helps us to form propositions has gaps in it and is less reliable.

What will almost certainly be transferred from the experience of L1 listening is something that appears to be a universal human attribute – an **effort after meaning**. We seem to be primed as a species to try to make sense of the information we hold, however incomplete it is. It is very likely that an L2 listener will support meaning building by using strategies to compensate for gaps in decoding. But, whether those strategies are effective or not, they do not constitute a normal part of L1 processing (except perhaps in circumstances of high noise). This means that the experience of listening to a second language is different in quality from that of listening to one's first.

On these grounds, it seems fair to conclude that systematic training in meaning building is useful to second language listeners and will assist them to develop an integrated set of listening processes. Like the preceding ones, this chapter therefore provides a description of the behaviour of an expert listener, with an examination of the challenges that L2 listeners face in acquiring it. There are then suggestions for types of exercise that might be used in the language classroom.

Meaning-building exercises need not be complex. A teacher might employ sets of specially designed sentences for learners to interpret or match to paraphrases; or might excise sentences from a recording that pose specific problems of understanding. Alternatively, the teacher might opt for a longer lesson in which several related aspects of meaning building are practised in conjunction with each other.

The way in which the exercises are presented is rather more varied than in previous chapters. While some are in the form of rubrics, others are examples of actual tasks from published materials. Some focus on a single element of the meaning-building process, while others show how several aspects of meaning building can fit into a standard comprehension lesson. A number of the exercise types that are described already form part of current methodology and materials, though their benefits in process terms are not always made clear to the teacher.

12.2 Contextual information

12.2.1 Types of outside knowledge

Writers often refer to the outside information that a listener brings to a piece of speech as 'world knowledge'. But other forms of knowledge may also be critical to understanding. They include knowledge of the specific topic, knowledge of the speaker, knowledge of the current situation and knowledge (or observation) of the setting. Let us briefly consider why all these types of knowledge are important.

- *World knowledge.* World knowledge operates at many different levels. Assume that a listener hears the following sentence in a radio programme for the partially sighted:

  Should you let your guide dog on to an escalator in the Underground?
  (*In Touch*, BBC Radio 4, 25 October 2005)

  World knowledge provides the background information that makes it meaningful. Underlying the sentence is an awareness (which the speaker assumes is shared with the listener) that a dog might be frightened of an escalator. But world knowledge also operates at word level. Thus, many encounters with dogs of different shapes and sizes enable us to conceptualise a group of animals which fall into the category DOG. We can interpret the compound noun *guide dogs* only if we know that blind people are sometimes provided with dogs trained to assist them. Something similar can be said of the word *Underground* as used to refer to the London metro. The mention of escalators (associated with underground trains in many countries) leads us away from a possible interpretation of *underground* as referring (say) to a spy network.

- *Topic knowledge.* Topic knowledge is part of world knowledge but can provide a more specific framework for what the listener hears. Somebody who is about to attend a talk on butterflies will go in with certain expectations. They may concern the aspects likely to be mentioned (lifespan, gestation, colouring, habitats) or questions which the talk might answer. They may also serve to trigger the process of spreading activation discussed in Chapter 10, foregrounding likely vocabulary items: BUTTERFLY → *caterpillar, chrysalis, antennae, nectar.* It has been shown that L2 listeners with a background in the subject of a listening passage succeed markedly better on tests of comprehension than those without (Long, 1990). Of course, a great deal may depend upon how conversant the listener is with the necessary vocabulary to represent concepts familiar from L1.

- *Speaker knowledge.* The advantage of prior exposure to the speaker's voice was noted in Chapter 10. But, when interpreting the message, it is also useful to know something of the speaker's background. This might relate to personal beliefs and attitudes. An environmentally concerned speaker who says *Who cares about carbon emissions anyway?* is counting upon the listener's knowledge of his views to mark out the utterance as heavily ironic. It might also relate to the speaker's role: a gunman who says *Put up your hands* anticipates a different response from a teacher who utters the same instruction. It also, very importantly, relates to the amount of experience that speaker and listener share. Thus, if a speaker mentions *that shop on the corner*, it is in the expectation that both shop and corner are familiar to the listener. Mention of *that place I went to on holiday last year* presupposes that the holiday has been discussed on an earlier occasion.

- *Knowledge of the situation.* Many speech events have an element of ritual about them and progress through a series of relatively predictable exchanges. Prior knowledge of the situation type (and of how it is handled in the culture of the speaker) assists the listener's understanding. In checking in at an airport, one can relatively confidently expect to hear, in this order: *Could I have your passport please? – Do you have any luggage? – Would you put it on the belt? – Did you pack this bag yourself? – An aisle seat or a window seat? – Here's your boarding pass – Boarding will be at Gate X – Have a good flight.* It is also important for the listener to have a clear idea of the type of information that a particular encounter will require. Bremer *et al.* (1993: 165) report that some immigrants expect interviewers to focus on facts and become confused when their personal views and preferences are solicited.

- *Knowledge of the setting.* Visual cues not only provide a contextual framework but also contribute to the way an utterance is interpreted. In real life, much spoken discourse makes use of reference to objects and people in the immediate environment of the speaker (*this picture, those children*). This might include the spatial relationship between speaker and listener (*Bring it here, on your left*). In addition, **paralinguistic cues** such as facial expression or gesture contribute significantly to the listener's understanding of what is being said.

Some of the sources of information that have been mentioned apply across languages: L2 listeners can readily transfer them from a native language context. However, in some cases, the ability to make use of contextual cues may be dependent upon an understanding of the culture and cultural assumptions that are associated with the target language. The listener may be unable to identify with how the speaker views the world, the form taken by ritualised encounters or the significance of certain gestures or facial expressions. This may restrict the extent to which the listener can make assumptions based upon external knowledge.

12.2.2 Schema activation

First language processing

The way in which world knowledge assists the building of meaning is often discussed in terms of schema theory. A **schema** (Bartlett, 1932) is a complex knowledge structure in the mind which groups all that an individual knows about, or associates with, a particular concept. The notion is a very vague one: it embraces world knowledge, large abstract concepts such as JUSTICE and word categories such as DOG.

A schema can be represented as operating in the form of a network of associated ideas. By way of illustration, an English speaker's schema for the concept APPLE might include the information shown in Figure 12.3, including appearance, function, other types of fruit, words that collocate with *apple,* etc.

Schematic information can be used in two ways to support understanding in listening. It can be used to predict what might be said: to repeat an earlier example, knowing that a lecture is about butterflies activates the relevant schema so that the listener is prepared for what she is

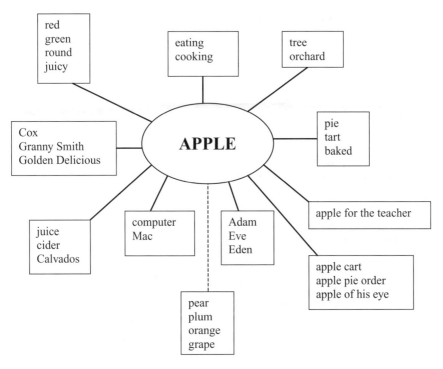

Figure 12.3   A schema for the concept APPLE.

likely to hear. But it also assists the listener in filling in information that the speaker does not specifically provide. A speaker might say: *He had cheeks like an apple*, leaving the listener to supply *red*; another speaker might say *I was working on my Apple*, leaving the listener to supply *computer*. If a speaker makes use of a word such as TABLE or CHAIR, it is on the assumption that certain notions of the shape and functions of these pieces of furniture are shared with the listener.

Closely associated with schema theory is another type of stored knowledge known as **script** (Schank and Abelson, 1977). This is a sequence of activities associated with a stereotypical situation. Scripts are particularly important to the listener in supplying information that the speaker does not specify. When a speaker says: *I answered the phone*, he does not feel obliged to mention the following details: *Somebody pressed buttons to form a number. An electrical connection was made. The phone made a buzzing noise. I heard the noise. I walked to the phone. I picked it up. I said 'Hello'.* Scripts thus permit a kind of spoken shorthand, where the speaker assumes that the listener shares certain pieces of stored knowledge and can be relied upon to add them to what is said. Without them, spoken interaction between human beings would be tedious indeed.

Second language practice

Schematic knowledge can be of considerable assistance to the second language listener. As well as embellishing the message that the speaker supplies, it can also be used to fill in gaps where decoding has failed. However, as already noted, problems of understanding may arise if there is a lack of fit between the schemas of the two languages. The possibility of a cultural mismatch is well illustrated by looking back at the schema for APPLE in Figure 12.3. Most obviously, the fruit may not be a familiar one outside temperate countries. In addition, a number of the associations depicted are specific to Western cuisine (*apple pie, cider*), to particular religious traditions (*Adam, Eve*), to an American product or to culturally transmitted ideas about teachers and pupils. Some of them concern idioms which occur in the target language but which are extremely unlikely to have parallels in L1.

So far as classroom practice is concerned, external knowledge can be activated *before listening* to a recording by asking learners to predict what the speaker will say.[1] This is very much part of standard practice, but it is important to explain in process terms why experienced teachers do it. The value of this kind of activity is that it:

- draws upon the listener's schematic knowledge of the topic;
- raises questions in the listener's mind which the speaker may answer;
- identifies possible scripts;
- starts a spreading activation process for words associated with the topic;
- identifies areas where concepts differ between languages.

External knowledge also needs to be activated *during listening* to amplify what a speaker says. This serves two main purposes:

- enriching the bare meaning contained in the propositions;
- supplying information that the speaker has taken as understood.

Tables 12.1 to 12.3 provide examples of the types of approach that encourage the use of external information before and during listening.

---

[1] The word *predict* and *anticipate* are used interchangeably by many writers on L2 listening, which can be confusing. Here, I use *predict* for the kind of activity that takes place before listening and *anticipate* for the kind of activity where learners suggest during listening what the speaker will say next.

Table 12.1 *Predicting using external knowledge*

Before listening

• *Content schema*
  You are going to hear a recording about *canals*.
  a. Brainstorm what you know about canals (in L1 or in L2).
  b. How much of this do you expect to hear in the recording?
  c. What words do you expect to hear which are associated with canals? Give words in L1 when you do not know them in L2.
  d. Do you know whether canals are still used today in L2-speaking countries? What for?

• *Background*
  The speakers are people who manage canals, people who work on canals and people who take holidays on them.
  e. How do you expect the attitudes of the groups to differ? Might they disagree?
  f. What differences do you expect between impromptu interviews 'in the street' and more formal interviews in studio conditions?

During listening

You will hear the presenter's introduction to the programme on canals.
  g. Check the list on the board to see if you were right in predicting what the presenter would say. Discuss with a partner.
  h. When you come across new words, decide if any of them could fit the words you predicted would occur, especially words in L1 that you do not know in L2.

12.2.3 The discourse representation

A listener's understanding of an utterance is also supported by recall of what has been said so far. The word *schema* is sometimes also used in this connection, with commentators referring to listeners 'constructing a schema' for a particular piece of discourse. To avoid confusion, the term 'discourse representation' is preferred here, and *schema* is reserved for long-term knowledge.

Table 12.2 *Using knowledge during listening*

Listen to the first part of the recording (about 20 seconds)

- *Content schema*
  a. What is it about? What do you know about this topic?
  b. How much of this do you expect to hear in the recording?
  c. What words do you expect to hear which are associated with the topic? Give words in L1 when you do not know them in L2.
  d. Do you know anything about this topic in L2-speaking countries?
- *Recording type*
  e. What is the recording? A conversation? A programme? A lecture? How do you expect it to begin and end?
- *Background*
  f. Who is the speaker you have heard so far? What is his/her view of the topic?
  g. How do you expect other speaker(s) to respond?

Alternative: Ask similar questions after extensive listening to the whole recording.

Table 12.3 *Activating a script*

- *Predicting.* You are going to hear a conversation in a restaurant between a customer and a waiter.
  a. Using L1, say what you expect the two speakers to say in an event of this kind. Might this be different in any way in the L2 culture?
  b. Now try to say what words you expect them to use in L2.
  c. Listen and check how accurately you predicted.
- *Anticipating.* You will hear part of a conversation.
  a. Say what the situation is.

  [Teacher plays a short section of recording of a situation that fits a script.]

  b. Say what words you expect to hear next.
  c. Listen to see if you were right. Then say what words you expect in the next part.
  d. Listen and check again.

As we have seen, a discourse representation has two functions: it is a record of what has been heard, a kind of 'work-in-progress' until the listening encounter finishes, when it may or may not be stored in memory. It also, like world knowledge, provides a background for new ideas as they come in. A listener (whether in L1 or L2) needs to constantly update the discourse representation. An expert listener **self-monitors** when doing so, checking each incoming piece of information to see if it is consistent with what she has understood so far. If it is not, then the listener needs either to revise her understanding of the new information or to revise her discourse representation. This is an important process for an inexperienced second language listener to employ, given the tentative nature of much of the information that is obtained. We will examine it in more detail in Chapter 13.

12.3 Words in context

We now consider the influence that context and co-text have on meaning at word level.

12.3.1 The fuzziness of word meaning

It is easy to assume that, once a vocabulary teacher has introduced a new word, it becomes fully established as part of a learner's repertoire. In listening terms, we might expect that a learner will recognise the word whenever it occurs in a recording. Indeed, much grading of listening material is based on notions of what does or does not fall within the target audience's vocabulary range.

We have already seen that this is a dangerous fallacy so far as decoding is concerned. The learner may have been exposed to the citation form of a word, but there is no guarantee that the word will be recognised when it occurs in connected speech. The assumption is also open to challenge in relation to meaning building. Learning the form of a word and attaching a dictionary meaning to it is not the same as mastering the word. Let us say that a learner has encountered the word COLD in the single context *cold water*. That does not mean that she will necessarily manage to find the appropriate meaning when she hears it in very different contexts such as *My food is cold, a cold colour, He was very cold towards us, the Cold War* or *The trail went cold*. The belief that she 'knows' the word may even lead to a serious misunderstanding when somebody says *I have a cold*. The point is that acquiring a word does not just entail associating a single meaning with it. It entails knowing how the meaning is shaped by the many co-texts in which the word occurs. It also entails establishing connections between words that often occur together.

A process view of listening

This is where most L2 listeners are at an enormous disadvantage compared with native listeners. The latter have had many years' experience of the target language; they have been exposed to all the likely contexts in which a given word might occur and the ways in which its meaning shifts. They do not have a single dictionary meaning for a word but a whole range of possible meanings. They are also familiar with how words change their meaning when they collocate with others (*heavy* and *smoker*, *blonde* and *hair*).

Word meaning in context is not an easy area for the language teacher to handle effectively. The listener needs exposure to multiple examples of a word; here, there is certainly a justification for continuing with the longer recordings that the comprehension approach favours. But it is difficult to raise learner awareness of the effects of context in any systematic way.

Two solutions might be considered. The first requires the teacher to examine the transcript of a recording with an eye to meanings that are determined by context. As part of preparing a listening lesson, instructors usually take great care to identify words that they believe are unfamiliar and might need to be explained. But they very rarely examine a tapescript for evidence of *known words used with unfamiliar senses*. These are more common than we realise and should not be ignored. Here is a relatively random example from a published listening course:

> I remember now I **look back** and I remember something that one of my mother's friends said to her and she said you won't really know **pain** or worry or suffering until you have children, and that is really **true** because worrying about yourself isn't anything but as soon as you have children those worries are just **huge** in fact it was all erm it it was nothing there was nothing **wrong** with her and it it was a **false** alarm but in a different way it changed my life.
>
> (Collie and Slater, 1995: 89)

A word used in a different sense from the one that was learned is as serious an obstacle to meaning building as a word that is not known. It might mislead the learners into making wrong assumptions and misinterpreting the text as a whole. Here *look back* refers not to a visual event but to the use of memory; the *pain* is emotional not physical and *true* is used in the sense of 'meaningful' (the speaker never really thought the idea was untrue). Learners might wonder how something abstract like a worry can be *huge*; they also have to recognise that the expression *nothing wrong with* refers to a problem or illness rather than an error or piece of bad behaviour, and that *false* carries a special sense when it occurs with *alarm*.

Table 12.4 *Raising awareness of contextual meaning*

'I'm going to say some sentences to you. Try to explain what they mean. You can use [first language] if you like.'

a. *The lawyer took out some **papers**.*
b. *You can **tell** they're rich.*
c. *She isn't very **close** to her brother.*
d. *I **found** him difficult to talk to.*
e. *I'm **afraid** I have bad news.*
f. *That's **quite** [completely] unacceptable.*
g. *I take **light** reading on holiday.*
h. *He lived in the Middle **Ages**.*
i. *She was **deep** in thought.*
j. ***Run** the water until it gets warm.*
k. *My boss was **chairing** the meeting.*
l. *The plane was **heading** for New York.*

Alternative: Get listeners to work out the meaning of some of the more transparent idioms in L2. Examples from English are *I don't buy that argument, too close to call, out of his depth, put your foot down, life in the fast lane.*

An alternative approach is for the instructor to devise a battery of sentences to dictate to learners, in which known words are used in ways that deviate from their dictionary definitions. The context should be clear enough to assist interpretation. Table 12.4 provides a few mixed examples appropriate for a low intermediate level.

12.3.2 Word ambiguity

First language processing

Listeners also use co-text in order to deal with ambiguity. When what they hear represents two possible words, they may not be able to attach the appropriate meaning until the end of the clause – and sometimes not even then. Consider the possible ambiguities thrown up by the sequence /raɪt/:

write the letter / the right letter
go right / go right ahead
'Make sure you take the right turning.' / 'All right.'
He writes about human rights.
They managed to right the boat.

An experienced listener fully conversant with the language has a number of means for resolving ambiguity of this kind:

- *Through collocation.* In the examples above, a native listener would understand the precise sense of *right* when it was used in conjunction with *turning, all or human.*
- *Through grammar.* The syntactic structure of the clause as a whole enables the listener to distinguish the two senses of /raɪts/ in *He writes about human rights.*
- *Through the wider meaning provided by the co-text* within which /raɪts/ appears.
- *Through the general context.* Schematic knowledge can help to determine which of two or more senses is more appropriate or more likely in a particular context.

Second language practice

These resources may not be available to L2 listeners because they depend upon an accurate decoding of the co-text. If listeners have not understood enough to resolve the ambiguity, they face the prospect of carrying forward two or more possible interpretations. In these circumstances, they often fall back on a word's most frequently encountered and therefore most likely sense. They may even go on to incorporate that sense into a discourse representation, leading to misunderstanding on a larger scale.

Issues of word ambiguity, like those of fuzzy meaning, tend to be overlooked in L2 listening lessons despite their potential for misleading the listener. It is a good idea to target homophonous words alongside new ones, and to get learners to disambiguate them in relation to the co-text in which they occur. In doing so, one raises awareness of potential problems and trains learners to use co-text more carefully. Table 12.5 suggests a number of exercises providing practice in disambiguation.

12.3.3 Unknown words

We now turn to the question of unknown words. Second language listeners deal with them by using *strategies*: i.e. techniques designed to overcome gaps in their language knowledge. Strategies will be discussed in detail in Chapters 15 and 16. But lexical strategies represent a special case. Rather than being short-term expedients, ways of 'getting by' until L2 proficiency improves, they draw quite closely on the kind of process that a listener might employ on hearing an unfamiliar word in her native language. It thus makes sense to consider them here alongside issues of word meaning.

Table 12.5 *Sample exercises on word ambiguity*

- *Awareness raising.* 'On your worksheet you will see two words for each sentence. Decide which word you hear. You will only have 1 second between sentences.'
  A. *I need to write my name.*   B. *We tried to put right a problem.*
  A. *I want to buy one, too.*   B. *I want to buy two.*
  A. *It's a road for bicycles.*   B. *They rode on bicycles.*
  A. *I told him his weight.*   B. *I told him to wait.*
  A. *Their son has brown eyes.*   B. *The sun's in my eyes.*
  A. *The patient came this week.*   B. *The patient became weak.*
  A. *There's no answer.*   B. *Do you know the answer?*

- *Double sense.* 'Look at the words on your worksheet and identify two possible meanings for each one. Then listen to some short sentences and decide which meaning is appropriate.'
    watch: *My watch is wrong. / Let's watch the birds.*
    rose: *I picked the rose this morning. / The sun rose quite early.*
    like: *What's he like? / What does he like?*
    safe: *The money's safe. / The money's in the safe.*

- *Revising interpretations.* 'You will hear part of a sentence. Suggest what words come next.' Teacher plays the first (ambiguous) part, takes suggestions, then plays the second part.
    In the exam, I had a hard ... seat to sit on.
    I'm looking for a light ... suitcase.
    I want a watch (= I want to watch) ... for my birthday.
    The park leaves ... its gates open.
    The children are looking ... very tired.
    My friend is taking ... off his jacket.
    The crowd is turning ... violent.

- *Known form, new word.* Teacher dictates sentences with familiar word form in a new sense, and asks for explanations. Allow long discussion before giving answers.
    The locks on the windows are very <u>sound</u>.
    They want to protect human <u>rights</u>.
    They <u>fined</u> him for parking his car here.
    They ran to the <u>bank</u> and jumped in.

- *Homophone interpretation.* When preparing a general listening activity, teacher identifies homophones in the tapescript. During the lesson, teacher replays sentences containing them and asks learners to explain them in their own words.

A process view of listening

First language processing

In listening to a talk or a programme on a little-known subject, a native listener might well come across words never heard before or only met in written form. This is not quite the same as a gap in L2 knowledge. The difference is that the native listener can be more certain that what she has heard *is* a new word. It also lies in the fact that a native listener usually has greater back-up resources in the form of a complete understanding of the co-text within which the word has occurred.

Confronted with a new word, a native listener adopts one of three approaches. She chooses to:

- ignore the word;
- accept an **indeterminate sense** for the word: enough to achieve a broad understanding (she might recognise that the word *linden* represents a tree without knowing exactly what type of tree);
- work out a precise meaning for the word from its co-text.

Second language practice

By tradition, second language listening instructors focus almost exclusively on the third strategy. After a comprehension session, they might replay short sections of text and ask learners to work out the meaning of new words within them. This approach has its limitations. It does not allow practice in the other possible means of dealing with a new word. It is useful to train L2 listeners to get by *without* some of the unknown words that they encounter (especially those listeners who feel insecure if they have not successfully decoded most of the input). It is also useful for the listener to be able to judge when an indeterminate meaning is quite sufficient to achieve an understanding of what has been said.

Furthermore, it is usually the teacher who identifies possible new words. In real-life exchanges, listeners have to decide for themselves that a word is a new one and not a variant form of a known one. That might sound like an easy decision, but it is not when the listeners in question are conscious of their uncertain phoneme values and limited decoding skills. In a study of the decoding accuracy of a group of L2 users (2008c), I discovered that in cases of uncertainty many of them preferred to assume that they had heard a known word which formed a rough match to the signal – even where that match did not make any sense in terms of the context – rather than accepting that a new word might be present. This is no trivial matter, since listeners in some cases go on to build an understanding of the passage as a whole that is based upon these mistaken matches.

226

As ever, there are conclusions for teaching. Given that L2 listeners seem to fall back so heavily upon approximate matches of this kind, there is a need for small-scale practice which trains them *to identify unknown words and to distinguish them from known ones that are similar in form.* Trainers also need to foster a much greater awareness among learners of the extent to which an apparent match is to be trusted. Does the listener feel 90% confident of the match she has made or only 10%? This must be closely combined with a procedure of checking possible mismatches against what follows, to be sure that they can be relied upon.

Table 12.6 reminds readers of some relatively standard exercises that ask learners to infer word meaning from different types of cue. Table 12.7 then suggests a number of additional exercises that provide practice

Table 12.6 *Inferring word meaning*

- *Approximate sense.* Teacher plays or dictates a series of sentences which provide a very general context for a target word. Learners give an approximate sense for the word.
- *Cognates.* Teacher dictates words which have cognates in L1 that are pronounced slightly differently. Learners attempt to transcribe words, then match to the word in L1. Words often shared by languages include *oxygen, international, taxi, television, computer, university*, names of countries and cities, etc.
- *Using known words.* Teacher dictates unknown words which contain known words as their stems, perhaps words with prefixes or suffixes added. Learners try to transcribe the words, then work out their meanings or write sentences which include them. For example: *unacceptable, continuation, indirect, distrustful, inclusive, revisited, differentiate.*
- *Use of co-text.* When planning a general comprehension lesson, teacher searches the tapescript for new words whose meaning is illustrated by the sentence in which they occur or by the immediately preceding sentence. Teacher records them on to a separate cassette. Use only new words which are important to an understanding of the text.
- *Use of world knowledge or topic.* Instead of pre-teaching new vocabulary, teacher prepares for listening by giving the topic of the recording and asking *in the native language* for predictions as to what the recording will mention. Teacher lists predictions on the board in L1. When new words occur, teacher pauses the recording and asks learners if the context suggests that they fit any of the L1 predictions on the board.

Table 12.7 *Dealing with unknown words*

- *Ignoring words 1*. Teacher plays a short passage (30 sec.) that is above learners' vocabulary level and asks questions for general understanding. Teacher replays and learners choose the five words they think are most important for a better understanding.

- *Ignoring words 2*. 'Are there any words you do not recognise? Are these words important to understanding the rest of the text or not?' Teacher plays a short passage (30 sec.) above learners' vocabulary level and asks questions for general understanding. Teacher then replays two sentences at a time, asking which unknown words are important for a better understanding.

- *New word or known 1*. Teacher dictates known words mixed with unknown words that closely resemble known ones. Learners try to identify and transcribe the new words. Consult lists of minimal pairs for material (for English, Baker, 2006).

- *New word or known 2*. 'Which word does not belong? Write it.' Teacher dictates sets of words, where the 'odd one out' is an unfamiliar word that resembles a familiar one.
    summer – autumn – string – winter
    purple – yellow – drown – green – orange
    cousin – sister – nephew – ankle – daughter
    drain – car – bus – ship – plane
    take – send – brick – fetch – carry
    ears – nose – mouse – eyes

- *New word or known 3*. 'Which words are new?' Teacher plays a short passage (30 sec.). Learners listen to identify new words. Teacher replays the passage; learners try to write down the new words using knowledge of L2 spelling.

in ignoring unknown words and in distinguishing between known and unknown words.

12.4 Speaker's intentions

As well as bringing outside knowledge to bear on an utterance, a listener very often has to guess the speaker's reasons for saying what he did. It is often a matter of putting in information that the speaker has taken for granted. We will call the process **inference** when the listener has to form connections between sentences or to supply missing background. We will call it **reference** when it is a question of tracking back to find out what words like *they*, *there* or *this* refer to. We will also look at ways in which the listener has to work out the full intentions behind the speaker's words.

12.4.1 Inference

First language processing

To explain how inference contributes to meaning, let us consider an example. The extract below is taken from a radio broadcast. In reading it, pretend that you have just tuned in and ask yourself the following questions:

What type of broadcast is it?
What are the roles of I and E?
What information would you carry forward from this extract as you
    continued to listen?
Is there information that the extract does not supply?

```
 1 I: what do you think
 2 E: well common SENSE + and and all of the experience
 3    round the WORLD demonstrate + that if you make ALL
 4    public places smoke FREE without exCEPtion + the policy
 5    WORKS very well + it is exTREmely popular + is the
 6    ONly way of protecting BAR staff + and ALL bar staff
 7    from exposure at work + and it has the ADDed knock-on
 8    effect + that about + if the IRish experience is anything to
 9    go by + about one in TWELve smokers will quit SMOking
10    + so it's very good for occuPAtional health + n it's very
11    good for PUBlic health + and I just DON'T understand
12    why the government doesn't do the OBvious + and get ON
13    with it++
14 I: what about the ARgument though + that if people can't
15    smoke + in + PUBS + then they'll just smoke more at
16    HOME putting their CHILdren at risk++
17 E: well all of the EVidence suggests that the OPPosite is true
18    + that was a STATEment that came from John REID
19    before the er manifesto page + and NONE of us in in
20    medicine + understand where on EARTH that figure is
21    co- + that proposal has come from + the evidence in
22    THIS country is that if you can't smoke in PUBlic +
```

(cont.)

> 23   you are + m + far LESS likely to go home and smoke in
> 24   front of your CHILdren + and indeed you're more likely
> 25   to quit smoking altoGETHer in which case the home
> 26   becomes smoke FREE ++
>
> (*Today* programme, BBC Radio 4, 26 October 2005)
>
> Upper case represents heavily stressed syllables; + and ++ represent pauses

Using your experience, you will probably have worked out that this is a news programme and that the extract is from an interview with an expert (E). As you read through the text, you will probably have assembled the following information, which might support your understanding of later stages of the interview:

a. The interview is about banning smoking in public places.
b. The context is a British one.
c. Government action is involved.
d. The expert is a doctor.
e. There is concern about bar staff being exposed to smoke while at work.
f. There is also concern that banning smoking in public may lead to people smoking more at home.

In addition, certain information has to be supplied from world knowledge which the listener may not possess. This includes:

• the identity of *John Reid* (a former British health minister);
• the role of *the manifesto* (banning smoking in pubs was part of an election proposal by the government);
• the relevance of *the Irish experience* (Ireland had already introduced a ban on smoking in pubs).

The extract seems to provide a neat example of how schematic information combines with information from the text to enable the listener to understand what is going on. In fact, it is not quite as simple as that. Of the six points listed above, only the last two are explicitly stated by the speaker. The others have to be inferred by the listener.[2] There is a favourable mention of *smoke-free* public environments, but no explicit reference to a ban on smoking. We guess the context is a British one because, halfway through, the Interviewer mentions *pubs*. The Expert says that the government needs to *get on with it* – suggesting but not saying explicitly that government intervention is expected, perhaps in

[2] Unless the listener already has an up-to-date schema for the issue being discussed.

the form of a law. The Expert refers to *us in medicine,* leading us to conclude that he may be a doctor.

Listeners, then, need to do more than draw upon contextual knowledge and the text-so-far. They also have to fill in gaps caused by information that the speaker has not supplied and connections that the speaker has not made. The reasons for those gaps are either (a) that the speaker assumes that certain knowledge is shared with the listener or (b) that the speaker relies upon the listener to make the connections without having them spelt out in detail.

We have already seen that much speech is a kind of shorthand, in which the speaker expects the listener to supply additional information from schematic knowledge (the example given earlier was the sentence *I answered the phone*). Similarly, speech becomes more efficient if the speaker leaves certain obvious connections unexpressed. Recall the example *I'm sorry I'm late. The traffic was awful.* The listener has to conclude, from the way the two sentences occur together, that there is a connection between the lateness and the traffic.

Second language practice

Attention is a limited resource, and human beings have to distribute it as efficiently as they can. A second language listener is fully capable of drawing inferences in L1; but, faced with the demands of unfamiliar sounds and vocabulary, she has to commit greater attention to decoding and to meaning at sentence level than she would normally. The result might be that she fails to make all the inferences that she would in her first language.

This is an area that the comprehension approach tends to neglect. It equates 'comprehension' with being able to report facts at sentence level that are expressed explicitly by the speaker. It rarely tests the extent to which the learner is capable of tracing implicit connections between sentences or between facts. To be fair, some exam boards now include 'global' or 'inferential' questions in their tests, but the issue receives relatively little attention in the classroom. One solution is for the teacher to provide additional comprehension questions that focus especially on the connections that the speaker has left unsaid. Examples for the 'smoking ban' text above might include:

a. What is the issue that is being discussed?
b. Which country is this interview about?
c. What two groups of people need to be protected and against what?
d. What does the speaker want to happen?
e. What is the profession of the person being interviewed?

A process view of listening

Table 12.8 Material for inferencing practice

Listen to these extracts with pauses between them. Explain the
connections between them using your first language.
a. *I longed to be an air hostess + until I discovered that planes
crashed + and then I decided I decided I'd be an air hostess
who worked on the ground.*
b. *Now a lot of people will say 'Oh dear this is something very
significant her dreaming of snakes' + but it's nothing to do with
any kind of erm ... double meaning that there may be + It's
because as a child I lived in the East + and I had many nasty
experiences with snakes.*
c. *I go into the supermarket + because I don't like shopping at all
+ and I go through as quickly as possible without any
interference from anybody that I might meet + 'cause I
generally meet the whole world in the supermarket + I pay up
as quickly as possible + and I put it in the car and I'm home.*
d. *There are lots of people who enjoy parties + but who can't
dance + now what I like about a party is that you're going to
meet + when you go to the party ... you don't know most of
the people there + But by the end of the evening if you could
have chatted even for a few minutes to different people + then I
feel that ... you know ... I've enjoyed the party + and I hate
parties where erm ... you only talk to one person or two people
+ and you're stuck with them for the whole evening.*

In all cases, learners should be asked to explain the reasons for their
answers.

It is also possible to design targeted exercises that practise making
connections between ideas. Here, one can use extracts from standard listening materials, with short pauses inserted to give learners time to form
their inferences. Those in Table 12.8 have been taken from authentic
informal recordings in Collie and Slater (1995: 81–7). Material of this
kind is especially useful because the connections are often much more
loosely made than they would be in a formal or scripted talk.

Learners can also be encouraged to practise inferencing at the level of
the whole text. They are used to being given a precise background by
their teacher for each recording that they encounter in class. However,
real-life situations are sometimes less clear-cut (e.g. when one tunes in to
a radio station in the middle of a programme or joins a conversation).
In these circumstances, listeners have to rely heavily upon inferencing

Table 12.9 *Sample exercise: text-level inference*

Ambiguous situation. What is the discussion about?
A: *What's got into him then?*
B: *I think he was expecting a bit more.*
A: *He got enough, dammit!*
B: *Yes, I know ...*
A: *Well, I don't have to give him any more, do I?*
B: *Not if you don't want to.*

(Maley and Duff, 1978: 66)

in order to establish a context for what they hear. Table 12.9 gives an example of the kind of recording that can be used.

12.4.2 Reference

First language processing

Another type of shorthand in speech makes use of pronouns and phrases to refer back to something or someone mentioned earlier. Looking back at the 'smoke-free' interview, ask yourself how a listener might manage to make sense of the following:

lines 4–5 *the policy/it*   line 7 *it*   line 10 *it's*   line 15 *they'll*
line 17 *the opposite*   line 18 *that*   line 19 *us*   line 21 *that proposal.*

We noted before that there is an important difference between the listener and the reader in that the listener cannot look back at a piece of text to check a link. The connection has to be made entirely in the listener's mind. Much will depend upon how accurately the listener has followed and can recall what has just been said. The listener thus has to remain constantly aware of the currently foregrounded topics against which pronouns may need to be matched.

The process might seem an easy one. Surely all the listener needs to do when interpreting *they'll* (line 15) is to be aware that *people* (line 14) is the current topic. In fact, it is not quite so simple as that. In the example given, there are two possible candidates available (*people* and *pubs*). The speaker could use *they* for either of them (an equally acceptable sentence would be *what about the ARgument though + that if people can't smoke + in + PUBS + then they'll lose all their customers*). So the listener has to carry forward both *people* and *pubs* – and the ideas associated with them – as current topics, and then has to decide which of the two is referred to when the speaker uses *they*.

233

A more complex case still is offered by *it's* (line 10) which has to be tracked back as far as *the policy* (line 4) and then even further back to establish what *the policy* refers to. In fact, *the policy* does not relate to a single person or thing but to a whole concept (*if you make all public places smoke free without exception*).

To make matters worse, pronouns are used more loosely in speaking than in writing (for examples, see Brown and Yule, 1983a: 216–22). There may be a lapse of time between the mention of a topic and the pronoun that refers back to it, as in the *it's* example. There may also be cases where a listener has to leapfrog a recent topic and track back to an earlier one. Consider the patterns of reference of the italicised words in the following piece of natural speech (Underwood, 1975: 107), which has three current topics running simultaneously: 'getting children to go to the cinema', 'community spirit' and 'children'.

> We're getting children into the habit of going to the cinema and perhaps *this* is something er which today we could describe as being a good thing since *they*'ve spent most of *their* early years at home and watching television and so on. It's getting *them* out, erm, getting *them* to sit with other people. The community spirit, I think, is very important and perhaps the cinema has got a part to play in *this*. Certainly, we don't make any money on *it*. *They* pay sixpence to get in, er, and, er, *they*, they buy ice cream and all the rest of it. But *it*'s not a profitable enterprise. But we enjoy doing *it*.

Second language practice

Again, the second language listener's ability to make references may be restricted by the way in which she chooses to distribute her attention. Especially in the early stages, concern with decoding is likely to limit the extent to which the listener carries forward an adequate awareness of the current topic. As a result, she may process pronouns and other instances of reference only at a very shallow level. The necessary connections may not always be made.

Teachers of reading have long been aware of this problem, and have devised a standard reading exercise where learners draw lines to link pronouns to the words that they refer back to. But tackling reference in listening demands a very different process in that listeners do not have words on the page to assist them. We have to find a way of drawing the learner's attention to small and sometimes barely perceptible items in a recording such as *it* or *this*. The easiest solution is to provide learners with short written extracts from a tapescript which provide examples of reference in the recording being used. They then have to listen in order to explain what the words in question refer to. There are examples in Table 12.10.

Table 12.10 *Sample exercises dealing with reference*

- *Making connections.* You will hear extracts from recordings in which people are asked about modern fashions in clothes. After each one, work out what the words **in bold** refer to, and write it down. Then compare your answer with others before you go on to the next extract.
  a. 've got **two** . . .
     I know **they** like to look different . . .
     things go a bit far . . .
  b. **they** haven't been washed . . .
     I feel sorry for **them** . . .

a. *The clothes that youngsters wear + well I'm not too keen + I've got two myself so I know the problem + I know they like to look different – don't want to wear the same clothes as us + but I do think things go a bit far.*
b. *Not even something bright and cheerful + jeans with holes in + crumpled shorts that look as if they haven't been washed for a week + to tell you the truth I feel sorry for them.*
> (adapted from Field and Wiseman, 1993: 172)

- *Backward and forward reference.* In the recording, you will hear sentences about outer space. Listen for the words below. Write R when you think that the words refer back to something already mentioned; write N when you think that they introduce a new subject.
  a. These craft / small rockets   b. Heavy clothing / the human body / the wearer   c. The danger   d. These dark patches

a. *Space travel would, of course, be easier if spaceships could take off from space stations outside the earth's atmosphere. These craft would orbit the earth, and small rockets would carry astronauts to and fro.*
b. *When in space, an astronaut has to wear a thick padded suit. Heavy clothing is necessary in order to keep the human body under pressure and to protect the wearer from small pieces of matter in the atmosphere.*
c. *Spacecraft would normally burn up as they entered the earth's atmosphere because of the friction of the air. The danger is avoided by covering them with thick shields against the heat.*
d. *Sunspots are much cooler than the surface of the sun and so shine less brightly. These dark patches on the sun can usually be seen in pairs.*
> (adapted from Field and Wiseman, 1993: 230)

12.4.3 Interpretation

First language processing

Finally, the listener will find it necessary to interpret an utterance as a whole. What is referred to here rather generally as 'interpretation' includes:

- recognising the speaker's intentions;
  Example: Speaker says *Is that really a good idea?*, meaning 'I don't want to do it.'
- recognising the speaker's ultimate goal;
  Example: Speaker says *It's very reasonable at that price*, in order to persuade you to buy something.
- allowing for understatement and vague language; Example: Speaker says *I had quite a shock*, meaning 'I was very upset.'
- coping with metaphor;
  Example: Speaker says *They're all at sea*, meaning 'they are very confused.'
- looking beyond what the utterance says to its implications.
  Example: Speaker says *Twelve of the fourteen passengers were unharmed*. This entails that two of them were injured or killed.

Successful interpretation is to some degree dependent upon linguistic knowledge. The listener needs to know that certain turns of phrase represent language functions such as threatening, offering, apologising, etc. and that certain idiomatic expressions are not to be taken at their face value. It may also be dependent upon cultural knowledge such as the extent to which native speakers tend to understate or use vague terms such as *quite a few*.

However, the last type of interpretation mentioned (the ability to think beyond what was said) is rather different in that it draws entirely upon intuition and world knowledge. It is the mark of a skilled listener; though how important it is depends upon the listener's goals. A casual observer at a press conference might come away with an accurate recall of all the information that was presented; but a journalist attending the conference might process the same information more deeply, seeking an angle on it or a coherent pattern for presenting it in writing. We will refer to this as **deep processing**.

Second language practice

Interpretation that depends upon linguistic knowledge lends itself very much to small-scale practice so far as a non-native listener is concerned. Tables 12.11 and 12.12 give examples.

Table 12.11 *Exercise in interpreting speaker language*

> *Language focus.* After a comprehension activity, teacher replays sequences in the recording which represent vague language or idiomatic language that is not transparent. Learners interpret, using L1.

Table 12.12 *Sample exercises: deciding speaker's goals*

> *Speaker goals.* 'You will hear pieces from six recordings. Do not worry if you don't understand everything. Just say what the main purpose of each speaker is.' Teacher plays short extracts – from, for example:
>
> (a) a radio/TV advertisement; (b) cookery instructions; (c) a speaker telling a personal story; (d) publicity warning of the dangers of smoking; (e) a campaigner protesting about global warming or animal rights; (f) a politician denying responsibility.
>
> Or teacher plays short extracts about a house or apartment as described by:
> (a) a possible buyer; (b) an estate agent; (c) an architect; (d) a burglar; (e) a builder maintaining it; (f) a conservationist.

Deep processing presents a rather more complicated case. We need to recognise that it makes heavy demands upon L2 listeners which take them well beyond listening for information. To illustrate this, let us imagine how a teacher might construct questions that test understanding of the following turn from the 'smoke free' interview.

> Well common SENSE + and and all of the experience round the WORLD demonstrate + that if you make ALL public places smoke FREE without exCEPtion + the policy WORKS very well + it is exTREmely popular + is the ONly way of protecting BAR staff + and ALL bar staff from exposure at work + and it has the ADDed knock-on effect + that about + if the IRish experience is anything to go by + about one in TWELve smokers will quit SMOking + so it's very good for occuPAtional health + n it's very good for PUBlic health + and I just DON'T understand why the government doesn't do the OBvious + and get ON with it +

The teacher might well ask about local facts, using questions such as: *Is the policy popular? How many smokers are expected to quit smoking?* The problem with these questions is that their wording echoes the words of the speaker. It is quite easy for learners to answer them correctly without fully grasping the point at issue. To test comprehension more reliably, a teacher/tester will generally reformulate the questions so that they paraphrase the speaker's words: *Do people like the idea?* Or the questions might refer to what the information entails rather than to what it says: *How many people are likely to continue smoking?* Or they might ask the listener to interpret the speaker's attitude: *How does the speaker feel about the government?*

This is relatively standard practice, and unlikely to change in the near future, so far as standard listening tests are concerned. But we should not lose sight of the fact that it takes us beyond listening 'comprehension' and into 'interpretation'. We are asking learners to show not just that they have understood something accurately but that they have *processed it in depth*. Some learners find it hard to employ these quite sophisticated interpretative processes, even in their first language. There is also the issue of whether questions of this kind sometimes ask listeners to process information at a level of complexity that the text in question would not normally require.

Despite these concerns, paraphrase plays such an important part in the international testing of listening (in multiple-choice and true/false items and even in simple open-ended questions) that we need to provide practice exercises where learners report not what is said but on its implications. Tables 12.13 and 12.14 give examples of exercises that demand this kind of deep processing.

Table 12.13 *Deep processing (for paraphrase)*

- *True/false updated.* 'Check these statements against information in the recording (they may not be in the same order and will not use the same words). If they are correct, mark with a tick. If they are wrong, mark with a cross *and correct them*. If they are not mentioned, mark with a question mark (?).'
- *Paraphrase matching.* 'Read sentences 1–10 below. Make sure you have fully understood each one. Then listen to ten recorded sentences numbered 1–10. Say if they mean the same as the sentences you have read, or not.' For a full example, see Table 5.2.
- *Collating.* 'Listen to two recordings. List four points where the speakers agree in the information they give and three points where they differ.'

Table 12.14 *Sample exercise: guided summary with paraphrase*

Summarise what you hear by completing the sentences below.
a. The first pilots navigated by using ...
b. Pilots often lost their way when ...
c. The pilots of the first passenger planes did not like flying during ...
d. It was not always easy for them to recognise ...

The earliest planes were quite dangerous to fly. They were light and frail and the pilot had to use a compass or the stars to navigate by. The pilot was quite likely to get lost in bad weather. Even when passenger planes came into service, there were still problems with navigation. Pilots were reluctant to fly at night because the lights on the runways were sometimes difficult to see.

12.5 Conclusion

This chapter has attempted to demonstrate that listeners do not simply 'receive' a message from the mouth of a speaker. On the contrary: listeners have to contribute a great deal in order to make complete sense of what they hear. They use an ongoing representation in their minds of what has been said so far in order to expand on the raw meaning of what has been decoded. But they also bring in their own outside knowledge: knowledge of the world, the topic, the speaker, the situation and so on. They use the same sources of information to restrict the meanings attached to words, making the words specific to the utterance in which they occur. They also have to supply gaps that speakers may have left unexpressed.

These are all processes that a second language listener is familiar with from L1. But it is optimistic to assume that they are processes that transfer automatically to L2. Many of the components which support them are missing if a listener has limited decoding skills and limited vocabulary and grammar. Certainly, an adult listener has world knowledge that can be carried over from L1, but that does not mean that she can apply it with confidence to input that has only been partially understood. Decisions on the relevance of a new piece of information are obscured by the fact that the information may be incomplete or uncertain. Even monitoring comprehension becomes more difficult. Inconsistencies may have arisen because the current utterance has not been correctly or adequately decoded; or they may have arisen because the listener has built up an incorrect discourse representation from earlier in the encounter.

Two factors conspire against the inexperienced L2 listener:

(a) a degree of uncertainty about the accuracy of decoding;
(b) the need to focus much more attention on low-level decoding operations than a native listener would, thus limiting the mental resources available for meaning building.

The consequence is that the operation is qualitatively different from one the learner would apply in L1.

This analysis points again to the critical part played by decoding in developing confidence and competence as an L2 listener. But it also signals a need for language learners to be given sustained practice in applying well-established meaning-building operations to the unfamiliar circumstances of listening to a foreign or second language.

Further reading

Brown, G. (1995) *Speakers, Listeners and Communication*. Cambridge: Cambridge University Press.

Brown, G. (2005) 'Second language listening'. Entry in K. Brown (ed.), *Encyclopaedia of Language and Linguistics*. Oxford: Elsevier.

13 Handling information

Lok's ears spoke to Lok."?" But Lok was asleep.
William Golding (1911–1993), British author, *The Inheritors*

The last chapter described how a listener constructs a deeper meaning representation from the bare message conveyed by the speaker's words. It was suggested that the meaning representation then contributes to a discourse representation, the listener's recall of everything that has been said so far. It does indeed, but the model shown in Chapter 12 was something of a simplification. Before the new piece of information is added to the discourse representation, it undergoes a certain amount of editing by the listener. The way in which it is handled and the way in which the representation is updated form the topic of the present chapter.

In dealing with incoming information, a listener is generally assumed to make a series of quite simple decisions. She has to decide:

- How relevant is this piece of information?
- How does it relate to what went before?
- Is it consistent with what went before?
- How does it fit into a hierarchy of other pieces obtained so far – some important, some less so?

Figure 13.1 (see p. 242) offers an expanded version of the model from Chapter 12, with these additional stages added. We will examine each of them in turn and consider how they are handled by an expert listener. As before, we will also examine how the processes are affected by the additional demands of listening in a foreign language, including the need to allow for gaps in the information that is obtained.

13.1 Selecting information

First language processing

Much of the information that a listener obtains may not be of huge importance. Some may repeat what has been said before; some may not be clear; some may not be relevant to the listener's purpose in listening. Occasionally, the speaker may have digressed and lost the thread of the conversation. Even among the useful pieces of information, some will be more central to what is being discussed than others. The listener therefore has to make judgements as to the relevance and importance of

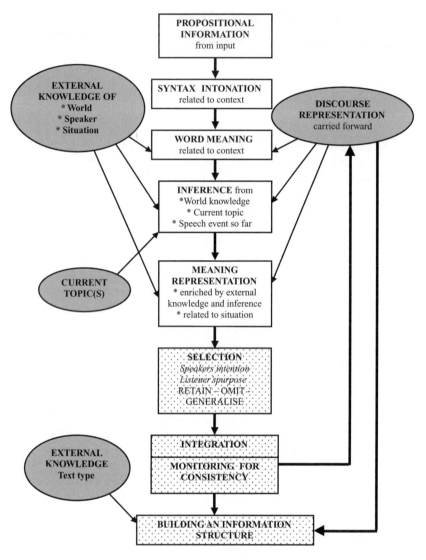

Figure 13.1   Building a discourse representation.

what she has understood. On the strength of these judgements, listeners
have one of three options (Van Dijk and Kintsch, 1983). They can:

- *abandon* (allow a piece of information to decay);
- *store* (retain a piece of information);
- *generalise* (retain a piece of information but with detail omitted).

Decisions about the relative importance of content are made at a *local level*. The listener might decide at the time of hearing it that a piece of information is redundant in that it repeats something that the speaker has said already. An L2 listener might decide that she has not decoded a piece of speech with sufficient accuracy to place any faith in the information that it appears to contain.

But other decisions are made at a more *global level*. Some units of information are downgraded or omitted from the discourse representation because they appear to be of low importance in the scheme of things, compared to others. Others (especially in L2 listening) might be omitted because they conflict strongly with the discourse representation built up so far and are therefore treated as tainted by possible misunderstanding.

An expert listener uses several criteria in arriving at decisions of this kind. First and foremost, she takes account of what she perceives to be the *intentions of the speaker*. The important thing is to determine in what ways an incoming piece of information contributes to the wider message that a speaker appears to be trying to transmit. A second consideration – and it is one that sometimes comes to outweigh the first – is the *listener's own goals*. Listeners have their own purposes for listening, which may not always be the same as those of the speaker. To give a simple example, a defendant in a court of law tries to present a positive picture of his actions, but the prosecuting counsel meanwhile listens out for loopholes. Similarly, if a speaker is only interested in one piece of information, she may decide to 'tune out' once she has received it. A good example is the way travellers process train or flight announcements. See Brown (1995: 24–9) for a thoughtful account of the gap between listener and speaker.

A further consideration is **redundancy**. Spoken discourse is often repetitive, with the speaker reiterating, rephrasing or revisiting information that has already been expressed. This applies as much to formal discourse (the lecturer returning to a point to ensure that it has been grasped) as it does to informal (the pub bore who gives his views on the political situation several times over). It seems especially to be a characteristic of lecturers who are addressing non-native listeners (Wesche and Ready, 1985).

The most important message to be drawn from this discussion is that listeners are not simply recorders of information. They make judgements about the information they receive: they select some, they omit some and they store some in reduced form. We should expect the same utterance to result in differently constituted messages in the minds of different listeners.

243

Second language practice

In the current form of the comprehension approach as described in Chapter 1, teachers set questions before the 'intensive listening' phase to ensure that learners direct their attention to the appropriate parts of a recording. The argument is that this procedure leads to more focused listening. It also avoids the kind of heavy memory demands that occur when a listener does not know what to listen out for and tries to make a mental note of every detail of a passage. But we should recognise that, by asking questions at all, the comprehension approach deprives the listener of the decision-making process that has just been described. *It is not the listener who decides what information to focus upon and what information to ignore but the person (teacher or tester) who sets the questions.* The learner is not given the opportunity of practising one of the most important components of the listening skill – the evaluation of information in terms of whether it does or does not contribute usefully to the discourse representation. Instead, it is the questioner's view of what is important in the text that prevails.

Testers and materials writers would no doubt defend their corner by saying that they aim to distribute questions across a test, paying heed to what is or is not important. The more enlightened even aim for a balance between local and global understanding. But that is not the point. The fact is that comprehension questions effectively do the work of selection. At some point in a programme of listening training, the listener therefore needs to be given the opportunity of making these decisions for herself, as would happen in a real-life context. One way of doing this is to ask learners to note-take from time to time, and then to collect and check their notes – looking not just at the accuracy of their interpretations but also at the importance that they have accorded to individual points, and the extent to which they have succeeded in separating new points from repeated ones. Table 13.1 gives examples of two other exercises designed to foster the idea that not all parts of an L2 text are necessarily of equal relevance.

Another approach is to expose learners occasionally to speakers who are not very coherent or to speakers who express their ideas in an unfocused way, going off at tangents or providing too much supporting detail. This type of material makes an interesting contrast with commercially produced recordings (especially those that are scripted), which tend to be coherent and well structured. A useful source, curiously enough, can be found in radio interviews, which these days tend to favour informality. Both interviewers and interviewed sometimes digress, ramble or express themselves unclearly. Table 13.2 gives examples of the kind of material that can be used.

Table 13.1 *Sample exercises: selecting relevant points*

- *Relevance.* You will hear an interview with somebody who claims to have seen a strange object flying over a city. As you listen, look at the summary below.
    Underline the points which you think are important.
    Put brackets round the points which you think are not important.
    Cross out the points which are not mentioned at all in the interview.

    (Field and Wiseman, 1993: 12)

- *Main points.* The facts listed below will all be mentioned in the first part of the talk about whales which you are going to hear. Listen to the recording and tick THREE which you think are the most important points made by the speaker.
    □ People are not concerned enough about the threat to the whale.
    □ Several types of whale may become extinct.
    □ The whale is protected.
    □ Some countries do not respect international law on whales.
    □ Hundreds of whales were killed last year.
    □ Some countries worry about the incomes of their fishermen.
    □ There are many different types of whale.
    □ The biggest whale is the Blue Whale.
    □ Some whales are quite small.

    (Field and Wiseman, 1994: 258–9)

Table 13.2 *Sample exercises: text-level inference*

- *Main point.* You will hear a wordy speaker being interviewed on the radio. Decide which of the following is the MAIN answer to the question he is asked.
    a. It depends on what you are like. b. It is not a settled life.
    c. You are often poor. d. It is very tiring.
    e. No other job is as good.
    — *Would you recommend a career as an actor?*
    — *Well, it obviously depends on the kind of person you are.*

    (cont.)

Table 13.2 *(cont.)*

> *And of course it's a very unsettled life; you can never be sure*
> *that you'll get work and you're often short of money. It's very*
> *tiring, too – more tiring than people realise. But really, I have*
> *to admit there's nothing else quite like walking on to a stage.*
>   (adapted from Field and Wiseman, 1994: 21)
>
> • *Unfocused speaker.* What is the discussion about?
> *Well, I was seventy-four and a half when I first went to Nepal*
> *and I'd never thought of doing such a thing, you know, at all,*
> *it was totally out of the blue. ... In the wild I really don't*
> *mind what my hair looks like but Elizabeth asks me every*
> *morning if her hair is looking right. Whenever we stop at a*
> *camp for more than a very short time, she insists on washing*
> *it and this is a tremendous palaver...One of the problems*
> *when you're trekking is to keep your clothes clean and*
> *one of the porters always does the washing and one of my*
> *vests floated away and I suppose it's gone into the Indian*
> *Ocean down the Ganges because, I mean, I never saw it again.*
>   (Geddes, 1988: 87)

Steps should also be taken to make L2 listeners aware of the redundant nature of much speech. It may boost their morale to know that a point missed the first time round is likely to recur if it is of importance and that a string of words which proved impenetrable may be paraphrased later by the speaker in a more accessible way.

But redundancy also represents a potential pitfall. There is the danger that an unwary listener will interpret information as additive rather than repetitive: will attempt to make two points out of what should have been only one. It is a worthwhile exercise to expose learners to short pieces of circumlocutory speech and to ask them to identify when a point is introduced for the first time and when it is revisited. Table 13.3 contains an exercise that raises awareness of redundancy and another that deals with the 'repetition versus addition' problem.

After deciding that a piece of information is worth conserving, the listener needs to add it to the other pieces that she has already assembled. Several processes are involved in integrating information into a discourse representation in this way. As a simple mnemonic, let us label them 'connecting', 'comparing' and 'constructing'.

Table 13.3 *Sample exercises: recognising redundancy*

- *Repetition.* You will hear three extracts. In each, identify the important sentence, then find another sentence which says the same thing in a different way. Listen again and write down the first two words of each of them.

  a. *We really have to get this message across: smoking is bad for your health. Smokers just don't realise the damage they're doing to themselves and of course to people around them. I can't stress this enough: smoking is a major cause of illness and early death.*
  b. *We see dead fish being caught and we hear about red tides and beaches being closed to the public. But it isn't necessary for the seas to be polluted like this. We need better sewage processing and we need much more control over factory waste. We can stop marine pollution if we try.*
  c. *They really had no choice. They had to clear the squatter areas. They were overcrowded and they had no proper facilities. There were thousands of people there, packed together in very basic conditions.*
  (adapted from Field and Wiseman, 1993: 217)

- *Repetition versus addition.* Listen carefully to the speakers. Where the second sentence adds something new, write +. Where the second sentence says the same as the first one, write R (repeat).

  a. *The meal was very expensive. What's more, they'd added the bill up wrongly.*
  b. *The price has gone up by a quarter. That's an increase of 25%.*
  c. *There was no damage to the vehicle. And the driver wasn't hurt either.*
  d. *He didn't like the film we went to. It just wasn't his kind of film.*
  e. *I can't say I agree with the idea. In fact, I think it's quite wrong.*
  f. *Most washing powders get stains out. But no powder is quite like Gloxo.*

[Teachers will find many real-life examples of redundancy and addition in extracts from lecture-style material.]

13.2 Connecting

First language processing

A relationship has to be established between the incoming information and the listener's understanding of the text so far. It is helpful to think of this as resembling the process of paragraphing that a writer employs when grouping like ideas together. The listener has to decide whether the new information:

- *extends a current point* (falls within the same 'paragraph') – in which case it might do what the expansion sentences in written paragraphs often do. It might explain or rephrase what has been said, it might exemplify it; it might counter it with an alternative; it might add details; it might mention a cause or an outcome.
- *marks a new departure* (starts a new 'paragraph'). Here, the listener has to work out how the new topic or idea is connected to the one that has just finished. Sooner or later, this will shape a view of the overall structure of the conversation, broadcast, lecture, etc.

The exercise in Table 13.4 is an application of this 'paragraph' notion.

The difficulty of making connections between pieces of information may depend upon the type of text involved. A tradition in reading holds that certain texts are, broadly speaking, more demanding because of how their ideas are linked. If this is true of reading, it is even truer of listening, given the listener's need to make connections under pressure of time and her inability to look back to check understanding. A *narrative* text, a set of *instructions* or the description of a *process* usually involve temporal connections and a chronological sequence of events, which are relatively easy for the listener to grasp. More demanding are general *descriptions*, which may require the listener to construct visual or spatial

Table 13.4   *New point versus continuing point*

> *Paragraphing.* 'Formal spoken texts are a little like written ones. They fall into "paragraphs". Listen to this talk about global warming. Whenever you think that the speaker is starting a new "paragraph", write down the first three or four words of it. Listen again and check your decisions. Compare your paragraphs with those of a partner; try to say how each paragraph is linked to the one before. Then listen again and make brief notes of what the speaker says in each paragraph.'

images. More complex still are expositions; here, as noted in Chapter 12, an important factor may be how much the listener already knows about the topic. Finally, the most demanding types of listening are likely to be *discursive*, the type of exchange that occurs in the for and against of academic seminars or the monologue delivery of lectures.

Second language practice

In making the connections required by the easier text-types such as narrative, instruction or description, an L2 listener can often rely upon non-language cues – for example, the order in which events are mentioned. But in cases of exposition or discussion, the listener has to focus upon the speaker's words in order to work out the direction that the argument is taking. A widely used technique for assisting learners (especially in academic contexts) is to train them to recognise **linkers** which serve as signposts to the speaker's intentions. The linkers might be single words or phrases (*However, Next, On the other hand, Alternatively*) or they might be more elaborate (*A very different approach to this problem is to . . . , Here's an example of what I've been saying . . .*). Linkers serve two major purposes:

- They might show logical connections between one topic and another (like the examples given so far).
- They might provide a framework for the talk as a whole: *By way of introduction, To summarise, What I'm going to talk about today is . . . , What I've been trying to say is . . .*

The 'linker' approach is a useful one, especially for learners who are preparing themselves for extended listening in academic contexts; it has been used to effect in successful teaching materials such as Lynch (2004). Table 13.5 suggests possible exercises to raise awareness of linkers.

However, this approach has certain practical limitations. Firstly, within-sentence coordinators (*and, but, or*) are often brief, weak and quite difficult to perceive; the same is true of some subordinators (*if, though, so*). Secondly, linking devices do not always take the form of a standard lexical item. Formulations such as *Mind you, Problem is that . . . , That's all very well but . . .* are more likely to introduce counter-arguments in informal conversation than conventionally taught items such as *However, Nevertheless, On the other hand*. The teacher needs to be alert to examples of these less recognised ways of marking relationships when preparing a lesson from a tapescript.

Most importantly, any careful examination of natural speech shows that linkers are not as frequent in listening as our experience of reading

Table 13.5 *Raising awareness of linkers*

- *Explicit teaching.* Teacher presents the linkers most likely to be encountered in the type of listening text to be heard – including those that actually occur. Learners listen solely for linkers and note down those they hear. In pairs or in full class, they discuss what the linkers convey. Learners listen again and add a brief note of what the speaker says after each of the linkers they have identified.
- *Noticing linkers.* As above; but learners identify linkers without previous guidance.
- *Identifying linkers online.* Teacher pauses after every linker. Learners use the linkers to anticipate what the speaker will say next.
- *Macro- and micro-.* Learners identify linkers, then listen again and say whether they relate to the overall structure of the text or link ideas between adjoining sentences.

leads us to expect and as some commentators have suggested. In conversational contexts, there is a tendency to use coordinators (*and*, *but*, *so*) relatively loosely. The job of connecting turns or ideas might be done not by linkers but by the speaker echoing previously used words or repeating a syntactic pattern. Even in academic discourse, linkers are often quite scarce. Because lectures are more planned than conversation, we tend to think of them as containing carefully placed signposts to assist the listener in connecting one main point to another. Linkers are certainly used quite extensively by speakers to provide a **macro-structure** for a talk, i.e. to mark out the 'paragraphs' of the argument. But they are used loosely or sparingly within these sections to mark the connections between individual ideas.

That does not mean that the 'linker' approach is redundant. By teaching the functions of linking words, we provide an important introduction to the range of logical connections that (expressed or unexpressed) join one topic to another. Some of the more common of these relationships are shown in Table 13.6, which is partly based on Quirk *et al.*'s account of the multiple functions of *and* (1985: 930–32). These provide the instructor with a point of departure; but they need to be taught as ways of thinking about the connections between units of information rather than as pieces of language that the listener has to listen out for.

Teachers have to come to terms with the fact that linkers cannot provide the whole answer. Much of the time, the listener may need to form inferences about connections which are very loosely represented by the

Table 13.6 *Basic logical links between a speaker's points*

---

addition (= *also*)   sequence (= *then, secondly*)
result (= *consequently, so*)   cause (= *the reason is*)
alternative (= *alternatively*)   contrast (= *by contrast*)
concession (= *however*)
comment (= *what I think is*)   digression (*by the way*)
example (= *for example*)   repetition (= *in other words*)
extra details (= *in fact*)

---

words *and*, *but* and *so*, or are not expressed by the speaker but taken as understood (see the earlier discussion of inferencing in Chapter 12). One way of practising this process is by supplying learners with a list of (say) five logical links taken from Table 13.6. The teacher then plays a recording which exemplifies the links, pausing after each piece of information for learners to say how it is connected to the previous one.

13.3 Comparing

First language processing

A second part of the integration operation requires the listener to compare incoming information against the discourse representation in order to check for possible inconsistencies. These inconsistencies might derive from the input. Maybe the speaker has made an illogical leap or has contradicted something said earlier. But they might also (especially in L2 conditions) result from a failure of understanding on the part of listener.

Self-monitoring plays an extremely important part in all language skills. For example, a speaker constantly monitors his utterances to ensure that they convey to the listener the meaning that he intended. In a similar way, a listener needs to identify problems of understanding at or shortly after the point when they occur so that she can repair the breakdown by asking for repetition or clarification. Of course, where the listening task is a non-participatory one, such conflicts cannot be resolved quite so easily. Instead, the listener has to pay special attention to what comes next to see if it sheds light on the problem.

Second language practice

Second language listeners often fail to monitor their understanding adequately. There seems to be a parallel here with research into the teaching of reading to children, which shows that many young readers do not detect inconsistencies in a text. They have to focus their efforts so much upon decoding the words on the page that they do not have spare attention to give to the overall picture they are building.

Investigating this apparent parallel, I asked adult L2 listeners to summarise a text which contained contradictory pieces of information (Field, 2005b). The listeners showed a strong tendency to retain the first of the conflicting items and to omit the second. Reporting the news story of the theft of a painting which was valued first at 10 million and then at 9 million pounds, the majority opted for the earlier figure and did not even comment on the inconsistency.

These were adult listeners who undoubtedly monitored their understanding quite rigorously when listening to a speaker in their first language. Why should they have changed their behaviour when listening to a foreign language? The answers have already been given more than once in this account of meaning building. Firstly, just like young L1 readers, their attention is diverted into decoding the text and away from checking information. Secondly, if they decide to tackle any apparent inconsistency, they have to deal with a double uncertainty. Is it the new piece of information that is unreliable or is it the discourse representation that they have built up? There is no hard evidence for either, other than what the listener carries in her mind. We will return to the question of how learners handle this kind of uncertainty in due course. For the moment, it is worth noticing that it is the first version of events that they tend to report.

The tendency of listeners not to check understanding provides a further reason for playing a recording twice in the difficult conditions of a listening test. The second play allows listeners to return to problematic areas which they may have been aware of in passing but left unresolved. It enables them to reconsider the evidence and compensates to some small degree for the listeners' inability to apply repair strategies (asking for clarification) whenever a breakdown of understanding occurs.

But we also need to find ways of encouraging L2 listeners to self-monitor in second language contexts. Table 13.7 provides examples of two simple exercises.

13.4 Constructing

First language processing

As more and more information is received and connected, a listener has to impose some kind of pattern upon the discourse representation being

Table 13.7 *Sample exercises: self-monitoring*

- *Inconsistency.* Without forewarning learners, teacher reads/plays a text which contains factual inconsistencies; then checks for general understanding. Teacher plays again; learners see how many inconsistencies they can spot.

  Over the years, the British government has imposed taxes upon many different things. In fact, it was a tax on tea which led to the American Revolution. One of the strangest was a tax on men's hats, which was collected from 1784 to 1811. It was based on a scale which ranged from three pence on cheaper hats that cost under four shillings to two pence on hats that cost more than twelve shillings. Shops selling hats had to buy a licence and also had to display a special sign. To make sure the tax was collected, the government printed labels which had to be pasted inside every hat that was sold. Both the sellers of hats and the women who wore them could be prosecuted if they avoided the tax. The tax lasted for 50 years, but was abolished in 1834.

- *Comparing two accounts.* 'You will hear the statements of two witnesses of a car accident.
  a. In pairs, decide on the points on which they agree.
  b. Now listen again and identify the points on which they disagree.'

built up. She might trace the development of a conversation though a series of brief turns; or she might recognise the overall **argument structure** of a lecture or a broadcast.

Spoken discourse does not consist of a linear series of idea units. It is usually hierarchical, with some units carrying more weight than others, and some dependent upon others. Many L2 listeners find it quite difficult to identify this kind of pattern. There may be gaps in their understanding of what was said, resulting in missing links in the chain of logic. But, even where they have grasped most of the speaker's points, they may find it difficult to establish how each contributes to the message as a whole.

A useful account of comprehension by Gernsbacher (1990) represents it as **structure building**. Each time a new piece of information comes in, a listener or reader has to decide whether to persist with a current meaning structure or to shift to a new phase (cf. the 'paragraphing' suggestion in

Hierarchical

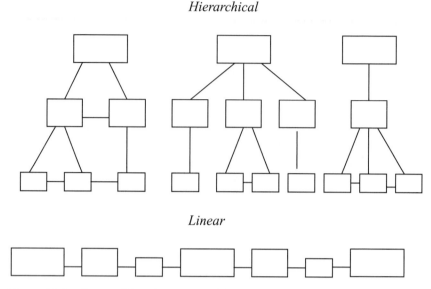

Linear

Figure 13.2   Successful and unsuccessful structure building.

Section 13.3). Less-skilled comprehenders shift too often. They thus fail to build a complex network of interrelated ideas but rely instead upon a string of small units of meaning. This in turn makes heavy demands upon memory – with the result that the poor comprehender retains much less of what has been heard or read. The two patterns of behaviour are displayed in a simplified form in Figure 13.2.

Building a complex structure like the one shown at the top of the figure is greatly helped by an understanding of how different types of speech event are organised. The knowledge is said to be stored in the form of schemas like those discussed in Chapter 12. The way these **formal schemas** assist listening is through analogy: the listener thinks back to her experience of other listening events that resemble the one in progress. For example, it pays to know that lecturers usually begin with an outline of what the lecture is to cover and end with a summary of points raised. In between, they are likely to adopt one of a limited number of discourse patterns, such as 'argument for – argument against' or 'problem – solution'. Similarly, in understanding the radio news, it is useful to know that the headlines are traditionally read first, followed by more extensive coverage of the stories that have been mentioned – in the same sequence as the headlines.

Second language practice

Listeners face a number of problems in building structures in a second language. As ever, there is the question of *attention* (the additional demands made by L2 decoding) and there is the question of *partial understanding* (important links in the chain may have been missed). These factors seem to have a particular impact upon a listener's ability to identify a speaker's line of argument. The listener's scale of priorities in meaning building seems to be heavily weighted towards smaller-scale operations. There may also be cultural impediments: speakers in the target language may structure their ideas differently, so that formal schemas carried over from L1 are misleading.

Two needs have to be addressed. Firstly, we should train learners to discriminate between major and minor points (Table 13.8).

Table 13.8 *Exercises on awareness of main and subsidiary points*

- *Locating main points.* (a) You will hear a summary in simple language of the recording you are about to hear. Discuss it, and make a note of the main points. (b) Listen to the full recording. Each time you hear one of the main points being made, put up your hand / write down two or three key words. (c) Listen again. Your teacher will pause at the main points. What extra information can you add?

- *Identifying main points.* On your worksheet you will see a list of main points that will be made by the speaker. They are not in the order in which they appear in the recording. As you hear the speaker making these points, number them. Note: the speaker will not use the same words as on the worksheet.

Secondly, we should help learners to recognise organisational patterns in a text. This can be a rather abstract exercise. A good way of tackling the issue concretely is to focus upon patterns of logic that occur at a local level. One of the more frequent is a **general–specific** sequence, of the kind that is often discussed when teaching L2 reading skills. A simple exercise might build on the 'paragraphing' idea put forward in Section 13.3. A teacher first asks learners to identify each new 'listening paragraph' in a passage and to write down its opening words. A second play then serves to draw learners' attention to the fact that, in many cases, these words mark the beginning of **topic sentences** of exactly the kind one encounters in reading. They are followed by expansions of various kinds, performing functions like those in reading texts: exemplification, explanation, restatement, result, contrast, alternative, comment, supporting detail. Table 13.9 suggests two variations on this general approach.

Table 13.9 *Sample exercises: topic sentences and expansions*

> - *Expansions.* (a) After you have listened to the recording, write down in your own words the [THREE] topics which the speaker covered. (b) Listen again. This time, write down the first two or three words of each of the sentences which introduced the three topics. (c) Now your teacher will play the recording, one sentence at a time. You must say if the sentence you hear
>   1. introduces a new topic.
>   2. gives an explanation of the sentence before.
>   3. gives an example.
>   4. provides evidence or extra details.
>   5. says the same as the sentence before but uses new words.
>
> - *Skeleton summary.* Your teacher will provide you with a skeleton summary of the text you will hear.
>   (a) Listen and write down the main points (A, B and C).
>   (b) Listen again and fill in the missing secondary points.
>   (c) Listen again and add figures from the recording that support the points. Sample summary:
>
>> A. Problems with .....
>>   1. ....
>>   2. ....
>>   3. ....
>> B. Solutions suggested by .....
>>   1. Solution 1 ....
>>   For ....
>>   Against ....
>>   2. Solution 2 ....
>>   For ....
>>   Against ....
>> C. Decision reached .....

It was suggested above that learners do not build the kind of complex structure that efficient listeners produce because their attention is too preoccupied with low-level matters such as decoding and tracing links between adjacent utterances. One way of counteracting this is to separate the lower-level and higher-level operations during listening instruction, thus reducing the cognitive demands upon the learner. It entails playing the recording twice: once for listeners to focus on acquiring information and once for them to trace the overall pattern of argument.

A more explicit approach might require learners to note down as much information as seems relevant during the first hearing – achieving the process of *selecting* (Section 13.3) but little more. Learners are then asked, singly or in pairs, to classify the main points they have listed as 'macro-' or 'micro-', and to reach conclusions as to the patterns of logic which link the former. Replaying the recording then permits them to evaluate these decisions and to revise them if necessary (see Table 13.10).

Table 13.10   *Exercises that separate information and text structure*

- *Two plays.* (a) Listen to the recording. Make notes of the important points made by the speaker. Check the points with a partner. Suggest how the points are connected. (b) Listen to the recording again. Check that you have followed the overall structure of what the speaker says. (c) One student will present his/her summary to the class. See if you agree.

- *Macro- and micro-.* (a) Listen to the recording. Make notes of what the speaker says. (b) Decide which of these are MAIN points and which are secondary points. Compare with a partner. Then listen again to check. (c) Now discuss with your partner what the connections are between the points. (d) Listen again and check that you have understood the arguments. (e) Discuss in full class.

Once again, the value of replaying the recording is indicated – here as part of a staged approach to two processes which learners will ultimately need to combine. The usefulness of dividing tasks in this way is supported by research carried out by Buck (1990), who concluded that listeners approach a recording in a different way when they hear it for the second time. *Listening to a replay (especially of longer monologue material) is not just a repetition of an earlier activity; it is qualitatively different from the first hearing because of the information that learners have acquired.*

13.5 The discourse representation: dealing with uncertainty

We have examined the decisions that a listener makes when adding new pieces of information to an ongoing discourse representation. We will now look briefly at the representation itself.

13.5.1 Indeterminate representations

First language processing

For a number of reasons, the discourse representation constructed by a listener is rather different from the one constructed by a reader. Readers have a permanent record available to them on the page and can therefore re-read to check understanding. In addition, if readers have trouble in constructing a representation (difficulties of decoding or difficulties of interpretation), they can take time to study the text in a way the listener cannot. The representation constructed by a listener is both less tangible in not being supported by physical evidence and hastier because of the onward progress of the speaker's voice. We should not be surprised if it is more rudimentary than the representation of a reader.

It is certainly the case that listeners show themselves more willing than readers to accept an **indeterminate representation,** one from which details may be missing. Rather than increasing the attention that they give to passages that contain technical vocabulary or complex argumentation, they satisfy themselves with a more general picture until such time as the input becomes easier to process.

Second language practice

Similar behaviour has been observed among those who are listening to a second language. Lund (1991) compared the way in which L2 listeners and readers represented the same text. The listeners reported more main ideas but fewer details than the readers. They were also more likely to invent new information or frame incorrect but plausible contexts.

Nevertheless, not all L2 listeners feel comfortable about accepting an indeterminate representation. Willingness to listen in this way appears to be a reflection of an individual's **listening style** or of their attitude to learning. Learners from certain cultures take a very localistic approach to second language listening (and to language learning in general) and are easily fazed by encountering unknown vocabulary, complex sentences

Table 13.11 *Exercises in accepting an incomplete representation*

- *Listening for gist (conversation)*
  'Listen to the recording. Do not expect to understand everything. Just tell me:
  How many speakers are there?
  What are they talking about?
  What is the point of view of each one?'
- *Listening for gist (monologue)*
  'Listen to the recording. Do not expect to understand everything. Now listen again and write down the [FOUR] points that the speaker makes.'
- *Paused listening*
  Teacher pauses a recording after each proposition.
  'You will hear a recording divided into short pieces. After each one, try to write down the most important word (the one that carries stress). Do not worry if you do not understand it; just wait for the next piece. Then look at the words you have written down. Try to work out the meaning of what you have heard so far. Listen again.'

or dense argument. Particularly with these listeners, it is important to provide practice that licenses an account that is accurate but not detailed. One way of achieving this within a traditional comprehension format is to establish the difficulty of the listening exercise not by reference to the language of the recording but by reference to the task that is set. The teacher might ask a group of elementary learners to listen to a pop song and identify how many times the singer uses the words *yesterday* and *tomorrow*. The teacher might ask them to listen to a piece of news and summarise in one sentence what has happened. This kind of lesson demonstrates to the more cautious learner that it is not necessary to understand everything in order to accomplish a listening task satisfactorily. See the more extended discussion in Chapter 14.

In addition, teachers can provide exercises that are specifically designed to encourage listeners to construct indeterminate representations. Table 13.11 covers questions that focus on gist, while Table 13.12 contains an example of a task that requires learners to report only a general context for what they have heard.

Table 13.12 *Sample exercise: working out context*

> You will hear the opening words from three sports commentaries. Listen for the stressed words and try to work out which sport is being described.
>
> a. *It's a fine day here and the teams have just come on to the pitch. The away team, you'll remember, with a new captain after Graham Hill sustained a leg injury in the last match they played. That, of course, was the match that got them into this final with an amazing four–nil win.*
> b. *And now into the ring comes Tony Green, lightweight champion of the world. He's coming forward for the referee to check his gloves, and then it's back to the blue corner.*
> c. *Welcome back to the centre court where the first match of the day has just begun. And it's Walker to serve ... a fine service, that, the ball just over the net...*
>
> (adapted from Field and Wiseman, 1994: 88)

13.5.2 Laying the foundations

First language processing

A listener begins to construct a discourse representation from the very beginning of a listening encounter. Even before the encounter, a wise listener attempts to predict what will be said, in terms either of the ideas that will be mentioned or of the words that are likely to be used. If the listening is participatory, the listener might speculate about the words the speaker might use and what an appropriate response might be. This kind of mental rehearsal is a useful technique for both receiving and producing language. If the listening is non-participatory (a lecture, a radio broadcast or a film), an efficient listener might, as discussed in the previous chapter, activate relevant schemas for the topic.

Second language practice

So far as listening instruction is concerned, thinking ahead before listening is a standard part of current classroom practice. Chapter 1 referred to the convention of using a pre-listening slot not only to provide a context for a recording but also to stimulate curiosity about what will be heard. Listeners then go on to check their expectations against what is actually said, so as to confirm or revise them. The result is a much more focused listening experience than if the listener approaches the encounter with no previous opportunity for reflection.

Of course, many real-life encounters are unpremeditated and/or unpredictable in terms of their content. In these circumstances, the beginning of an encounter requires an exceptionally high level of attention from the L2 listener. Precisely because there are no clear presuppositions, the listener has to work hard to lay the foundations for a discourse representation and to predict the direction that the speaker is likely to take.

So, one way or the other, L2 listeners pay special heed to the early parts of a listening passage as the basis for constructing an initial discourse representation. This suggests that the opening sentences of the passage carry particular weight.[1] The level of difficulty of a text is thus reduced if the first part explicitly specifies the areas that are to be addressed. But the level increases if the first part is introductory or relates to areas that are irrelevant to the main discussion.

In principle, listeners should be sensitive to the fact that any representation which they construct early on in a listening event is provisional and must be tested against new evidence as it comes in. In practice, many of them do not seem to operate in this way. Instead of rejecting an early hypothesis when it is disconfirmed, they come to rely upon it and may even reshape later information to make it fit their initial expectations.

Why do L2 listeners cling to a provisional discourse representation even in the face of contrary evidence? One reason is that a lack of confidence in their decoding skills and the transitory nature of the signal makes them cautious about the accuracy of the bottom-up information they receive. But there also seems to be what might be called an **investment principle** at work. Having invested time and thought into constructing a discourse representation, the listener seems reluctant to abandon it. The notion that 'a bird in the hand is worth two in the bush' seems to carry the day. In test conditions, dropping a provisional representation might amount to having to start all over again part way through listening. In addition, the tape is rolling on remorselessly, and, while focusing on incoming information, the listener may not have sufficient spare mental capacity to start rethinking established assumptions.

There is nothing wrong with using provisional discourse representations to guide listening; but learners appear insufficiently sensitive to the danger that a wrong representation will distort understanding. Teachers need to design their pedagogy so as to encourage L2 listeners to construct and carry forward hypotheses; they also need to ensure that

---

[1] Gernsbacher (1990) refers to this as the *advantage of first mention*.

Table 13.13 *Exercise in building a discourse representation*

- *Initial representation*
  Listen to the first 20 seconds of the recording.
  a. What do you think it is about? Discuss with a partner.
  b. What are the main points made by the speaker? Discuss with
     a partner.
- *Approximate representation*
  c. How sure are you of your answers in (a) and (b)? 20%?
     80%? Did you disagree with your partner?
- *Checking understanding*
  d. Listen carefully to the next 20 seconds. Is there anything you
     want to change? Discuss in pairs.

---

learners test these hypotheses against subsequent evidence. Table 13.13
suggests questions that encourage learners to construct a discourse representation as the recording proceeds but, importantly, to keep monitoring
it to be sure it is correct.

    Clearly, in this exercise it is important for a teacher to adopt the kind
of non-interventionist stance recommended in Chapter 3 and to leave
it to the learners to resolve and rethink any contradictions that occur
during the course of the recording. As learners become more competent
at checking their representations, the teacher can extend the excerpt that
is played.

13.6 Anticipation

One aspect of higher-level processing much highlighted in teacher manuals has not so far been discussed: the value of anticipating what the
speaker will say next. In its strongest form, the argument goes as follows: *Good listeners use the text-so-far to anticipate what a speaker
is going to say. This enables them to 'tune out'. All they need to do
is to monitor the actual words that are used to see if they confirm
their expectations. In this way, they gain a respite from the demands of
listening.*

    This version of events may perhaps derive from Goodman's (1967)
much-criticised account of reading as a 'psycholinguistic guessing game'.
In terms of our current state of knowledge of language processing, it does
not hold water. The reasons were briefly discussed in Chapter 8. Firstly, a

'good' native listener does not find decoding effortful; it is usually highly automatic, whereas the process of anticipating and checking what a speaker will say next makes enormous demands upon the attention. The 'anticipation' account thus suggests that we employ an onerous process to spare ourselves one that is effortless. The second reason for distrusting the account is that, as this chapter has tried to show, listening is an extremely demanding and complex activity. Large reserves of the expert listener's attention are dedicated to integrating incoming information into the discourse representation that has been established so far. This forms the listener's primary goal at this level, a goal that might be severely compromised if at the same time the listener were trying to anticipate the speaker's next words.

That said, one should not dismiss the 'anticipation' account entirely. The listener's priority is to build and sustain an up-to-date discourse representation; but there is definite value, *when pauses in the discourse allow*, in using the representation to anticipate what is to come. As we have already seen, some kind of expectation of what a speaker is going to say leads to more focused listening, in which the listener confirms or revises earlier presuppositions. Note, however, that this is very different from the argument that the listener uses anticipation to spare herself the effort of decoding.

Training in 'anticipation' is sometimes included in listening skills methodology. Two types of exercise are employed, one relating to meaning and one to form. In one, the teacher pauses the recording and asks learners to anticipate what will happen next. In the other, the teacher plays the first half of a sentence and asks learners to anticipate the wording of the remainder. In the light of what has just been argued, should we abandon these types of activity?

My answer would be no. But we should revise what we claim to be their purpose. Instead of urging the value of 'anticipation training', we might regard the first exercise as providing listeners with a breathing space in which they have to construct a discourse representation of what has been heard so far, one which is rather deeper than the model they might form while engaged in listening. After the pause, they will need to check that representation (and indeed the expectations they have formed) against what actually comes next. In other words, the exercise provides training in two processes which are unequivocally part of good listening: the construction of an ongoing mental model of what has been said and the constant monitoring of understanding. The exercise also, of course, emulates what an expert listener normally does at the end of a speaker's turn: namely, exploit any pause in order to anticipate what direction a conversation will now take.

Similarly, the second exercise provides practice in the process of syntactic parsing. We have seen that listening proceeds online, with the listener constructing provisional word matches as the speaker proceeds. Pausing an utterance in the middle obliges the listener to engage in this online process, in terms of both the words used and the grammatical pattern that is beginning to emerge. Once again, the value lies less in what is to come than in establishing good practice in relation to what went before.

13.8 Conclusion

We have now finished examining the processes used by an expert listener. In Appendix 1 you will find a comprehensive list of the decoding processes that have been discussed, and in Appendix 2 a list of the meaning-building processes. This lengthy exposition, over six chapters, has had several important goals. Firstly, it has aimed to correct a number of misconceptions concerning the process of L1 and L2 listening and to address a number of questions left unanswered by the all-pervasive comprehension approach. If future teachers of the skill are better briefed, they will be more able to evaluate the materials which they use and the practices which they adopt.

The second goal has been to draw attention to the challenges which face someone who wishes to acquire listening competence in a second language. Again, this is an aspect which the simple solutions of the comprehension approach have tended to obscure. It is to the advantage of any instructor to have a close understanding of what goes on in the minds of second language listeners, and of the processes in which they engage.

A third goal, in Chapters 8 to 11, was to underline the important and sometimes neglected contribution made by decoding skills to successful listening. The ability to match input to words efficiently is a fundamental need of L2 listeners in that it frees their attention for meaning building and thus enables them to perform in ways that more closely resemble native listeners. Decoding should therefore be awarded high priority in the early stages of any listening programme.

The exercises proposed in Chapters 12 and 13 promote the transfer to L2 of meaning-building operations. These processes are in the main already established and used to effect in L1. But it was argued that they are not necessarily brought into play when a learner is listening to a foreign language, because of the unfamiliarity of the experience and gaps in understanding. The purpose of the exercises that have been recommended is thus not to train learners from scratch but to ensure that well-practised L1 processes are applied in the special conditions of L2 listening.

It is important to note that the processes modelled in these exercises are restricted to those that form part of general listening competence. They entail using context, forming inferences, building meaning structure and so on in the way a native listener would. Similar processes can also be used to serve a very different purpose: namely to compensate for gaps in understanding. In this form, they might assist the L1 listener occasionally in conditions of noise; but they are much more vital to an L2 listener with uncertain decoding skills and limited vocabulary and grammar. These techniques, characterised as strategies, have not been considered so far but will come to the fore in the next and final part of this book, when we examine ways of equipping the learner to cope with real-life listening encounters.

A progressive programme of exercises of the kind exemplified in these six chapters aims to equip a learner with a competence that will in due course ensure successful decoding and meaning building. But while the listener is acquiring these skills, she needs to hold her own somehow in the real world of conversation, TV broadcasts, lectures and so on. She needs to be able to extract, if not the whole of a speaker's intentions, at least sufficient for the bare bones of the message to be understood. We therefore turn now to the kinds of expedient that enable the listener to cope with L2 input despite limited experience and limited linguistic knowledge.

Further reading

Chaudron, C. and Richards, J. (1986) 'The effect of discourse markers on the comprehension of lectures'. *Applied Linguistics*, 7: 113–27.
Gernsbacher, M-A. (1990) *Language Comprehension as Structure Building*. Mahwah, NJ: Erlbaum.

Part V: The challenge of the real world

14   Real speech

Remember there's always a voice saying the right thing to
you somewhere if you'll only listen for it.
Thomas Hughes (1822–1896), British educationalist

So far, I have argued strongly in this book for an approach to L2 listening which builds the skill incrementally. But there is a problem with any developmental approach of this kind. At the same time as learners are acquiring the relevant processes, they also need to make use of the skill. In the case of ESL learners, they may have to survive in the world outside the classroom; in the case of EFL learners, they may be confronted with examples of the target language which they wish to access. It is therefore important to balance the gradualistic approach recommended here with one that equips learners as early as possible to deal with everyday listening encounters in L2. If we do not do this, the learner is likely to feel a strong sense of frustration and even to conclude that the effort put in to small-scale exercises is not feeding through into listening competence.

The remainder of the book tackles the issue of how we can equip a learner with limited linguistic knowledge to meet the challenge of real-life listening. In this chapter, we consider an issue that has been touched upon a number of times but not discussed in depth: the role of recordings that expose the learner to the unscripted speech of the world outside the classroom. In subsequent chapters, we examine the strategies that learners employ when they have to make sense of natural spoken language that has not been simplified or slowed down to fit their supposed learning needs.

14.1 Authentic recordings

14.1.1 What is 'authentic'?

The notion of authenticity has been much discussed. It has been claimed that it should apply not only to the materials used in teaching but also to the circumstances under which they are used. It would be rash to pretend that the listening lesson can ever fully replicate the circumstances of the type of listening that takes place outside the classroom – or indeed that the tasks and exercises that we set bear anything more than a superficial resemblance to those in which real-life listeners engage. So the focus of this discussion will be entirely on the use of 'authentic recordings' – recordings of people speaking naturally and without the purposes of language learning in mind.[1] Morrow's (1977) definition of 'authenticity' will serve us well: he relates it to 'a stretch of real language, produced by a real speaker or writer for a real audience and designed to carry a real message of some sort'.

If one adopts a definition of 'authentic' based upon original purpose, it means that authentic recordings should be taken to cover a wide spectrum of styles from formal (an interview) and even 'read aloud' (the radio news) to very informal (a pub conversation). One cannot assume that 'authentic' is synonymous with 'conversational'. More meaningful ways of contrasting authentic listening recordings with those that are not authentic are in terms of:

- **graded** versus ungraded. Purpose-written materials make certain assumptions about the level of linguistic knowledge of the target user: at lower levels of L2 proficiency, they aim for simple syntactic structures and high-frequency vocabulary. Some recordings may also employ a reduced speech rate in the belief that it assists decoding. By contrast, authentic recordings are subject to no such constraints.

- **scripted** versus unscripted. Purpose-written materials are performed by speakers who operate in studio conditions and read aloud from a script. The script may well have been written in a way that attempts to reproduce many of the features of written conversation; but it is not spontaneous and its rendition is very much dependent upon the acting skills of the performers.

Both contrasts should be treated as to some extent relative. Thus, it is perfectly possible to grade authentic recordings; the difference is that one checks them for language level *after* the recording has been collected rather than before. One might even edit them, if necessary, by excising any complicated sequences. As for scripting, we have already noted that authentic recordings include certain types such as news broadcasts, dramas or talks which have their origins in a written text. Nevertheless, the terms 'ungraded' and 'unscripted' are useful because they serve to remind us of the precise reasons for wishing to employ authentic recordings in the first place.

---

[1] To this, one might add 'or without a non-native listener in mind' so as to exclude 'foreigner speak' and non-standard forms such as Voice of America's Special English.

14.1.2 Graded versus ungraded

Let us assume that the result of grading the language in a listening passage is that the majority of the passage in question is understood by the listener. It is an enormous assumption, because it ignores the important distinction (to which attention has often been drawn) between knowing a word or grammatical pattern and recognising it when it occurs in connected speech. However, let us adopt it for the sake of argument. If the L2 listener becomes accustomed to hearing only language that is familiar, then she will not have been adequately prepared for the experience of listening outside the classroom. In the real world, speakers may make adjustments to reflect the assumed level of the non-native listener, but they do not consistently edit out words, expressions and grammatical forms that the listener does not know. In order to function effectively as an L2 listener, *a learner needs extensive experience of handling input in which a proportion (sometimes a large proportion) of the language is not known and recognised.* She needs to acquire techniques for dealing with conditions of uncertainty that simply do not occur in L1 listening. From this point of view, it is essential that a listener is given practice in handling recorded material which contains passages that go beyond what she is capable of producing as a speaker, and that she learns either to ignore these passages or to devise ways of inferring their meaning from the wider context. Exposing a listener only to graded material is like feeding a child exclusively on baby food and then wondering why the child cannot cope with an adult diet.

We should also be wary of jumping to the conclusion that a simplified text is necessarily easier to process than an authentic one. Consider the following exchange (I give rather an extreme example in order to make the point):

A: *Where do you buy your FOOD?*
B: *I DON'T LIKE supermarkets + I buy my meat at a BUTcher's + I buy my fruit and vegetables in the MARket + they're cheaper there + I buy other things in a CORner shop + it's open late at NIGHT.*

If anything, the simplified syntax and lack of cohesion end up obscuring the patterns of thought which link the sentences. Furthermore, the conversation bears very little resemblance to the way in which real speech is shaped by the speaker's need to plan ahead while he is in the course of speaking. Compare this alternative, which more closely resembles natural speech:

A: *where do you buy your food?*

B: *well, I'm not too keen on supermarkets, so I get my + meat in a BUTcher's + FRUIT and VEG + I get in the MARket 'cos they're much CHEAPer + and then other sort of + EVeryday things you know + BUTter and MILK and BREAD and suchlike + I get in our CORner shop + handy because it stays open LATE*

There are several features here which, far from complicating matters, positively assist the listener. There are planning and hesitation pauses as well as fillers (*sort of, you know, and suchlike*). The speaker employs them to gain time for forward planning; but they also give the listener time to review what has been heard. The central topic of two of the sentences is brought into prominence by ignoring the standard Subject–Verb–Object word order and moving it to the beginning. This obviously assists a listener who is processing input on a word-by-word basis. While the syntactic structure remains rather loose, logical connections are made between the different points. The text thus not only gives the listener a better flavour of real-life listening but, in processing terms, may actually be easier to follow.

14.1.3 Scripted versus unscripted

Similar points can be made about scripted texts. Here, the first imponderable is whether the writer of the script has an ear that is sufficiently sensitive to the rhythms and idioms of everyday speech. Even if we assume that he does, the script will have been made available to the actors in the form of neatly typed sentences, beginning with a capital letter and ending with a full stop. The sentences may contain the odd *erm* or *well* inserted by the writer, but in general they will be complete and well formed. They will be uttered ready-made and will therefore lack the characteristics of speech that is being planned online, while a conversation is actually in progress. In these circumstances, the content of scripted recordings is bound to be phonologically different from natural spontaneous speech. It is vital that we also make use of material that has not been specially written, so as to expose learners to the hesitations, false starts, fillers and incomplete utterances that they are likely to encounter.

There are, of course, certain problems in obtaining and using speech that is unscripted. It is necessary to gain the permission of the speakers if one is recording conversations, and their normal behaviour may change markedly if they know that they are being recorded. The quality of the recording may not be as good as it would be in studio conditions, while external noise may add unfairly to the demands placed upon the listener. Furthermore, much of the content of everyday speech is, frankly, boring and not at all motivating for a language learner to listen to.

Such objections are quite routinely heard, and they have led publishers and examination boards to explore possible middle ways between scripted and authentic material. They have come to rely quite heavily upon two solutions:

- **re-recording**, in which an authentic text is transcribed and then recorded again by actors in a studio;
- **improvisation**, in which actors are given a set of general instructions and asked to act out a monologue or dialogue along the lines suggested.

These types of recording are often described rather enigmatically in publisher's blurbs as 'semi-authentic'. The claim is sometimes made that a particular set of materials contains 'a mixture of authentic and semi-authentic passages', though the vast majority often prove to be semi-authentic.

A few years ago, I identified listening passages from international tests which were representative of the four types of recording (scripted, authentic, re-recorded and improvised) and played them to various groups of overseas teachers. The teachers showed a high level of accuracy in identifying the source of each passage. This suggested that each type was phonologically distinctive and, importantly, that the re-recorded and improvised recordings did not really reproduce the features of authentic speech.

The re-recorded text had none of the hesitancy or false starts which characterise speech that is being planned on the fly. The neatness of the turn-taking provided evidence that a script was involved, and sentence endings were clearly and consistently marked with pauses which showed that the actor had encountered a full stop. As for the improvised recording, it contained hesitation and overlapping turns like those in real-life contexts, but both features seemed to be by-products of the need to keep finding new ideas so as to keep the conversation going.

The conclusion is clear. When speakers are armed with a script, it is extremely difficult for them to simulate the online planning that takes place during spontaneous speech and gives rise to pauses, unfinished utterances, ragged turn-taking and so on. If the teacher's goal is to expose the learners to the rhythms and discourse features of natural speech, it is worthwhile, wherever possible, to make use of recordings that really are authentic in origin.

14.2 Sources for authentic recordings

But where are such recordings to come from? There are relatively few published courses that exclusively feature authentic material. Among the best and most varied are the old Underwood recordings (1975, 1976), to which some readers may still have access, though the accompanying exercises are limited in scope and now out of print. Of more recent 'skills series' courses, the one that stands out for variety of topic and voices is Collie and Slater (1995). For students of American English, there is a valuable recent resource in Hauck, MacDougall and Isay (2001). For academic English, Campbell and Smith (2007) provide a range of well-chosen lecture material.

The alternative is for language teachers to collect their own recordings. In the past, discussion of the practicality of doing so was often muddied by the confusion between 'authenticity' and informality. There was an assumption that truly authentic recordings consisted of personal conversations; hence the concerns expressed about the boring and inconsequential nature of authentic materials and the problems of 'noise'. However, if we adopt a definition of 'authentic' as 'designed without language learning in mind', it is evident that there is a wealth of material available from radio, TV and the Internet. The original recording is always of a high standard, and, as the world moves over to digital transmission, it can be downloaded by a teacher with no loss of sound quality.

The issue becomes not how to obtain the material, but how to select from what is available. It is here that the points outlined in the last section become relevant. The goal must be to ensure firstly that the learner is exposed to the rhythms of everyday speech and secondly that she is given adequate practice in making sense of input that is only partly understood.

A great deal will depend upon the needs of the learners. For a group that anticipates going on to study in the target language, the principal concern will be to obtain lecture and seminar material covering a range of different presentational styles. For the more general learner, two considerations might be uppermost:

> To what extent is the language of the text representative of natural speech in the target context?
> To what extent does the performance of the speakers embody elements of the spontaneity which characterises unrehearsed speech?

To put it more concretely, one might prefer a recording of an ordinary individual talking about his or her life (Underwood, 1975; Collie and Slater, 1995; Hauck, MacDougall and Isay, 2001) over an equally 'authentic' radio discussion of a political issue, in which speakers weigh their words so as to put across a point of view coherently. One might prefer a broadcaster such as the late Alistair Cooke, who famously improvised from notes, over a radio drama in which the actors, however convincing in their roles, tend to pause in predictable places and allocate sentence stress very consistently.

The criteria that have just been suggested are not as limiting as they might sound. There has been a sea change in the style of radio and TV presentation in the past 30 years, and a cult of informality has developed. Broadcast interviews are much more loosely constructed than they used to be, with the interviewer following lines of enquiry as they emerge rather than rigidly pre-planning a set of questions.[2] Presenters of news programmes like to sound chatty and may end up improvising and presenting their ideas in a fragmented way. Even the weather forecast is sometimes constructed ad lib by the presenter around a number of main points. A further extremely rich source of unplanned language can be found in the increasing prevalence of vox pop and 'fly on the wall' programmes on most American and European broadcasting networks and some Far Eastern ones. In all these instances, speech is being planned and delivered spontaneously and with minimal scripting; this means that it bears a much closer resemblance to natural everyday speech than does (ironically) the delivery of dialogue in a soap opera or Hollywood movie.

Though spontaneity represents a useful criterion, a place still needs to be made for more controlled types of presentation such as news broadcasts, pre-scripted talks, train and plane announcements, dramas, documentaries or advertisements. One cannot claim that they possess the spontaneity of unplanned speech, but they certainly represent a particular speech genre with which the learner may have to deal in a target language environment. The value of using authentic versions resides in the fact that their presentational style will be unequivocally the style which is associated with the genre in question, and not a simulation.

McGrath (2002: 106) provides a useful set of guiding principles for choosing authentic materials, which apply as much to the teaching of listening skills as to other areas. They are (with my own comments added to make connections to listening):

• Relevance (to syllabus, to learners' needs): *To what extent does the recording represent the type of spoken input that a learner will encounter? How relevant is the listening task to real-life contexts?*

---

[2] Beware, though, of politicians, who, for all their apparent informality, have often carefully rehearsed all possible answers to an interviewer's questions. Note their lack of hesitation pauses, their use of carefully polished chunks and the regularity with which they place their sentence stress.

- Intrinsic interest of topic/theme: *How easy is it to create interest in the topic at a pre-listening stage? How familiar is the topic – bearing in mind that topic knowledge is a factor which facilitates understanding?*
- Cultural appropriateness: *Is there any culture-specific content in the recording which would (a) reduce its comprehensibility to listeners from other cultural backgrounds; (b) potentially cause cultural offence?*
- Linguistic demands: *Is the critical vocabulary in the recording (i.e. words central to an understanding of the topic) likely to be familiar to the listener? To what extent does the task rely upon the ability to decode the linguistic content? To what extent can the task be achieved without a full understanding of the linguistic content?*
- Cognitive demands: *How complex are the ideas in the recording? How dense are they? How complex are the relationships between the ideas? How complex is the overall argument structure?*
- Logistical considerations, e.g. length, audibility: *How long is the recording (allowing for the fact that it may need to be replayed four or five times)?*
- Quality: *How good is the quality? How clearly do the speakers articulate?*
- Exploitability: *To what extent does the recording lend itself to extended tasks which clearly indicate comprehension at both local and global levels?*

14.3 Who benefits from authentic recordings?

There is a conservative view that the proper place for authentic recordings is in listening courses designed for learners at more advanced levels. The belief is that it is better to start listeners off with graded/scripted recordings which permit the materials developer to control content, before exposing them to the greater demands of authentic ones.

A case can certainly be made for using simplified materials in the early stages of L2 learning. Self-confidence and motivation are important factors in fostering 'can do' attitudes towards the daunting task of listening to speech in an unfamiliar tongue. Learners are easily deterred if they are asked to make sense of strings of sounds which they are entirely unable to deconstruct. It is therefore critical to present them with listening exercises which they feel are within their competence.

So can a case be made for using authentic recordings during the early stages of L2 learning? There can be no doubt of the answer if one harks back to the purposes outlined above for using such materials. *We use authentic recordings to expose the listener to the natural cadences of the target language and to train the learner in the unfamiliar process of extrapolating meaning from a piece of speech that may only partly have been understood.* On this analysis, experience of authentic speech is as important to the novice as it is to the more advanced learner. If we limit the early listener's experience to scripted material, we deny her the opportunity of hearing what L2 really sounds like. If we limit the listener's experience to what has been graded to fit her language level, we are not equipping her to cope if and when she comes face to face with the target language in the outside world.

Some teachers may well respond that their learners have little or no opportunity to travel to areas where the target language is spoken. But today that is no longer the issue. Thanks to globalisation and satellite communications, learners have increasing possibilities of contact with other languages, even within the bounds of their own country. Some of the most productive language learning can take place in the world outside the classroom – but only if the learners are adequately equipped to take advantage of any examples of the target language that they may encounter (Field, 2007). The experience might entail as little as identifying a few dislocated words in a film, a pop song or a radio broadcast. But achieving this simple piece of decoding in relation to natural language may mark the first step towards the deconstruction of complete messages. Very importantly, learners' motivation is boosted enormously by evidence that they can apply classroom learning to instances of L2 in the real world.

It is wrong to treat the function of the listening teacher as limited to assisting learners to make sense of set texts. Equally, if not more, important is the need to equip learners to deal with the examples of L2 which they meet outside the classroom, and to enable them to make use of such encounters to add to their repertoire of linguistic knowledge. We should not just be training learners to meet the requirements of the curriculum; we should also be providing them with listening skills which enable them to continue acquiring L2 once they have left our care. For this reason, it makes sense to ensure that learners have experience of authentic speech from an early stage.

But how practical is it to introduce authentic recordings to L2 learners at an elementary level of proficiency? The first consideration is adequate preparation. Learners only find their first encounter with natural speech disheartening if they expect (on the basis of their experience with scripted materials) to understand every word. It is a question of mind-set. If learners are forewarned that their understanding will be partial – and above all if they are allowed the opportunity to form and discuss hypotheses and to hear multiple-plays – they are by no means daunted by an authentic piece of listening material. Indeed, the reverse is often true: learners report that they find it extremely motivating to get to grips with samples of the real language rather than a text that has been artificially simplified.

There are at least three ways in which a teacher can ensure that an authentic recording falls within the listening competence of the learners:

- *Simplifying the task.* The most commonly applied principle is to counterbalance the increased linguistic difficulty of the text by simplifying the requirements of the task that is set (see Anderson and Lynch, 1988: 87–96, for a discussion). To give a very simple example, several years ago, I featured a Frank Sinatra recording of a song called *Good night, Irene* in the very first programme of a BBC series for beginners. The song ran as follows:

  > *Irene, good night, Irene.*
  > *Irene, good night.*
  > *Good night, Irene, good night, Irene.*
  > *I'll see you in my dreams.*

  The producer expressed some concern: this was, after all, the first programme and only two of the words in the song were within the learner's vocabulary. But all the learner was required to do was (as the reader has probably already guessed) to count how many times Frank Sinatra said the words *Good night*. The point is that it is not necessarily the language that makes a piece of listening difficult; ease or difficulty also resides in the task that is set. It is perfectly possible to use a listening passage which is well beyond the learner's level, provided that what is demanded of the learner is correspondingly simple. If one notches up the text, one notches down the task.[3]

  In this spirit, first approaches to an authentic text can make use of the very general types of question that are often used in the 'extensive listening' phase of a lesson:

  > *How many people are speaking? Who are they? Where are they?*
  > *What are they talking about?*
  > *What are their attitudes to the topic / to each other?*
  > *Can you identify three important points that they make?*

---

[3] Incidentally, the BBC received positive feedback from learners – illustrating the earlier point about the motivating effect of exposure to authentic language.

Learners can also be supported in advance of listening by telling them where to direct their attention:

> *Listen carefully to the first two sentences.*
> *Listen carefully when I raise my hand.*
> *The word X is very important in this text. Listen carefully, to find out what the speaker says about it.*
> *Listen out for the following words.... What does the speaker say about them?*

- *Grading the texts.* There is no reason why one cannot grade authentic recordings in very much the same way as scripted ones. Once a teacher has collected a large enough sample of recordings, it becomes relatively easy to identify those which are more accessible to a lower-level learner by virtue of:

  - more frequent vocabulary;
  - simpler syntax;
  - simpler and less dense ideas or facts;
  - a degree of redundancy, with ideas/facts expressed more than once;
  - a degree of repetition, with the same form of words repeated;
  - a very specific context or genre of communication which to some extent pre-determines how participants behave.

A precedent can be found in the work of Thorn (2006) who, having collected more than 80 recordings of informal interviews, found it possible to grade content from elementary level upwards, chiefly using linguistic and perceptual criteria.

By way of illustration, here are two brief samples of natural speech which are very simple in vocabulary and syntax. The first is a recorded conversation; the second is a piece of broadcast material. Neither requires a high level of linguistic knowledge on the part of an L2 listener.

Conversational speech at an elementary level

I'm just **teach**ing (.) two of my daughters to drive (.) one's already got a provisional licence cos she's seventeen (.) the other's **sixteen** so she can't get a provisional licence until her **birth**day (.) h so (.) with **her** the **young**est Sarah (.) we have to go to a big **car** park at the supermarket (.) we just **drive** round **there** (.) but it's quite useful I mean (.) she can get to know the **basics** there

(Langford, 1994: 102–3)

KEY (.) brief pause   **bold** = sentence stress

Off-air recording at an elementary level

[Panel discussion] I think the **key** words that John . . . said (.) were on occasion the public transport system works okay (.) it really is pretty disgraceful I think (.) really on the whole in **this** country compared to the rest of **Eur**ope (.) the public **transp**ort system (.) and I travel round quite a **bit** (.) is really not very **good** (.) I mean the **trains** (.) you go to **Switz**erland (.) you go to **France** (.) you go where**ver** (.) they all seem to work much **better** (.) and we just don't seem to be able to get the **simple** things right (.) and that's what I think **both**ers me so much (.) and it's **expen**sive as well (.) so you're getting a **worse** service and you're paying **more** for it.

(*Any Questions?* BBC Radio 4, 25 January 2008)

Features helping understanding include the shortness of each group of words, simple ideas and simple relationships between them, focal stress on important words and the tendency of a speaker (especially in the second extract) to repeat and rephrase what he says.

- *Staging the listening.* A third approach is to provide graduated activities which require the learner to build up an understanding of the recording little by little. The most obvious technique is to begin with extremely simple tasks, then (replaying the text each time) to progress to ones that demand a closer understanding. Other possibilities include:

  - pre-playing selected key sentences from the recording before the recording as a whole is heard;
  - pre-playing and analysing the first few sentences of the recording before considering the text as a whole, thus enabling learners to activate appropriate schemas and to normalise to the speaker's voice;
  - pre-playing a scripted summary or even a re-recorded version of the recording;
  - providing a gapped tapescript for learners to complete, with the most critical pieces of the text (i.e. those which contribute most to an understanding of it) omitted;
  - asking learners to listen out for certain critical words, before playing the text for general understanding.

With short to medium-length video recordings, there is also the widely adopted option of pre-playing the sequence with the sound omitted, so that learners can draw preliminary cues from the context, from facial expression and from gestures.

To summarise, there is every reason why teachers should introduce authentic recordings early on in a learner's exposure to L2. There are ways of achieving this without demanding too much of the learner and thus damaging morale.

14.4 Graded and authentic: the interface

An eclectic approach to text authenticity has thus been proposed. It accepts that for novice listeners a mixture of small-scale practice activities and scripted recordings may be appropriate, but it stresses the importance of early exposure to authentic recordings.

This means that early learners find themselves exposed to input which is quite diverse in its phonology and language, on a gradient which runs from formal scripted speech to informal authentic. Teachers very much need to take account of the decoding problems which may arise from this mixture of types of speech: especially when learners have to change from the controlled delivery of scripted recordings to the more fragmented style of natural ones.

The clash of styles is not an argument for unduly delaying the introduction of authentic recordings. A switch from scripted to unscripted has to take place at some point, and may, in fact, prove to be more of a shock when a teacher postpones exposure to authentic speech until later on. It may then prove more not less difficult for learners to adjust, since they will have constructed well-practised listening routines for dealing with scripted and/or graded material, which may have become entrenched.

The solution is to give rather more careful consideration than at present to building bridges between the two types of input. A two-pronged attack is needed, combining exercises which raise awareness of the differences between pre-prepared and spontaneous speech with exercises which provide focused practice in processing conversational features. In both cases, the focus will be on the more informal end of the spectrum, since it is here that problems are most likely to occur.

Awareness raising can take a number of simple forms:

- listening first to a re-recorded version and then to the original authentic one;
- focusing on a short section of an authentic text, transcribing it and analysing what makes it distinctive;
- comparing tapescripts after listening first to a scripted and then to an authentic recording;
- using analytical exercises such as those in Cauldwell (2003), to recognise the extent to which forms become reduced in conversational speech;

281

- providing a gapped tapescript for completion, with features omitted which appear to characterise authentic informal speech;
- at a higher level, turning a piece of authentic conversational English into an appropriately constructed written text.

Some of the differences will be perceptual. A piece of natural conversational speech is likely to include a higher degree of assimilation than a piece of scripted speech, and reduced forms are likely to be more frequent. The duration of weakly stressed function words may be greatly reduced, and it is worthwhile playing authentic examples of the more frequent L2 function words in a number of different sentence contexts, to make learners aware of the extent to which their pronunciation can vary.

There are likely to be differences in the language that is used, as this extract from an interview with a taxi driver (Underwood, 1975: 134–5) illustrates:

Er, well, I don't think you could, erm, I don't think there's any taxi-driver in London who could take you to every street in London, know 'em all off by heart, because there's ... we, I, I don't know how many streets there is, but there's ... it's a fantastic memory and I don't think there's anybody in the world could remember all the names of the streets in a city as big as London.

They may include instances of non-standard grammar where a speaker focuses so much on sentence planning that he breaks quite basic rules (*how many streets there is*). It is also worthwhile drawing learners' attention to the fact that the grammatical structure of continuous natural speech is very unlike what might be expected in a written text. In real life (as shown in the example above), speakers frequently use long sentences which are linked by coordination rather than subordination.

Even the vocabulary of authentic speech is likely to be rather different. A scriptwriter has time to choose words that precisely encapsulate what he wants to express. By contrast, the natural speaker sometimes finds that the most appropriate word is difficult to retrieve under time pressure and makes do with a **general term** or superordinate (*people* for 'participants', *things* for 'ornaments', *nice* instead of 'well-made', *tune* instead of 'aria'), with a circumlocution (*those plants that eat flies, a shop that sells fancy cakes, a monk who doesn't speak*) or with an approximation (*a bit like bread, sort of round*). The consequence is that the onus is sometimes on the listener to work out the speaker's intended sense.

Besides introducing learners to these features of authentic speech, it is useful to give them practice in dealing with those that might most impede understanding. The procedure can follow the lines of the decoding exercises proposed earlier in the book. The exercises can be small-scale, with the teacher asking learners to listen to short pieces of input and to write down what they think they hear. The material for transcription is much more effective if it is excised from recordings of authentic speech rather than delivered by the teacher. The ideal approach is to pick out several short sections of a recording which exemplify a single conversational feature. This helps learners to identify some of the features when they encounter them and trains them to ignore others (e.g. fillers and filled pauses) which contribute nothing to the meaning of the passage.

Table 14.1 provides a list of the kinds of conversational feature that a teacher might wish to target. Most are the consequence of the online planning which occurs in spontaneous speech but which is conspicuously absent when an actor reads from a script.

Table 14.1 *Features of conversational speech for listening practice*

Filled pauses: Sounds such as *er, erm*. These sounds are specific to English; and there is a strong possibility that a non-native listener will identify the sound *er* as the indefinite article, *a*.

Fillers: Words such as *well* or sequences such as *you know, I mean* inserted into a sentence carry no real meaning but, like *er* and *erm*, serve to give the speaker time to plan what to say. The L2 listener sometimes tries to incorporate them into the meaning representation.

False starts: The speaker begins a sentence in a particular way, then has a change of mind and begins again (*I don't think you could, erm, I don't think there's any taxi-driver...*).

Repetitions: The same word or phrase is said twice or three times (*I, I...*).

Contracted forms: In addition to verbal contractions (*I've, he's*), the word *them* is often shortened to *'em* (*know 'em*).

Ellipsis: Subject pronouns are sometimes omitted. In the extract above, there is an example of a dropped relative pronoun (*there's anybody in the world could remember...*).

The challenge of the real world

14.5 Conclusion

The use of authentic recordings in listening is not just a faddish option put forward in the belief that the classroom must at all costs emulate the conditions of real-life communication. It is clear that true 'authenticity' cannot be achieved in the language classroom – and perhaps least of all in the listening classroom. But the value of recordings which are not scripted or graded resides in the fact that they:

a. represent a form of speech that is markedly different, both phonologically and syntactically, from purpose-designed materials;
b. provide the learner with a listening experience that approximates to a real-life one in that parts of the input (sometimes large parts) will not be understood.

On this analysis, the use of authentic recordings at some point in a listener's development can be seen as a necessity. In fact, a case can be made for introducing them as early as possible on a 'surrender value' principle: even if learners withdraw from language study before the end of their programme, they will at least have been exposed to the cadences of natural speech in L2 and will have shared the experience, common to L2 listeners, of constructing meaning from scant evidence. The key to using authentic recordings early on lies in choosing tasks which the learners are capable of achieving, even if much of the linguistic content of the recording is beyond their current state of knowledge.

That said, we should not lose sight of the fact that exposing learners to a combination of scripted and authentic recordings is potentially confusing, given the considerable differences between the two. Teachers need to take steps to ease the transition from one to the other by introducing learners gradually and systematically to the features of natural connected speech which may cause them problems of decoding. This can be done by means of simple transcription exercises like those already proposed as part of a process approach, which focus on each of the features in turn.

One should also be careful of jumping to general conclusions about the nature of L2 listening that are based upon the graded materials traditionally used in the language classroom. Those materials were and are designed with a view to ensuring that almost all the input is accurately decoded by the listener, so that the need to fall back on compensatory information from outside the input is relatively small. We must accept that decoding real-life discourse is different in kind and a much more partial and approximate affair. This question will return in Chapter 15, where we will ask how much of a piece of authentic recording is recognised by a typical intermediate-level listener and how much may have to be provided by strategic guesswork.

284

Further reading

Buck, G. (2001) *Assessing Listening*. Cambridge: Cambridge University Press, Chap. 6.

Field, J. (2007) 'Looking outwards, not inwards'. *ELT Journal*, 61/1: 30–38.

McGrath, I. (2002) *Materials Evaluation and Design for Language Teaching*. Edinburgh: Edinburgh University Press, Chap. 6.

15 Listening strategies

The more faithfully you listen to the voices within you, the better
you will hear what is sounding outside.
Dag Hammarskjold (1905–1961), UN Secretary General

A developmental approach of the kind recommended in the earlier part of this book takes time. So how is the L2 listener to survive meanwhile? Even if learners are provided with graded and scripted input in class, they are bound to judge their own expertise in listening by their ability to understand speakers of the language in the real world. And if teachers make use of authentic recordings, then it is important for them to support learners in making sense of material that has not been simplified to suit their level of language.

Learners need to be given a sense of achievement early on in the listening experience. Their commitment is greatly increased by evidence that they can understand natural everyday speech in the target language. It is threatened when they find that they do not have the means of coping, even with simplified material. They need a means of puzzling out the meaning of what they hear, despite the disadvantages imposed by their limited knowledge of L2 and their limited ability to recognise sounds, words and phrases in the target language.

A concerned teacher will want to ensure that novice listeners can decode some minimal portion of the input and that they can then make use of the information they obtain in order to construct a rough idea of what is being said. This constitutes a lifeline for those living in a target-language environment. But it is essential even to those who are not, since it equips them to notice, learn from and respond to examples of the target language that they might encounter outside the classroom. The ability to understand at least some of what is heard casually has enormous effects upon motivation and convinces the learner of the value of studying a second language.

This perspective on L2 listening suggests, then, that an additional further goal of the instructor is to equip the learner to engage in listening which is *strategic*: which does not aim for complete understanding but tries to make as much as possible of the reduced amount of information that the listener has managed to extract from the signal.

It should be made plain that the strategies we are considering here are **compensatory** ones, employed by the learner to deal with an actual or anticipated breakdown in communication. They are mainly responses to an immediate problem of understanding, but might also be ways of avoiding a problem that previous experience has taught the listener to expect. We will not in these chapters be discussing a very different type of strategy that makes use of listening to assist the learning of grammar and vocabulary.

The focus of discussion has now moved on from the behaviour of an expert listener. The type of listening that we will be considering is characteristic not of the first language listener,[1] but of the second language one. Our concern will be with the expedients that learners employ when there is a mismatch between their listening competence and what a listening task demands (Corder, 1983). We will try to maintain a sharp distinction between these strategies and the normal *processes* of listening that were discussed earlier.[2]

Of course, the performance of most learners is a combination of the two. They make use both of acquired L2 processes and of strategies that compensate for gaps where the processes have not yet been acquired. We sometimes think of strategies as short-term expedients, but that is not necessarily the case. Many learners come to rely heavily upon techniques that have proved productive, and incorporate them into their listening behaviour. In this respect, they go on operating in ways that are markedly different from those of an expert listener.

15.1 Strategies and the listening instructor

Teachers wishing to promote more effective listening behaviour need to give careful thought to learner strategies. It is useful (and very much in line with the process approach advocated earlier) to establish what contribution accurate decoding makes to learners' listening and thus how important strategies are in making up for gaps in what has been decoded. This is true whether one is using authentic or purpose-written material. In addition, an understanding of strategies can support and inform the way in which we approach instruction. Teachers might incorporate strategies into a listening programme in one of three ways. They might:

a. draw upon knowledge of strategy use to interpret the decisions made by learners about the recorded material they hear;
b. raise learner awareness of listening strategies: both their potential value and their possible dangers;

---

[1] Except, of course, in conditions where there is a great deal of noise or the input is unreliable.
[2] Though we may need to allow for some overlap: for example, both L1 and L2 listeners have to deal with unfamiliar words.

c. include specific instruction that aims to increase strategy use and to ensure that learners match their strategies more effectively to the problems they seek to resolve.

The ways in which listening strategies are described and categorised by researchers do not in general serve the purposes of the classroom very well. Some accounts try to fit the special circumstances of the listening skill into a model designed for strategy use as a whole. Others rely on categories that are abstract and not easy for instructors to apply or exemplify. Commentators do not always recognise the importance of establishing a connection between a particular problem of understanding and the type of response that is most appropriate. This chapter therefore seeks to establish a practical framework for thinking about second language listening strategies: one which enables instructors to shape their approach to strategy use quite closely to the ways in which learners perform.

Once a general framework has been established, an attempt will be made to list a representative sample of strategy types. Specifying the strategies used by L2 listeners is made more complicated by the fact that we do not have the kind of psycholinguistic evidence that was drawn upon in earlier chapters when describing standard listening competence. There is certainly a strong tradition of research into L2 learners' *beliefs* as to what strategies they use; but that is not the same thing as showing that strategies X, Y and Z have psychological reality or exist in the precise forms that we tend to assume (compare the similar reservations expressed by some commentators about sub-skills). We know relatively little about online strategy use: how a particular strategy is matched to a particular problem of understanding, how two or more strategies become combined or which strategies produce the most reliable results. That is why the list of strategies proposed towards the end of this chapter relies to some extent upon intuition (though it draws upon the work of a number of specialists).

15.2 How strategic is L2 listening?

We first ask how strategic second language listening really is and how crucial this kind of behaviour is to the listener's ability to derive a message from the input. What proportion of the input do L2 listeners typically succeed in decoding and what proportion has to be supplied by informed guesswork?

If we adopt the Stanovich principle outlined in Chapter 8, we can assume that there is a relationship between how much a listener manages to decode from the speech signal and how much she relies upon the cues provided by co-text and world knowledge. If the product of decoding is not sufficient to build a message, she will compensate by falling back on strategies that make use of external information.

To investigate how much learners actually manage to decode, I used a **paused transcription** method (Field, 2008c). Learners hear an authentic recording into which pauses have been inserted at irregular intervals. Whenever one of these pauses occurs, they have to write down the last few words they heard before it. Because the pauses are unpredictable, the listener processes the text normally, without focusing undue attention at word level.[3]

The recording used was an authentic interview with a cinema manager (Underwood, 1976: 106–8). The groups of words that learners had to report included both function and content words. All the words were frequent enough to be within the vocabulary of the listeners; in fact, the listening material had been produced for use at their proficiency levels.

The task was given to 95 mixed nationality learners of English, graded by their school as of intermediate level and above. Figure 15.1 shows how successfully they decoded two typical extracts ('programme which changed each week' and 'expect a higher standard of entertainment'), chosen because they are typical.

The front profile in each represents the results for 30 learners graded at Level 5 (roughly, intermediate) on the English Speaking Union's scale of proficiency, showing what proportion of the group managed to identify each of the words of the extract. It can be seen that, on average, only around 25% of the group identified a word. The white profile gives the results for 45 learners classified as being between Levels 6 and 8 (upper intermediate to low advanced). Here, decoding skills are better overall, but they still fall far short of 100% recognition of each word. It is not until Level 9, a high advanced level, that performance at all resembling that of native listeners is achieved. For the sake of comparison, a similar group of native listeners undertook the task. Their accuracy with most words was 100%, and it did not drop below 96%.

It is plain that the L2 listeners succeeded in decoding far less of the input than their teachers tended to assume. It is not a question of linguistic knowledge: the language of the text should have been well within their range. But it appears that the ability to *recognise* known vocabulary and syntax may fall well behind the ability to produce it.

The relatively low levels of word recognition that are shown here strongly reinforce the arguments in previous chapters for training listeners in decoding. They also demonstrate the extent to which L2 listening

---

[3] It is perfectly reasonable to ask a listener to report such words because (see Chapter 12) they remain in the listener's mind until the end of a clause is reached.

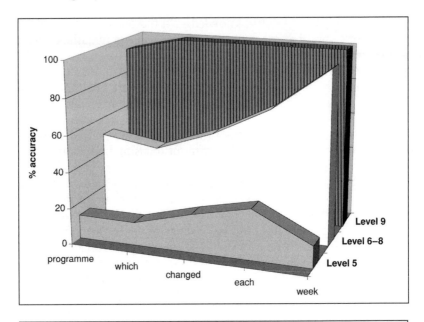

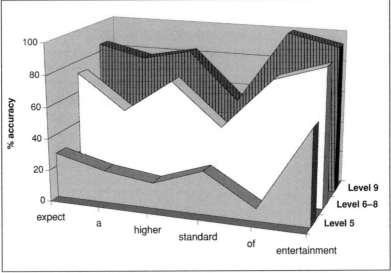

Figure 15.1   Decoding accuracy on two simple extracts.

is, for many learners, a strategic operation, where gaps in 'bottom-up' information have to be compensated for by informed (and sometimes uninformed) guesses. A model of second language listening has to recognise that, at least at lower levels of L2 knowledge and expertise, a listener is likely to be quite heavily dependent upon using strategies. It cannot be assumed that she will listen in ways that are similar to those she employs in L1, given the reduced part played by decoded input.

Nor will a language-based solution serve to reduce strategy dependence. The problem for the learners in Figure 15.1 was not linguistic knowledge, since most of the language in the targeted sequences was within their L2 repertoires. A crash programme of vocabulary or grammar would not greatly assist. What they lacked was the ability to deconstruct the input effectively.

The evidence just considered shows that learners succeed in decoding rather less than we tend to assume. It suggests that second language listening is heavily dependent upon compensatory strategies until quite a high level of proficiency is reached. For many learners, strategic behaviour seems to be critical to success in understanding the target language. From this, we might conclude that, if learners are to operate effectively as listeners, they need to have a sufficient number of techniques at their command to deal with the problems of decoding that will inevitably arise. At the very least, a case can be made for raising awareness of the benefits that strategy use can bring. But one might go further and ask whether listening instruction should include programmes with the specific purpose of training learners to use strategies.

15.3 L2 listening as a strategic activity

We will now look more carefully at what strategy use entails and the potential risks that it brings. Here is a simple example, in which the conditions of L2 listening are roughly simulated in visual form. Look at the exchange in the panel below, and see if you can work out what the conversation is about and where it is likely to have occurred.

A minimally informative dialogue

Speaker A: dooggninrom
Speaker B: dooggninrom + wohhcumeraehtoranges
Speaker A: eryehttwentylayirhcae
Speaker B: sey + revoereht
Speaker A: thgir + dloucievahthree
Speaker B: erehouyera + stahtsixtylayir
Speaker A: sknaht + serehahundredlayireton
Speaker B: sknaht + fortylayirregnahc

The challenge of the real world

In recorded form, I have played a similar example many times to groups of listeners. It takes around three hearings for them to identify the words *oranges, twenty, three, sixty, hundred* and *forty*. From this, they manage to conclude, on the basis of having decoded only six words, that the conversation probably takes place in a market or greengrocer's with Speaker A buying three oranges at twenty each, paying for them with a hundred note and receiving forty change.

This is an example of what was termed in Chapter 12 the 'effort after meaning'. The listener first strives to identify familiar strings of sounds (just as the reader's eye picks up familiar strings of letters). They form 'islands of reliability' in an otherwise uncertain setting. The listener then forms a hypothesis, based upon world knowledge, about the situation that connects these words.

In this way, strategy use supplements incomplete input by drawing upon outside information. However, the information must be used with some caution, and always weighed carefully against any evidence that the input provides. There are two complicating factors here:

- *Confidence*. L2 listeners, especially novice ones, treat with some caution the information extracted from decoding because they do not fully trust their own ability to identify sounds in the target language or to match sounds to words. Some place undue faith in a strategic interpretation based upon world knowledge and co-text.
- *Processing demands*. Decoding the input does not come easily to the less experienced L2 listener: it is not automatic and so makes heavy demands upon attention. The listener may find it less challenging to rely upon external information. This pattern has been observed in weak L1 readers, who prefer to rely upon contextual cues because decoding the text makes heavy demands upon their attention.

These factors lead some L2 listeners to rely upon external evidence rather than trusting the evidence of their ears. The problem is recognised by researchers, even those who are primarily interested in the effects of context. For example, Long (1990: 72) acknowledges that background knowledge 'can have dysfunctional effects on comprehension'.

A parallel danger arises when individual words trigger interpretations of what has been said. Less experienced second language listeners seem to focus much of their attention at word level (Field, 2004, 2008c). But, of course, whether this approach contributes usefully to larger-scale understanding depends critically upon how accurately the word in question has been identified and matched to the appropriate sense. A listener who interprets *in disguise* as *in the skies*, or *her system collapsed* as *her sister collapsed* (Bond, 1999) will create entirely wrong expectations as to what might come next. Likewise, someone who accesses the most frequent sense of *sentence* in *a long prison sentence* or *late* in *my late uncle* will activate schemas that are inappropriate.

Strategy use, then, is a valuable way of supporting L2 understanding when one's linguistic knowledge or listening experience is limited. But it also carries dangers which the instructor needs to recognise and the student has to learn to avoid.

15.4 Types of strategy

Let us now attempt to identify in a very general way the types of strategy that a learner might employ. Second language strategies have become a complex area in terms of the terminology used and the concepts involved. The account given here will be as straightforward as possible and will keep quite strictly to the needs of the classroom.

15.4.1 Generally recognised strategy types

As already mentioned, there are many detailed taxonomies of learner strategies. However, there is little agreement between writers as to what should or should not be included. This is partly because those who work in this area interpret the term 'strategy' in widely different ways. As a result, the specifications that have been produced conflict with each other both in what they list and in the categories they employ. In some of them, the strategies that are cited are very various: ranging from specific to very general, from those that map on to recognised psychological processes to those that certainly do not.

In addition, few of these proposals are directly relevant to the needs of the listening teacher. Commentators on strategies tend to compile general lists which supposedly embrace all four skills but in practice take speaking as their point of departure.[4] The result is that quite a lot of what they cover is not relevant to listening. It also means that they fail to take full account of the circumstances which distinguish listening from the other skills – most importantly, the fact that the listener cannot control the speed of the input and has to respond in a way that is constrained by time. These factors have an enormous impact upon the types of strategy that a listener can employ.

---

[4] Oxford (1990) comments very pertinently that the communication strategies that are subjected to analysis tend invariably to be those related to speaking – but then expresses the rather odd conclusion that *communication strategy* is not an appropriate term if we include reading, writing and listening.

An approach to classifying language learner strategies that has been much quoted was proposed by O'Malley and Chamot (1990: 44). It divides strategies into:

- **metacognitive**: 'planning for, monitoring or evaluating the success of a learning activity';
- **cognitive**: 'operat(ing) directly on incoming information, manipulating it in ways that enhance learning';
- **social-affective**: 'interacting with another person to assist learning'.

The O'Malley and Chamot categories are mentioned because the reader with an interest in listening is likely to come across them. They have been adopted by a number of respected listening researchers, such as Vandergrift, Goh and Graham, who have used them to effect. However, there are reasons for not adopting them here. Firstly, they are not very transparent, either to the listening instructor or (very importantly) to the learner. The distinction between *cognitive* and *metacognitive* is quite difficult to explain. It is also quite a fuzzy distinction. Strategies that are 'metacognitive' in one context may turn out to be 'cognitive' in another. If I plan to listen out for stressed words in an utterance, the strategy qualifies as metacognitive; but if I just do it, it becomes cognitive.

But perhaps the most important consideration is that the O'Malley and Chamot account does not differentiate between two very different types of strategy. It groups strategies that assist the learner to *acquire* the language (learning strategies) with strategies that assist the learner in *using* it (communication strategies).[5] This is well illustrated if you look at the definitions that I have quoted. In discussing listening, it is quite important not to blur the boundaries between the two. **Learning strategies** (using listening as a way of acquiring new linguistic knowledge) are usually much more intentional than **communication strategies** (dealing with immediate and often unexpected problems of understanding). We are really only concerned here with the latter. The argument presented in this book has taken the line that listening is a skill to be developed in its own right. Incorporating learning strategies into listening practice (rather than into general language instruction) runs the risk of taking us back to the idea that one of the main goals of the listening lesson is to add to linguistic knowledge.

[5] O'Malley and Chamot are chiefly concerned with learning strategies (hence the title of their 1990 book). But the definitions of their three types of strategy (e.g. p. 99) also embrace what they term 'problem solving'; and it is clear that among their strategies are some that assist learning in certain circumstances and communication in others.

Table 15.1   *Examples of communication strategies in listening*

- Listener A decodes only a few words: *better ... left ... road ... drive ... see ... sign ... Ontario.* Using the sequence in which the words occurred, she guesses that the speaker is advising her to turn left at the road ahead and to go on until she sees a sign to Ontario.
- Listener B only manages to decode the words *greenhouse gases ... keeping ... heat ... atmosphere ... water ... reduces ... heat ... lost ... surface.* From her knowledge of the topic, she reconstructs the lecturer's point.
- Listener C believes she has heard the speaker mention *a radio ham.* She notes that this is a tentative match and checks it against what comes next.
- Listener D comes across a new word in the utterance: *I've never really liked ******* though they say it's healthier than butter.* She uses world knowledge and the rest of the sentence to work out the meaning of the word.
- Listener E is not sure whether the speaker said *to the park to meet her* or *to the parking meter.* She carries both hypotheses forward and checks them against what comes next.
- Listener F understood very little of what was said. But she knows that speakers tend to repeat themselves, so she decides to ignore it.
- Listener G thinks that the speaker said something about *a sexy phone*; knowing the speaker, she considers it unlikely. She asks the speaker to repeat what he said.

15.4.2 Response types

So let us take a fresh look at the types of strategy that learners use, with the needs of the instructor in mind.

Table 15.1 gives examples of several types of strategy that a listener might employ in conditions of uncertainty, with Listener A's most closely resembling the example given earlier. It will be noted that they do not always involve the use of 'context'. The table illustrates the wide range of problems of understanding that occur in L2 listening and the wide range of techniques available to a listener for dealing with them. A first observation is that they do not all seem to be of an equal level of importance or frequency. Listener A's – forming hypotheses based upon external knowledge or upon co-text – seems to be more fundamental, and that is why it has been used throughout this chapter as an example of strategy use. David Mendelsohn, a specialist in listening strategies, presents it (1994) as central to strategic behaviour.

But what the table also shows very clearly is that there is a close relationship between the problem and the solution that the listener brings to bear. It is not enough to apply a strategy: one has to apply a strategy *that is appropriate to the situation*. The strategy is successful only if it goes some way towards dealing with the potential or actual problem of understanding. Precisely how far it needs to go will depend upon the communicative needs of the listener.

We will return to the question of the relationship between problem and solution in Chapter 16. For the moment, let us consider how one might categorise strategies in terms of the listener's response. A useful classification was proposed some time ago by both Corder (1983) and Faerch and Kasper (1983) and has been used since by others including Dörnyei and Scott (1997). It distinguishes between **avoidance** (sidestepping the communication problem), **achievement** (tackling the problem) and '**repair**' (seeking help in putting the problem right).

As often happens when writers analyse strategies, the types mentioned here were chosen very much with second language *speaking* in mind; but they adapt well to the circumstances of the listener. A strategic listener might:

- *Avoid*: (a) ignore what has been said in the hope that it is not of major importance
           (b) accept a very general version of the speaker's meaning;
- *Achieve*: attempt to construct a meaning on the basis of incomplete bottom-up evidence;
- *Repair*: appeal to the interlocutor.[6]

These three *response types* are very broad, but they provide a useful starting point. They account for all the examples in Table 15.1, with the first five representing different types of achievement, Listener F representing avoidance and Listener G repair. Their merit is that they refer to phenomena that are concrete and demonstrable.

15.4.3 Adding metacognition

The strategy types proposed so far include strategies that O'Malley and Chamot (1990) would classify as 'cognitive' and 'social-affective'. What

---

[6] Vandergrift (1997) makes a distinction between repair strategies which focus upon a single word or phrase and those which relate to the complete utterance.

Table 15.2 *Pro-active strategies of L2 listening*

- Listener H realises that her decoding skills are weak and therefore rehearses in her mind what the speaker is likely to say before meeting him.
- Listener I thinks carefully before listening about what level of detail she needs to extract from the speaker, so she will not be bothered by passages she does not understand.
- Listener J knows that the demands of decoding a lecture in a second language may prevent her from remembering all the information she has obtained. From time to time, she mentally rehearses the lecturer's points so far.
- Listener K thinks about the topic before listening to a recording. She tries to predict what words she will hear, then listens out for them.
- Listener L has been told by her teacher to look carefully at the wording of the questions in a test, then to listen out for similar words in the recording.
- Listener M knows that she has special difficulty in decoding L2 spoken by hesitant speakers. She gives extra attention to their utterances.

they have in common is that they relate to circumstances where a listener has to form an immediate response to an unpredicted and probably unpredictable problem of understanding. They take place under pressures of time and are what one might term reactive strategies. But we now need to consider a rather different type, exemplified in Table 15.2.

Unlike the ones discussed so far, these patterns of behaviour are not reactions to a specific breakdown of understanding. Instead, they employ various kinds of forward planning that might extend to a whole encounter. The behaviour is still strategic in that it is a means of dealing with what the listener perceives to be a weakness in her listening competence. But what distinguishes these strategies from those in Table 15.1 is that they contain an element of pre-planning. We will refer to them as **pro-active** strategies.

These processes would be called 'metacognitive' by many commentators but they comprise a much smaller set than the O'Malley and Chamot one. There are no examples in the table that support the learning of language as against the communication of meaning. Also absent are the kinds of technique that *any* listener (expert or novice, native or non-native) employs in order to build a meaning representation, to enhance recall or to focus attention. These are taken to be part of the normal listening process and are already covered in Chapters 12 and 13. Among them are techniques that afford useful aids to study, regardless of whether one is studying in a first or a second language (for example, note-taking, formulating questions about the topic before listening, attaching concrete images to abstract ideas). They support the retention of information rather than compensating for the lack of expertise of the L2 listener.

It is useful to recognise the role played by pro-active strategies; indeed, Vandergrift (2003) maintains that metacognitive strategy use becomes especially important as learners become more proficient in the second language. On the other hand, we should not lose sight of the fact that the opportunity to make use of pre-planning occurs only in a minority of listening events. It is relevant in circumstances where the listening is *non-participatory* and quite *extensive*. These more deliberate strategies might serve an important purpose for those who are contemplating extended lecture listening of the kind that takes place in English for Academic Purposes, or for those who plan to take international tests of listening. But they have a limited role in the normal circumstances of conversation (the exceptions are those employed by Listener H and Listener M). Instructors need to take this into account when considering which strategies are most likely to be appropriate to the needs of their learners.

To summarise, we have now identified four types of strategy:

- *Avoidance strategies.* Learner gets by without the missing or uncertain piece of input.
- *Achievement strategies.* Learner attempts to make maximum sense of what has been decoded.
- *Repair strategies.* Learner appeals for help.
- *Pro-active strategies.* Learner plans her behaviour in a way that might enable problems of understanding to be avoided.

Of these, the first three have been called 'reactive' in that they constitute an immediate response to a specific problem of understanding. They are shaped by constraints that are special to listening: most importantly, the fact that the input is transitory. This means that these strategies are characterised by the need for rapid decision-making. The fourth type is pro-active in that the listener attempts to minimise problems by anticipating them. We have noted that most strategies in this group are applied in a restricted set of listening events.

15.5 A listing of L2 listening strategies

Having marked out these boundaries, I will now try to list some of the more important communication strategies that occur in second language listening. In undertaking this exercise, one does not need to start from scratch. A possible line of attack is to consult one of the general taxonomies that are available and to adapt it to provide a set of strategies that are relevant to the behaviour of a listener.

A detailed list of strategies was put together by Dörnyei and Scott (1997). One of its strengths is the fact that it focuses narrowly on communication strategies. Another is that the authors went to considerable lengths to ensure that their strategy types corresponded quite closely to those of earlier commentators in the field. It is thus a compendium of the ideas of several of those who have written about strategy use. However, a disadvantage is that, here as elsewhere, many of the strategies are identified with speaking rather than listening in mind.

The list of strategies that is provided below draws partly upon Dörnyei and Scott (hereafter D&S) but adapts their items to make them refer specifically to listening. Other strategies have been added by me. Like D&S, I adopt the three 'response type' categories of avoidance, achievement and repair; but their fourth category, *stalling*, is not included. Practising stalling strategies would not seem to be a productive use of class time, unless the learner is intending to participate in an oral exam where she needs to buy time to form a reply.

The tables that follow constitute a tentative proposal for a set of strategies for listening. The lists are intended to be indicative rather than comprehensive. They aim to focus attention on aspects of L2 listening performance which are entirely strategic (in the sense of compensatory) rather than forming part of any standard listening process. It should be stressed that the purpose is to provide guidelines for professionals who wish to think about this area. There is no intention of providing a definitive account. We should be very aware of the dangers of setting taxonomies of this sort in stone and using them as a yardstick to measure learner competence.

- *Avoidance and achievement.* The strategies in Table 15.3 are arranged with the message-based ones first, followed by those that are based on sounds and on words. Clearly, the strategies are not all of equal importance or frequency. As already noted, the most critical is item 4, a kind of macro-strategy which features **hypothesis formation** (Mendelsohn, 1994) and testing. Note the large subset of devices (strategies 7 to 12) available to the listener for cracking the code of speech at word level.

Table 15.3 *Avoidance and achievement strategies*

- **Avoidance strategies**
  1. *Message abandonment*: abandon the message as unreliable
  2. *Generalisation*: accept a version of the message that is not very specific
  3. *Message reduction*: accept a partial message but remain aware of gaps in it
- **Achievement strategies**
  4. *Hypothesis formation*: infer meaning, using incomplete evidence from the input
  5. *Translation*: construct a message by converting words into L1
  6. *Key words*: listen for words associated with the topic, paying attention to the words around them
  7. *Prominence*: focus attention on words bearing sentence stress
  8. *Reliability*: focus attention on lexically stressed syllables
  9. *Approximation*: accept an indeterminate sense for a word (*oak* = some kind of tree)
  10. *L2 analogy*: use analogy with other words in L2
  11. *L1 analogy*: seek cognates in L1; work out the word's spelling by means of L2 spelling rules
  12. *Similar sounding words*: accept an approximate lexical match
  (loosely adapted from Dörnyei and Scott, 1997, with additions)

Table 15.4 *Repair strategies*

- **Repair strategies**
  1. *Direct appeal for help*: 'I don't know what that means'
  2. *Indirect appeal for help*: Listener signals lack of understanding
  3. *Request for repetition*: 'Sorry?' 'What was that?'
  4. *Request for clarification*: 'What do you mean?'; listener repeats utterance with rising intonation
  5. *Request for confirmation*: 'Do you mean …?'
  6. *Summary for speaker to comment on*: Paraphrase of speaker's message
  7. *Other checking strategies which parallel speaking strategies*: circumlocution, use of approximate words, switching into L1
  (based on Dörnyei and Scott, 1997, with additions)

Table 15.5 *Pro-active strategies for listening*

- **Pre-listening**
  1. *Task evaluation*: matching the amount of strategy use to the depth of listening that is required
  2. *Rehearsing*: anticipating in one's head the words that a speaker might use
  3. *Activating appropriate schemas*, related to the topic
  4. *Anticipating likely issues*: forming questions in advance
- **During listening**
  5. *Counting points*: mentally numbering the main points
  6. *Retrieval cues*: associating a word or an image with a main point made by the speaker
- **Post-listening**
  7. *Review*: mentally rehearsing the main points made by the speaker
  8. *Application*: relating the main points to information from elsewhere
  9. *Reflection*: thinking about the angle taken by the speaker

- *Repair.* Repair strategies (Table 15.4) represent a point where the teaching of listening interacts with the teaching of speaking skills. Providing the learner with the correct forms of words to use when requesting clarification is simple to do but carries considerable benefits. Note the strategies that are brought together under item 7. Many of the techniques used in speech production to get round a gap in vocabulary knowledge are also used by listeners to check that an unfamiliar word has been correctly understood.

- *Pro-active strategies.* The strategies of use cited by D&S are exclusively cognitive and social ones. We should add a group of metacognitive techniques that are closely associated with listening. Those listed in Table 15.5 draw upon my own observations but have been influenced by the work of commentators such as Goh (1997), Graham (2006) and Vandergrift (1999). They come with the important rider that they may only be relevant to certain types and contexts (particularly academic ones). In these situations, an important factor is **task evaluation**. The instructor needs to ensure that the learner is able to assess what depth of listening is required, and to apply the strategies that will be most effective in achieving the goal desired.

The strategies are organised in Table 15.5 according to where in a listening event they are likely to occur. This table is presented with some reservations. To me at least, the strategies listed here seem different not just in the level of cognitive engagement but also in the function they serve. Whereas those in Tables 15.3 and 15.4 are clearly *compensatory* in that they are designed to deal with potential or actual breakdowns in communication, those in Table 15.5 might best be described as *supportive* in that they constitute ways of listening more effectively.

15.6 Conclusion

The purpose of this chapter has been to mark out the areas of strategy use that seem particularly relevant to a second language listening programme. With this in mind, the chapter has focused upon the strategies adopted by L2 listeners in order to deal with an immediate or potential problem caused by a breakdown of understanding. Strategies are conceived of as expedients which assist listeners to achieve meaning at a time when their decoding ability and knowledge of L2 are not sufficient to give them access to much of the word-level information in an utterance.

These communication strategies are (so far as possible) distinguished from the processes which make up the expertise of a skilled and experienced listener, and which the L2 learner aims to acquire as part of her long-term competence. They are also distinguished from a very different type of strategy, which makes incidental use of listening in order to add to the learner's repertoire of grammar and vocabulary.

It has been assumed that, as L2 proficiency improves, the need to rely upon strategic behaviour declines. The paused transcription evidence examined above suggests, however, that strategy use remains an important part of the L2 listening experience for learners up to quite an advanced level. During this period, there may be a considerable gap between input in the form of the speaker's words and intake in the form of the proportion of those words that are successfully decoded by the listener and available as a foundation on which a message can be built.

Three categories of strategy were proposed, based upon the form taken by the listener's response. A listener might avoid a breakdown of understanding, attempt to resolve it or seek assistance in repairing it. In addition, a further set of strategies provides support in noticing, storing and retaining information. When we turn to strategy training in the next chapter, we will need to consider whether these different types of strategy demand different approaches to training.

Further reading

Cohen, A. (1998) *Strategies in Learning and Using a Second Language*. London: Longman, Chap. 2.

Cohen, A. D. and Macaro, E. (eds.) (2007) *Language Learner Strategies: Thirty Years of Research and Practice*. Oxford: Oxford University Press.

Dörnyei, Z. and Scott, M. L. (1997) 'Communication strategies in a second language: definitions and taxonomies'. *Language Learning*, 447/1: 173–210.

Faerch, G. and Kasper, G. (1983) 'Plans and strategies in foreign language communication'. In G. Faerch and G. Kasper (eds.), *Strategies in Interlanguage Communication*. London: Longman, pp. 20–60.

Macaro, E. (2001) *Learning Strategies in Foreign and Second Language Classrooms*. London: Continuum, Chaps. 1–3 and 8.

Vandergrift, L. (2003) 'Orchestrating strategy use: toward a model of the skilled second language listener'. *Language Learning*, 53: 463–96.

16 Strategy instruction in second language listening

Education is the ability to listen to almost anything without losing your temper or your self-confidence.
Robert Frost (1875–1963), American poet

A simple framework for communication strategies in listening was proposed in the last chapter, based upon three types of listener response. A listener might avoid a problematic stretch in an utterance, might attempt to decode it by using various types of cue, or might appeal to an interlocutor for help. In addition, we recognised a fourth group of strategies, chiefly employed in contexts where listening is a planned exercise.

Some concrete examples of strategies were given within these categories, with a view to helping instructors to recognise strategy use in learners and to assess its effectiveness. But so far we have not considered whether teachers should attempt to make learners aware of the value of strategies or to instruct them in strategy use.

Strategy training is quite a contentious area. Some commentators have argued strongly that it represents a good use of class time and produces tangible benefits. Others have been more sceptical. There is also the question of how extensive the training should be. Should teachers simply raise learners' awareness of the types of strategy that can be employed? Or should they devise a detailed programme of strategy practice? In addition, there is the question of how explicit and how targeted strategy training should be. Should teachers just supplement general listening practice with tasks that encourage strategy use? Or should they introduce strategies one by one and provide exercises that focus on each in turn?

It is not easy to arrive at clear answers. The situation is complicated by the fact that, as already noted, we do not have empirical evidence of strategy use that resembles the detailed models of expert listening that were presented in earlier chapters.

16.1 Is strategy instruction useful?

Compensatory strategies bring considerable benefits to second language listeners, enabling them to overcome some of the limitations imposed by their incomplete knowledge of the target language and uncertain decoding skills. This suggests that instructing learners in how to use these strategies might be of value and might assist them to communicate better in L2. However, we need to consider briefly a number of objections that have been raised to the general principle of strategy training.

16.1.1 Some reservations

Firstly, it is sometimes said that it is not necessary to teach communication strategies because learners already possess them in their first language. If we accept that human beings are strongly motivated by an 'effort after meaning', then surely we can assume that they will transfer the appropriate techniques into L2 performance as and when they need them.

A second objection to strategy training concerns how effective it is likely to be in the case of learners who, for one reason or another, are not temperamentally inclined to use strategies. Some learners, especially the less extrovert, may not feel a strong compulsion to achieve communication in the target language. Others may simply not be 'strategic' in the way they handle any type of problem or uncertainty. Others still may have cultural assumptions about learning which stress the importance of mastering details. Can we be sure that changing the behaviour of a learner in a classroom exercise will have sustainable effects on the way the learner behaves when confronted with a communication difficulty in the real world?

Some practical concerns have also been raised. They include whether strategy instruction is a productive use of class time, whether teachers need special training in how to handle it and how relevant learners find it.

16.1.2 Instruction in listening strategies

Let us now consider these reservations in relation to the specific needs of a listening programme. It is true that learners have experience of using similar strategies in their L1: for example, when dealing with speech that occurs in noisy conditions. But, as already pointed out, second language listening carries with it a very different set of circumstances. More of the input is likely to be missing due to the listener's limited decoding skills, and what is available may not be entirely reliable. There is scope, in other words, for greater uncertainty. Mendelsohn (1994: 46) claims from experience that many strategies used in L1 listening are not automatically transferred to a second language context. Some learners seem to behave strategically when confronted with passages of L2 speech, while others do not. Even among those who do employ strategies, there are many who do not use them as constructively as they would in their native language.

Strategy use does indeed vary from one L2 listener to another, both in terms of how frequent it is and what types of strategy are employed. But there is evidence that listeners who have been made aware of strategies perform better than those who have not. It has even been suggested that strategy training is helpful precisely for those whose temperament and listening style make them hesitant to form hypotheses on the basis of scant evidence.

Perhaps the strongest argument for including strategy training within listening classes is the need to ensure that listeners can make some minimal sense of what is said to them, at an early stage in their mastery of the L2. Learners often become frustrated with standard listening classes when they see few signs of progress and remain unable to deal with everyday encounters in the target language. Practice in employing strategies helps them to take their first steps in cracking the code of connected speech in L2. Even small breakthroughs in understanding can have a considerable effect upon motivation.

Feedback from learners supports the view that strategy training contributes usefully to a listening programme. Their comments in interviews and learner diaries suggest that it improves their confidence and enables them to extract more from L2 input than they might otherwise. A case study by Goh and Taib (2006) noted that even young learners (ten Singaporean pupils of 11 and 12) recognised the benefits. One of the reports quoted (p. 232) is especially encouraging:[1]

> I am able to concentrate on the text better and ignore distractions. Try to prepare myself before the exams ... If I miss any information, I will take note of where they can be found and be extra attentive during the second reading. I am able to calm myself if I ran into any difficult and unknown words and try to guess their meaning ... If the speaker is too fast, I will catch only the important points of the passage that can help me in my questions. My listening ability has improved and it also help me to catch more information when I communicate with others, watch TV or listen to radio, etc.

Graham (2006) looked at how listening tasks were handled by British learners of French who had *not* generally received strategy instruction. Graham reports that awareness of strategies among the group was low and the few strategic techniques that were applied were very hit and

---

[1] Though, even at this age, it includes test-taking strategies as well as those specific to listening.

miss. Here is an illustration of a word-focused approach that is used in a very undirected way (p. 177):

> usually I just find a word I know, try and make it out . . . Doesn't always work 'cos it's so fast and I find I'm still concentrating on what is said before when it moves on to the next bit.

Graham (p. 178) compares this account with that of a learner who had received training:

> I can work out like intonations and stuff . . . I can pick up the gist of it and then, you know, get a few words and then, like, cos my teacher taught me how to, like, if you've got a French word and you don't know what it means, try to find an English word which sounds similar . . .

These and similar reports suggest that training has an effect both upon learners' faith in their listening ability and upon the way in which they go about a listening task. Some learners may find their way quite naturally into using strategies, but others seem to need help.

Any concerns about the wise use of class time are thus dispelled by the tangible benefits strategy training can bring. As for the other practical concerns, a great deal depends upon how strategy training is introduced. There are ways of going about it that are heavy on time and that demand special training. I attempt in the sections that follow to make suggestions for methods that are efficient, that engage the learner fully and that grow out of established practice.

16.2 Strategy instruction in a listening programme

We will assume, then, that training in strategy use can form a valuable additional strand in the teaching of L2 listening. It complements the kind of developmental approach that was explored earlier in the book by helping the learner to make sense of spoken input in the early stages of what may be quite an extended listening programme. Writers such as Mendelsohn, Vandergrift, Goh, Macaro and Graham have argued for its inclusion alongside more general listening practice. Mendelsohn (1994: 38) even goes so far as to suggest that strategy use is the key to listening success and that it should therefore form the principal part of any programme.

This last recommendation perhaps needs to be qualified. Both the need to employ strategies and the type of strategy used are closely connected to the proficiency level of the learner. Strategies (of the compensatory kind that is our chief concern here) are more critical for learners in the earlier stages of listening acquisition than for more competent listeners.

They provide a recipe for survival at a time when listening skills and linguistic knowledge are not adequate to the task of analysing the speech signal.

On these grounds, one can make a strong case for greater strategy training in the early days of a listening programme but rather less as listening skills improve. We should not lose sight of the fact that compensatory strategies are an expedient: their purpose is principally to enable the learner to function adequately in the short term.

If we are to introduce strategy training, what form should it take? An occasional session dedicated to strategy use seems to be greatly preferable to a crash course that delays practice in other areas. It is important to bear in mind that strategy training is not a substitute for intensive practice in decoding or for extended exposure to L2 input. Only by developing improved and more automatic decoding skills will the learner, over time, reduce her dependence upon strategy use.

There are two ways in which a teacher can present strategies to learners and encourage their use. The first consists of *raising awareness* that strategies exist and demonstrating their value in achieving communicative goals. Here, listeners are asked to reflect upon their own performance in a listening task, to consider the ways in which it is strategic and to assess the success or failure of the techniques they used. This kind of activity could well take place at the end of a conventional listening session. Alternatively, a session could be restructured, with the teacher pausing the recording from time to time, checking understanding and then exploring with the class how understanding was achieved. This accords well with the kind of non-interventionist and diagnostic approach that was advocated in Chapters 3 and 5.

A difficult decision has to be made about how explicit awareness raising needs to be. On the one hand, the teacher might name strategies, model them and ask learners to identify them in their own behaviour; on the other, learners might simply be asked to comment in L1 or in L2 on the way in which they dealt with a specific problem. Here, some care has to be exercised. Reflecting on strategy use often provides useful insights and can help to shape future behaviour. But excessive emphasis on categorising strategies intellectualises a technique that should be instinctive and may even inhibit learners.

The second possibility is to provide *strategy practice*. The teacher gives examples of how to use a strategy when handling a short piece of recorded speech and then encourages learners to employ it in a longer piece of listening. What is important here is to choose both recording and listening task with care to ensure that they are appropriate to the strategy that is being targeted. This means that they contain challenges to the listener that would be likely, in natural conditions, to give rise to the strategy. It also means that the strategy represents the most direct and effective way of dealing with these problems of understanding.

So far as strategy practice is concerned, the instructor has to bear in mind that listeners must not only learn to use particular strategies in controlled conditions but also to integrate them into their general listening behaviour. It is by no means easy to ensure that this latter goal is achieved. The best that one can do, once again, is to look for authentic recordings or to set tasks within the general listening programme that seem likely to demand a particular strategic response.

16.3 An explicit approach to listening strategies

The general model of strategy training that has evolved in North America and elsewhere accords importance to the *explicit* teaching of the different strategies – i.e. to making learners intellectually aware of the functions that each performs. The model has some or all of the following characteristics:

- Strategies are introduced individually.
- Strategies are explained explicitly to learners and even sometimes named.
- Strategies are modelled for learners to emulate.
- Strategies are practised in controlled tasks.
- Learners evaluate their own use of the strategies in less focused listening tasks.

Another characteristic of this approach is that communication strategies like those exemplified in Chapter 15 are often taught alongside very different types of strategy: those that assist in the learning of language or the retention of information.

Many specialists in language learner strategies favour this type of 'direct' instruction (the term comes from O'Malley and Chamot, 1990: 153), and it is not my intention to challenge it as a general model. But it is relevant to consider whether it meets the specific needs of the listening teacher; and here a number of quite serious reservations present themselves.

They are mainly related to the practice of presenting strategies individually and discussing them in depth. The most obvious constraint is class time. Listening sessions are often lacking in this particular commodity – especially if they have already been extended to include the types of small-scale exercise that were advocated in earlier chapters. In addition, the purpose of teaching listening strategies is not well served if we dwell too long upon single examples.[2] We must not lose sight of the main goal: to equip learners as rapidly as possible with a range of techniques that will help then to deal with everyday encounters.

There is also the question of how to choose the strategies to target. There are plenty of taxonomies of L2 learner strategies, though, as already noted, they are often designed with speaking rather than listening in mind. But it is important to bear in mind that these taxonomies are based upon the intuitions of specialists. As with sub-skills, there is no guarantee that they represent actual psychological processes. That may seem academic; but the important issue is that we cannot take it for granted that the strategies in question can actually be divided up and separated out in the ways proposed. A very important question in strategy instruction is whether strategies ever really operate individually or whether they can only function effectively in 'bundles'. It may be that, when a listener tries to compensate for a breakdown in understanding, what she draws upon is not knowledge of a single strategy but previous experience of having used a whole complex of strategies, with each dependent upon the others. To give a very obvious example, 'hypothesis formation' is of little value unless it is accompanied by 'self-monitoring' in the form of checking the hypotheses against later input.

A rather different way of looking at this issue is to say that using strategies demands making choices, and that one of the purposes of a strategy programme should be to equip a learner with an awareness of what the choices are. This helps her to opt for one strategy out of several that is most likely to resolve the problem of understanding that has arisen. Again, taking a very simple example, let us say that a learner encounters an unknown word in a piece of speech. Among her options are: to ignore the word, to accept an indeterminate idea of what the word means, to infer the word's meaning from its context or to get by without the utterance as a whole. Clearly, she cannot really make the best choice unless (at some level of her mind) she recognises all the alternatives. Here is a second way, then, in which strategies cannot be treated as standing alone but are quite closely interdependent.

'Direct' programmes also reflect the belief that learners have similar needs. As already noted, strategy use in listeners seems to be quite individual. Learners differ greatly in how willing they are to make strategic choices; they also respond in different ways to the same problem of understanding. In most groups, especially mixed nationality ones, there will be **risk takers,** who are ready to infer the sense of a new word from

---

[2] An exception is the macro-strategy of 'hypothesis formation', which appears to be central to much strategy use.

its co-text or to form hypotheses on the basis of incomplete evidence. But there will also be **risk avoiders,** who are uncomfortable about rushing to conclusions until they have accumulated a body of hard evidence in the form of words and chunks of language which they have recognised. The difference may sometimes be the result of cultural background. Certain education systems foster an intuitive and holistic approach to information gathering; while others set great store by assembling and analysing details. Other factors have been shown to influence strategy use across all language skills. They include gender (with females apparently more strategic than males), age (with adults able to deploy a greater range of world knowledge) and motivation (with some learners keener to communicate than others).

This means that listening instructors must expect learners to vary considerably in the extent to which they employ strategies and in the types of strategy they use. We need an approach to training that somehow accommodates these differences in behaviour. Whereas a risk avoider needs to be encouraged to form hypotheses on the basis of incomplete evidence, a risk taker might need to be restrained from making unfounded assumptions. The drawback of teaching listening strategies one by one on the 'direct' model is that we may end up training some learners in techniques which they already employ and training others in techniques which they are temperamentally unlikely to use.

16.4 The problem–solution issue

There is one further major objection to a 'direct' approach so far as listening is concerned. Compensatory strategies are used for a purpose. What counts is not just the strategy that is used but whether the strategy succeeds in resolving the problem that gave rise to it. Is it appropriate? And is it effective? Cohen (1998: 69) expresses the issue very concisely: 'strategies are not inherently "good" or "effective," but rather need to be evaluated in terms of their effectiveness for the individual learner in the completion of the language task at hand'.

The relationship between problem and solution is often ignored in programmes of instruction. But its importance becomes clear when we consider what is known about the impact of strategy instruction on how listeners perform. When researchers and teachers investigate the effects of 'direct' training upon listening, they generally find, encouragingly, that learners make greater use of the strategy that was taught. However, some of them have also reported (a) that listeners are not necessarily able to *use the strategy in conjunction with other strategies* (see the discussion above); and (b) that listeners are not necessarily able to apply *the strategy appropriately when new circumstances demand it.*

The conclusion one draws from point (b) is that many compensatory strategies in listening are closely linked to the problem of understanding that made them necessary. A listener would respond differently to the problems posed by an unknown word, a failure of decoding or an inability to trace connections between the speaker's points. Similarly, a listener would respond differently when 90% of a stretch of speech had been understood from the way she would if only 10% were available. The choice of strategy varies from one situation to another and from one state of knowledge to another.

If we look at listening strategies from this perspective, it becomes clear that the challenge to the learner is not just to find a strategy, but to find one that addresses the problem in hand.[3] In order to achieve this, a listener needs to be able to trace parallels between the present set of circumstances and similar ones that she experienced at moments in the past. She then needs to recall which strategies were employed successfully on those past occasions. Effective use of achievement strategies in particular depends not so much upon the knowledge of what strategies are available (though of course that information is helpful) as upon the ability to find analogies between a present crisis of understanding and previous ones.

So practice in using individual listening strategies is not enough. The learner also needs a context for them. She needs to build up a record of past problems and associated solutions to which she can refer.

Of course, the 'referring' that takes place does not draw upon logic and reason. It does not involve a detailed analysis of the characteristics of the current problem, followed by a careful evaluation of possible responses. That might be possible in writing or reading, or even in pre-planned speech. But it is simply not possible under the time constraints which apply to listening. For the listener, adopting a particular strategy is a sort of instinct: a memory trace of 'what it felt like' when a similar problem occurred before, which then triggers a recall of how the listener responded.

The ultimate goal for the listening instructor is thus to achieve rapid and appropriate problem–solution connections. Nevertheless, in the early stages of strategy training, it is obviously helpful to introduce a degree of intention into the matches that are made. There will also

---

[3] Important research such as the Nijmegen studies into how Dutch learners compensate for lexical problems (Poulisse, 1990) confirms that the task has a strong effect on the strategy that is chosen.

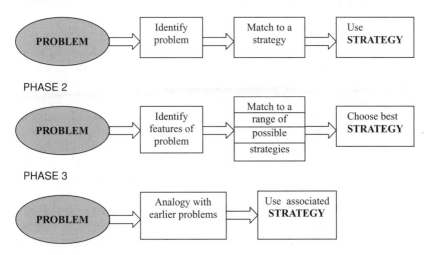

Figure 16.1   A staged approach to strategy instruction.

be an element of trial and error for the learner. A strategy instructor needs to:

- identify different types of problem of understanding;
- establish links between problems and their solutions in the form of strategies;
- establish links between alternative strategy solutions;
- enable learners to assess which strategies are productive and which are not.

With these targets in mind, one might see the strategy development of a learner (especially a learner who is not strategic by temperament) as passing through three phases. In the first, the learner makes simple one-to-one matches between problems and solutions. In the second, she recognises the characteristics that link certain problems; and the fact that certain solutions represent alternative ways of handling the same problem. In the third phase, she should have accumulated enough experience of strategy use to be able to match an incoming problem quite closely to a memory trace of an earlier one.

This model (shown in Figure 16.1) may help to guide the way in which instructors think about strategy training. Instructors might direct learners' attention: firstly, towards specific problems of understanding; secondly, towards the characteristics that some problems share and the choice of solutions; thirdly, towards a comparison with earlier experiences.

313

16.5 Strategy training in context

Let us now consider how the points made in the previous section might affect the methodology that is adopted when presenting listening strategies – most particularly, strategies of *achievement* and *avoidance*. It would seem to be sounder to adopt an approach that proceeds from problem to solution rather than one that focuses principally upon the solution. It would seem preferable to provide opportunities for strategy use within a task that has a real communicative goal, thus enabling learners to build up their experience under conditions that resemble those of real life as closely as possible. It would also seem advisable to allow learners a degree of freedom to decide which of the available strategies she feels most comfortable with.

There are two ways of achieving these goals: a local one and a more general one. The first focuses on awareness raising. The teacher collects a series of short extracts, ideally from authentic recordings that have caused problems of decoding or problems of general understanding in the past. The extracts should be only three or four sentences long, but sufficient to provide the listener with a limited amount of context. The teacher then proceeds as in Table 16.1.

As the learners' familiarity with strategies improves, the teacher can extend the final discussion, guided by the phases of strategy development identified in Figure 16.1. From matching a strategy to a problem, one can move on to look at alternative strategies and to examine which precise

Table 16.1 *Local approach to strategy practice*

First play. Teacher plays a single extract. Learners discuss in pairs what it means. They use their first language.

Second play. Learners listen again and decide if they wish to keep to their interpretation or change it.

Feedback. Pairs report to the whole class, using L1. They make clear how confident they are about their interpretations. Class attempts to decide who was right.

Strategy review. Pairs say how they arrived at their interpretation. Teacher might list simple mnemonics on board for the strategies used, making use of words from the text rather than terminology.

Final play. Teacher plays the extract again and indicates which pair was most accurate. Discussion of why that pair's strategy was successful.

characteristic of the problem encouraged learners to choose the strategy they favoured.

An alternative is to introduce and practise strategies as part of a larger listening task. This kind of *task-based* approach works especially well with many strategies of avoidance and achievement (though we will later consider exceptions). It corresponds more or less to what O'Malley and Chamot (1990: 153) call 'embedded instruction'. Strategy instruction along these lines resembles a standard listening comprehension lesson of the kind described in Chapter 1. But the recording needs to be chosen on the grounds that it is likely to throw up problems of understanding; for this reason, authentic recordings are preferable. The way in which the teacher handles the text needs to be redesigned in order:

(a) to make the learners aware of the strategies they have used and of how effective they are – in other words, to show learners their own personal strategy preferences;
(b) to create conditions where learners employ strategic behaviour to resolve problems of understanding, report on what strategy was chosen and review other options that might have been taken.

In these ways, the learner begins to form matches between problem and strategy and to lay down a set of strategic experiences.

A lesson of this kind might follow the stages outlined in Table 16.2. Note that the suggestion is not that *all* listening sessions should take this form, but that, from time to time (perhaps once every four or five sessions), it might be useful to dedicate a whole teaching period to an activity designed to promote the development of strategies.

The value of this approach is firstly that it enables listeners to deal with their own problems of understanding in their own way. Within their pairs, they can focus on, discuss and hopefully resolve any problems which they as individuals may have encountered. But it also obliges risk avoiders to engage in hypothesis formation by making informed guesses as to what has been said; and it obliges risk takers to do what they often signally fail to do – namely, check their interpretations against other evidence in the recording.

The approach centres on a single macro-strategy which all learners, regardless of listening style, need to acquire. The process of listening is driven by an 'effort after meaning' which, in the absence of sufficient decoded information from the input, must entail:

• forming hypotheses;
• possibly carrying forward two or more alternative interpretations;
• assessing the relative strength of the hypotheses;
• testing the hypotheses against what comes next.

315

Table 16.2 *Modelling strategy use: a lesson format*

- *Pre-listening*
  Establish context. Create motivation for listening.
  Pre-teach only critical vocabulary.
- *Extensive listening (whole recording)*
  General questions on context and attitude of speakers.

- **Intensive listening 1** (first 20–30 seconds of recording)
  Learners take notes of the words or chunks which they
    recognise.
  Learners compare notes in pairs.
- **Intensive listening 2** (replay)
  Learners revise the words they have written and add to them.
  Learners compare notes in pairs.
  They discuss (in L1 or L2) their interpretation of what they
    have heard.
- **Intensive listening 3** (replay)
  Learners check their interpretation and discuss it.
  Pairs discuss their interpretation with the whole class.
    (Teacher does not provide answers.)
- **Intensive listening 4** (replay)
  Class discusses interpretations and chooses between them.
  Teacher gives pointers and/or feedback.
- **Awareness raising**
  Successful individuals report on why they chose a particular
    interpretation.

The teacher then repeats the intensive listening cycle with a further
20–30 seconds of the recording.

- **Final listening**
  Class listens with tapescript. They mark the areas they found
    difficult.
  Class and teacher review problems and how they dealt with
    them.

But although it features one overall strategic goal, the learner has to draw upon many of the strategies that are often recommended for practice (listening for key words, listening for stress, inferring meaning from context) in order to achieve it.

The advantage of this approach over more 'direct' ones is that the structure of the lesson shapes the target behaviour that the learners are required to adopt. What they acquire is *procedural* knowledge of strategy use (hands-on 'knowledge how') rather than declarative knowledge ('knowledge what'). The approach also embodies a view of listening methodology which has informed the whole of this book but was especially discussed in Chapter 5. It features:

- *multiple replays* of short pieces of a recording for individual deconstruction;
- *learner collaboration*, resulting both in greater participation and in increased motivation to listen with a view to proving that one's own interpretation is the correct one;
- *minimal intervention* by the teacher.

Importantly, it also addresses the problem of the limited time that is sometimes available for listening practice, since it does not entail taking time out for targeted strategy practice.

If instructors feel that the format is rather short on provision for awareness raising, they can extend the phases in which learners report on why they made a particular choice. This enables learners to reflect upon the problems they have just encountered (possibly using L1) and the remedies they adopted. It might perhaps feed into a brief note-taking activity in which the strategies employed are recorded in a listener diary.

In addition, many of the techniques recommended in Chapter 5 for identifying learner problems as part of a diagnostic approach can also be used to raise strategy awareness. One that I have found especially useful is to video record a listening comprehension session of (say) 20 minutes. The second half of the lesson is then used to replay the recording, pausing whenever a member of the class seems to have encountered a listening problem. This leads to discussion of what the problem is and how the individual tried to resolve it. The strength of this approach is that the video enables the learners to relive the experience of the lesson and thus to recall their own strategic behaviour more clearly than they might without the visual trigger.

Some familiar strategies will come to the fore during discussion. They include making approximate lexical matches, listening for stressed words, using world and topic knowledge, seeking cognates with words in L2, using a knowledge of L2 morphology, assuming SVO word order and so on. But an additional issue that may need to be discussed is the point at which a particular interpretation begins to appear so unreliable that it is put to one side. Learners need to be given practice not simply in forming hypotheses but also in *rejecting* them.

An important consideration is to ensure that, once adopted in response to a particular task and listening passage, strategic behaviour is then extended appropriately to other listening events. With this in mind, it is useful to review learners' previous discoveries about their own behaviour at the beginning of each new strategy session, and, at the end of the session, to draw attention to the points at which they have re-used a previously taught technique. This assists them to trace useful analogies between previous problems and present ones.

The approach outlined in this section is especially relevant to situations in which the listener chooses to adopt strategies involving *achievement*. However, it is important for the instructor never to overlook avoidance as an option. One of the marks of a successful L2 listening strategist is the ability to make judgements about how much effort it will take to resolve a problem of understanding. If the problem is complex, if the solution is very demanding upon the listener's attention or if there is very little evidence to support the solution, then the wisest move is to get by without the stretch of speech that caused the difficulty. There is also the possibility of accepting an imprecise version of the speaker's message, which may be all that the situation demands. One of the strengths of a task-based approach is that it obliges the learner to make this kind of judgement.

16.6 Generalisable strategies

The discussion so far has represented listening strategies as demanding an appropriate response to a very specific breakdown of understanding. But we should beware of assuming that this is necessarily the case with all strategies. One can identify a small number of strategies of achievement which are not dependent on a particular context but can be used across a range of listening texts. These particular strategies fit in much better with a 'direct' approach. They can be practised one by one, by means of short micro-listening sessions.

They especially consist of strategies that apply at word level. Some of them require the listener to single out parts of the input for special attention. Examples might be: listening out for words bearing sentence stress or predicting the speaker's words. Table 16.3 mentions a number of strategies of this type, together with suggestions for micro-listening exercises which a teacher might use in order to practise them. Others, also at word level, involve dealing with unfamiliar words. They were discussed in some detail in Chapter 12,[4] where Tables 12.6 and 12.7 give examples of the kinds of targeted practice that can be provided.

---

[4] They were included in Chapter 12 as a matter of convenience, but it was made plain that they have a strong strategic element in them.

Table 16.3 *Generalisable strategies of achievement*

- *Key words.* In a pre-listening session, learners brainstorm words associated with the topic of the listening passage. Learners are then told to listen out for the words they have listed and to focus only on what is said about those words.
- *Sentence stress.* Learners hear a set of sentences (ideally excised from an authentic text). They write down the word in each sentence which carries sentence stress.
- *Prominence.* Learners listen to a short authentic recording that is complex in language, in which the speaker speaks fast or in which the sound level has been lowered. They note down the words which carry sentence stress. They then try to construct hypotheses as to what the speaker is talking about. Teacher may need to replay several times.
- *Reliable syllables.* Learners practise listening to stressed syllables in a very short piece of speech with volume level reduced. They try to guess the identity of the whole word from the syllable.
- *Given and new.* Learners listen to samples of recorded speech and note how the initial part of an utterance often sets the topic while the end brings in new information. They listen to sample sentences and report the new point in each.

The strategies identified accord well with a 'direct' approach. Even so, we should not lose sight of the fact that employing them in a real-life listening situation makes considerably greater demands than just practising them on their own. When encountering an example of an unfamiliar word, the listener not only needs to know how to use a particular strategy but also has to make a choice between all the options that are available. In addition, she has to take full account of strategic considerations such as how important the word is to the message, how much of the co-text has been understood and how certain it is that the word is a new one rather than a variant of a known one. So, while certain achievement strategies can certainly be demonstrated singly, the true test of the competent user remains whether she can apply them appropriately to a specific instance.

What marks out most of the strategies mentioned in this section is that they are not just short-term expedients but continue to be valuable to the L2 listener as L2 proficiency increases. They seem to fill a grey area between strategies and processes, where what starts out as a strategy to focus attention on a particular aspect of the input ends up as a long-term process that is integrated into general listening behaviour.

16.7 Repair strategies

Repair strategies differ from the others in two important ways. Firstly, they require a decision by the listener about whether to interrupt the speaker's flow of speech and at what point. Secondly, they are heavily reliant on language: they require the listener to master a range of formulae (*Sorry? Would you mind saying that again? I didn't quite get that*). This is somewhat of a simplification, as they also require an understanding of patterns of L2 interaction (when it is acceptable to interrupt the speaker and when not) and specific listening skills relating to the way in which a speaker marks that he has come to the end of his turn. Nonetheless, in practical terms, repair strategies form quite an easy target for teaching. Like the small group of achievement strategies just considered, they are *generalisable*. They do not need to be demonstrated in relation to a specific context. Once mastered, they can be used by the learner across a range of different problems of understanding.

The necessary formulae can be taught like any other part of a programme of functional language. They can be subdivided into:

- Requests for repetition: *Sorry? What was that? I didn't quite catch that. Could you say that again?*
- Direct appeals for help: *What does X mean? Sorry – could you explain X? I'm not quite sure what an X is.*

Learners need to be carefully directed so far as the intonation of *Sorry?* is concerned. They also need to be directed away from problematic expressions such as *Excuse me?* or *Pardon?* (UK) / *Pardon me?* (US), where they often experience cross-cultural difficulty in understanding the precise pragmatic area covered. Alongside the forms of language, there are a few techniques which can be taught individually. They include:

- repeating the speaker's words with a rising intonation;
- repeating the speaker's words up the point where the problem arose;
- negative back-channelling in the form of a filler such as *er* or *um*.

Learners sometimes fail to signal a breakdown of understanding simply because they are unable to determine the right point at which to do so. A programme in repair strategies should therefore also include activities to raise their awareness of turn-taking conventions in the target language. The best way of doing so is by playing short authentic conversations to them and asking them to identify the kinds of signal that speakers provide when they are finishing their turns. This gives them a degree of confidence when they intervene to request clarification or repetition. Turn-yielding cues they should be alert for in English speakers include (drawing on Duncan, 1972) a decline in the pitch of the speaker's voice or in loudness; the last syllable of the utterance continuing for longer than usual; the end of a syntactic structure; the utterance trailing away into fillers such as *er, you know*.

It is also useful to sensitise learners to the dangers of providing back-channelling signals which may give the impression that they fully understand when they have not. Nodding and smiling are problematic for learners whose cultures use them as markers of respect rather than to show understanding or agreement.

16.8 Pro-active strategies

Finally, let us consider pro-active strategies, which represent yet another special case. As noted in Chapter 15, they are much more likely to be used in certain types of listening context – those that are not time-constrained in the way that conversational listening is and those that require close listening and recall of information. Academic listening is perhaps the most obvious example.

The category as defined here was limited to strategies which are strictly compensatory in that they anticipate problems of understanding due to the learner's limited knowledge of L2. This means that pro-active strategies are used:

- *to evaluate a task* by deciding what level of comprehension is necessary in order to meet the task demands;
- *at a pre-listening stage* to create a mental set. Examples: activating appropriate schemas related to the topic; devising questions in advance or identifying certain areas of interest; anticipating in one's head the words that a speaker might use;
- *during listening* to record specific words or pieces of information. Examples: mentally counting the points the speaker has made; establishing retrieval cues by associating a word or an image with a main point;
- *at a post-listening stage* to ensure the storage of information from the message. Examples: mentally rehearsing the main points made by the listener; relating the main points to information from elsewhere.

It is worth noting that the strategies in the 'during listening' stage come at the potential cost of divided attention. While the listener is engaging in this kind of metacognitive monitoring, she may fail to keep adequate track of what is being said. So sometimes training in these areas can be counterproductive.

Some teachers might feel the need to pay special attention to pro-active strategies in a training programme. One possible situation is where learners are preparing for academic listening; another is where learners expect to take an international test. But the small group of strategies that involve prediction also have some general applications – for example, they can support listening to TV or radio programmes, even when listening principally for entertainment.

Table 16.4 *Integrated training in pro-active strategies*

- *Task evaluation 1.* Learners study the task before hearing the recording. They discuss how great their attention to detail needs to be.

- *Pre-listening.* Teacher tells learners the topic of the text. Then learners
  (a) brainstorm likely vocabulary
  (b) suggest what issues or topics are likely to occur
  (c) devise their own questions for the speaker to answer
  (d) are given two or three minutes to mentally rehearse the actual words that the speaker might use.

- *During listening.* Learners are trained to
  (a) take selective notes
  (b) review speaker's points at critical stages in the talk or when the speaker pauses
  (c) establish retrieval cues (perhaps single words) to assist recall
  (d) mentally count each of the speaker's points.

- *Task evaluation 2.* After the first play of the recording, learners say whether they find it difficult or not. They say why. They then estimate the extent to which they will need to use strategies to extract the information they need.

- *Post-listening.* Listeners are asked to
  (a) mentally list the main points
  (b) list the speaker's main points, then decide which are of primary importance (here, summary is much more effective than comprehension questions)
  (c) say how the points added to their knowledge.

Although it is worthwhile drawing attention to these strategies, especially with the types of learner group just mentioned, it may not be necessary to devise practice exercises that target them individually. The fact is that the traditional classroom listening lesson already sets up the kind of conditions that are necessary: namely time to predict and monitor and a need for close listening. The best way of handling these strategies is therefore to introduce and explain them explicitly (after all, they are strategies which a learner handles in a much more deliberate way). But the instructor can then go on to integrate them into a general comprehension lesson. Table 16.4 suggests how this can be achieved.

16.9 An eclectic approach to instruction

An approach to strategy instruction has been proposed which many readers will find unconventional. But there are good reasons for arguing that 'direct' approaches to presentation and practice do not always meet the needs of the listening class.

The first consideration is time. Listening programmes do not have unlimited time to give to strategy instruction. The type of instruction described elsewhere in this book is vital if the learner's listening competence is to be advanced and her dependence upon strategies is to be gradually reduced. It therefore makes sense for us to combine strategy work with other listening practice so far as is possible.

Secondly, the direct approach offers a 'one size fits all' solution. Those who adopt the approach do not allow for the fact that listeners are very diverse in the strategies they use, in how they use them and in how much they use them. Nor do they take account of the fact that the type of strategy that is chosen is, in many cases, heavily dependent on the problem that gave rise to it. Different problems lead to different strategies.

A further objection to a 'one size fits all' approach is that, just as learners are various, so are strategies. The set of categories proposed in Chapter 15 was partly designed with the needs of instruction in mind. Repair strategies, for example, can chiefly be presented in terms of the formulaic language that the learner needs to master. But practical considerations also suggest a further distinction between those strategies that are *generalisable* and those that are not. The former group includes repair strategies, pro-active strategies and a limited number of strategies of achievement. They lend themselves to 'direct' presentation and practice, since the instructor can be relatively confident that, after training, they can be widely applied, regardless of context. The only major constraint is that, at a later stage, learners will need to be shown that some of them are alternatives, between which a choice has to be made.

By contrast, many other strategies (particularly strategies of achievement and avoidance) represent a reaction to a specific problem of understanding. It was argued that in these cases we cannot separate the solution from the problem. We need to judge learners' performance not by how frequently they use strategies but by how appropriate their strategies are to the situation in hand. If one accepts this view, then 'direct' instruction does not really fit the bill. It seems better to incorporate strategy practice into an extended listening comprehension lesson, reshaping the methodology in ways that encourage learners to behave strategically. The predominant strategy in this kind of lesson involves forming and testing hypotheses about the speaker's message, but the learner also draws upon a range of other more localised strategies.

We need to recognise that what we call strategies covers a very wide range of techniques, some more intentional than others, some closely linked to language, some generalisable across different contexts and some not. Teachers need to shape the methods they use to the types of strategy they wish to practise – even if that means some inconsistencies in their methodology. An eclectic approach seems to be what is called for: one that reflects the circumstances of strategy use and the varieties of strategy type – and one that allows learners some opportunity to follow their individual inclinations.

Further reading

Cohen, A. (1998) *Strategies in Learning and Using a Second Language*. London: Longman, Chaps. 4–5.

Dörnyei, Z. (1995) 'On the teachability of communication strategies'. *TESOL Quarterly*, 29/1: 55–85.

Field, J. (2000) "Not waving but drowning": a reply to Tony Ridgway'. *ELT Journal*, 54/2: 186–95. Also: 54/3: 307.

Macaro, E. (2001) *Learning Strategies in Foreign and Second Language Classrooms*. London: Continuum, Chap. 6.

Mendelsohn, D. J. (1994) *Learning to Listen: A Strategy-Based Approach for the Second-Language Learner*. San Diego, CA: Dominie Press, Chaps. 3–4, 7–8.

Ridgway, T. (2000) 'Listening strategies: I beg your pardon?' *ELT Journal*, 54/2: 179–85.

Vandergrift, L. (1999) 'Facilitating second language listening comprehension: acquiring successful strategies'. *ELT Journal*, 53/4: 73–8.

Part VI: Conclusion

17   Fitting it together

The eye is the organ of temptation; the ear of instruction.
Aristotle (384–322 BC), Greek philosopher

There have been two broad goals behind this book. One was to examine first and second language listening in depth in order to assist teachers to make more informed decisions in their choice of materials, methods and tasks. The other was to propose approaches to practising the skill which might produce more tangible results than those currently in use: approaches which aim to produce better listeners rather than simply providing more opportunities to listen. A wide range of ideas and possible approaches has been discussed. The purpose of this final chapter is to place them in a wider framework by providing some broad guidelines as to where the priorities of listening instructors should lie.

17.1 Possible approaches

A number of different approaches to the teaching of L2 listening have been put forward. Let us briefly review what the options are.

1. *A process approach.* The principal recommendation made here was for a programme introducing learners in a systematic way to the processes that contribute to expert listening. It would consist of practice exercises, each of which focus upon a single aspect of the skill. They might target (a) features of the language that are likely to cause difficulties of decoding or meaning building for the L2 listener; or (b) processes that have been shown by research to form part of L1 performance. Many of these exercises can make use of transcription and be as short as ten minutes. In decoding, the goal of practising a single aspect so intensively is to develop the automatic processing that characterises skilled listening. In meaning building, the goal is to encourage the learner to transfer processes already well established in L1 but not employed in the unfamiliar circumstances of listening to a foreign language. See Chapter 7 and Chapters 9 to 13.
2. *A task-based approach to strategy instruction* that raises awareness of strategy use and links it to the circumstances that give rise to it. The approach adapts existing methodology with a view to promoting strategy use in comprehension sessions. The goal is to equip learners

with techniques that enable them to decode and understand as much as possible of the input they encounter in real-life contexts, at a time when their knowledge of L2 and experience of L2 listening are both in the process of development. See Chapter 16.

3. *A targeted approach to certain more generalisable strategies*, which demonstrates and practises the strategies individually. It is chiefly suitable for repair strategies and for 'pro-active' achievement strategies where some premeditation is possible. See Chapter 16.

4. *A diagnostic approach* to general comprehension work, where the teacher's goal is to identify the processes which have led learners to give particular answers. These insights lead on to practice exercises like those that feature in approach 1. See Chapter 5.

5. *Autonomous listening practice*, in which learners are free to listen and re-listen to passages in order to tackle problems of understanding that may be specific to the listener. See Chapter 3.

6. *Gradual exposure to authentic materials* from an early stage of listening development, with a view to ensuring that learners become familiar with the sounds, rhythms, vocabulary and syntax of natural speech. See Chapter 14.

7. *Awareness-raising sessions* to draw attention to features of authentic connected speech that learners may encounter. See Chapter 14.

At times, I may have given the impression that these seven approaches are alternatives, but we should really regard them as interdependent. It is pointless to contemplate a long-term programme of listening development unless one also makes short-term provision for the learner's communicative needs, in the form of strategy training. Similarly, a process approach should not simply rely upon a checklist of possible problem areas but should also draw upon evidence about where the problems of a particular group lie, obtained from the kind of diagnostic exercise outlined in approach 4. As for exposure to authentic speech, it remains a necessity, whatever type of practice is being offered.

Even the comprehension approach (one further way of tackling L2 listening) has an important part to play, despite the criticisms that have been levelled against it here. It is not enough to practise specific techniques in isolation; teachers also need to provide more extended listening tasks, in which the processes that have been acquired can be employed more freely and in conjunction with each other. All the approaches except the last depend at some point upon giving the listener the opportunity of hearing longer passages.

So there is no suggestion that the CA should be completely abandoned. But there should certainly be differences in how teachers apply the approach. Proposals were made in Chapters 3 and 4 for making it more flexible, more demanding in what it requires of the learner and broader in scope. There must also be differences in how we view the reasons for using the approach. The aim should not be to check whether learners are capable of answering questions correctly, but to provide them with more extended and less controlled listening, in which they can apply the techniques they have learned. The teacher's function is no longer to arbitrate between right and wrong but to train the learners adequately beforehand and to check during the sessions that they are employing processes and strategies that are appropriate and effective.

A second reason for retaining an approach based on general understanding is that it provides listening experience. Expertise in any skill is achieved by applying it frequently and across a wide range of contexts. More specifically, expertise in listening entails being able to cope with a wide range of speaking styles, voices and varieties of the L2. On the exemplar theory mentioned in Chapter 10, each new voice and each new encounter lays down traces for the listener which broaden the scope of what she is capable of decoding. A listener who has recognised the sound [əʊ] or the word *actually* in twenty voices and twenty contexts has a stronger impression of the ways in which they vary than one who has only practised recognising them when modelled by a teacher.[1]

17.2 Some priorities

Since each of the approaches just described carries its own benefits, we need to consider how to combine them into a coherent programme. Which are more critical in the early stages of listening development? Are any of them more important overall? Are some dependent upon others? Curiously, the question of coordinating different types of listening instruction has received relatively little attention. Despite the large and growing literature on strategy training, for example, there have been few attempts to explain how it might fit into more general practice activities.

Here are some initial thoughts that an instructor might wish to consider. They draw upon points made elsewhere in this book.

- Process is central. Teachers need to practise appropriate listening processes from the outset and to show learners where potential problems

---

[1] Until recently, it would have seemed hopelessly idealistic to recommend that teachers in many EFL contexts exposed their learners to a wide range of target language speakers. Advances in technology have now provided plenty of material for those who are fortunate enough to have internet connections. But we still have to direct learners to ensure that the material they encounter is relatively accessible both in terms of its language and in terms of its cultural assumptions.

may arise. Otherwise, there is a danger that inefficient routines or routines not relevant to L2 will become entrenched over time and resistant to change.

- Decoding needs to be a major target in the early stages. Without some minimal level of decoded input, the learner is unlikely to be able to form any general impressions as to what is being said. In addition, a learner with efficient decoding routines has more attention to spare for meaning building.
- Decoding practice should focus first on word recognition. This is partly because of evidence that less experienced listeners focus their attention at this level, and partly because identifying words with some degree of confidence provides the listener with 'islands of reliability' upon which hypotheses can be built.
- Meaning building that draws upon general context has to precede meaning building that draws upon co-text. Co-text cannot be assumed to be available until a certain level of decoding ability has been achieved.
- Practice in handling information (i.e. selecting important points and recognising lines of argument) should come quite late in the programme. Learners need to become competent in basic processes before they can shift attention to wider issues of meaning.
- Strategy instruction is vital in the early stages of listening development. It enables the learner to unlock the code of speech and achieve some minimal understanding despite limitations of language. The ability to make sense of what a speaker says is an important motivating factor for the early language learner. It also ensures that the learner does not become impatient with a progressive listening programme of the type proposed.
- Learners need to be given the opportunity to integrate individual processes and strategies into general performance, using them in conjunction with each other and making choices between them.
- A diagnostic approach performs a useful function in highlighting processes or strategies that are misapplied and in need of practice. It also enables the teacher to check on how effectively training feeds into general performance.
- Learners need to be given access to samples of authentic speech from quite early on, but with tasks that are appropriate to their level. Early learners also need to become familiar with features such as false starts, hesitations and fillers.

This set of priorities points to a heavy focus upon strategy instruction in the early stages of a listening programme, to equip the learners with basic survival techniques. A similar purpose is served by exposing learners at the outset to limited samples of authentic speech. There is likely to be a need for training in listening processes throughout the learner's development, but the emphasis should be on decoding at the start, since it provides the key to skilled performance.

17.3 A multi-strand programme

Table 17.1 offers a tentative proposal for a multi-strand programme, in which the different approaches are mutually supportive. I have identified five strands in all: process training, strategy training, exposure to authentic speech, diagnostic activities and general comprehension work. Six stages of development are shown, relating not to the learners' knowledge of the language but to their listening competence. The stages should not be treated as set in stone. We can assume that they will vary from one group of learners to another and that there will often be overlaps, with progress in one of the strands falling behind progress in others. Some stages (especially Stage 3) may last much longer than others.

The Table 17.1 should be regarded as a very rough guide to where an instructor's priorities might lie. The grey tone indicates areas that merit special attention at a particular stage of listening development. There is an early emphasis on strategy instruction; the use of diagnostic approaches and more extended comprehension tasks is delayed; exposure to authentic recordings increases as decoding skills become more competent.

- *Process development.* This is the most important strand of the programme, for all the reasons that have been given in this book. The first line of attack is to develop learners' ability to recognise words in connected speech by means of small-scale transcription exercises and tasks related to lexical segmentation. Decoding skills are then tackled, with a view to practising them intensively and achieving a greater degree of automaticity. Gradually, meaning-building tasks are introduced as well – but those that require the manipulation of information and the formation of argument structures are delayed until decoding has reached a satisfactory level. Finally, process work becomes largely remedial: addressing specific failures of understanding in comprehension exercises.

- *Strategy training.* A high priority should be given to strategy training in the early stages of acquiring the L2, when listening experience is very limited. The first way of supporting learners is to equip them with formulaic repair strategies so that they can tell a speaker that understanding has failed. It is useful to demonstrate to them that they

Table 17.1 A multi-strand approach to L2 listening development

Stage	process development	strategy training	authentic speech	diagnostic procedures	comprehension tasks
1	basic: lexical	repair; avoidance; word-based	exposure		graded, short; max. two voices; narrative; instructional
2	decoding	achievement; reliance on context	simple texts; awareness of characteristics	limited use	short; conversational
3	decoding; meaning building	achievement; increased use of co-text	increased use; transcription	diagnose poor processing	medium length; two+ voices; descriptive
4	decoding; meaning building	generalisable	mainly authentic	inform process work	medium length; expository; major varieties
5	handling information	remedial	mainly authentic	inform all aspects	longer; discursive
6	remedial	remedial	only authentic; focus on idiom	focus on language	longer; two/three texts; other varieties

do not need to master everything that is said; they should be shown that parts of the input are redundant and can be ignored ('avoided') if not fully understood. The teacher can also focus upon ways of building hypotheses around words that have been successfully identified; this capitalises upon the process work being done on word recognition. At a second stage, achievement strategies can be modelled and practised by means of the task-based approach recommended in Chapter 16. However, the recordings used will need to be short and simple. The teacher can expect learners to draw on general contextual cues but should not rely upon the assumption that they will have built up a clear picture of the conversation as a whole. At Stage 3, co-textual cues increasingly become available, paving the way for a much more extended coverage of achievement strategies. At some point, perhaps at the next stage, the teacher will wish to introduce the more generalisable and pro-active types of strategy, which can be taught individually. Finally, as the learners become more skilled in listening processes, the main concern will be with strategies that have become fossilised or strategies that are misapplied in the course of extended listening exercises.

- *Authentic speech.* There is a gradual increase in the proportion of authentic materials that are used. Learners are first exposed to occasional short samples, and given simple tasks to perform that are appropriate to their level. At a second stage, transcription and awareness-raising exercises introduce them to the features that characterise authentic speech. Comparisons are made with the scripted materials which they are more familiar with. Transcription continues to be used at Stage 3 to tackle problems of decoding. Later work might focus on idiomatic features of spoken language which are unfamiliar to learners. Throughout, exposure to authentic speech should be coordinated with strategy training, since the latter equips learners to deal with recordings beyond their current level of linguistic knowledge.

- *Diagnostic procedures.* Diagnosing learners' problems would seem to have little value in the early stages of listening development; there would simply be too many issues for the teacher to target in any systematic way. However, from Stage 3 onwards, diagnosis performs a useful function in identifying problems of processing that would benefit from remedial practice. In the later stages, the teacher might investigate *any* breakdown of understanding in order to remedy it. There might finally be a traditional focus on repairing gaps in the learner's language knowledge.

- *Comprehension tasks.* The function of these tasks is to enable learners to integrate listening practices acquired elsewhere and to extend their experience of dealing with different types of connected speech. The column includes brief suggestions about how one might grade the recordings that are used. They relate to the length of the passage, the number of voices, the type of passage and the range of accents. These are drawn from the factors identified by Brown and Yule (1983b: 80–89) in their analysis of the causes of listening difficulty. Clearly, the difficulty of the task that is set also needs to be taken into account (see the suggestions in Chapter 4).

17.4 The importance of listening

The busy language teacher may well feel that the programme just outlined is unrealistically ambitious. In a syllabus that has to cover pronunciation, grammar and vocabulary, not to mention the other three skills, how is a class likely to get time to cover more than a fraction of what has been proposed?

To this, my answer would be: it is a matter of priorities. At the moment, instructors tend to seriously underestimate the importance of listening practice. When they find themselves short of time, it is quite often the listening session that gets cut. Alternatively, listening is relegated to voluntary attendance in a language centre. To some extent, this attitude is understandable. Developing listening competence in learners can be frustrating. Progress is often slow and difficult to spot. Spoken language is less tangible and more difficult to handle than written. There is also the dead hand of the methodology we use, which seems ineffectual in its present form.

But we need to reflect much more carefully than we do at present upon the relevance of the skill and upon the ways in which it contributes to success in learning a language. Acquiring the ability to understand what L2 speakers say is not an optional extra. On the contrary: listening is the principal means by which learners expand their knowledge of the spoken forms of the target language. It opens up access to language used in natural contexts. It is also, if we are honest, a much more effective and efficient channel for picking up grammar and vocabulary than a lesson delivered by a teacher to a group of learners in a session of some 40 minutes. This is not to question the value of instruction, just its priorities. If we have to make a choice between practising the Third Conditional for the fourth time in the hope of finally getting it right or committing time to developing a transferable skill that may just do the job for us – then perhaps we should in future be bold enough to go for the second option.

In addition, we should not overlook the fact that listening competence has a critical effect upon learner motivation. Aspiring L2 users quickly become defeatist if they are unable to understand a native speaker in conversation or to make sense of the simplest airport announcements, street directions or phone messages. They do not simply give up as listeners; they often give up as language learners too.

This discussion has brought us full circle: back to the arguments for teaching listening with which this book began. We badly need to take the skill more seriously. We need to challenge the view that L2 listening competence somehow comes about of its own accord; or the view that acquiring L2 listening is a slow process that brings few obvious rewards; or the feeling that we do not possess a methodology that enables us to tackle the skill in the way we would wish. We need to give prominence to listening in language programmes as the skill that will be of most use to learners in the world beyond the classroom. If this book has done anything to achieve this shift of perspective, then it will have served its purpose.

Appendix 1

Decoding processes

1. Phoneme level
1.1 Phoneme recognition in a range of contexts
1.2 Discriminating consonants
1.3 Discriminating vowels
1.4 Recognising consonant clusters
1.5 Extrapolating spellings from sounds

2. Syllable level
2.1 Recognising syllable structure
2.2 Recognising syllable stress
2.3 Treating stressed syllables as more reliable
2.4 Using stressed syllables as access codes
2.5 Using weak syllables to locate function words

3. Word level
3.1 Lexical segmentation
    3.1.1 Rhythm-based strategies
    3.1.2 Using prefixes and suffixes as boundary markers
    3.1.3 Using fixed stress (where appropriate)
3.2 Recognising variant forms of words
    3.2.1 Allowing for cliticisation
    3.2.2 Allowing for resyllabification
    3.2.3 Recognising weak forms of function words
    3.2.4 Recognising assimilated words
    3.2.5 Allowing for elision
    3.2.6 Recognising reduced words within intonation groups
3.3 Recognising complete formulaic chunks
3.4 Using awareness of word frequency
3.5 Current activation
3.6 Spreading activation (word networks in the mind)
3.7 Distinguishing known and unknown words
3.8 Dealing with unknown words: infer – generalise – ignore
3.9 Automatic lexical access

4. Syntactic parsing
4.1 Building syntactic structures during pauses and fillers
4.2 Using planning pauses to demarcate syntactic structures
4.3 Distinguishing planning and hesitation pauses
4.4 Using intonation groups to demarcate syntactic structures

Appendix 2

Meaning-building processes

1. Word meaning
1.1 Narrowing word sense to fit context
1.2 Dealing with word ambiguity
1.3 Inferring meaning of unknown words

2. Syntactic meaning
2.1 Relating syntax to context
2.2 Interpreting speaker's functional intentions
2.3 Forming inferences from syntactic information

3. Intonation meaning
3.1 Recognising given/new relationships
3.2 Distinguishing given/new and contrastive and emphatic stress
3.3 Relating contrastive and emphatic focal stress to context
3.4 Recognising finality
3.5 Recognising the end of a speaker turn
3.6 Using intonation to identify questions in statement form
3.7 Distinguishing a confirmation request from a more open question
3.8 Distinguishing echoes and challenges
3.9 Distinguishing neutral – emotive – withdrawn intonations

4. Using contextual knowledge
4.1 World knowledge
4.2 Topic knowledge
4.3 Speaker knowledge
4.4 Knowledge of situation
4.5 Knowledge of setting

5. Using schematic knowledge (including scripts)
5.1 Predicting what will be said
5.2 Triggering spreading activation
5.3 Inferring what the speaker has not expressed
5.4 Allowing for culturally determined schemas

6. Context/co-text and meaning
6.1 Using context and co-text to narrow down word meaning
6.2 Using context and co-text to infer pragmatic meaning
6.3 Using context and co-text to infer word meaning

7. Using inference
7.1 Inferring information the speaker has left unsaid
7.2 Inferring connections between pieces of information that were not made explicitly

8. Making reference connections
8.1 Carrying forward current topics
8.2 Dealing with imprecise reference

9. Interpreting the utterance
9.1 Interpreting speaker language
9.2 Deep processing

10. Selecting information
10.1 Considering relevance
10.2 Considering redundancy: addition versus repetition
10.3 Dealing with incoherence

11. Integrating information
11.1 Connecting new information to previous
    11.1.1 Recognising locally connecting linkers
    11.1.2 Recognising 'signpost' linkers
    11.1.3 Recognising links not marked by linkers
11.2 Monitoring for consistency
11.3 Structuring the discourse
    11.3.1 Recognising topics and sub-topics
    11.3.2 Using formal schemas

12. Forming and checking provisional discourse representations
12.1 Forming the basis for a discourse representation
12.2 Accepting an indeterminate representation
12.3 Checking, revising and upgrading a discourse representation

Appendix 3

A guide to phonetics and phonology

Listening requires the listener to **decode** spoken language, turning a group of sounds into words, phrases and clauses. Where possible, the input to the listener is represented in this book using the conventional letters of the English alphabet. However, at certain points, it has been necessary to show the speech signal in terms of the actual sounds it contains – especially when demonstrating that certain words are markedly different in their spoken forms from the way we represent them in writing. Here, I make use of a standard set of symbols which form part of the International Phonetic Alphabet (**IPA**), and which have been chosen by international agreement to represent the characteristic sound contrasts of English speech.

Many pre-service teacher training courses, both national and international, give attention to the teaching of pronunciation and to the sound system of the target language. However, it may be that some readers have not had the benefit of an introduction of this kind. For them, this very brief appendix aims to explain the symbols that are used in the book and what they signify.

Any language can be thought of as consisting of a limited set of sounds (called **phonemes**) which serve to distinguish between words that might otherwise be identical. Examples in English might be /b/ and /d/ in *bed* and *dead* or /ɪ/ and /iː/ in *fit* and *feet* or /k/ and /g/ in *back* and *bag*. (The contrasted pairs of words are called **minimal pairs**.)

Consonants and vowels

I will use English as an example, since it is the main language of exemplification in this book. Table A3.1 shows the phoneme symbols used to represent the consonants that occur in most varieties of English. You will notice that, when we write individual phonemes, we put a slash at the beginning and end (/ /) to distinguish them from ordinary spellings. We do the same at the start and finish of words or whole sentences that have been transcribed.

Here are some points to look out for:

a. Consonants can be classified according to *how* they are formed and to *where in the mouth* they are formed. You do not need to concern yourself too much about these characteristics as they are not widely discussed in this book.

340

Table A3.1 *English consonants*

/p/	pat	/b/	bat
/t/	tug	/d/	dug
/k/	cap	/g/	gap
/f/	fan	/v/	van
/θ/	thing	/ð/	this
/s/	sue	/z/	zoo
/ʃ/	ship	/ʒ/	measure (*written* s)
/tʃ/	cheap	/dʒ/	jeep
		/m/	met
		/n/	net
		/ŋ/	sing
		/w/	wet
		/l/	let
		/r/	red
		/j/	yet
		/h/	hit

b. Note that the consonants appear in two columns. The first eight rows consist of pairs that are formed in the same way and in the same part of the mouth, but that differ in one important respect. The one on the left is termed **voiceless** because it is not usually accompanied by a vibration of the vocal cords. The one on the right is termed **voiced** because, in many of its occurrences, it does require vocal-cord vibration. You can try this out by contrasting /f/ and /v/, with your hands over your ears. The remaining consonants in the right-hand column do not have a partner but are generally voiced.

c. You will note that many of the phoneme symbols are standard alphabetic letters. They are the easy ones to recognise, but remember that they can sometimes represent a number of different spellings. For example, /f/ represents not only F in *five* but also the sound at the beginning of *phone* and at the end of *enough*. Beware too of /j/, which does not represent the sound at the beginning of *jam* but the one at the beginning of *young*.

d. Notice that there are certain two-letter sequences in the spelling system such as SH- which we tend to think of as a double sound because of their spelling; they actually represent a single sound.

e. Finally, notice that some consonants are limited as to what part of the word they can occur in: /ʒ/ and /ŋ/ never occur at the beginning of an English word.

Table A3.2 *Simple and complex vowels and diphthongs (southern British English)*

Vowels

Short			Long	
/ɪ/	hit		/iː/	heat
/e/	head			
/æ/	hat			
/ʌ/	hut		/ɑː/	heart
/ɒ/	hot		/ɔː/	hoard
/ʊ/	foot		/uː/	hoot
/ə/	about		/ɜː/	hurt

Diphthongs

/eɪ/	hate		/əʊ/	boat		/ɪə/	here
/aɪ/	height		/aʊ/	bout		/eə/	there
/ɔɪ/	boil					/ʊə/	cure

Triphthongs

/aɪə/	fire	/aʊə/	flower

Table A3.2 shows the set of vowels, together with phonemes that are made by combining vowels. The vowels vary greatly between different varieties of English; the ones that are given here by way of example are those of standard southern British English. Some points to note:

a. Vowels are made by positioning a part of the tongue (front, middle or back) either near to the top of the mouth (close) or lower in the mouth (open). These distinctions need not be of concern for present purposes.
b. A **diphthong** involves a movement from one vowel position to another. It is thus transcribed as two vowel symbols, though it is treated as a single sound. A **triphthong** involves three such positions and consists of three symbols.
c. The vowels on the right are often referred to as **long vowels** and are indicated as such by the use of a colon (:); they sometimes, but not always, take longer to say than those on the left.
d. Vowels do not form pairs in the way that some consonants do. Those that are paired horizontally here have certain similarities in terms of tongue position.

e. The vowel /ə/, known as **schwa**, has a special identity in that it occurs only in **weak** (unstressed) syllables such as the ones at the end of *never* or *America*.

It is important to bear in mind that phonemes are 'ideal' forms in a language. They are part of an abstract **phonological** system in the mind of a listener. If one listens to the way in which they are actually produced, it quickly becomes clear that they vary greatly from one word to another, from one speaker to another and from one occasion to another.

When we aim to represent *the actual sounds that a speaker produces* (as against the standard dictionary pronunciation), we use square brackets ([ ]) instead of slashes. This tells the reader that these are real **phonetic** sounds rather than phonemes. Strictly speaking, these variant forms of the phonemes of the language are termed **phones**, but for the sake of simplicity they are often referred to in this book simply as 'sounds'.

Word stress and weak quality

In many of the world's languages, content words (nouns, verbs, adjectives) of two or more syllables have one syllable that is marked out as more prominent than the others. *Notice that this is a characteristic of the word; it is present wherever the word is used.* In a large proportion of these languages, the stressed syllable is constant: it might be the first or the penultimate or the last in every word. In English, however, its location varies from one word to another. As an extreme example, compare the different stress patterns of

PHOtograph   photoGRAphic   phoTOgraphy.

Stress is marked in several ways: by a movement in the pitch of the voice, by making a syllable longer or by making it louder. When using a phoneme transcription, stress is indicated by a vertical superscript line, as on the first syllable of /ˈpesɪmɪst/. In the present book, it is sometimes indicated by capital letters where the standard English alphabet is used: *PEssimist.*

The converse of the stressed syllable is that a word may have one or more syllables that are **unstressed**. This means that they are noticeably less prominent than the other syllables; in English, unstressed syllables often contain the weak vowel schwa /ə/. Consider the unstressed syllables of *banana* (first and third) or *manager* (second and third). Many function words such as *of* or *to* or *for* have a **weak form** with schwa; it is in this form that they usually occur when they are used in connected speech.

Intonation

A speaker produces speech in small groups of words. The words are usually clustered around a single syllable which bears additional **focal**

stress on top of the normal lexical stress. The movement of the speaker's voice (or **intonation**) marks out the word in question as the most important one in the group. An important feature to note is that the key word is also highlighted by reducing the other words around it in length or in prominence. This means that some of the words may end up very different from their standard dictionary forms.

Intonation is often used to draw attention to a new topic that has been introduced; but it also serves to mark contrast and emphasis.

Further reading

Ashby, P. (1995) *Speech Sounds*. London: Routledge.

Brown, G. (1990) *Listening to Spoken English*. Harlow: Longman, Chap. 5.

Dalton, C. and Seidlhofer, B. (1994) *Pronunciation*. Oxford: Oxford University Press.

Gimson, A. C. (1994) *Gimson's Pronunciation of English*. 5th edn (ed. A. Cruttenden). London: Edward Arnold.

Kenworthy, J. (1987) *Teaching English Pronunciation*. Harlow: Longman.

Roach, P. (2000) *English Phonetics and Phonology: A Practical Course*. Cambridge: Cambridge University Press, 3rd edn.

Glossary of listening-related terms

access code: stressed syllable of a word that may help the listener to locate it in her mental vocabulary.

accommodate (accommodation): adjust one's speech rate, pronunciation, vocabulary and/or grammatical patterns to resemble those of an interlocutor.

achievement strategy: a strategy that attempts to make sense of parts of an utterance that have not been understood.

acoustic features: characteristics of the sound wave reaching the listener's ear which indicate that a particular **phoneme** has been produced.

activation: process that foregrounds a word in the mind as a likely match for what has been heard; better matches receive more activation than poor ones.

anticipation: (as used here) working out what the speaker is likely to say next.

argument structure: the way in which a speaker links the different points that are made.

articulators: the parts of the vocal tract (lips, tongue, palate, teeth) that are used to form speech sounds.

assimilation: adjusting a speech sound to make it easier to move from one articulatory position to another. In English, the final sound of a word might be changed to anticipate the sound at the beginning of the next word.

auditory scanning: process of listening to a recording to find answers to a set of questions.

authentic recordings: recordings which were not made with language learning in mind.

automatic: employed in a way that is rapid and accurate, and that makes minimal demands upon attention.

automaticity: see automatic.

avoidance strategy: a strategy that consists of getting by without the parts of an utterance that have not been understood.

back-channelling: sounds and words to signal that the listener has understood and/or is still listening.

behaviourist: based on a view of language as habitual behaviour acquired by learning the appropriate response to a stimulus.

bottom-up: describes a process that builds smaller units into larger ones (syllables into words and words into phrases).

chunks: small groups of words that commonly occur together.

citation form: the 'idealised' form of a word, heard when a speaker articulates it precisely and on its own.

cliticisation: attaching a word or an abbreviated form of a word to the end of the previous one (e.g. *did + n't → didn't, they + are → they're*).

co-articulation: the way in which the pronunciation of a phoneme is influenced by the phoneme that occurs before or after it in the syllable.

Glossary of listening-related terms

cognitive strategies: strategies that depend upon rapid mental processes.

cognitive validity: whether a language test requires candidates to perform processes that are similar to those they would employ in a real-life context.

communication strategies: strategies that, in listening, attempt to redress gaps in decoding or understanding.

compensatory processing: using contextual information to fill gaps where decoding has been unsuccessful.

compensatory strategy: a type of strategy that attempts to make up for a gap in decoding or understanding.

comprehension approach: the standard approach to the teaching and testing of second language listening in which learners listen to a recording in order to find answers to comprehension questions.

consonant clusters: groups of consonants that commonly occur together, at the beginning or end of a syllable.

context: outside information brought to bear by the listener – including world knowledge, topic knowledge, knowledge of the speaker and awareness of the situation. Sometimes used more widely to include the listener's understanding of what has been said so far.

co-text: the words that a speaker has used so far, which help to create a **discourse representation** in the mind of the listener.

critical word: a word in a listening passage without which it would be impossible to understand the speaker's main point.

current activation: a process that foregrounds a word in the mind of the listener because it has been heard recently.

declarative knowledge: factual information stored in the mind.

decoding: analysing the sounds in the speech stream with a view to matching them to words, phrases and sentences.

deep processing: reflecting upon a speaker's message in a way that identifies its wider implications.

diagnostic approach: approach in which a teacher uses answers to a comprehension task to discover where learners' listening problems lie.

discourse representation: the listener's interpretation of what has been said so far.

effort after meaning: the desire to make sense of a text, even when it appears inconsistent.

elision: missing out a sound in order to make a word or two adjoining words easier to produce.

ellipsis: words missed out by a speaker that a listener has to infer.

epenthesis: insertion of a vowel sound before or within a **consonant cluster**, with (e.g.) *sport* becoming [sɪ'pɔːt].

exemplar view: a view that we store in our minds multiple examples of words that we hear, allowing us to recognise many different variants of a single word.

expansions: additional information added to topic sentences by the sentences that follow them.

expertise: highly skilled performance in a task.

extensive listening: a preliminary hearing of a recording, to identify the main points.

'extensive' listening: recent term for listening for pleasure.

false starts: pieces of speech where a speaker begins a sentence in a particular way, then has a change of mind and begins again.

filled pauses: sounds such as *er*, *erm*, used to fill gaps when a speaker is hesitating or planning what to say.

filler: a meaningless word or group of words that buys a speaker time for planning.

focal syllable: the syllable that carries focal stress and serves to identify the most important word in an intonation group.

formal schema: knowledge of the conventional patterns that certain speech events follow.

formulaic chunks: small groups of words that commonly occur together and are likely to be stored in the mind as a unit.

frequency: how often a word occurs in speech.

function words: words which do not have a clear dictionary meaning but perform a grammatical role.

functions: ways of expressing intentions, such as refusing, apologising, threatening, offering.

general term: a word such as *thing* or *people* which does not refer precisely to what the speaker intends.

generalisable strategy: (as used here) a strategy which is relatively independent of the problem that gave rise to it and so can be used in a number of similar contexts.

general–specific: a discourse pattern where a general statement is followed by a specific example.

given: an element in a sentence that has previously been mentioned.

graded recording: recording where the grammar and vocabulary have been simplified to suit the level of the learner.

hesitation pauses: pauses where the speaker has forgotten or changed his mind about what to say.

hypothesis formation: constructing an idea of what a speaker has said based upon incomplete information.

improvised recording: studio recording made by voice actors without a script.

indeterminate representation: a generalised understanding of the intended message.

indeterminate sense: an imprecise sense for a word, with which an L2 listener sometimes has to be satisfied.

inference: connections between sentences or background knowledge which a listener has to supply because the speaker has not mentioned it explicitly.

information processing: a model which shows a listener taking a piece of speech through several stages and reshaping it at each one.

input: the speech that reaches a listener's ear: sometimes assumed to be **acoustic** in form, sometimes assumed to have been analysed by the listener into **phonemes**.

Glossary of listening-related terms

integrated skills: approach to language skills practice in which a theme is handled in different ways across two or more skills.

integrating information: adding new information to a representation of what has been said so far.

intensive listening: listening to a recording to report details.

interactive: combining information that is both **bottom-up** and **top-down**.

interactive approach: an approach where learners are encouraged to share their impressions of what has been heard.

Interactive Compensatory Hypothesis: a theory that the amount of contextual information used by readers (and, by extension, listeners) depends upon how accurate and complete their decoding has been.

interactive listening: situation where a listener has to respond to the speaker.

interpretation: (as used here) the meaning attached to an utterance by a listener, including assumptions about the speaker's intentions.

intonation group: a group of words produced together as a unit and clustered round a syllable that has **focal stress**.

investment principle: the theory that a listener is reluctant to abandon a provisional hypothesis about what has been heard, having put effort into constructing it.

jigsaw listening: an activity where learners work in pairs or threes, each learner having heard a different version or a different part of a recording.

'key words': strategy of listening for words that are closely associated with the topic or for words provided by a test rubric.

learning strategies: strategies for noticing, recalling or retaining aspects of the target language.

levels of representation: different units into which a listener might divide a piece of speech (phoneme, syllable, word, phrase).

lexical access: gaining information about a word (including its meaning) from its entry in the mind.

lexical phrases: multi-word items of vocabulary such as *in front of.*

lexical segmentation: locating word boundaries in connected speech, where there are few pauses between words.

lexical stress: consistent stress on one syllable of a word, which helps the listener to identify it.

linguistic knowledge: knowledge of the sounds, vocabulary and grammar of the language (including word meanings).

linkers: connecting words or phrases which serve as signposts to the speaker's intentions. They might show logical connections between topics or they might provide a framework for a complete talk.

listener anxiety: the fear that connected L2 speech is too difficult to make sense of.

listening centre: part of a language teaching facility set aside for independent listening practice.

listening style: a learner's individual approach to the challenges of L2 listening.

listening type: a listening situation characterised by how local it is and by how much attention it demands.

macro-structure: the major 'headings' in a piece of spoken discourse and the connections between them.

meaning building: (a) adding to the bare meaning of what a speaker says by drawing upon outside context and upon what has been said so far; and (b) selecting relevant information from what a speaker has said and building it into an overall discourse pattern.

meaning representation: a **proposition** expressed by a speaker, to which contextual information has been added by the listener.

mental set: a motivated or enquiring attitude towards a listening passage.

metacognitive: involving an understanding of one's own mental processes; often used for strategies that consist of planning how to listen.

micro-listening task: a short practice exercise lasting from five to ten minutes and usually focused upon a single aspect of listening.

minimal pair: a pair of words that are different in only one phoneme (e.g. *pack/back*).

'new': an element in a sentence that has not previously been mentioned. *See* 'given'.

non-interventionist approach: an approach in which the teacher encourages learners to solve listening difficulties for themselves.

non-participatory: a situation where the listener is not expected to contribute as speaker.

normalise: adjust to the pitch and speed and quality of a speaker's voice.

online: analysing what is said immediately after the speaker has said it.

operation: used here for a major component of listening that employs a set of closely linked processes.

paralinguistic cue: additional information about an utterance provided by facial expressions or gestures.

parsing: tracing the grammatical structure that links a group of words.

paused practice: listening exercise where the teacher pauses the recording and asks learners to repeat what they have just heard or to anticipate a response.

paused transcription: a research method that consists of pausing a recording sporadically and asking listeners to report the last few words heard.

phoneme: one of a set of sounds which make up a language's phonological system.

phoneme discrimination: distinguishing between two sounds of a language that are easily confused.

phoneme variation: the way in which the sounds of a language vary according to the sounds that adjoin them, the type of speech and the speaker.

phoneme–grapheme correspondence: rules that link sounds to spellings.

pitch: level (high or low) of a speaker's voice.

pitch movement: the upwards or downwards movement of a speaker's voice.

post-listening: a period after a teacher has played a recording, used for reviewing any issues that have arisen during listening.

pragmatics: the way in which the speaker intends his words to be taken by the listener (as a threat, an offer, etc.).

Glossary of listening-related terms

prediction: (as used here) suggesting in advance what words and ideas are likely to occur in a text.

pre-listening: a period before a teacher plays a recording, used for preparing learners for listening.

pro-active strategy: (as used here) a strategy that involves an element of intention or planning.

procedural knowledge: knowledge of how to perform an action or sequence of actions.

process: a mental activity which contributes to a skill.

process approach: an approach based upon training learners in the different processes which have been shown to contribute to skilled listening.

process of listening: how a listener makes sense of what a speaker says.

product of listening: a listener's interpretation of what a speaker has said with no indication as to how the interpretation has been arrived at.

prognostic approach: an approach where a teacher attempts to predict where listening problems will arise.

proposition: an abstract representation of a single idea, independent of the context in which it was expressed.

real time: refers to the way in which the speech signal reaches the listener over time.

recursive: describes an activity where a language user can look back and check.

reduction: (as used here) the way in which words may become reduced in length and reshaped if they do not have a prominent role in an **intonation group**.

redundancy: natural repetitiveness of speech, where speakers often reiterate or rephrase information they have already given.

reference: tracking back (or sometimes forwards) to find out what words like *they*, *there* or *this* refer to.

reflective phase: a period where an independent listener considers problems that may have arisen and their likely causes.

rehearsal: turning over in one's mind a response to a speaker.

rehearsing: anticipating in one's mind the words that a speaker might use.

reliability: the ability of a test to produce the same range of scores wherever and whenever it is applied.

repair strategy: a strategy in which a speaker is appealed to for help if understanding breaks down.

repetition: the same word or phrase said twice or three times as a speaker hesitates.

re-recorded: recorded by voice actors from a transcript of natural speech.

resyllabification: redistribution of syllables in connected speech. The consonant from the end of a word is sometimes attached to a following word that begins with a vowel (*find out* → *fine doubt*).

risk avoider: a listener who is reluctant to form conclusions about a speaker's meaning when there are gaps in decoding or understanding.

risk taker: a listener who is prepared to form conclusions about a speaker's meaning despite gaps in decoding or understanding.

routine: used here for a set of processes that has become automatic through repeated use.

schema: a complex knowledge structure in the mind which groups all that an individual knows about, or associates with, a particular concept.

script: a sequence of activities associated in the mind with a stereotypical situation.

scripted recording: recording that has been specially written and recorded by voice actors.

self-monitor: check one's understanding to ensure that it is consistent.

signal: the sequence of sounds and rhythmic patterns that reaches the listener's ear.

social-affective strategies: strategies that involve interpersonal relationships or emotion.

speaker variation: the way in which speakers vary in terms of their voice, speech rate, accent, etc.

speech stream: the sequence of sounds and rhythmic patterns that reaches the listener's ear.

spelling extrapolation: working out the spelling of a word that has been heard.

spreading activation: a group of words becoming **activated** (foregrounded) in the mind because they are associated with a word that has just been heard.

strategy: (as used here) a technique used by a listener to compensate for gaps in decoding or understanding.

stressed: more prominent than other syllables. Especially used of **lexical stress**.

stress-timed: describes the supposed rhythm of a language, characterised by roughly equal periods of time between stressed syllables.

strong syllable: syllable with a full-quality vowel.

structure building: building a pattern from the points made by a speaker, in a way that reflects their relative importance.

sub-skills approach: an approach to listening and reading which consists of dividing the skill into a set of component parts and practising them individually.

syllable-timed: describes the supposed rhythm of a language, characterised by syllables of roughly equal length.

task: a listening exercise which involves form-filling and similar activities rather than answering questions.

task evaluation: matching the amount of strategy use to the depth of listening that is required.

testwise strategies: techniques that rely upon information given in a test rubric rather than in the listening passage.

text-so-far: what the listener has heard up to now.

Threshold Level: a level of vocabulary beyond which the transfer of L1 skills becomes possible because enough of a text can be understood.

top-down: strictly speaking, describes a view of listening as a process that uses larger units in order to identify smaller ones (e.g. uses word-level information to recognise phonemes).

Glossary of listening-related terms

topic sentences: sentences that introduce a sub-topic, in the way that the first sentence of a paragraph often does in reading.

tuning out: withdrawing attention from a speaker.

weak form: a reduced form of a function word, usually containing /ə/. It is the most common form of the word; the **full form** might be used for emphasis.

weak syllable: syllable with a weak-quality vowel such as /ə/.

word variation: the way in which words vary according to the words next to them, to the type of speech, and to their importance in an **intonation group**.

working memory: a component of memory which holds short-term information and works upon it. Limited in how much it can hold and therefore how much attention can be allocated to a task.

References

Abbs, B., Cook, V. and Underwood, M. (1968) *Realistic English Dialogues*. Oxford: Oxford University Press.

Alderson, J. C. (1984) 'Reading in a foreign language: a reading problem or a language problem?' In J. C. Alderson and A. Urquhart (eds.), *Reading in a Foreign Language*. London: Longman.

Alexander, L. G. (1967) *First Things First*. London: Longman.

Anderson, A. and Lynch, T. (1988) *Listening*. Oxford: Oxford University Press.

Archibald, J. (1998) *Second Language Phonology*. Amsterdam: John Benjamins.

Ashby, P. (1995) *Speech Sounds*. London: Routledge.

Bachman, L. (1990) *Fundamental Considerations in Language Testing*. Oxford: Oxford University Press.

Baker, A. (2006) *Ship or Sheep?: An Intermediate Pronunciation Course*. Cambridge: Cambridge University Press.

Bartlett, F. C. (1932) *Remembering*. Cambridge: Cambridge University Press. Reissued 1995.

Bates, E. and MacWhinney, B. (1987) 'Competition, variation and language learning'. In B. MacWhinney (ed.), *Mechanisms of Language Acquisition*. Hillsdale, NJ: Erlbaum, pp. 157–94.

Blundell, L. and Stokes, J. (1981) *Task Listening*. Cambridge: Cambridge University Press.

Bond, Z. (1999) *Slips of the Ear: Errors in the Perception of Casual Conversation*. San Diego, CA: Academic Press.

Bradford, B. (1988) *Intonation in Context*. Cambridge: Cambridge University Press.

Bremer, K., Broader, P., Roberts, C., Simoniot, M. and Vasseur, M-T. (1993) 'Ways of achieving understanding'. In C. Perdue (ed.), *Adult Language Acquisition: Cross-Linguistic Perspectives*. Cambridge: Cambridge University Press, pp. 153–95.

Brown, G. (1986) 'Investigating listening comprehension in context'. *Applied Linguistics*, 7/3: 284–302.

(1990) *Listening to Spoken English*. Harlow: Longman, 2nd edn.

(1995) *Speakers, Listeners and Communication*. Cambridge: Cambridge University Press.

(2005) 'Second language listening'. Entry in K. Brown (ed.), *Encyclopaedia of Language and Linguistics*. Oxford: Elsevier.

Brown, G. and Yule, G. (1983a) *Discourse Analysis*. Cambridge: Cambridge University Press.

(1983b) *Teaching the Spoken Language*. Cambridge: Cambridge University Press.

Buck, G. (1990) 'The testing of second language listening comprehension'. Unpublished PhD thesis, University of Lancaster.

(2001) *Assessing Listening*. Cambridge: Cambridge University Press.

Byrne, D. (1981) 'Integrating skills'. In K. Johnson and K. Morrow (eds.), *Communication in the Classroom*. London: Longman, pp. 108–14.

References

Campbell, C. and Smith, J. (2007) *English for Academic Study: Listening*. Reading. Garnet Education.

Carr, T. H. and Levy, B. A. (eds.) (1990) *Reading and its Development: Component Skills Approaches*. San Diego: Academic Press.

Cauldwell, R. (2003) 'Streaming speech BI: listening and pronunciation (British and Irish voices)'. At www.speechinaction.com/streamingspeech_course_menu.htm.

Chaudron, C. and Richards, J. (1986) 'The effect of discourse markers on the comprehension of lectures'. *Applied Linguistics*, 7: 113–27.

Cohen, A. (1998) *Strategies in Learning and Using a Second Language*. London: Longman.

Cohen, A. D. and Macaro, E. (eds.) (2007) *Language Learner Strategies: Thirty Years of Research and Practice*. Oxford: Oxford University Press.

Collie, J. and Slater, S. (1995) *Cambridge Skills for Fluency: Listening 3*. Cambridge: Cambridge University Press.

Corder, S. P. (1983) 'Strategies of communication'. In G. Faerch and G. Kasper (eds.), *Strategies in Interlanguage Communication*. London: Longman, pp. 15–19.

CRAPEL (1999) 'Un outil multimédia pour apprendre les langues étrangères'. (J-M. Debaisieux and O. Régent). Downloadable from: www.univ-nancy2.fr/CRAPEL/publications_melanges_24.htm.

Cruttenden, A. (1986) *Intonation*. Cambridge: Cambridge University Press.

Cutler, A. (1990) 'Exploiting prosodic probabilities'. In G. Altmann (ed.), *Cognitive Models of Speech Processing: Psycholinguistic and Computational Perspectives*. Cambridge, MA: MIT Press/Bradford Books, pp. 105–21.

   (1997) 'The comparative perspective on spoken-language processing'. *Speech Communication*, 21: 3–15.

Dalton, C. and Seidlhofer, B. (1994) *Pronunciation*. Oxford: Oxford University Press.

Daly, D. (2006) 'Learner evaluation of a ten-session intensive listening programme'. Paper presented at BAAL/CUP seminar 'Research perspectives on listening in L1 and L2 education', University of Warwick, UK, 12–13 May 2006.

Doff, A. and Becket, C. (1991) *Cambridge Skills for Fluency: Listening*. Cambridge: Cambridge University Press.

Dörnyei, Z. (1995) 'On the teachability of communication strategies'. *TESOL Quarterly*, 29/1: 55–85.

Dörnyei, Z. and Scott, M. L. (1997) 'Communication strategies in a second language: definitions and taxonomies'. *Language Learning*, 447/1: 173–210.

Duncan, S. (1972) 'Some signals and rules for taking speaking turns in conversation'. *Journal of Personality and Social Psychology*, 23: 282–92.

Ellis, G. and Sinclair, B. (1989) *Learning to Learn English*. Oxford: Oxford University Press.

Faerch, G. and Kasper, G. (1983) 'Plans and strategies in foreign language communication'. In G. Faerch and G. Kasper (eds.), *Strategies in Interlanguage Communication*. London: Longman, pp. 20–60.

Field, J. (1983) *New Cambridge First Certificate English Practice*. Basingstoke: Macmillan.

(1988) *Successful Listening: Form 4*. Hong Kong: Macmillan Hong Kong.

(1998) 'Skills and strategies: towards a new methodology for listening'. *ELT Journal*, 54/2: 110–18.

(1999) 'Key concepts in ELT: bottom up and top down'. *ELT Journal*, 53/4: 338–9.

(2000) '"Not waving but drowning": a reply to Tony Ridgway'. *ELT Journal*, 54/2: 186–95. Also: 54/3: 307.

(2001a) 'The changing face of listening'. In J. C. Richards and W. A. Renandya (eds.), *Methodology in Language Teaching*. Cambridge: Cambridge University Press, pp. 242–7.

(2001b) 'Lexical segmentation in first and foreign language listening'. Unpublished PhD dissertation, Cambridge University.

(2003) 'Promoting perception: lexical segmentation in L2 listening'. *ELT Journal*, 57/4: 325–34.

(2004) 'An insight into listeners' problems: too much bottom-up or too much top-down?' *System*, 32: 363–77.

(2005a) 'Intelligibility and the listener: the role of lexical stress'. *TESOL Quarterly*, 39/3: 399–423.

(2005b) '"A bird in the hand": first mention and the second language listener'. Paper presented at BAAL Annual Meeting, Bristol, UK.

(2007) 'Looking outwards, not inwards'. *ELT Journal*, 61/1: 30–8.

(2008a) 'Revising segmentation hypotheses in first and second language listening'. *System*, 36: 35–51.

(2008b) 'Bricks and mortar: how does a second language listener process input?' *Tesol Quarterly*, 42/3.

(2008c) 'The L2 listener: type or individual?' *Working Papers in English and Applied Linguistics in Honour of Gillian Brown*. Cambridge: RCEAL.

Field, J. and Wiseman, A. (1993, 1994) *Use of English: Developing Skills*. Hong Kong: Macmillan, 2nd edn.

Gardner, D. and Miller, L. (1999) *Establishing Self-Access: From Theory to Practice*. Cambridge: Cambridge University Press.

Geddes, M. (1988) *How to Listen*. London: BBC Publications.

Gernsbacher, M-A. (1990) *Language Comprehension as Structure Building*. Mahwah, NJ: Erlbaum.

Gimson, A. C. (1994) *Gimson's Pronunciation of English* 5th edn. (ed. A. Cruttenden). London: Edward Arnold.

Goh, C. (1997) 'Metacognitive awareness and second language listeners'. *ELT Journal*, 51: 361–9.

Goh, C. M. (2000) 'A cognitive perspective on language learners' listening comprehension problems'. *System*, 28: 55–75.

Goh, C. and Taib, Y. (2006) 'Metacognitive instruction in listening for young learners'. *ELT Journal*, 60/3: 222–32.

Goodman, K. (1967) 'Reading: a psycholinguistic guessing game'. *Journal of the Reading Specialist*, 6: 126–35.

References

Graham, S. (2006) 'Listening comprehension: The learners' perspective'. *System*, 34/2: 165–82.

Grellet, F. (1981) *Developing Reading Skills*. Cambridge: Cambridge University Press.

Grosjean, F. and Gee, J. (1987) 'Prosodic structure and spoken word recognition'. *Cognition*, 25: 135–55.

Hansen, C. and Jensen, C. (1994) 'Evaluating lecture comprehension'. In J. Flowerdew (ed.), *Academic Listening*. Cambridge: Cambridge University Press, pp. 241–68.

Hauck, M. C., MacDougall, K. and Isay, D. (2001) *Twelve American Voices*. New Haven: Yale University Press.

Hockett, C. F. (1955) *A Manual of Phonology*. Baltimore: Waverly Press.

Holec, H. (1985) 'On autonomy: some elementary concepts'. In P. Riley (ed.), *Discourse and Learning*. Harlow: Longman, pp. 173–90.

Kelly, P. (1991) 'Lexical ignorance: the main obstacle to listening comprehension with advanced foreign language learners'. *IRAL*, 29 (2): 135–49.

Kenworthy, J. (1987) *Teaching English Pronunciation*. Harlow: Longman.

Koster, C. J. (1987) *Word Recognition in Foreign and Native Language: Effects of Context and Assimilation*. Dordrecht: Foris Publications.

Langford, D. (1994) *Analysing Talk*. Basingstoke: Macmillan.

Laver, J. (1994) *Principles of Phonetics*. Cambridge: Cambridge University Press.

Long, D. R. (1989) 'Second language listening comprehension: a schema-theoretic perspective'. *Modern Language Journal*, 73: 32–40.

(1990) 'What you don't know can't help you'. *Studies in Second Language Acquisition*, 12: 65–80.

Lund, R. J. (1990) 'A taxonomy for teaching second language listening'. *Foreign Language Annals*, 23/2: 105–15.

(1991) 'A comparison of second language listening and reading comprehension'. *Modern Language Journal*, 75: 196–204.

Lynch, T. (1995) 'The development of interactive listening strategies in second language academic situations'. In D. Mendelsohn and J. Rubin (eds.), *A Guide to the Teaching of Second Language Listening*. San Diego, CA: Dominie Press, pp. 166–85.

(2004) *Study Listening*. Cambridge: Cambridge University Press, 2nd edn.

(2006) 'Academic listening: marrying top and bottom'. In A. Martinez-Flor and E. Usó-Juan (eds.), *Current Trends in Learning and Teaching the Four Skills within a Communicative Framework*. Amsterdam: Mouton, pp. 99–101.

Macaro, E. (2001) *Learning Strategies in Foreign and Second Language Classrooms*. London: Continuum.

(2006) 'Academic listening: morning top and bottom'. In A. Martinez Flor and E. Uso-Juan (eds.), *Current Trends in Learning and Teaching the Four Skills within a Communicative Framework*. Amsterdam: Mouton, pp. 99–101.

McDonough, J. and Shaw, C. (1993) *Materials and Methods in ELT: A Teacher's Guide*. Oxford: Blackwell.

McGrath, I. (2002) *Materials Evaluation and Design for Language Teaching*. Edinburgh: Edinburgh University Press.

Maley, A. and Duff, A. (1978) *Variations on a Theme*. Cambridge: Cambridge University Press.

Meara, P. (1997) 'Towards a new approach to modelling vocabulary acquisition'. In N. Schmidt and M. McCarthy (eds.), *Vocabulary: Description, Acquisition and Pedagogy*. Cambridge: Cambridge University Press, pp. 101–21.

Mendelsohn, D. J. (1994) *Learning to Listen: A Strategy-Based Approach for the Second-Language Learner*. San Diego, CA: Dominie Press.

Morais, J., Cary, L., Alegria, J. and Bertelson, P. (1979) 'Does awareness of speech as a sequence of phones arise spontaneously?' *Cognition*, 50: 323–31.

Morrison, B. (1989) 'Using news broadcasts for authentic listening comprehension'. *ELT Journal*, 43/1: 14–18.

Morrow, K. (1977) 'Authentic texts in ESP'. In S. Holden (ed.), *English for Specific Purposes*. London: Modern English Publications, pp. 13–17.

Munby, J. (1978) *Communicative Syllabus Design*. Cambridge: Cambridge University Press.

Nuttall, C. (1996) *Teaching Reading Skills in a Foreign Language*. Oxford: Heinemann, 2nd edn.

Oakeshott-Taylor, A. (1977) 'Dictation as a test of listening comprehension'. In R. Dirven (ed.), *Listening Comprehension in Foreign Language Teaching*. Kronberg: Scriptor.

O'Malley, J. M. and Chamot, A. U. (1988) 'How to teach learning strategies'. In A. U. Chamot, J. M. O'Malley and L. Kupper (eds.), *The Cognitive Academic Learning Approach (CALLA) Training Manual*. Arlington, VA: Second Language Learning, pp. 121–2.

(1990) *Learning Strategies in Second Language Acquisition*. Cambridge: Cambridge University Press.

Osada, N. (2001) 'What strategy do less proficient learners employ in listening comprehension? A reappraisal of bottom-up and top-down processing'. *Journal of the Pan-Pacific Association of Applied Linguistics*, 5: 73–90.

Oxford, R. L. (1990) *Language Learning Strategies: What Every Teacher Should Know*. Boston, MA: Heinle and Heinle.

Palmer, H. E. (1922) *The Principles of Language Study*. London: Harrap. Reprinted Oxford University Press, 1964.

Pawley, A. and Syder, F. H. (1983) 'Two puzzles for linguistic theory'. In J. C. Richards and R. W. Schmidt (eds.), *Language and Communication*. London: Longman, pp. 191–226.

Pemberton, R., Toogood, S., Ho, S. and Lam, J. (2001) 'Approaches to advising for self-directed learning'. In L. Dam (ed.), *Learner Automomy: New Insights. AILA Review*, 15: 16–25.

Perfetti, C. and Roth, S. (1981) 'Some of the interactive processes in reading and their role in the reading skill'. In A. M. Lesgold and C. Perfetti (eds.), *Interactive Processes in Reading*. Hillsdale, NJ: Erlbaum, pp. 269–97.

Poulisse, N. (1990) *The Use of Compensatory Strategies by Dutch Learners of English*. Dordrecht: Foris.

References

Prowse, P. (2001) 'Success with extensive listening'. Cambridge University Press website at: www.cambridge.org /elt/readers/teacher/articles/current4.htm

Quirk, R., Greenbaum, S., Leech, G. and Svartvik, J. (1985) *A Comprehensive Grammar of the English Language*. Harlow: Longman.

Richards, J. C. (1983) 'Listening comprehension: approach, design, procedure'. *TESOL Quarterly*, 17: 219–39.

Ridgway, T. (2000) 'Listening strategies: I beg your pardon?' *ELT Journal*, 54/2: 179–85.

Roach P. (2000) *English Phonetics and Phonology: A Practical Course*. Cambridge: Cambridge University Press, 3rd edn.

Rost, M. (1992) *Listening in Language Learning*. Harlow: Longman.
    (1994) *Introducing Listening*. Harmondsworth: Penguin.

Schank, R. C. and Abelson, R. P. (1977) *Scripts, Plans, Goals and Understanding*. Hillsdale, NJ: Erlbaum.

Sheerin, S. (1987) 'Listening comprehension: teaching or testing?' *ELT Journal*, 41/2: 126–31.
    (1989) *Self-Access*. Oxford: Oxford University Press.

Shockey, L. (2003) *Sound Patterns of Spoken English*. Oxford: Blackwell.

Spolsky, B. (1990) 'Oral examinations: an historical note'. *Language Testing*, 7/2: 158–73.

Stanovich, K. E. (1980) 'Toward an interactive-compensatory model of individual differences in the development of reading fluency'. *Reading Research Quarterly*, 16: 32–71.

Tauroza, S. (1993) 'Recognizing words in continuous speech: how important are word-final consonants?' *ELT Journal*, 47/3: 211–27.

Thorn, S. (2006) 'Real lives, real listening'. London: The Listening Business. At: www.thelisteningbusiness.com.

Tsui, A. and Fullilove, J. (1998) 'Bottom-up or top-down processing as a discriminator of L2 listening performance'. *Applied Linguistics*, 19: 432–51.

Underwood, M. (1971, 1975) *Listen to This!* Oxford: Oxford University Press.
    (1976) *What a Story!* Oxford: Oxford University Press.
    (1989) *Teaching Listening*. Harlow: Longman.

Ur, P. (1984) *Teaching Listening Comprehension*. Cambridge: Cambridge University Press.

Urquhart, S. and Weir, C (1998) *Reading in a Second Language: Process, Product and Practice*. Harlow: Longman.

Van Dijk, T. A. and Kintsch, W. (1983) *Strategies of Discourse Comprehension*. New York: Academic Press.

Vandergrift, L. (1997) 'The Cinderella of communication strategies: reception strategies in interactive listening'. *Modern Language Journal*, 81/4: 494–505.
    (1999) 'Facilitating second language listening comprehension: acquiring successful strategies'. *ELT Journal*, 53/4: 73–8.
    (2003) 'Orchestrating strategy use: toward a model of the skilled second language listener'. *Language Learning*, 53: 463–96.
    (2004) 'Listening to learn or learning to listen?' *Annual Review of Applied Linguistics*, 24: 3–25.

Voller, P., Martyn, E. and Pickard, V. (1999) 'One-to-one counselling for autonomous 24 learning in a self-access centre: final report on action learning project'. In D. Crabbe and S. Cotterall (eds.), *Learner Autonomy in Language Learning: Defining the Field and Effecting Change*. Frankfurt: Peter Lang, pp. 111–26.

Weir, C. (1993) *Understanding and Developing Language Tests*. Hemel Hempstead: Prentice Hall.

(2005) *Language Testing and Validation: An Evidence Based Approach*. Basingstoke: Palgrave Macmillan.

Wesche, M. and Ready, D. (1985) 'Foreigner talk in the university classroom'. In S. Gass and C. Madden (eds.), *Input in Second Language Acquisition*. Rowley, MA: Newbury House, pp. 89–114.

White, G. (1998) *Listening*. Oxford: Oxford University Press.

Wilson, J. J. (2008) *How to Teach Listening*. Harlow: Pearson Education.

Wilson, M. (2003) 'Discovery listening – improving perceptual processing'. *ELT Journal*, 57/4: 335–43.

Wray, A. (2002) *Formulaic Language and the Lexicon*. Cambridge: Cambridge University Press.

Index

360

Index

Index

radio and TV broadcasts 5, 48, 270, 275
reading 1, 6, 14, 21, 22, 27–8, 37, 38, 43–4,
     80, 99–100, 105, 107, 234, 248–9,
     255–6, 312
reading in listening tasks 23, 55–6, 80
real time 4, 38
real-world input 5, 31–2, 54, 59, 277
recorded material, grading 118–19
recording 58–9, 158–9, 261
     authenticity of 269–85
recording a class 72, 84, 317
recursion 27, 38, 45–57
reduction 143, 152–7, 195–7
redundancy 243, 246–7, 279, 333
reference 212, 229, 233–5
reflective phase 92–4
rehearsal 71–2, 260, 297, 301, 321,
     323
remaking the message 37, 209
remedial practice 88–91
repair formulae 320
repair strategy 70, 71, 296, 320–1
replay 31, 38, 41, 43–5, 46, 47, 51–3, 75,
     83, 159, 162, 226, 252, 257, 276, 278,
     280, 317 (see also multiple-play)
re-recording 273
response types, strategic 295–6
resyllabification 144–5
rhythm 143–4, 172–3, 274, 276–7, 284
Richards taxonomy 100–2
risk avoider 311
risk taker 310–11

schema 216–20
schwa 343
script 217–18
scripted recording 270, 272–3, 281–3
selecting information 241–5
self-diagnosis 92–4
self-monitoring 221, 248, 251–3, 258
self-study 46–56, 71–2, 91–4, 328
semi-authentic 273
simplification 271–2
single interpretation 30, 40, 41
skill 9
skill training 79, 98–9, 110
skilled vs unskilled listening 131–2,
     135–8
social-affective strategy 294
sound, of a language 30, 79, 85, 86–7, 107,
     113, 115, 126–7, 127–9, 140, 141–62,
     165–7, 167–72, 231, 292 (see also
     phoneme)
sound–spelling relationship 170
speaker attitude 200–5
speaker intentions 228–39, 243
speaker interruption 320

speaker knowledge 130, 215
speaker omissions 231, 239, 249–51
speaker variation 119, 157–61
speaking strategies 293, 296
speech rate 119, 158, 160, 270
speech signal 27, 28, 85, 125–9, 140–60,
     163–84, 186, 261, 286
speech stream 126, 140–62
spontaneous speech 272, 274
spreading activation 164–5, 182–3, 215,
     218
Stanovich principle see Interactive
     Compensatory Hypothesis
storage of language 165–7
strategies, task-based approach 315–17
strategy 8, 9, 32, 117, 286–303
     achievement 296, 298, 299–300, 314–20,
          323
     avoidance 296, 298, 299–300, 314–20
     pro-active 296–8, 321–3
     repair 296, 298, 300–1, 320–1, 322
     varying definitions of 293
     vs process 297, 298, 299
     word-level 224, 226
strategy appropriacy 296, 311–13, 324
strategy awareness raising 291, 308, 314–15,
     317
strategy categorisation 288, 293–8
strategy choice 310, 319, 323
strategy instruction 287–8, 291, 304–24,
     330, 331–3
     'direct' 309–12, 319, 322, 323
     'embedded' 315–7
     effects 307
     explicit 308, 309–11, 322, 323
     format 314–17
strategy types 293–8
strategy use, variation in 305–7, 310–11,
     322
stress, fixed 179
stress, focal/sentence 101, 104, 115, 187,
     194–7, 198–205, 260, 275, 280, 294,
     300, 316–19
stress, word 101, 111, 146, 172, 174–7,
     178–80, 343
stressed syllable 143–4, 172, 174–7, 178–80,
     194, 316–19
stress-timed 172, 184
structure building 253–7
study techniques 298
style of delivery 158
sub-skill 9, 98–108, 110–13, 118, 288,
     310
sub-skills approach 98–108, 110–11
subtitles 55
suffix 151, 178–81, 227
SW pattern 143–4

364

Index